3rd edition

CONCEPTS OF INTERNATIONAL POLITICS
in global perspective

Charles O. Lerche Jr.
Abdul Aziz Said

School of International Service
The American University

Prentice-Hall, Inc., Englewood Cliffs, New Jersey 07632

Library of Congress Cataloging in Publication Data

Lerche, Charles O.
Concepts of international politics.

Bibliographies.
Includes index.
1.–International relations. I.–Said, Abdul Aziz, joint author. II.–Title.
JX1308.L4 1979   327   78-10311
ISBN 0-13-166033-0

© 1979, 1970, 1963 by Prentice-Hall, Inc.,
Englewood Cliffs, N.J. 07632

All rights reserved. No part of this book
may be reproduced in any form or
by any means without permission in writing
from the publisher.

Printed in the United States of America

10 9 8 7 6 5 4 3 2 1

Editorial/production supervision: Jeanne Hoeting
Cover design: Jorge Hernandez
Manufacturing buyer: Harry P. Baisley

Prentice-Hall International, Inc., *London*
Prentice-Hall of Australia Pty. Limited, *Sydney*
Prentice-Hall of Canada, Ltd., *Toronto*
Prentice-Hall of India Private Limited, *New Delhi*
Prentice-Hall of Japan, Inc., *Tokyo*
Prentice-Hall of Southeast Asia Pte. Ltd., *Singapore*
Whitehall Books Limited, *Wellington, New Zealand*

FOR HERKY, RIYAD, AND JAMIL

Contents

Preface   XIII

Introduction: Changing Foci of Analysis 1

Development of the Study of International Relations 2
Present State of the Art 5
Recent Trends in International Relations Theory 11
The Approach of this Study 14
Recommended Readings 17

PART I
THE ACTORS:
THE STATE IN GLOBAL POLITICS 19

1   The Nature of Foreign Policy 21

Politics: The Struggle to Maximize Values 21
>*The Nature of Politics 21.   Social Values and Foreign Policy 23. Value Content of Foreign Policy 23.   Foreign Policy and International Politics 24.   Ascriptive Politics 25.*

Interests, Goals, and Objectives 27
>*From "Social Values" to "National Interest" 27.   Ends and Means in Foreign Policy 28.   The Nature of an Objective 28. The Common Objectives of States 29.*

Policy and the Strategic Decision 31

*The Meaning of "Policy" 32. The Need for Priorities 32.
The Classic Compromise 34. Initiatives and Responses 35.*

Types of Foreign Policies   36

The Policy of the Status Quo 37. The Policy of Revisionism 38.

Recommended Readings   39

2 Government and Policymaking   40

State Organization for International Action   40

*Government and Foreign Affairs 40. The Head of Government 41.
The Foreign Minister and the Foreign Office 42. The Diplomatic
Service 43. Other Departments 44.*

The Policy Process   45

*The Process of Decision 46. The Analysis of Situations 47. The
Choice among Alternatives 48. Evaluating and Revising
Decisions 49.*

Factors Influencing Decisions   50

*The Appreciation of the Problem 50. The Cost/Risk Calculation
51. The Domestic Aspect: Consensus 52. The Incompleteness of
Information 53. The Pressure of Time 54. National Style 55.
Commitments and Precedents 56.*

Recommended Readings   57

3 Capability in Action   58

The Concept of "Capability"   58

Definition 58. The Function of Capability 59. Influence and Coercion in Capability 60. Capability and "Power" 61.

Capability Judgments in Foreign Policy   61

What Is a Capability Judgment? 61. Judging the State's Own Capability 62. Capability Judgments of Other States 62.

Factors in Capability Analysis   63

*Analytical Point of View 63. The Policy Context 64. The Situational Base 65. Relativity of Capability 65. Capability:
A Dynamism 66.*

Elements and Factors of Capability   66

*The Major Categories 67. The Tangibles 68.
The Intangibles 71.*

Recommended Readings   74

4 The Implementing of Decisions   76

Political Techniques: Diplomacy   77

> The Nature of Diplomacy 77. The Functions of Diplomacy 78. Success and Failure in Diplomacy 79.

Economic Techniques: The Carrot and the Stick   81

> The Rationale of Economic Methods 81. Persuasive Economic Techniques 82. Coercive Economic Techniques 83. Conclusions on Economic Techniques 84.

Psychological Techniques: Propaganda and Culture   85

> The Nature of Propaganda 85. Propaganda as a Foreign Policy Tool 86. The Role of Subversion 87. Cultural Techniques in Foreign Policy 88. Cultural Imperialism 88.

Military Techniques: War and Its Approximations   89

> War in Foreign Policy Calculations 89. Technology, Nationalism, and War 90. The Appropriateness of War 91. Military Techniques Short of War 92.

Recommended Readings   93

Part II
The Global Political System: Actors and Their Relations   95

5 Ideas and Patterns of Global Politics   97

The System of States   97

> The Characteristics of the System 97. The State in the System 99. The Interstate Relationship 100. The Pole of Order and the Pole of Disorder 101.

Equality and Inequality in Global Politics   101

> The Political Inequality of States 103. The Trend Toward Greater Inequality 104.

Power Politics   104

> The Assumptions of Power Politics 105. Power Status in World Politics 106. Patterns of Power Politics 107.

The Regularities of Global Politics   109

> Patterns of Equilibrium of Power 109. Multiple Balance of Power 110. Simple Balance of Power 110. Integration of Power 111. Methods of the Balance of Power 112.

Recommended Readings   114

6 New Conditions of Global Politics 116

The States of the World 116

> The Contemporary Global System 117. Origins of the Nation-State System 118.

The Rise and Decline of the Traditional International System 121

> The Old International Order 121. The Emerging System 122. Diversity and Integration 124.

Nonstate Actors in Global Politics 125

> Bloc Actors 126. International Organizations 127. Regional Actors 130. Transnational Actors 131. Nongovernmental Organizations (NGOs) 132.

Recommended Readings 133

7 Conflict and Adjustment 135

The Nature of Conflict 135

> The Sources of Conflict 136. Types of Conflict 136. Objectives of Conflict 139. Balancing-Objective Conflict 139. Hegemonic-Objective Conflict 141. The Tactics of Conflict 142.

The Adjustment of Conflict 143

> Pacific Settlement 144. Coercive Procedures Short of War 147. Forcible Procedures: The Role of War 148.

The Relationship of Force and Political Conflict Resolution 149

> The Changing Nature of Force 149. The Changing Nature of Conflict 150.

Recommended Readings 151

8 Limitations on State Action 153

Morality as a Limitation: What is a Moral Consensus? 154

> The Moral Problem in International Politics 154. The Rupture of the Moral Consensus 155. Morality and Foreign Policy 156. Morality, Interest, and Power 156. The Rise of International Morality 157. The Restraining Effect of Moral Consensus 159.

International Law 159

> *The Subject Matter of International Law 160. Political Conception of International Law 161. Third World Attitudes toward International Law 164. Recent Trends in International Law 166.*

The Calculus of Prudence in Statecraft 167

> *Rationality and Prudence in Statecraft 167. The Role of Probability 167. The Virtues of Half a Loaf 168. The Relativism of Decision 168.*

Recommended Readings 169

Part III
The Substance of Global Politics: Major Issues of our Age   171

9 War and Arms Control   173

Total War and the State System 174

> *The Possibility of Catastrophe 174. The Invalidation of "Victory" 175. The Rethinking of Political Values 175. The Disappearance of Decision 176. Decision by Consensus 177.*

Political Effects of the New Warfare 177

> *The "Balance of Terror" 177. The Declining Credibility of Military Force 179. The End of Status 180. The Utility of Military Force Today 181.*

New Doctrines and the Military Dilemma 183

> *The Importance of Military Doctrine 183. The Doctrinal Crisis: Is This a New Era? 184. Doctrines of Total War 185. Doctrines of Limited War 189.*

The Arms Race, Arms Control, and Transfers 191

> *The Arms Race 192. Strategic Arms Limitation 193. The Future of Arms Control 194. The Role of Political Decision 195. Arms Transfers 195.*

Recommended Readings 196

10 Ideology, Nationalism, and Prestige   198

Ideology and World Politics   198

> The Nature of Ideology 199. Ideology and Foreign Policy 200. Ideology: Myth and Reality 202.

Ideological Formulations in World Politics   203

> The Soviet Approach to the World: A Form of Communism 204. The United States Approach to the World: A Form of Democracy 205. Third World Approach to the World 207.

Nationalism: Old and New   210

> Traditional European Nationalism 210. Nationalism in the Third World 212.

The Prestige Race   213

> What is Prestige? 213. The Race for Prestige 214.

Recommended Readings   215

11 Humankind, Technology and the Ecosystem   216

Energy   217

> Fossil Fuels 217. Nuclear Energy 217. The Second Industrial Revolution 218. Nuclear Energy and World Politics 218. Solar Energy 219. Appropriate Technology 220.

The Conquest of Space   220

> The Breakthrough into Space 221. The Space Race 222. Political and Military Considerations 223. Cooperation in Space 224.

The Population Problem   226

> Causes of the Population Problem 226. Political, Social, and Economic Effects 227. Avenues of Solution 228. Population Pressure and the Shape of World Politics 229.

Mass Communication   229

> Mass Media in World Politics 230. Image Projection in Foreign Policy 230. Destructive and Constructive Applications 231.

Production, Consumption, Distribution   232

> New Production Techniques 232. Rising Consumer Expectations 233. The Problem of Distribution 233. Political Significance 234.

Computers   235
Recommended Readings   236

Introduction: Changing Foci of Analysis

There is no intrinsic advantage of any one model of analysis of world politics. Explanations of human behavior generally reflect the popular theories or the dominant culture in a given era. In the heyday of Darwin, Spencerian biological ("survival of the fittest") models came into vogue. Earlier, as an outgrowth of the impact of Newton, mechanical ("balance of power") models were favored. In the present era statistical models have prevailed in all the sciences, both physical and social.

The value of choosing a particular frame of reference for any inquiry is not that it gets us any closer to the ultimate truth of the matter; rather, it provides a ground on which to stand. The choice of a frame of reference is a strategic issue. Thus it must be determined by its *utility* to the researcher—in terms of manipulative convenience, commonality with viewpoints familiar to prospective users, dramatic impact, or whatever. In any event, selection of a frame of reference for research is a value choice, with all the responsibilities that such a choice entails.

Our analytic tools and research doctrines do not evolve independently of our cultural milieu. Conversely, they also have their effects on us. The claims of scientific objectivity are overstated. Our limited conceptions of what is possible confine the boundaries of our awareness and often act as barriers to understanding. In addition, our underlying assumptions can limit the content of our awareness. While it is true that making assumptions about our surroundings helps us achieve a stable consciousness, our world of assumptions is intrinsically culture bound and conservative. Accordingly, our paradigms or models constitute, at best, local roadmaps and must not be taken for world atlases.

A troublesome aspect of the present day study of international relations has been the adoption of the logic and methodology of Western scientific materialism that defines knowledge primarily by the evidence of reason. Such a rational and linear map of human knowledge is fragmentary. It shows only features that could be proved to exist, leaving important areas of world politics unexplored. The result is an incomplete chart with human values and meanings faintly drawn. Subtle nuances of reality that do not fit are viewed as absurd and mysterious.

The impatience of the rationalists with ambivalence has caused them to trade the risk of error which accompanies the search for universality for the certainty and comfort that comes from parochialism. Only when we develop the view that *being is one,* that human consciousness consists of analytic and holistic modes, can we begin to view the individual parts of reality as well as the whole. The complementary functioning of the analytic and rational and the intuitive and holistic is a measure of human creativity. When we reconcile the two we come to terms with ourselves and bridge the gap between appearance and reality without which there can be no vision. We see humanity as a whole.

Much of the study of international relations denies the existential interpretation of experience by forcing theorists into the role of detached observers. Accordingly, recent methods of study do not seek to explain the human condition from the standpoint of someone actually participating in the process. Yet only by acting as conscious participants can we connect international relations to the reality of our experience in the world. The social world thus becomes what it is—the product of our experience and choices—a drama where we emerge as human beings by pursuing goals of our own choosing.

For this reason, those who deny that we can ever bridge the gap between subjectivity and objectivity fail to realize that subjectivity is not a threat to objectivity but is the promise of its possibility. We should develop a complete view of world politics at the risk of errors of theoretical accuracy. Specialism—the idea that the study of any single subject can be conducted in isolation from every other subject, that the scientific or philosophical pursuit of truth must be conducted independently from ethical implications undermines reality.

The effort to construct such cause-and-effect analyses of human behavior excludes human motives and the moral significance of human behavior. Reality is a succession of intertwined events, each capable of influencing the other.

Development of the Study of International Relations

Four major trends can be discerned in the development of the study of international relations. Beginning shortly before World War I and continuing throughout the interwar years, attention was focused on diplo-

12 Interdependence, North-South Relations, and Development 238

Interdependence, Integration, and Convergence 238
> *Integration 238. Interdependence 240. Convergence Theory 240.*

North-South Relations and the New Economic Order 243
> *The New International Economic Order? 244. The North-South Dialogue 246.*

Development and Approaches to Development 247
> *Approaches to Development 248. Beyond Economics toward Adaptation 252. Development: Problems and Prospects 254.*

Recommended Readings 256

13 Multinational Corporations 258

Historical Evolution of Multinational Corporations 258
Goals of the Multinational Corporations 262
Multinational Corporations and "Nation-States" 265
The Crisis-of-Development Theory 274
Regulating the MNCs 276
Recommended Readings 278

14 Ethnic Nations and Terrorist Groups 279

Ethnic Nations 279
> *Nations vs. States 281. Roots of Ethnic Conflict 283.*

Ethnicity and Development 286
> *Ethnic Nations and Foreign Policy 290. Neoethnic Groups 291.*

Terrorist Groups 294
> *Terrorism as a System 294. Goals and Objectives of Terrorists 295. Legal Control of Terrorism 298. Responses to Terrorism 299.*

Recommended Readings 301

15 Human Rights 302

International Concern for Human Rights 303
The Western Context of Human Rights 307
Marxist and Neo-Marxist Views of Human Rights 310
Human Rights in the Third World: The Islamic States as an Illustration 312
Human Rights in the World Order 316
Toward Global Human Rights 318
Recommended Readings 320

Conclusion: Beyond the Geopolitical System 322

Recommended Readings 330

Index 331

Preface

We live in a new era of global politics. Despite some continuity, the environment—the stage setting of international relations—is undergoing a shift from the historic focus on nation-states as the predominant actors in a world environment organized around coalitions, blocs, and ideological groupings toward a more complex, differentiated, even cosmopolitan order where other kinds of actors wield significant influence. The new global system deemphasizes the importance of distance, introduces such issues as interdependence, integration, North-South relations, development, human rights, and nuclear proliferation, and brings into the spotlight such new actors as multinational corporations, ethnic nations, and terrorist groups. The domestication of international politics and the internationalization of domestic politics is no doubt a disturbing trend for the policymakers who must plot the course of action for their respective states. The global system is simultaneously more parochial and less geographic than the international system of nation-states we are leaving behind. New bonds of community clash with the traditional barriers of geography that formerly separated peoples and states.

The nature of power is undergoing a radical transformation as well. Power is increasingly defined in terms of the maldistribution of information. Inequality, long associated with income, is now beginning to be connected with technological factors and with political and economic control over the global exchange of information. The traditional exercise and conduct of foreign policy which developed in nineteenth-century Europe and which mainly concerned themselves with such geopolitical concepts as the balance of power, the nation-state, national interest, and ideological competition and imperialism are receding from the nomenclature of present and future world political discourse. Such a transformation promises that foreign policy and the bureaucracy that attended its growth will never be quite the same. The new nomenclature of global politics will accordingly emphasize the kinds of new actors and issues envisioned by this third edition of *Concepts of International Politics*. The present volume covers the range from decision makers as actors to the global system as an actor.

The Introduction of the present edition updates our brief survey of the study of international relations and explains our revised treatment of the subject matter. It is disconcerting to ask ourselves questions that undermine long-held assumptions, particularly when those assumptions are attended by an effusion of literature that seeks to explain and legitimize them. Perhaps it is fantasy to believe that any of us can relieve ourselves of the old assumptions, and yet our theories and methodologies should be oriented toward discovering whether those assumptions are consistent with present realities. Our theories and methodologies, predicate to the study of international relations, too often evolve a separate identity and life of their own.

Part I, The Actors: The State in Global Politics, introduces the notion of ascriptive politics and underscores the cultural context of political activity. The perspectives of the concepts treated are broadened to accommodate the emerging politics of transnational exchange. Part II, The Global Political System: Actors and Their Relations, places emphasis on the nature of the new pluralistic environment. The treatment reflects the increasing integration in the global system and its implications to the relationships between various types of actors. Part III, The Substance of Global Politics: Major Issues of Our Age, has undergone total revision. The chapters on war, ideology, technology, and development are updated, and we have expanded our treatment to include new sections on interdependence, integration, and North-South relations. This edition includes new chapters on multinational corporations, ethnic nations and terrorist groups, and human rights. The concise nature of the first two editions remains intact.

Acknowledgments

My coauthor in other volumes, Luiz R. Simmons, helped me to develop the new outline. My student assistants have provided me generous assistance. Allen Hibbard, Dean Millot, and Samuel Olens gave up their whole summer to undertake research for this volume. Joel Busch and Jonathan Davis collected data to update the chapters on multinationals and ethnicity, respectively. Elizabeth Brodbine, Steven Kolodny, and Steve Hyjek investigated the chapters on technology and international law. Eric Benisti, William Toca, and Richard Schultz labored over proofreading. My colleagues at The American University, Professors Theodore Couloumbis, Hamid Mowlana, Howard Cottam, Robert Kirchner, Mohammed Mughisuddin, and Deb Sarkar, gave me constructive criticism. Colonel William Taylor and Captains Daniel Kaufman and James Borowski of the West Point Military Academy contributed invaluable insights to the chapter on war and arms control. My students Alain Sportiche and Ricardo Sarti shared with me their thoughts on integration and convergence theory and North-South relations, respectively. The generous support of my friend, Stan Wakefield, Political Science Editor, Prentice-Hall has been invaluable. Jeanne Hoeting, Production Editor, has provided me with constructive criticism and sound advice. Ethylon Butler and Gregory Ford typed the final manuscript with great efficiency and good humor. Last, but not least, my wife Elizabeth has given me constant support and encouragement.

A.A.S.

matic history. In the interwar years, another concentration was on current events. At the same time, a trend became prominent based on the assumption that international conflicts could be solved by a study of international law and organization. From the beginning of World War II to the present, the study of international relations has been motivated by a "realist" viewpoint, stemming from an empirical orientation.

These trends should not be characterized as clear demarcations, since they have often run parallel to each other or arisen in response to a preceding trend. Contemporary writing incorporates the ideas expressed in all of these trends. Each one contributes in some degree to the advance of the field.

During the period of concern with diplomatic history meticulous attention was paid to historical detail and historical method. The "discipline" was replete with lucid accounts of particular periods or significant diplomatic events. The diplomatic historian sought to explore fully a given historical event, utilizing a maximum quantity of documentary evidence. This historial orientation precluded the development of a theoretical or propositional core for the "discipline."

The second trend arose as a reaction to the diplomatic historian's lack of emphasis on current events. It focused on current events to the virtual exclusion of the historical record. These essentially descriptive efforts, based almost exclusively on *New York Times* accounts and divorced from historical antecedents, were necessarily superficial and speculative. Again, theoretical inquiry was either disavowed or considered unfeasible.

The third trend, professing innovation and borrowing from the first two approaches, turned to the problems of international law and international organization. Its exponents asserted that the task of the scholar was to work toward the transformation of society and the creation of international institutions. This activist position was largely inspired by the establishment of the League of Nations, by the hopes associated with its inception, and by the goal of communicating the ideas of the League to the world, particularly the isolationist-inclined United States. A single belief attracted most of these scholars—the belief that establishment of a strong international organization would resolve the perplexing issues of international politics.

In general, the scholarship of the early interwar period was optimistic. Simply solving the technical and procedural problems of establishing a world government, it was thought, would bring peace within our grasp. Consequently, research tended to focus exclusively on international law and the constitutional and procedural difficulties of international institutions. However, by 1939 historical and practical realities overtook this optimistic approach. The political turmoil in Europe and the Far East in the 1930s, the rise of dictators, and the impotence of the League of

4 INTRODUCTION

Nations in the face of these events contributed to a feeling of despair and cynicism among scholars and the world at large.

Cynicism and disappointment overtook the academic community, particularly in the United States, during World War II. The reformist approach to the study of international relations was jettisoned. The prevailing academic judgment was that the faith of the reformers had been misplaced; individuals were neither perfect nor perfectible; reason and morality had no role to play in the study or practice of international relations; institutions could never be reformed nor war eliminated. Power —usually crudely identified as military strength—was considered the only absolute in the affairs of nation-states, and power politics was thought to be neither immoral nor irrational, only inevitable.

This sour verdict, compounded equally by disillusionment and immediate wartime pressures, continued over the postwar period. It received intellectual underpinning with the appearance, in 1948, of an outstanding contribution to the theoretical approach to international relations: *Politics Among Nations* by Professor Hans J. Morgenthau. International politics, according to Professor Morgenthau, is a struggle for power. States are impelled by the urge to amass, protect, and manipulate power; power is the single "national interest" of everyone. He argued that this clue to the behavior of states would unlock the riddles of international politics and provide the scholar with the insight to understand the process and to give useful advice to the policymaker.

This was (and is) widely advertised as the "realist" approach to international politics, as opposed to the "idealist" proposition of the interwar years. It swept the field for six years after its publication. Morgenthau was not directly challenged until the early 1950s. Then, when students took a second look at his doctrine, they came to appreciate that this type of "realism" was simply pessimism and cynicism about human motivations. Debate rocked the academic community. Morgenthau's doctrine, it was argued, ignored all the evidence that, although we were obviously not angels, neither were we beasts. Today the "realist-idealist" controversy is a good deal less significant, and even Professor Morgenthau is less insistent on the crucial importance of the concept of power.

But although Morgenthau's "realism" is no longer taken seriously, and the "power concept" is not so militantly urged, his real contribution to the field is greater than ever. In his pioneering work, he showed us how to think systematically about international politics—in other words, to think by means of *concepts* rather than in terms of institutions or events. The purpose of such conceptual thinking is to discover valid generalizations about states' behavior rather than determine policies for dealing with particular situations. Morgenthau started us thinking about the *causes* of state behavior in general and social science terms. Even those students who rejected his suggestion that states are basically motivated by a quest for power acknowledged something new—the necessity of discovering the true motivations of states. Students of international relations had been convinced for two generations that history, politics, law, and philosophy were their only sources of insight—that sociologists and psychologists also had a great many interesting things to say about international issues.

As the power concept lost its attractiveness and "realism" its appeal, the true Morgenthau influence began to be felt. Younger scholars, excited by the challenge, undertook to emulate Morgenthau and began to think systematically and conceptually. Certain universities—Harvard, Princeton, Yale, Chicago, Northwestern—became centers of this enterprise that soon began calling itself, with considerable justification, the "scientific" study of international relations. Today, a typical college-level introductory course in international relations—the most accurate indicator of the state of the field—is likely to be a theoretical course concerned with explaining the global political system and establishing a set of generalizations about the actions and interactions of states and other actors in political settings. No longer do students learn details about the foreign policy of France between 1958 and the present as an end in itself. That sort of material is important only for illustrating a generalization or a broadly applicable rule.

Present State of the Art

Today we are all theorists. We analyze the data that come before us, not only for their intrinsic interest or even their policy relevance, but also in an attempt to develop a *conceptual system*—roughly, a workable scheme for classification of data that will make it possible to deal with universals rather than particulars. Those of us who have become "policy oriented" —who want governments to adopt our action formulas—are obliged to take our stand on whatever momentarily convincing theoretical and "scientific" insights we may possess, and to use them as a basis for ordering contemporary data. For a scholar, it is a tremendously exciting field of study, alive with ideas, hypotheses, schemes, and theories; although there may not be as many theories as there are theorists, there is unquestionably a host of ideas wandering around seeking converts. Approving critics talk of a "healthy ferment" within the field; disapproving ones characterize it as one of "unrelieved confusion."

Nevertheless, we may make certain preliminary generalizations about the present state of the study of international relations. First, it is a young field: young in the freshness of its approach and in the chronological age of its students. Only a few of the "old masters" of the profession are generally regarded as productive and provocative today.

Second, the contemporary study of international relations is oriented to a search for explanatory rather than descriptive factors. Value judgments are universally admitted to be relevant to the practice of foreign policy, but since they are subjective, they do not always lend themselves to rational and scientific analysis. The student, therefore, tends to concentrate on discovering the unspoken rules that govern cause-and-effect relationships in the affairs of states and other actors. This may be a weakness. For when scholars suspend their normative judgment, the function of evaluating policies falls to political leaders, journalists, and manipulators of the mass psyche. In any case, modern authors, in a self-conscious attempt to avoid the softheadedness of the utopians or the frozen cynicism of the neo-Machiavellians, usually beg the question of value judgments and seek to liberate themselves from the thrust of day-by-day crisis.

Third, modern students of international relations are by and large interdisciplinary in their orientation and background. Although political science and political understanding are, of course, crucial, so are a host of other kinds of knowledge and insights: economic, demographic, geographic, sociological, psychological, anthropological, linguistic, theological, and so on.

Today there is something of a bias toward the "behavioral" social sciences. These disciplines, it is felt, can help us achieve a total understanding of individual human behavior and thus open the way for their prediction and control. This Promethean urge is offset to some extent by a rising interest in what may be called the "philosophy of science" or the study of the validity and logic of our approaches to gain knowledge. Sober reassessment of our nature will inevitably return us to fundamentals and relieve us of many of our contemporary apprehensions about the potentialities of such intoxicating phrases as the "culture concept," the "iron law of oligarchy," and "small-group dynamics." Sociologists and anthropologists have opened new horizons for us, but they are no better able to resolve all our doubts than were their intellectual forerunners, the philosophers, the jurisprudents, and even the economists.

Finally, the study of international relations today is iconoclastic. Its students attack each other vigorously and the academic scene is littered with the debris of repudiated conceptual schemes.

This lack of consensus is reminiscent of the period of flux and controversy through which the science of astronomy passed after being liberated in the Middle Ages by Copernicus from the geocentric theory of Ptolemy. Dozens of students thronged the observatories and laboratories of the Western world, taking advantage of their new intellectual freedom to observe and classify to their hearts' content. Inevitably they began to hazard generalizations, many of which were proved wrong by their colleagues. Only out of such probing and checking can progress toward valid generalization be achieved in a field where the data can be observed (and classified), but not manipulated.

So much for generalizations about the field. What are contemporary scholars actually concerned with as they try to organize a vast and constantly growing body of data into useful and valid categories? Recent thinking in international relations encompasses five major categories.

We find first a concern with *pretheory* (or theoretical models setting up initial assumptions) and with theory itself—just what theory will look like when it is completed and perfected. This involves a good deal of interest in how "scientific" the field of international relations may expect to become, particularly the question of whether we will ever be able to predict events or must be forever confined to the explanation of events after they occur.

A second major concern of conceptual thinking today is over the various stages of the *process of research*. Since the 1960s scholars have been asking many new questions about the action and interaction of states. Out of this effort has come some appreciation of the data we must acquire before we can give any convincing answers. The search for different sorts of information has led to the development of an entirely new subfield of quantitative methods, comprising new techniques of research and the adaptation of others drawn from the behavioral sciences. The general assumption being that, if scientific knowledge of the world can only be acquired by the observation and classification of quantitative data, then the study of international relations must in some way make use of quantification in its search for scientific truth. Some of us have fallen into the trap laid by the scientific materialists, who contend that only things which can be counted, weighed, measured, or observed can be called "real" (or, by extension, "true"). Most of us, however, try to blend our quantitative work with qualitative analysis and humanist insights.

Qualitative inputs into quantification are improving current quantitative international relations research activities at the stage when concepts are being transformed into symbolic numbers. Quantification initially moved the field from the traditional viewpoint that all questions are particular and unique, but today theorists and empiricists are working together to ensure that the meanings of our concepts are conveyed by our data. Although discovering and understanding patterns of similar and recurrent situations so one might predict the outcome of future events continues to be the primary goal of quantitative research, many more research reports address unique situations unexplained by current theoretical generalizations.

Quantitative methods utilize symbolic language for the analysis of international relations. Mathematical symbols are substituted for verbal characteristics of entities. The purpose of quantitative methods is to avoid diffuse theorizing and to achieve precision in our analyses. Concepts become variables and are submitted to statistical techniques which produce results used to explain the original concepts as well as relationships between those concepts. In this manner, students of international relations seek to take advantage of the technological revolutions in computers and mathematics and to tap the potential for improved data analysis. Data thus organized and analyzed enhances explanations of national and international events.

Quantification covers a broad spectrum of modern research approaches. Examples of a few, follow. *Content analysis,* borrowed from the scientific study of communications, has opened new vistas in such areas as threat perception and symbols of interaction between elites as well as peoples. *Mathematical formulation* of internal relationships, taken from the pioneering work of Lewis Fry Richardson, has come in for some searching reexamination. Using various devices of political *gaming* or *simulation,* researchers have created simplified models of situations in the form of "games" played by human subjects whose actions and reactions are carefully observed and analyzed. This approach has been materially aided by the advance of computers, and projects are now aimed at simulating the behavior of national states.

Another of these approaches is *decision making,* which attempts to determine how decisions are made in practice by delineating several complex clusters of variables which affect the decision-making process at different critical stages. *Cybernetics,* referred to as "communications engineering," suggests different ways of examining the concept of *feedback.* Originally developed by Norbert Wiener, and introduced into political science in the work of Karl W. Deutsch, the explanation of feedback is seen as the missing link in the study of actions and reactions between individuals and states, and describes the manner in which communications control the interaction process.

The third and fourth major concerns of present-day intellectual enterprise require some semantic clarification before their content can be summarized. One of the troubles confronting students of international relations is the imprecise use of terminology. Descriptive terms that should be distinguishable are used as synonyms: *international relations, world politics, global politics, international politics,* and *transnational politics* are only a few names given to the overall field. (These, incidentally, are all drawn from the titles of standard textbooks in the field—including our own—all of them presumably about the identical body of subject matter!) Modern scholars, despairing of ever achieving semantic agreement by converting others to their viewpoint, have begun making their definitions operational by using one single term to refer to only one relationship, and then remaining true to that use.

International relations theory can be said to encompass two kinds of theories: action theory, dealing with an actor as it moves within the system, and interaction theory, dealing with the relations of actors to each other. Action theory is the realm of foreign policy analysis, and interaction theory is that of international politics.

Thus the third contemporary concern is in the area of *action theory*—the way actors and decision makers analyze their situations, select their objectives, and decide upon and execute courses of action. Here some of the most important and interesting areas of inquiry are being explored: ends-means analysis, decision making, capability analysis, and the influence of the structure and functioning of society or environment on the foreign policy of an actor in global politics.

The fourth concern has been the area of *interaction theory:* the sphere of international politics (*politics* rather than *relations,* because the actors are national states and other organizations and groups rather than mere individuals). Here there is much less agreement on definitions and premises than in action theory. The range of speculation and hypothesizing runs from systematic models of the entire global system, at one extreme, to very detailed examinations of specific forms of interaction at the other. There is a further differentiation between studies that investigate the "patterns" of interaction and those that concentrate upon the behavior of the actors engaged in interaction. Areas of analysis in interaction theory include balance theory, equilibrium theory, value theory, game theory, "challenge and response" theory, "image" theory, "expectation" theory, "dependency" theory, "development" theory, and a host of others.

The fifth major concern is what we may broadly call *systems analysis:* the development of testable hypotheses about the global system itself, as distinct from separate actors. By and large this has taken two major forms: (1) a questioning of the concept of "actor" in the international political sense, and (2) a fresh look at the role of environmental factors in the relations of actors. The first form concentrates on the nature of the national state today and the direction of its evolution, the changing concept of the individual and the social group as factors in global politics, and the evolving role of international entities (such as international and regional organizations and "security communities") and transnational actors (such as multinational corporations) as self-energizing actors in the system. The second form concentrates on factors external to human actors, refining concepts like "environmental determinism," "the global social system," "social change," "order," and "community" as they are relevant to the behavior of actors in world politics. Those concerned with the changing concept of "actors" are considered action theorists; those dealing with environmental factors are interaction theorists.

A *system* can be defined as a whole made up of interrelated parts. Systems analysis is a conceptual device which utilizes this idea of systems and applies it to empirical reality for the purpose of categorizing and understanding different phenomena in our complex world.

Systems analysis in its broadest context can be viewed as consisting of four basic elements: (1) the *system* itself, which can be repeatedly broken down into subsystems; (2) its *environment,* or all of reality outside the system; (3) *inputs*—those factors which influence the system and bring about changes in it; and (4) *outputs* emanating from the system—the system's responses to inputs. In analyzing a system, the analyst first attempts to distinguish between the system and the outputs produced by it. In this way the analyst can register how the system changes (i.e., maintains itself) and thus better understand how it operates.

With the possible exception of the universe, no system is perpetually self-maintaining. However, there do exist systems that can respond on their own, to a limited extent, to inputs. The human organism is one of them. Minor wounds will heal without medical attention; most maladies are overcome in a healthy body by means of inherent defense mechanisms; the general system of the body is constantly maintained by the continuing creation of new cells to replace the old. When the body can no longer handle inputs, the human system breaks down and life ceases.

Social and political systems function in much the same way as the human body. Social systems in general, and political systems in particular, are at least partially self-maintaining. A political system, such as the state, responds to the demands of inputs by issuing outputs that will hopefully counteract stresses created by the inputs.

Systems analysis has not been a completely useful tool for analyzing the behavior of the global political system and its subsystems. A principal difficulty is our inability to define explicitly the distinct components of the system and the environment. The problem of delineating the boundaries of a system is especially acute when dealing with social systems. In viewing international relations, we must ask: What is and what is not to be regarded as political in human behavior at the global level? If the political system is viewed as the aggregate of the political activities or roles of its members, where do we draw distinctions among political, social, religious, and economic activities?

Thus, while systems analysis is a useful theoretical tool, operationally it runs into great difficulties in meeting its first task—that which must be dealt with by a specific system.

Recent Trends in International Relations Theory

We can best appreciate the direction this vast array of theoretical enterprise is taking by comparing it with its primary source, traditional political theory. Two logically related trends are discernible in the transition from traditional political theory to recent theories in international relations.

The first trend is the revision of the traditional image of the *political person,* who, according to the prior image, is rational in either political, economic, or moral terms. Such classically oriented theorists as Charles Beard, Hans J. Morgenthau, and Jacques Maritain retain this image of the political person derived from Platonic, Thomist, or liberal sources.

Such other recent leading figures in international relations as Kenneth Boulding, Herbert Kelman, Harold Lasswell, David McClelland, and Charles Osgood, influenced to a greater or lesser degree by the behavioral sciences, have rejected the classical image of the political person. They are instead attempting to understand that individual in terms of psychological motivations or sociological conditionings. They speak of the "images," "cognitive structures," "values," "needs for achievement," and "stereotypes" which govern the behavior of political actors. Dismissing the doctrine of human reason, they assume that human consciousness is a function of fluid settings.

The second trend is revision of the image of *political community* held by traditional political theorists. The classical image was formalistic. Traditional theorists dealt in such grandiose abstractions as national ethos, the state, realism, sovereignty, and the public philosophy. Such theorists as Raymond Aron, E. H. Carr, Louis Hartz, A. D. Lindsay, and Walter Lippmann employ such concepts gleaned from classical sources.

Other theorists in international relations, such as Gabriel Almond, David Apter, Karl Deutsch, David Easton, and Richard Snyder, have discarded the classical image of the political community in their attempt to make the traditional abstractions measurable, or at best tangible. According to them, the state is a decision-making process, while sovereignty becomes no more than the state's situational capabilities. The public philosophy is simply those values which the political system allocates at large. These writers look for linkages among the social, economic, and cultural system of collectivities and the political systems. They employ indices, variables, and empirically based concepts to analyze all political communities.

The new directions in theory of international relations have resulted in greater awareness of political reality. Empiricism has replaced the narrow moralism and legalism that prevented traditional political theorists from seeing the political collectivity for what it is. Multilevel analyses of causation have replaced simplistic economic and, power-politics, interpretations of political action. In a sense, recent theorists can feel proud for having liberated the study of international relations from the strictures of traditional political theory.

A primary weakness of recent theory is its failure to take into account human motives as expressed in terms of values and ideologies. Perhaps recent theorists have overreacted to the traditional political analyses of such "isms" as constitutionalism, capitalism, nationalism, communism, and imperialism. Yet political theorists need to recognize the methodological significance of values and the substantive relevance of ideologies. That is, they must always explicate all the assumptions underlying their analyses and recognize that ideological factors are crucial determinants of political realities. Many theorists seem to overlook the fact that the political world is not free of values.

Another weakness of recent theorists is that a large number of them view politics as nothing more than the interaction of tensions, conflicts, and diffuse pressures which stem from groups and subgroups throughout the world. Many recent theorists of the behavioral persuasion have discounted the individual as a real actor. The individual is almost abolished, and only tensions, desires, frustrations, and pathological tendencies remain. This trend in the field can be called *reductionism* because the complex nature of the human behavior of individuals is reduced to a few ambiguous, but manageable, concepts. As a result of this reductionist movement, recent theory has developed a world view that lacks stability and boundaries. Analyzing such esoteric factors as childhood fantasies, swaddling practices, and even mail flows produces conclusions of doubtful political relevance.

Of course, the problem today is that there is no commonly accepted criterion of what is germane to politics. Without making certain assumptions, if only for immediate purposes of analysis, theorists cannot proceed from method to substance. This is not to say that theorists in international relations should return to the rationalistic and formalistic womb of traditional political theory. Nonetheless, every theoretical field of study has to include some constants, and the study of international politics is no exception.

Many theorists' interests have resulted not only in new substantive insights, but also in the strict compliance to formal methods of research. At times it seems that model building in the social sciences has become an end in itself. In refuting the accusation of "scholasticism," theorists argue that their approaches are not scholastic nor formal, and that they disdain universals and are concerned with the real, specific things found in the world. This argument cannot be accepted. The proposed general theories recently put forth are almost without exception based on formalisms of some type. An example is the incoherent accumulation of data which represents only synthetic theoretical advances and has yielded nothing more than statistical profiles and collections of stereotypes.

The formalism that is present in a great deal of our research methods has also led to fragmentation within the study of international relations. Methodological cults do not communicate with one another because there are no common grounds. For instance, many research analysts speak in jargon that is unintelligible to all except the initiated. Although some advocates of conceptual rigor do promise that time will yield a new synthesis or concensus for analyzing international politics, the fruits of the past three decades do not imply this happy ending.

Theory, generally understood by its strict definition, does not explain very much about international relations. In many cases, knowledge of human behavior in one period is simply translated into the jargon of the next, with little increase in understanding. Understanding means knowledge sufficient to predict behavior, and there is an absense of evidence that Alexander the Great had any less understanding of the probable behavior of his opponents than General Westmoreland, two thousand years later, had of his.

Finally, many of the approaches and methods of recent theorists have tended to distort political realities. Having invested so much effort in developing methodologies, theorists who subsequently turn to substantive analyses are often trapped. By making all political realities fit their theoretical models, they have confused reality with the products of their own minds. Rather than confront reality, they often merely refine their techniques, retest their theorems one against the next, strengthen the logical coherence of their models, and close every possible gap or hole left in their systems. Because their methodological systems are so perfectly self-contained, they fail to account for many substantive factors of political relevance dealt with by the traditional, historical, institutional, or ideological approaches.

So we see that empiricism has often led to an examination of nonpolitical, even trivial, phenomena. Reductionism has tended to cloak political reality behind a behavioral metaphysics. Logical consistency has resulted at times in rigid formalism. Lurking beneath "value-free" analyses are generally disguised judgmental assumptions and unresolved (and perhaps unresolvable) moral issues. These weaknesses, however, are not intrinsic to the theoretical study of world politics. The pitfalls can be overcome when theorists reconcile their methodological fervor with the imperatives of substantive analysis.

The success of the scientific revolution in the physical and biological sciences through reductionism—explaining matter by its particles, and explaining biological processes by chemical and physical ones—became popularized in the social sciences. The study of economics was reduced to the study of psychological-rational particles, and psychology to a study of biological and mechanical units. In international relations the reductionist process attempts to explain the behavior of actors in psychological, economic, and mathematical-statistical terms.

The cultivation of technical and quantitative competence, and the discovery of psychological, economic, and sociological factors in the study of international relations, have been valuable. The emphasis on method rather than substance, however, has produced a situation in which the study of international relations is defended in terms of the methods used rather than of the problems treated or the issues explained.

More recently, economists and psychologists seem to be reappraising their earlier aspirations and expectations. The effort to interpret all interactions in terms of behavioral determinism has confounded the best efforts of the social scientist. Students of international relations must pause to ponder their methodological direction. The task of discovering and classifying regularities, stable relationships, and uniform sequences cannot be performed without first understanding the creative disorder of human interventions and strategies.

The study of international relations can adapt creatively to the challenges that confront us. It can explore the possibilities of human solidarity, which can overcome both despair over the future and its adverse, technocratic conceptions of the future, and develop an ecological harmony between the individual and nature. We cannot afford to abandon our search for new explanations nor our resolve to construct new research tools and methodologies. Tools and methods do not constitute a separate branch of knowledge. Their value is determined by their contribution to the intellectual tradition of scholarship.

The Approach of this Study

Politics can be analyzed usefully and instinctively from any of three points of view. First, we can inquire into the motivations and tactics of individual political actors as they move within the political system. Second, we can examine the political system itself—the social structure within which the political actors move—in order to understand the processes of political action and the opportunities and limitations affecting its members. Last, we can focus on the substance of political action to discover what the actors are concerned with and the possible social consequences of their political maneuvering.

In this book we shall look at global politics from each of these points of view. Part I is a discussion of the individual political actor—in this particular case, the state and its foreign policy. This will include a study of the problem a state faces in relating the ends it seeks to the means at its disposal. The relationship is obviously two-way: Ends without means add up to futility; means not related to relevant ends culminate in frustration. Both the attempts and generalizations about ends (via such notions as national interest and the calculus of ends) and the renewed interest in such concepts as strategy and ideology reveal the important relationships.

This study then examines foreign policy decision making and the environmental factors influencing it. We turn next to the progressively subtle methodology of discovering the effective range of choice open to the policymaker at any given time. The once-sovereign word *power*, as representing an analytically useful concept, is challenged. *Power*, in a sense, betrayed its advocates by being simultaneously too broad and too constricted. It concealed a fatal imprecision beneath a facade of great clarity. We substitute *capability* for the old idea of *power* and divide it into two more sharply defined terms: *influence*, which refers to the ability of the state to gain consensus by persuasive devices short of force, and *coercion*, the province of force pure and simple, as one state attempts to bend the other to its will. Finally, we study the various means employed by policymakers to implement foreign policy decisions.

Part II centers on the global political system, both in theory and in practice. Our effort here is devoted to a study of the patterns of interaction among states and the assumptions underlying them. We begin by examining the concepts of sovereignty, independence, power politics, the balance of power, and the regulating mechanisms of international politics and their implications to transnational relations, that is, international relations involving actors other than states. This book does not attempt to develop a rigid and overall set of categories of interaction. We question the assumption that any one of these concepts is the proper focus for the study of international and transnational politics.

"Balance of power," a phrase that refers to a condition, can easily become "balanced power," which refers to a relationship of interaction. *Equilibrium theory* seems a natural derivation from the notion of balance. Many studies of power, control, and capability essentially seek to learn more about what is balanced in an equilibrium and what falls out of balance and creates disequilibrium, tension, and crisis. The very idea of deterrence clearly stems from analysis of balance-type interaction; mutual deterrence is a classic type of balance or unstable equilibrium.

Even many of those who reject *balance* as a useful interaction concept acknowledge the need for a "central" or "organizing focus," some key interaction concept that will provide the framework for more elaborate analysis. This was the rationale of the original Morgenthau "power thesis." *Politics Among Nations* was more a study of interaction than of action, more an analysis of international politics than a study of the foreign policy of states. When Morgenthau postulated the search for power by all states, he sought primarily to provide the motivation necessary to set interaction patterns in motion. We argue that the proper focus for our study of interaction is *value theory*, since all politics is a struggle for the maximization of competing value systems. Because this clashes with the "value-free" orientation of present-day conceptual debate, however, this approach so far has relatively few supporters among interaction theorists (although many more among analysts of the foreign policy process).

We examine next the barrage of exertive influences, changing conditions, and emerging directions in the present global system. We analyze the sources and changing nature of conflict, the relationship of force to conflict resolution, and the restraints upon conflict.

Part III deals with the substance of global politics and is organized as a discussion of actors and issues affecting the entire system and its members: war, ideology and nationalism, technology, interdependence, integration, north-south relations, development, multinational corporations, ethnicity and terrorism, human rights, and order are all studied in detail.

The following pages will provide you with a map to identify the main features of international and transnational relations. You will be exposed to the concepts that are in daily use among academic students and practitioners of this great human drama. You will be initiated into some of the operational hypotheses of the field, and have now been alerted to the widespread lack of consensus among us. It is now appropriate for you to inquire what relevance all of this abstract system building has for you.

Every action that an individual makes in the world is postulated upon a theory; every interpretation we make of an event is grounded in certain operational (perhaps unconscious) generalizations about the world and our place in it. There is no more vicious (and effective) theorist than the individual who says, "I don't have any theory, I just let the facts speak for themselves," for such a person advances a simplistic explanation—which is hence very appealing. Of course, even the supremely "objective" facts of history must be interpreted anew to each generation. History itself teaches us nothing; historians, however, teach us a great deal—and even the most dedicated historical scholars have a theoretical base that governs the inclusion and exclusion of data in the history they write.

So we all base our actions on theory. There is no question about the role of generalization, hypothesis, and relationship between events in human endeavor. The real questions are not whether responsible officials use theory in their judgments, but whether their theoretical foundations are explicit and self-conscious, or concealed, implicit, and often misunderstood. There is a second and equally important reason why practical persons can benefit from theoretical discussion: in the process they may discover that the generalizations upon which they proceeded in the past are inconsistent, incomplete, or perhaps even wrong. There is always the possibility, therefore, that a personal inventory of one's working concepts might result in their overhaul, or at least in their clarification, strengthening, or elaboration. What we are suggesting is that, since you will probably never be able to dispense with theoretical and conceptual considerations in your encounter with international relations, there is a reason for you to become acquainted with the broad body of such discussion that is going on in the academic community and among serious students of all sorts.

We have already pointed out the determination of most current thinkers to avoid normative judgments and all questions of "good or bad" and "right or wrong." Speaking personally, this is a tendency we find utterly deplorable. Only when we focus on the problems that divide the world and not just the problems induced by one's own method of knowing, and only when we approach these problems not merely with the tools of a laboratory but also with human compassion, will be able to see the resemblance among all of us. We are all one.

Neither scientific truth nor human freedom benefits from new thinking that implies a suspension of moral judgment on the objects of inquiry. These are not mathematical symbols or hydrocarbon molecules that the scholars are studying; their subject matter consists of living, feeling human beings. It would be cold comfort, if we were all blown up in a cloud of radioactive dust, to realize that the scientific scholars knew exactly why this was happening. Individuals live by the things they cannot prove, and we lose much if in our search for the reasons for human behavior, we forget the truth about us is not as important as the miracle that we exist at all.

As you deal with the problems of global politics, never forget that you are engaged in something that matters in the here and now, as well as in the awful scales of truth. Be logical, scientific, rigorous, objective, and honest; but above all, be compassionate. Think in terms of concepts, as we feel you must; but never forget to think like a human being.

Recommended Readings

ALMOND, GABRIEL, and G. BINGHAM POWELL. *Comparative Politics Today: A World View.* Boston: Little, Brown, 1974.
COPLIN, WILLIAM D., and CHARLES W. KEGLEY, eds. *Analyzing International Politics: A Multimethod Introduction,* New York: Praeger, 1975.

DAHL, ROBERT A. *Modern Political Analysis* (3rd ed.). Englewood Cliffs, N.J.: Prentice-Hall, 1976.

DEUTSCH, KARL W. *The Analysis of International Relations* (2nd ed.). Englewood Cliffs, N.J.: Prentice-Hall, 1978.

HAAS, MICHAEL. *International Systems: A Behavioral Approach*, New York, Chandler, 1974.

KAPLAN, ABRAHAM. *The Conduct of Inquiry: Methodology for Behavioral Science.* San Francisco: Howard Chandler, 1964.

KAPLAN, MORTON. *System and Process in International Politics.* New York: John Wiley and Sons, 1957.

LIEBER, ROBERT J. *Theory and World Politics.* Cambridge, Mass.: Winthrop, 1972.

MCCLELLAND, CHARLES A. *Theory and the International System.* New York: Macmillan, 1966.

MORGENTHAU, HANS J. *Politics Among Nations,* (5th ed.). N.Y., ALFRED A. KNOPF, 1973.

———. *Scientific Man Versus Power Politics.* Chicago: University of Chicago Press, 1946.

ROSENAU, JAMES N., VINCENT DAVIS, and MAURICE A. EAST. *The Analysis of International Politics.* New York: Free Press, 1972.

ROSENAU, JAMES N. *In Search of Global Patterns,* New York: Free Press, 1976.

SINGER, J. DAVID. *Quantitative International Politics.* New York: Free Press, 1968.

SULLIVAN, MICHAEL P. *International Relations: Theories and Evidence.* Englewood Cliffs, N.J.: Prentice-Hall, 1976.

WRIGHT, QUINCY. *The Study of International Relations.* New York: Appleton-Century-Crofts, 1955.

I

*THE ACTORS:
THE STATE
IN GLOBAL POLITICS*

The Nature of Foreign Policy

1

This book is a guide to the ideas we use in the discussion, study, or practice of global politics. Our subject matter is first international and transnational, dealing with relationships among states as well as between them and nonstate actors. It is also a "political" study; the kinds of relationships in which we are primarily interested are those that we shall define as political. There are many relations other than political—for example, economic, cultural, interpersonal—but we shall consider these less on their own merits than in terms of their impact on the political behavior of peoples, governments, states, and other actors.

Politics: The Struggle to Maximize Values

Politics is a common word in the English language that refers to an equally familiar phenomenon. However, precise definition of the word is usually rather difficult. Individuals have strong emotional responses to the concept; any definition cannot help but reflect the definer's biases. Since the words *politics* and *political* will appear repeatedly throughout this book, it is important that we make our meaning explicit at the outset. Our first undertaking, therefore, is a definition of *politics* and a demonstration of how political concepts are expressed in a state's foreign policy.

The Nature of Politics

Politics is the organizational activity of individuals seeking to maximize their convictions about social values. Through political action, individuals attempt to realize their differing notions of the "public good."

22   THE ACTORS

Thus politics is really a *process*—a means to a value-centered end—which is meaningless except in terms of the values that give rise to political action.

Such a definition of *politics* covers a wide range of activities—as it must, since political acts include virtually the entire spectrum of human activity. The definition is, however, quite explicit in emphasizing *social values* as the roots of politics. Since these shared ideas of "the good" are what make political action unique, almost any human action can, with an appropriate value motivation and organizational setting, be termed *political*. Without the value drive or the organizational nexus, the same action is in the strict sense *apolitical*.

Human beings do not agree on any single inclusive set of social values. Struggles reflecting differing value judgments are therefore an integral part of the political process. Achievement of a political goal is normally at the expense of other political actors who have their own, different goals and aspirations. Thus the range of political action may extend from agreement and cooperation between political actors to the various zones of partial agreement or total opposition and conflict. The experienced political practitioner possesses strategies and tactics designed to attain the highest feasible level of value satisfaction.

These two ingredients of politics—the value-rooted ends of action and the political climate of struggle and disagreement—are as clearly demonstrated in world politics as they are in the more familiar environment of electoral politics in a democracy. Foreign policy consists of a state's attempt at realizing, on the global plane, what it conceives as good. It is the fact that foreign policy is rooted in values that makes nationalism so intense today and makes resolution of conflict so difficult. World politics thus takes place in a climate of disagreement and conflict—a fact that would seem to require no demonstration. In its key aspects, then, global politics is the same sort of social process as politics at any level; with appropriate conceptual adjustments, insights derived from world politics are broadly applicable to internal political relations, and vice versa.

Within any political system, disagreement and conflict over values takes place within a larger value consensus that helps hold the system together. Such agreement on fundamentals gives rise to the system in the first place and makes political action possible. We shall see later that the global system incorporates such a consensus (although only imperfectly grasped by many states), and that political action on the global plane is feasible only in its terms.

Social Values and Foreign Policy

Each society, especially when it deems itself a "nation" and is organized into a state, has a social code that contributes to its peculiar identity and which activates and energizes all political action. If the prevailing concepts of "good" and "evil" could be realized within the boundaries of the state itself, they would have little or nothing to do with world affairs. However, ever since the Industrial Revolution and the dawn of modern nationalism, national value structures have impinged upon the world outside their borders; social values have thus become intimately connected with questions of foreign policy.

Certain aspirations, needs, and wants are widely shared in any society. Many of these require governmental action to attain even partial fulfillment, and individuals look to their political leaders to act on their behalf. Obviously, one area of value preference in which public agencies are the only effective actors is that of international and transnational relations. Individuals or subgroups of a society cannot function adequately in the interest of the entire group; only officials armed with the authority and sanctions of society at large can deal with extrasocietal problems. Foreign policy, therefore, is the exclusive province of government, because only government can act on behalf of all the people individually and of the society collectively.

Governmental action in the world arena is determined by the set of social values controlling the society at large. Before the birth of political consciousness in the states of Europe, international politics consisted only of the relations of kings; mass attitudes and preferences had no foreign policy relevance. The rise of nationalism made foreign policy "democratic"—in the sense that governments became obliged to structure their international efforts to reflect the value judgments of the people. Analysis in modern foreign policy making is thus basically a procedure for translating the value preferences of a society into a workable frame for governmental action.

Value Content of Foreign Policy

From an analytical point of view, we must avoid becoming overly specific about the social values that underlie foreign policy. Values are seldom self-evident, and the concepts of good and evil that a government chooses to pursue always stem from a mixture of sources within the society. We can identify at least five differing versions of "good" that are usually combined in a single foreign policy:

1. *The good of individual citizens*—primarily the wish to be secure in their person, beliefs, and property against threats from outside their society.

THE ACTORS

2. *The good of the society at large*—collective values, normally including preservation of the social system, maximization of its prestige, protection of its ideology, and so on.
3. *The good of the state* (the juristic personality)—most commonly including self-preservation, security, well-being, and the "strength" of the political unit.
4. *The good of "special-interest groups" in the state/society*—which tend to be included to the maximum extent possible within the operative notion of the general interest and contribute largely to the shaping of public policy on specific issues.
5. *The good of the government itself and of its personnel*—values peculiar to membership in a public community that inescapably find expression in foreign policy.

Thus the values maximized by the state in foreign policy are varied in origin and substance. Officials charged with policy making shape this broad spectrum of needs and wants into some semblance of integrity and apply the resulting *value synthesis* to international politics. The policymaker may compromise among competing values, accepting some at the cost of rejecting others, or he may find some other rationalizing device. Policymakers cannot, however, avoid the necessity of building their approaches to world affairs on a foundation of value choices.

Foreign Policy and International Politics

The base of any foreign policy is a state's mission to maximize its value synthesis. Once it moves onto the global scene, however, it encounters other states and actors, each seeking accomplishment of its own value-derived goals. Thus world politics is basically a contest of values in which the moves are determined less by objective environmental conditions than by the judgments individuals make about those conditions.

In this respect, world politics is not dissimilar to domestic politics. There is a significant difference between the two, however, that makes the global variety peculiarly perplexing and fascinating to its students. Although domestic politics go on within a well-understood set of rules that cover the range of permissible action and are enforced by social and governmental mechanisms, no such structure inhibits the practice of world politics. States are free to pursue their value purposes as far as their wishes and strength will permit; they are normally checked by the strength of other states and only occasionally by institutional mechanisms.

World politics, because of the highly internalized motivations of its practitioners and the lack of universal limitations on approved action, is ever on the verge of explosion. The values that go into foreign policy are deeply held and powerful; the restraints are relatively few and relatively impotent. In many respects, therefore, world politics is a manifestation of the political process in its most crude form.

Ascriptive Politics

Politics is also a cultural activity. Depending on the culture in which it is studied, it can be intensely rationalistic and competitive or it can be hierarchical and passive. This is what we mean when we use the term ascriptive politics.

World politics is a particular species of politics. The actors are states and other groups and organizations, not merely individuals, and the environment is neither competitive nor hierachical, but *amniotic*—responding to the desires and needs of actors in neither a rational manner nor by means of a hierarchical process. The consensus or rules which characterize both competitive and hierarchical systems are conspicuously absent.

In order to impose some kind of order on our understanding of world politics, the study of international relations has insisted that in spite of the differences which characterize the internal politics and cultures of states, the external politics of these states can be conceptualized by certain common norms and attitudes. By making these assumptions we ignore the broad spectrum of human cultures. World order does not necessarily mean a world that operates on universally agreed upon cultural values.

Recent studies of international politics have concentrated on discovering the common denominators of relations among states from which a calculus of war and peace could emerge. The reductionist emphasis on common denominators has often obscured the multifaceted nature of the phenomenon of politics. Are all states motivated by the desire to maximize power, or to accumulate wealth? Or is it only the imperial and acquisitive states?

What has occurred over the last three decades is the reshaping of our concept of politics to accommodate various theories of political behavior. Although there is a chicken-and-egg quality to this debate, we can discern certain contours of the phenomenon of politics and its relations to theories of politics. *Scientific politics,* as it is called, proceeds from the assumption that all states share a common agenda in world politics, the only differences being quantitative. Presumably the Bahamas would like to exercise the power of the Soviet Union but is constrained by size, population, resources, and industry.

The problem with such theories is that they seek to reduce the external behavior of states to a formula without examining states' internal environments, a wholly arbitrary and artificial separation of a political organism. Such theories reinforce the perception that external politics is governed by one set of rules and internal politics by another.

The fact of the matter is quite different. Although the absence of universally held norms compels each state to assert its interest in terms of similar demands, the character or nature of those demands arises from a specific sociopolitical culture. Theories of international politics have concentrated on the technique of conflict resolution, but have perhaps consciously avoided the content of the conflict. Theory has been preoccupied with the how of politics but not the why. In the world arena—an environment characterized by an absence of consensus and no enforcement machinery—how states are left to resolve their differences is only limited by resources and moral reservation.

But what has theory of international politics contributed to our appreciation of *why* states have differences? It is clear that such differences do exist. The oil-rich states are not as concerned with an "energy crisis" as the oil-poor. The state surrounded by oceans is not as concerned with "security" as the states surrounded by traditionally hostile enemies. The "scientific" study of international relations has tended to tell us how states resolve their difficulties but has not elucidated the reasons why they have them. Consequently, we have had little success in constructing paradigms of what kinds of states are likely to clash with others and what can be done to prevent such collisions.

The recognition that politics is essentially an ascriptive phenomenon—that it is culture specific and that the values and goals which states seek to maximize are a reflection of these factors—makes us attentive to these differences and less likely to believe that "they" think precisely as "we" do.

Perhaps one example will suffice:

> The United States underestimated the will of the North Vietnamese to resist aerial bombardment. This tragic miscalculation, it now seems, was a logical outgrowth of the belief that the North Vietnamese, as a state, shared certain common objectives with the U.S. American policymakers determined that since the U.S. would have responded to the threat of bombing to save its industries, so too would the North Vietnamese.

This was not a casual miscalculation but the logical outcome of the belief that all states have a breaking point which could be methodically determined. Our emphasis on the common denominators which the North Vietnamese presumably shared with other states obscured the context of their demands, the nature of the conflict, and the tenacity of their resistance.

Our theories of international relations have not equipped us to predict dysfunctionalism in the global system. This is because the pursuit of common denominators has caused us to emphasize what is similar in the politics of states, not what is different. It is the differences with which ascriptive politics is primarily concerned and by which the calculations of war and peace ultimately are determined.

Interests, Goals, and Objectives

Our discussion up to this point has established that foreign policy is purposeful and that value judgments are the basis upon which a state proceeds in world politics. The state, however, must act in the real world; it cannot function effectively on behalf of values that remain abstract, absolute, and undefined. No foreign policy can really achieve "freedom," "power," "justice," "honor," or even "peace"—to cite a few of the more common values ascribed to foreign policy—except in concrete terms and in relation to specific situations. The policymaker must translate "values" into "objectives" before he can begin to act.

From "Social Values" to "National Interest"

The key concept used by a policymaker in applying value judgments to the realities of political action is "national interest," a notion notoriously vague and difficult to define. It may be considered as the general, long-term, and continuing purpose which the state, the nation, and the government all see themselves as serving. It is rooted in the social consciousness and cultural identity of a people and includes all the disparate ideas of the "good" that we have noted. In practice it is synthesized and given form by the official policy makers themselves.

We cannot be more specific in defining the content of national interest, since both its value roots and the process of its synthesis are peculiar to the history and institutional makeup of any given society. We can, however, be quite explicit about its function. As the overriding purpose governing the state's relations with the outside world, national interest serves two purposes: (1) It gives policy a general orientation toward the external environment, and (2) more importantly, it serves as the controlling criterion of choice in immediate situations. National interest, in other words, dictates the nature of the state's long-term effort in foreign policy and governs what it does in a short-term context.

National interest thus manifests itself as an application of a state's values to its place in world politics. It is, within the terms of its social origin, relatively slow to change, and its change is evolutionary rather than revolutionary. National interest provides the necessary measure of consistency to national policy. A state consciously adhering to its national interest in a rapidly changing situation is more likely to maintain its balance and continue to progress toward its goals than it would if it changed its interest in adapting to each new situation.

Ends and Means in Foreign Policy

Developing a definition of national interest (which may remain an abstract concept) is the first step in formulating a foreign policy, even though it remains an abstract concept. Before the concept may actually serve as a guide to action, the policymaker must grapple with a classic problem: reconciliation of ends and means.

The ends of state action in world politics—realization of the national interest and such national goals as may be derived from it—are postulated a priori. Before policy can be made, the policymaker must somehow mesh the facts of the problem, including whatever means are available, with the conceptual system formed by the set of ends. In specific policy situations, one of the most difficult problems faced by policymakers is how to determine of the most appropriate relationship between abstract ends and concrete means.

Ends, in theory, determine means. In a situation permitting several possible courses of action, the one chosen should most directly advance the national interest. In practice, however, there is always a temptation to allow means to determine ends, to decide that the objective most easily attained is the one the state should seek. Intermediate ends—ends that, if achieved, are intended only to serve as means to still further ends—tend also to acquire an absolute relevance in themselves as ends.

The effectiveness of a state's foreign policy will inevitably suffer if there is any confusion in the ends-means relationships, any loss of appreciation of the value roots of policy, or any reluctance to remain firmly committed to long-range concepts of interest. Governments that succumb to these dangers quickly find themselves on the strategic defensive and largely at the mercy of others who know more precisely what they are trying to accomplish. There is no substitute for a clearly rationalized and thoroughly understood purpose in foreign policy, especially in the contemporary period of great change in the global milieu.

The Nature of an Objective

State action in foreign policy is always in pursuit of an *objective*—that state of affairs which the state feels is most in its national interest in a particular *situation.* An objective may call for some change in the existing situation or for the protection and preservation of a desirable set of existing relationships. It is crucial, however, that formulated objectives be realistic.

Objectives are defined in practice by applying the concept of national interest to the generalized situation in which policy is being made. Before a particular objective is so defined, an intermediate value judgment is often made concerning a *goal,* defined here as the most desirable future state of affairs regarding a particular *issue.* Adoption of a goal, since it is based on relatively fixed factors, helps policymakers evaluate the dynamic forces that will shape the particular objective selected.

Thus, for any single policy situation, the relations between the national interest, the postulated goal, and the selected objective are largely functions of different time spans of analysis. National interest is a long-range factor: Its interests will presumably keep the state involved in the problem forever, or at least as long as the political system endures. A goal is considered operational for as far into the future as can be anticipated analytically. As long as the general shape of the situation remains constant, the postulated goal will be in effect. Any drastic change, however, would require selection of a new goal more in harmony with the nature of the problem. An objective is immediate or short-range in its time component. It is the state of affairs considered attainable in terms of the forces operative at the moment of decision.

The ends-means relationship is central to the choice of an objective. While the goal represents the best conceivable state of affairs, the objective is actually the closest approximation to the goal that decision makers believe feasible. The postulated end of state action in most situations does no more than point out the direction in which the state should move. The distance it actually goes along this imaginary line depends on the means the state has available for use in the situation.

The Common Objectives of States

After arguing, as we have, that each state's set of interests, goals, and policy objectives is unique, it may seem somewhat contradictory to suggest that it is possible and useful to discuss "the common objectives of states." The uniqueness of state purpose is confined to matters of detail, but the general problem of foreign policy presents itself to all states in the same fundamental terms. States are compelled, by the logic of sovereignty and the inexorabilities of the political system in which they function, to seek the same kinds of satisfaction. At least conceptually, we may divide the objectives of any foreign policy into six categories, remembering that each state defines its purpose within each category in such specific language as suits its dominant interest:

SELF-PRESERVATION. Analytically, self-preservation must be considered an ubiquitous objective of state action. The "self" to be preserved—which action is deemed a supreme good—is the collective entity of the state and its human and territorial manifestations. A state's desire for existence, if it wishes to remain a state, is self-evident. States normally act so as to maximize their chances of survival in the world; for most this is simultaneously the highest and most basic purpose of foreign policy.

SECURITY. Second in importance to self-preservation is the objective of security. Since existence for any state is never absolutely certain, each is impelled to arrange its relations with the rest of the world so as to maximize its possibilities for continued existence. This is usually called a "search for security," but real security is clearly unattainable under the prevailing conditions. What the security objectives of states amount to are no more than the reduction to a practical minimum of all visible and conceivable threats. A measure of insecurity is really an inescapable cost of doing business in the state system.

WELL-BEING. Third in the list of common objectives of states is well-being. After the higher-priority objectives of self-preservation and security have been satisfied to the maximum permitted by the state's situation, the state tries to improve the actual conditions of existence of its citizens. This well-being, in both conceptual and practical terms, is the welfare of the collectivity rather than that of individuals. The unit of calculation here is "the economy," and the measures of prosperity tend today to be those familiar "macroeconomic" concepts, "gross national product" and "rate of economic growth." Of course, there may be no real clash between collective well-being and the economic welfare of individuals, and even when such a conflict develops it is only seldom on an explicit "guns-or-butter" basis. In cases of unavoidable divergence of interest, however, the normal pattern of political value choices dictates that collective well-being takes precedence over any individual or group interests.

PRESTIGE. Another common objective of state action is prestige. States normally act so as to appear impressive to others, in order to receive deference and status concessions from them. The achievement of a satisfactory prestige level is one of the more frustrating problems of foreign policy: how much prestige and status is "enough" in a given context? It is obvious that any politically self-conscious people have a strong urge to be well thought of by others and to seek concrete evidence of its prestige. One serious complication regards the criteria for prestige: A state may wish prestige in certain terms but receive it in other terms. A reputation for high level of artistic achievement, for example, is of little significance to a state that wants to be known as a major military power. The difficulties implicit in any attempt to "win" prestige, however, have not served to deter states from the attempt.

IDEOLOGY. Of great importance to some states is the promotion and/or protection of ideology. The present century, far more than any since the sixteenth, is an age of total belief systems, and a number of states, both large and small, have made both the protection and promulgation of their ideologies a major element in foreign policy. As a foreign policy objective, ideology, with its implications of proselytization and messianism, again raises questions of the explicitness and attainability of goals and of the criteria of success and failure in foreign policy. There is, furthermore, some contemporary evidence that even the more militant ideologically oriented states have had some second thoughts about the practicability of seeking to vindicate their ideologies by the processes of world politics.

POWER. Finally, we must take note of power as a common objective of states. As we shall point out later (Chapter 3), power considerations belong more in a discussion of the means of foreign policy than in a catalogue of the ends of state action. Yet accumulating more power may be an indispensable preliminary step to the accomplishment of a goal, and for "reasons" of prestige or demands of security a state may overtly establish an increase in power as a major objective of policy. Certainly it is a serious oversimplification to state flatly that all politics is a struggle for power and that every primary motivation is the urge to augment its store. Yet it is undeniable that, realistically or not, many states legitimize power as an appropriate end of state action.

Policy and the Strategic Decision

The tension between ends and means is never greater than when a state's policy makers are deciding whether or not to act and, if so, what steps should be taken first. An objective must be selected and a course (or courses) of action launched. Officials must serve the interests and goals already formulated and yet act in situations permitting only a limited range of means. The choices are often extremely difficult; policy decisions must be in the largest sense strategic. Unable to accomplish everything they wish, states must weigh the competing claims on their resources and capabilities and decide not only which of their goals they can hope to achieve at the moment but also the relative importance of different areas of action.

The Meaning of "Policy"

A *policy* is here understood to be a course of action designed to attain an objective. Although we shall defer detailed analysis of policy-making until Chapter 2, certain larger aspects of the concept of policy are appropriately considered here.

We should first note a semantic difficulty. The *foreign policy* of a state usually refers to the general principles by which a state governs its reaction to the international environment. Such catchwords as *isolationism, balance of power,* or *imperialism* are often, if somewhat inaccurately, used to characterize particular foreign policies. On the other hand, if a policy is defined as a course of action oriented to a single objective, a state has as many policies as it has objectives. Thus *foreign policy* and *foreign policies* have completely different meanings. Probably the best way to avoid confusion is to keep in mind that *foreign policy* (singular) is usually phrased in terms of goals, whereas *policies* (plural) are formulated in terms of objectives.

Second, a policy always involves both *decision* and *action,* with decision perhaps the more important ingredient. Action on behalf of an objective can result from policy only if the decision itself indicates clearly what the policy maker had in mind both as to objective and procedure. As a result, the formalized decision (the "policy paper") normally includes at least three elements of clarification and guidance for anyone concerned with its implementation: (1) formulation of the objective in the most precise terms possible; (2) the nature of the action to be undertaken, stated with sufficient clarity to guide and direct the state's other officials; and (3) the forms and perhaps the amounts of national power to be applied in pursuit of the objective.

A third factor bearing on policy is reflected in the final point in this list. A policy decision normally calls for the commitment of resources, the assumptions of a risk, or both. This is the cost/risk factor in policy making, which we shall examine later. Here we need only keep in mind that, in foreign policy as in life, everything has its price. Often the most excruciating problem in policy determination is deciding how much effort should be made in pursuit of an objective in view of competing claims of other goals and limitations in the state's resources.

The Need for Priorities

No state can accomplish everything it wishes in its foreign policy; almost by definition, a state's reach exceeds its grasp. Objectives and goals tend to be formulated in absolute terms—a government speaks of "security," "peace," "freedom," or "growth," never of "partial security," "relative peace," "a measure of freedom," "limited growth." The ends of policy are unlimited, but the means are sharply limited both in logic and in fact. Even large and powerful states must budget their efforts as carefully as a family allocates its available funds.

Thus every state must possess a system of priorities that governs its policy choices. Some questions are simply more important than others in terms underlying social values. Some priorities, indeed, are literally absolute, such as self-preservation; unless the state exists, any other purposes are really beside the point. Others, while clearly critical, must take second place to those of the highest priority. As the scale of priorities is elaborated, each intermediate objective takes its place in relation to all others.

Priority ranking of interests, goals, and objectives is critical in determining the relative claim that each has on the state's resources, energy, and "worry time." Such a set of criteria of intrinsic importance is a major determinant of policy. A state, for example, is always willing to give in on a low-priority goal in order to gain ground on a higher-priority one. Overall strategies are established on a priority basis; long-term commitments of power can be made intelligently only on the principle of "first things first."

A state that attempts to conduct its foreign policy without having established priorities, or with its priority system vague and imprecise, rapidly discovers priorities imposed upon it by force of circumstance. When there is no real sense of the relative importance of different problems, all issues tend to become equally significant; in many cases, each problem is dealt with as if it were of absolute priority. Top priority thus tends to be assigned on the basis of what's happening now rather than long-term criticality.

The "importance" of issues is determined in every case by the internalized values of the state. No one outside a state can say unequivocally what ought to be the priorities of its policy; even self-preservation has no more importance than a state chooses to give it, and cases can be found where states voluntarily chose to go out of existence in order to achieve certain other values. The priorities that a state applies are its own, peculiar to its world view and appropriate to no other society.

Thus far we have been using the concept of "importance" as if it were an absolute, and as if priorities flow automatically from a single unified system of values. In practice, however, many different kinds of concerns are important to a state, and determination of the appropriate criterion of priority is frequently a serious problem in policymaking.

One of the more common conflicts of policy is between a *functional* or *procedural* ("means") *priority* and a *substantive* ("ends") *priority*. Priorities of means and priorities of ends, in other words, often apply in different ways and impose hard choices. A state may be vitally interested in preserving the principle and practice of peaceful change in world affairs in general (a procedural priority), and yet may at the same time be under great pressure to use force to make an important gain in its level of security (a substantive priority). There is, unfortunately, no easy or simple answer to this dilemma; governments resolve it again and again on an ad hoc basis.

Time pressures often lead to a confusion of priorities. Every government finds itself in situations where a particular move must be made immediately—even though the issue is intrinsically minor and the step will in some way hurt another enterprise of greater long-term significance but of less immediate relevance. In most cases the officials concerned make every effort to avoid irreparable damage to their long-range and higher-priority concerns while dealing with immediate issues. Only by accident or almost excusable carelessness will a government become so engrossed in its immediate problems as to permit more significant long-range issues to go by the board.

A final consequence of an unclear priority system should be noted. If a government faces a priority choice without being sure of its own criteria of importance, it may refuse to make any choice at all. Its policy effort will therefore be expended in an attempt to put off making a decision—"buying time." If the breathing space it wins is used to resolve the priority dilemma, it may deal effectively with the difficult choice when it arises again. If, however, the time bought is frittered away uselessly and the need for a similar decision comes again, there may be much less favorable conditions of choice.

The Classic Compromise

The task of the policymaker, as the cliché puts it, is to "reconcile the desirability of the possible with the possibility of the desirable." No other formulation of foreign policy so well epitomizes the task of the responsible policymaker.

Much of our preceding discussion has been leading up to this point. In any policy situation, the state has a range of ends, all desirable in terms of its interests, that can be arranged in order of preferability. Some are attainable with ease, some only by great effort, and others are beyond the range of attainability. On the other hand, the state also has a range of action open to it: It has the capacity to produce a number of different outcomes. Some of these may be highly desirable, others neutral, and still others inherently undersirable. On the "graph of priorities," the two curves of desirability and possibility cross at the point of decision. The mission of the policymaker is to ensure that the action takes place as high as possible on the curve of desirability.

Foreign policy normally consists of enterprises involving partial commitments of resources for the accomplishment of partial purposes. As a rule, a state does not count on obtaining either all it wants or all it can get in any situation. Rather, it attempts *to get all it can of what it wants.* The policy decision is thus always a compromise.

Initiatives and Responses

The "strategic decision" in all states is marked by a relative emphasis on prudence and restraint. Strategy is a cautious enterprise. The consequences of failure in statecraft may be so destructive that rational policymakers refuse to give themselves the benefit of any analytical doubt in setting a course of action.

Thus it follows that, for the vast majority of states, policy is more responsive than it is initiatory. In an environment of so many dangers and threats, policymakers attempt first to rationalize the conditions of existence within the system before they seek to bring about changes in their own behalf. Only after a state has dealt adequately with stimuli arising from outside itself does it feel free to launch its own enterprises. Responding to challenges takes precedence in allocating a state's resources. Initiatives are thus undertaken only with as much capability as is considered to be in excess of its forseeable needs.

Of course, the key notion in this relationship is—as so often in foreign policy—that of "adequacy." In one sense no state can respond completely to all challenges produced by the external environment. Absolute security is, as we have noted, unattainable. But even within the limits imposed by risk, difficult decisions of adequacy and the allocation of resources and effort plague policy making.

Some states possess relatively extensive capability to undertake initiatives—either because of especially fortunate situations or, more commonly, relatively optimistic interpretations of the nature and extent of challenges and the necessary responses. In other words, states with greater prowess in scientific achievement, technological innovations, and military power have greater freedom to assert themselves against lesser states. If powerful states have an interest in environmental change, they are able to blend desirability and possibility at a comparatively high level. This is a common characteristic of the strategy adopted by Communist states. Other states, however, interpret their requirements as demanding that a large proportion of their capability be committed to a range of responses, with only a modest surplus left for the initiation of policies. Modern democratic states are often accused of exercising so much caution in foreign policy analysis that their policies are purely responsive. Fundamental differences in policy arise from such differences in the interpretation that states make of the effective environment and their capacity for initiative, as well as from their internalized image of their world role. We shall examine these variations and their implications in the next section.

Types of Foreign Policies

Throughout this chapter we have stressed the basic role played in foreign policy by social values and the image of national and state purpose. Now we examine the content of purpose so as to distinguish the different ways states structure their missions.

Every society, speaking through its leaders, applies its value structure to the generalized world environment. In the process, it cannot escape passing judgment on the relationship between itself and all others. Such a verdict can be affirmative; that is, the society may be basically satisfied with its place in the world and seek no major changes in the international structure. On the other hand, the conclusion may be negative; the society may decide that its place in the world is unacceptable. Either decision determines all subsequent discussion of foreign policy.

If the society is willing to accept indefinitely its place in the general shape of the world, its overall international purpose will become a conserving (not necessarily *conservative*) one. If, however, it decides to reject the role it is playing at the moment, it may choose to bring about change in the global order in its own interest. Every state in the world, at some time and in varying ways, has made such a choice and then based a foreign policy on it.

Such a selection of a generalized category of purpose is a pure value judgment. There are no objective criteria by which an observer can anticipate what evaluation of the environment a people will make. The elements that produce the eventual conclusion are embedded in their social dynamics and assume unpredictable and often eccentric forms.

Some years ago, students felt they could meaningfully categorize this duality of purpose by classifying states as "haves" or "have-nots." Unfortunately, this division was not sufficiently explicit about what the "have" states possessed that produced satisfaction and what the "have-nots" lacked that made them dissatisfied. In some cases a level of material well-being apparently served as the crucial criterion; in other cases, considerations of status and prestige; and in still others, obvious dissatisfaction with a historic role or nostalgia for former eminence; and so on. The best we can say is that a state is satisfied with its world role if its critical values are receiving adequate fulfillment. Dissatisfaction means that certain critical categories of value needs are not being met. Each state is the final judge of the determinants and of how high a level of satisfaction is adequate.

It is from this idea of purpose that the controlling concept of national interests develops. The "general and continuing" end for which a state acts is derived from that state's interpretation of its role in the global order. A state thus uses the concept of purpose to interpret data from the external environment and measure its degree of success or failure in foreign policy.

The Policy of the Status Quo

The policy orientation that we call "status quo" arises from a concept of purpose that stresses satisfaction and conservation. States that assume this role develop policies with a number of distinguishing traits.

Before examining the content of a policy of the status quo, we must define the sense in which we are using this common but often misunderstood concept. The status quo state seeks to preserve its own status vis-à-vis the rest of the global system. A status quo posture does not necessarily imply enthusiasm for the details of the existing state of affairs, but rather a judgment that the overall pattern of value satisfaction extracted by the state from the global system is the most favorable it can hope for by any reasonable expenditure of effort. Thus a status quo policy by no means condemns the state to inflexible defense of all the details of an established order. Indeed, an enlightened status quo position—particularly when held by a major power—leaves ample room for change and initiative. What *is* considered beyond major modification is the state's relation to the system as a whole.

Status quo policies, therefore, are defensive in strategic orientation. However, often they may call for tactical offensives. The controlling notion of national interest of status quo states is couched in such terms as *defense, preservation,* and *neutralization,* rather than *offense, change,* and *advantage.* Status quo policies seek the stabilization of relationships rather than their modification. They normally press for wide adoption of all manner of institutional and procedural restraints on the outer limits of state action.

A state following a status quo policy accepts conflict as a condition of existence, but seldom initiates it. When caught in an overt struggle, it consciously attempts to avoid escalation of the conflict, works for resolution of the dispute at as low a level of tension as possible, and is normally willing to view an inconclusive outcome as a victory—since it is left in possession of whatever prizes it had at the beginning of the disagreement. It is axiomatic that status quo states never initiate major wars.

The policy of the status quo, whether followed by a large or a small state, seeks to maintain a stabilized set of international relationships that include the relatively advantageous situation the state now enjoys. As a result, status quo policies tend to be marked by restraint in conception, caution in execution, and acceptance of only a comparatively small burden of risk. Operationally, their strength lies in their capacity to anticipate situational change and to develop rapid and effective responses to it. When status quo policies are prevalent in the global system, the general atmosphere is of relative quiet and relaxation; change is slow, evolutionary, and limited in extent.

The Policy of Revisionism

The second type of foreign policy—which flows from rejection of the current international status and role of the state—is known as *revisionism*. It is in almost every conceptual aspect the polar opposite of the policy of the status quo.

Revisionism aims at the favorable modification of the state's overall position in the global system. It does not necessarily operate on the assumption that all international relationships are fluid and subject to change, but only those that it feels are crucial. It will accept no solutions to those points that epitomize its dissatisfaction except those that give it the measure of fulfillment it demands.

A policy of revisionism is strategically offensive. National interest demands major environmental change in the state's favor, and policy is directed toward the discovery or creation, and complete exploitation, of opportunities for effective action. A revisionist state will not seek or agree to a stabilization of international relationships until it achieves what it seeks. Revisionist states, therefore, are normally cool to proposals for the organization of world politics that might in any way inhibit their carefully guarded freedom of action.

Revisionist states not only accept conflict, they actively seek it as long as it offers a hope for the rational attainment of an objective. They will normally accept a higher level of tension in a dispute, are less adverse to escalation (at least up to a point), and are much more resistant to accepting a stalemate or a draw than are status quo states. In a struggle between the two types, it is typically the revisionist state that begins the conflict and sets its terms; in any such controversy short of all-out war, it is usually the revisionist state that also decides how long the dispute will continue. Major wars have usually begun by states that were revisionist in orientation, at least at the time the critical decision was made.

A revisionist policy is characterized by relative daring in conception, optimistic calculation of factors of cost, and willingness to carry a relatively large burden of risk. Its operational advantage lies in its capacity to bring about situational change or capitalize quickly upon it. A historic period dominated by revisionist policies, therefore, is marked by a high level of tension in politics and a rate of change that is both rapid and extensive.

Recommended Readings

BAILEY, THOMAS A. *A Diplomatic History of the American People* (9th ed.). New York: Appleton-Century-Crofts, 1974.
BELOFF, MAX. *Foreign Policy and the Democratic Process*. Baltimore: Johns Hopkins Press, 1965.
BLOOMFIELD, LINCOLN P. *In Search of American Foreign Policy: The Humane Use of Power*. New York: Oxford University Press, 1974.
DAHL, ROBERT A. *Who Governs?* New Haven: Yale University Press, 1961.
FRANCK, THOMAS, and EDWARD WEISBAND. *World Politics: Verbal Strategy Among the Superpowers*. New York: Oxford University Press, 1972.
LASKI, HAROLD J. *An Introduction to Politics*. New York: Barnes & Noble, 1962.
LASSWELL, HAROLD D. *Politics: Who Gets What, When, and How*. New York: Meridian Books, 1961.
LERCHE, CHARLES O. *Foreign Policy of the American People* (3rd ed.). Englewood Cliffs, N.J.: Prentice Hall, 1967.
MACHIAVELLI, NICCOLO. *The Prince and the Discourses*. New York: Modern Library, 1950.
MORGENTHAU, HANS J. *In Defense of the National Interest*. New York: Alfred A. Knopf, 1951.
OSGOOD, ROBERT E. *Ideals and Self-Interest in America's Foreign Relations*. Chicago: University of Chicago Press, 1953.
PLATO. *The Republic*. Translated by Allan Bloom. New York: Basic Books, 1968.
RAPOPORT, ANATOL. *The Big Two: Soviet-American Perceptions of Foreign Policy*. New York: Pegasus, 1971.
ROSENAU, JAMES N., ed. *Domestic Sources of Foreign Policy*. New York: Free Press, 1967.
THUCYDIDES. *History of the Peloponnesian War* (trans. Rex Warner). London: Penguin Books, 1977.

Government and Policymaking

2

We have already established that states act purposefully in world politics, and that an essential part of the process of foreign policy is making and implementing decisions. Our next inquiry, therefore, is into the ways states organize themselves for their international and transnational contacts and the considerations that influence their decisions.

State Organization for International Action

Government and Foreign Affairs

In the delicately balanced and perilous world of today, foreign affairs is one of the principal concerns of all states. For a small state the problem may involve no more than the basic issue of survival. For the larger states there are also usually a variety of positive objectives that each hopes to attain. Each state's task in the global arena is unique, but they all consider foreign policy a matter of high priority and major import.

As might be expected, therefore, all governments organize themselves for foreign affairs with considerable care. No matter how inefficiently or casually a state conducts its domestic policy, no state can afford to function in world politics for very long at any except the maximum level of effectiveness. Foreign policy establishments in any state reflect the best that the society is capable of producing.

Organization of foreign policy is roughly identical in all governments. Atop the organizational pyramid stand the heads of government, testifying by their active role to the basic significance of world affairs. The head of government is directly assisted by whatever close advisory and administrative apparatus the government boasts, whether a "cabinet" of the British type, a "revolutionary council" of an authoritarian regime in the Third World, a "presidium" as in the Soviet Union, or a less institutionalized cabinet-executive office arrangement, as is the case in the United States. The principal foreign affairs specialist in the government is the foreign minister (in the United States, the secretary of state), who heads the administrative department concerned with foreign policy and is the principal official adviser to the head of government. In all states, other departments participate directly in foreign policy decisions. Financial and military experts are almost always consulted, and economic ministers (on questions of trade or development) have become just as important. Legislative bodies play roles dependent on their constitutional place, but foreign policy is primarily an executive prerogative, only occasionally inhibited by legislative interference.

A real part in decision making or policymaking (we are using these terms synonymously), is played by the representatives a state maintains abroad. Diplomatic personnel are ubiquitous today, and economic, cultural, and military representatives are growing in number. The information they relay to their home governments obviously affects policy; in addition, they conduct many negotiations themselves.

The Head of Government

The head of government—president, prime minister, or dictator—is the key figure in all foreign policy decisions. According to international practice, the head of government alone officially speaks for the state in international relationships. As the political leader of the people, the head of government exercises ultimate authority in the area of foreign policy. No institutional arrangements can eliminate or blur this responsibility.

The head of government may structure the foreign policy mission in any of a great variety of ways. The head of government naturally seeks advice and information to guide foreign policy decisions, but may rely on the opinions of subordinates or trust only personal judgments and intuition. The head of government may function entirely within the official apparatus or may rely more on informal and unofficial sources of recommendations—for example, the Communist party in the USSR, the National Security staff in the Unites States, "the Establishment" in Great Britain, or the "Revolutionary Council" in a Third World dictatorship. The heads of government may confine their personal attention only to issues of massive and general import, leaving detailed implementation to subordinates, or they may intervene into the decisional process in matters of great detail and short-run impact.

The peculiar function of the head of government lies in the province of political leadership. Whatever the controlling internal dynamics may be, the head of government must somehow translate the prevailing value pattern and operative consensus of mass public opinion into foreign policy terms. Whether a dictator or a popularly chosen leader, the task of the head of government as the visible symbol of national unity is to formulate national purposes and give them expression in the form of concrete objectives. Under modern conditions, heads of government expend an ever-increasing proportion of their effort in maintaining this link between a changing global environment and the political community which they lead. Their policy decisions therefore tend to become increasingly general, symbolic, and direction-setting, and less concerned with immediate operational choices.

The Foreign Minister and the Foreign Office

Foreign ministers in most states have a peculiarly taxing role. They must be specialists and technicians concerned with the innumerable complexities of day-to-day decisions. They must also have an appreciation of the larger internal and external political problems with which their respective chiefs are faced. Simultaneously they must be administrators (as each is the head of the foreign office and foreign service of that state), policymakers or decision makers (insofar as permitted by their superiors), and advisers.

In many cases, another task is added to this multiple responsibility: high-level negotiation. Modern transportation and communication (and the need for quick decisions) have given the foreign ministers of all leading powers and of many smaller ones a roving commission to travel widely and conduct all important negotiations among themselves, either bilaterally, before the United Nations, or in some form of "conference." Obviously, foreign ministers faced with complex and protracted discussions of a problem cannot always obtain workable solutions, and organizational strain and dilution of effort are predictable consequences of their profession. Whatever the disadvantages, foreign ministers' meetings (and their logical outgrowth, "summit" meetings among heads of government) have become a normal feature of international political life.

The foreign office of each state constitutes the primary grouping of expertise on international matters within the government. Generally speaking, its domestic personnel (e.g. State Department personnel in the United States) are relatively few, although some significant increase has taken place in recent years. It is normally organized into subsections that reflect the nature of its task. There is usually a breakdown by geographic areas corresponding to the state's involvement in various parts of the world, and also what the U.S. Department of State terms "functional bureaus," each of which focuses on a special function in a global context.

A foreign office thus has a dual mission: to communicate with its own personnel abroad and with foreign diplomatic missions in its own country. In performing this dual role, foreign office personnel make a vast number of policy decisions at all but the highest level of importance. The foreign office also acts as a source of policy recommendations that flow upward to the higher decisional levels: the foreign minister, the cabinet, the head of government, and staff members. In this respect, foreign policy bureaucrats often, by defining alternatives and selecting data, materially influence the ultimate decisions.

In most states, foreign office personnel form a part of the inner bureaucratic elite within the government. The nature of their responsibilities tends to confer an aura of preferment upon them as well as create some residual envy and resentment in officials of other departments. As foreign policy responsibilities have become diffused throughout many executive agencies (as has been the case in most powerful states), intragovernmental rivalries have impeded the optimum mobilization of national effort. This has been particularly true in the United States.

The Diplomatic Service

Every state maintains a network of diplomatic missions abroad—one in each state with which it conducts relations. Each state in turn acts as host for similar missions sent by other states. Thus communications flow in a dual channel: A message may go directly from the foreign ministry to the resident ambassador of a second state, or it may go to the state's ambassador abroad for delivery to the other state's foreign minister.

Each mission abroad is led by a "chief of mission," usually titled "ambassador." The function of the ambassador is multiple: representation before the host government, acting as a channel of communications, reporting information, performing a public relations task before the people of the host country, maintaining contact with the nationals who are subject to the jurisdiction of the host country, and (sometimes) conducting negotiations. The present century has seen a great magnification of the public relations and representational roles of ambassadors, and a corresponding diminution of the function of negotiation. Though in some respects regrettable, substantial elimination of the ambassador as an important decision maker was inevitable as soon as instantaneous communication and rapid transportation made it possible for higher officials to conduct negotiations themselves.

Embassies vary in size and structure according to the importance of the states to each other and the prestige each wishes to cultivate. Regardless of size or detailed organization, however, some degree of functional specialization among embassy personnel is the rule. For purposes of reporting and representation, different officers concentrate on political, economic, cultural, and labor matters; specialized (nonforeign office) representatives for military, scientific, commercial, agricultural, and various other affairs are also frequently found, at least in the embassies of larger and more prosperous states.

Most governments rotate diplomatic personnel between assignments abroad and tours of duty in the foreign office. There is much to be gained by this practice. Policymakers at home gain an appreciation of the problems faced by diplomats abroad, while the missions themselves gain insight into the large dimensions of national policy and into the difficulties of decision making which confront their own governments.

Complicating the task of diplomats abroad in recent years has been proliferation of what the United States calls "operating missions"—task forces charged with executing, within a host country, programs that have already been negotiated diplomatically. The exact status of the operating mission vis-a-vis the resident diplomatic staff has proved troublesome for American officials and has caused considerable tension. Other states that have adopted this device of implementing policy have encountered the same sort of problem. Since the lines of control and authority of the operating mission and the diplomatic mission do not coincide, jurisdictional conflicts must often be resolved by higher administrative personnel, sometimes even the foreign minister or a similar government official.

Other Departments

The centrality of foreign affairs to most governments is clearly demonstrated by the wide involvement of other departments in the matter. Every government brings a broad spectrum of insights and capabilities to the process of making and executing foreign policy.

Two departments are virtually universal participants: the agency charged with raising and allocating public funds (the Treasury Department in the United States, the Exchequer in Britain, the Finance Ministry in many states) and the military establishment. Each brings its special orientation to matters of world affairs.

Foreign policy for major states is very expensive. Questions of national survival, security, and interest are a top-priority charge on the state's resources. Any major foreign policy decision (and most minor ones) involves some charge on public finance and requires the active or tacit approval of the appropriate department. Matters of taxation, furthermore, touch sensitive nerves in the body politic, and general political considerations cannot help but affect any decision to commit public funds to international purposes. In an era in which most governments are taxing their citizens to the practical maximum and any increase will touch off resistance, great caution is required before increasing the foreign policy budget.

By far the largest share of expenditure for foreign policy purposes—at least for the most important states—goes for the military establishment. Most governments today are committed to the maintenance of as large a military force as is practicable. Security is the motivation in the majority of cases, but in others the dominant factor is clearly a search for prestige. We must also keep in mind that the military machine in many Third World states is an instrument of government and political leadership.

These considerations all have the same effect: Military leadership and the armed forces are actively involved in foreign policy making in almost all states. Their special point of view includes a distrust of "politics" as a bargaining tool and a strong preference for direct methods, attitudes which can and often do put the military at odds with the foreign office.

Increasingly important in almost all states today is the finance ministry (treasury) or the ministry of planning. In developed states, its primary concern with foreign policy lies in the area of international investment and trade; in less developed states, it is more involved with the problems of modernization and development. At times its recommendations may be absolutely controlling, as is the case in the Third World. Because the economic health of a state has a direct effect on the amount of resources it may commit to world politics, no government can indefinitely ignore the economic consequences of its policy. This fact alone would make economic specialists important in foreign policymaking.

Other agencies usually play a role more periodic and irregular. Perhaps special mention should be made of whatever organization the government maintains for propaganda. Modern mass communications are a powerful tool of domestic leadership and an effective instrument of policy. Propaganda experts are thus of great or even critical importance. Other departments with foreign policy responsibility, including intelligence agencies, tend to be called into the decisional process as their special orientations dictate and as the particular problem demands.

The Policy Process

The entire foreign policy organization of a state exists for the purpose of making and executing decisions to advance the state's interests. Because the basic ingredients of the decision-making process are substantially identical in all states, we turn our attention now to the policy process within any government.

The Process of Decision

Analytically, we may conceive of foreign policy decisions as flowing from the appreciation of a fluid and only imperfectly perceived situation by the corps of official decision makers. In this effort they use criteria of interest and purpose stemming from their social milieu and professional background, modified by their peculiar institutional setting. Although national interest as a concept has deep social roots, its expression in any decisional situation is undertaken by the responsible decision makers.

Thus the steady input of information to the decisional hierachy undergoes constant analysis and evaluation, as officials attempt to determine which events so affect the nation as to require decision and possibly action. These stimuli come from the "external setting." For most states the majority of data is simply noted and disregarded as peripheral to the national interest. Only a few major states have such widespread concerns as to make their involvement almost total. Only those matters judged to have policy relevance are actually analyzed and enter the process of decision.

The bulk of state activity in world affairs, therefore, may be thought of as "reaction" or "interaction": responses to stimuli external to the state. A portion of any foreign policy consists of "action" in the pure sense—efforts undertaken in response to domestic factors so as to modify the environment in a desired way. The norms of strategic decision making ordinarily make this matter of lower priority than the crucial business of response and adaptation to external stimuli, many of which are actually or potentially hostile. A state's first responsibility is to ensure its continued existence and effective range of choice; only after it has done all it can to guarantee its participation in the system can it attempt to bend events to its purpose.

If foreign policy is thus the application of a set of internalized criteria of judgment to a dynamic external situation, we may conceptualize the process as consisting of the following steps: (1) establishment of the original criteria; (2) determination of the relevant variables in the situation; (3) measurement of the variables by the criteria; (4) selection of an objective; (5) elaboration of a strategy to reach the objective; (6) the decision to act; (7) the action itself; and (8) evaluation of the results of the action in terms of the original criteria.

We must keep in mind that this formulation is an abstraction applicable only to a single problem, and that in practice the procedure is never so clear cut. States conduct many decisional operations simultaneously. Each analysis has its own peculiarities, and each affects all the others and is affected by them. Very few decisions go to completion without being modified by changing circumstances, and many enterprises are dropped before completion because time and new concerns have rendered them obsolete. In spite of these practical warnings, the schematic presentation is valuable because it distinguishes the various intellectual operations involved in a foreign policy decision.

The Analysis of Situations

Having decided that a situation merits decision, officials undertake a situational analysis in some depth, with a twofold purpose. Initially they seek to discover the manner and extent of their involvement in the situation under scrutiny in order to determine the most advantageous objective for their government. (In Chapter 1 we noted that "objectives" derive from concrete situations in contrast to "goals," which are postulated a priori.) The second purpose of their analytical effort is to discover the different courses of action the situation makes possible, independent of their relative desirability.

Situational analysis ordinarily requires consideration of three distinct sets of factors: (1) the general pattern of forces operative in the area of decision that lie beyond the control of any single state; (2) the particular policies being followed by other states—at least the important ones—in the given context; and (3) one's own capabilities for action in light of the first two factors. In theory, this analysis is as objective and cold-blooded as professional skill can make it. However, so many intangible factors must be weighed and evaluated that no government can be more than approximately accurate in this effort.

Only after situational analysis can an objective be selected. This point is of central importance in the decisional process. Then, only after the objective has been selected can the situation be reanalyzed for determination of the optimum course of action.

It should be emphasized once more that the situational context of a decision is analyzed at least three times. The first analysis stresses long-term factors so as to develop a working concept of interest. The second focuses on middle-range aspects in order to suggest an objective. The third analysis concentrates on short-run and immediate variables; this emphasis produces alternative strategies and policy declarations in the narrow sense.

The Choice among Alternatives

The key concept in the analysis of policy is "choice"; a decision maker must preserve, at any stage in the process, the maximum range of choice. In practice this results in formulating opportunities (or imperatives) as a set of alternatives for action.

Strategically, the principle of alternatives is often formulated in negative terms: "Never put yourself in a situation in which you have only one possible course of action." As long as a state retains a choice of tactics, its opponent must go to the trouble of devising responses to each one. A lack of alternatives, however, condemns a state to a predictable response and to facing predetermined counterstrategy. Decision making as a choice among alternatives is thus a way of examining all opportunities and of exercising whatever strategic advantages may be derived from forcing uncertainty and risk on the decision makers of other states.

Thus the approach to making a decision is usually seen in terms of all the alternatives open to the state in the particular context, together with estimates of the probable outcome of each alternative. This spectrum of choices forms the ultimate agenda of the "decisional unit," whether a single policymaker or a group. The alternative selected is that which promises the greatest gain or, as often happens, the least loss in terms of the current criteria of choice.

We must understand that the range of alternatives is seldom a set of many bad choices combined with only one "right" one. Most often, the real range of choice is fairly narrow and the policy and interest differentials among the various alternatives are relatively small. Selection of one is often difficult, especially when pressures of time or administrative necessity rush the decisional process. No state can dispense entirely with alternatives, however obscure their differences may be in a particular situation. Policy cannot be made for long on an ad hoc basis, nor can any government afford to give up the flexibility that the alternatives approach contributes to decision making.

Basing a decision on a choice among alternatives, especially if the courses of action are not mutually exclusive, makes it much easier for a state to adapt itself to the consequences of errors or unforeseen circumstances. If the selected course of action fails to evoke the hoped-for response, it will be possible to shift to another line of policy without going through the entire process again.

In rapidly moving situations, it is not uncommon for a state to launch a course of action with no clear idea of its ultimate outcome. However, the general line of attack is the result of a choice among alternatives, and contains within itself further alternatives. One (perhaps several) of these will be adopted, depending on the nature of the response to the state's initial step. Thus policy is kept abreast of situational change—and with a consequent gain in effectiveness if implementation is forceful. We must admit that such extreme flexibility is usually beyond the capability of most states. Only relatively powerful states can afford actively to maneuver with several alternative approaches available, each equally within its competence to pursue.

The usual method of testing the validity of a choice is to take its initial steps tentatively and leave an escape route open if the judgment proves to have been faulty. In such a case, a state can hold its losses to a minimum while preserving the freedom to strike later on a different tack. Only after the correctness of its assumptions and the accuracy of its situational analysis have been reasonably confirmed does a state permit itself to become fully committed to its initial choice of action.

Evaluating and Revising Decisions

Throughout this discussion of the policy process, it has been evident that the effectiveness of state action depends on the extent to which the action is responsive to the actual situation. Since decisions are always made upon incomplete and inaccurate information, prudence would demand constant evaluation of the results of decisions and immediate revision of policies that are not producing the desired effect.

Here modern communications media are of great utility to the policymaker. In an earlier age the policymaker would have to wait weeks or months to learn the response to a move. Today information is received within a much shorter period—sometimes instantly. In this sense the process of evaluation and revision is much simpler.

But in another way, modern conditions complicate the task of making decisions. Events today move even more rapidly than decisions, which are, after all, made by human being subject to fatigue and bad temper. Furthermore, the very complexity of foreign policy leads major states to implement their decisions by relatively fixed commitments and long-term "programs"—both extremely difficult to change even in circumstances of stress. A third factor that makes evaluation difficult is the pressure of the foreign policy business. When new problems crowd in on the decision maker, it is more likely that these problems will be dealt with than those associated with the agonizing reappraisal of earlier decisions (to see if they worked out as expected).

It is therefore not uncommon today for a particular policy to be utterly invalidated by an unexpected train of events which would have been anticipated by adequate evaluation and revision. Major powers with extensive and complicated networks of commitments are particularly prone to this danger. Although constant evaluation is the most necessary for them, it is also usually the most difficult. Smaller states, with less margin for error and with a narrower range of concerns, have proved much more adept at adjusting their policies to even modest situational evolution.

Factors Influencing Decisions

Foreign policy is not made by electronic computers; it is formulated by individuals who lack mathematical precision but who do possess judgment. We have seen that a policy decision incorporates a choice. What factors influence the selection of one course of action rather than another?

The Appreciation of the Problem

Decision making must begin with an understanding of what the decision itself is about. No policy can be chosen without an appreciation of the problem the decision is to affect. This truism is often overlooked in much of the discussion of policymaking in the United States.

To begin with, probably no two officials in any government see the same set of facts in identical "problem" terms. Each brings a distinct personality, professional and organizational bias, and intuitive skill to bear on the task, and each may have personal sources of information. A large part of the "Tower of Babel" effect in policymaking—especially in Western democracies—flows from this variance in the overall appreciation of the policy environment among those charged with responding to it. One significant task of leadership, whether political or professional, is to make sure all subordinate decision makers follow standard criteria of problem identification.

Confusion sometimes stems from the semantic trap laid by the word *problem.* Strategy is a cautious business at best, and the natural tendency (at least in Western languages) to conceptualize "problem" as an obstacle to be overcome and pressures to be resisted only reinforces this danger. If "problem" is instead understood to be the factor in a situation that demands solution, and if it is borne in mind that, in logic, a "problem" can be as much an opportunity as an obstacle, the possible deadening effect of the idea can be minimized. It is as "problematic" to determine ways of capitalizing on an unexpected advantage as it is to develop a strategy to lessen the effect of misfortune.

A crucial element in any problem analysis is the early selection of an objective worth the state's effort. This is the essence of *strategy,* defined as a plan for the employment of resources for the attainment of a predetermined end. On the broadest foreign policy scale, such a plan may accurately be termed a *national strategy*. Since all operational decisions are made in terms of postulated goals, the identification and evaluation of strategic objectives constitute a major step in the process of problem identification. This task is more complex than it might seem at first.

Even if decision makers have a firm grasp on national goals and an adequate comprehension of the situation, they ordinarily encounter difficulty in formulating objectives. One set of possible objectives will be attractive because of its intrinsic *desirability,* while another group has *feasibility* in its favor; rarely will a single objective rank high on both scales. The task of the decision maker thus beset by opposing constructions of the problem is to strike the best possible balance between the desirability and feasibility of the objectives the individual perceives, and to act on the basis of this compromise.

The Cost/Risk Calculation

A second major factor that affects foreign policy decisions is the cost/risk calculation. No state can count on getting anything free in world politics. Furthermore, even with the maximum intellectual and physical effort, any policy carries with it some risk of failure. The twin cautions of cost and risk tend to sharply limit the real range of choice of the policymaker.

In considering a possible line of action, decision makers dare not give themselves the benefits of any doubt. In establishing a possible-cost factor, they must assume the worst possible consequences of their move. Only then are they free to take action. Of course, the "worst possible consequences" are those that are actually foreseeable in the light of the policymaker's supply of information. If "possible" were taken literally, every decision would be a peace-or-war choice, for war is a *possibility* in any international confrontation. Cost factors are actually estimated in terms of the range of probabilities open at any time. A decision to act really means that the decision maker feels that the objective sought is worth the highest price that anyone will actually charge the state.

Determining the risk involved in the projected course of action, conceptually a second step in analysis, is usually conducted simultaneously with the calculation of cost. "Risk" here refers to the relative odds in favor of success. Assessing risk is necessary in decision making simply because of unforeseen contingencies that perpetually endanger the peaceful interaction of states. The evaluation of risk is an acknowledgment of the element of guesswork in all foreign policy.

For each alternative that demands a decision, the state establishes an "acceptable burden" of risk—the amount of failure that its policy will tolerate. The degree of acceptability of such a "calculated" risk is determined by two sets of interlocking factors: the importance of the objective being sought (a value judgement), and the seriousness of the consequences of failure (an analytical conclusion). For important objectives, a state will accept great risk of failure; for lesser objectives, less risk.

The factors of cost and risk as determined by the decision makers define limits within which decisions must fall. No rational policy choice would dictate action in behalf of an objective that might cost too much if the risk of having to pay that price is beyond the level of acceptance. Thus, policymakers find themselves hemmed in by analytical inhibitions and practical counsels of prudence.

The Domestic Aspect: Consensus

Another limit upon the decision maker is internal (domestic) in its effect. Regardless of form of government or political philosophy, any foreign policy apparatus is bound by popular consensus and limited to whatever area of permissibility mass attitudes may allow. This is not to encourage the unsophisticated view that "all foreign policies are democratically inspired." The consensus that restricts decision makers may be entirely synthetic and the result of a planned campaign of deceptive mass propaganda. But regardless of its origin or degree of sophistication, consensus plays a key role in staking off the area of free decision the policymaker enjoys at any given time.

As long as war remains the ultimate sanction of state policy and wars are fought by entire populations, consensus will govern decision making. No government can safely be divorced from the active support of its populace. Mass identification with foreign policy issues, although an enormous source of strength to all governments, is also in this sense a debilitating factor that often deprives officials of the capacity to follow their best professional judgment.

In practice, popular consensus imposes varying degrees of constraint. Given a wide area of permissibility and dealing with matters of lesser import, decision makers often operate without specific reference to mass reaction. The more narrowly and specifically popular consensus focuses, however, the more officials feel its impact.

There is an interesting relationship between the dimensions of breadth and intensity of consensus. A broad grant of discretion to government ordinarily implies a relatively low level of mass identification. When a government increases the intensity of its popular support on a particular issue, it pays the price of narrowing its permissible alternatives, at least as interpreted by the consensus. Thus the paradox: the closer to war a situation drifts, the more public attitudes become inflamed, and the less control policymakers exercise over events. In gaining popular support against the worst circumstances, governments often sacrifice their ability to capitalize upon more favorable circumstances.

Consensus is most obvious when it is most specific. Periodically—especially in moments of crisis—mass attitudes will seize upon a particular issue or problem of policy and insist on a (usually oversimplified) position. Since mass response to problems rarely takes into account either enough relevant data or practical range of choice, such manifestations are almost always sources of annoyance to decision makers. Policy personnel in democratic and dictatorial states alike dread such developments and make considerable effort to keep popular attitudes excited but safely below the boiling point. When consensus does break out of control, policymakers may ignore and defy popular demands only at their own risk, and even then for a brief time span.

The Incompleteness of Information

We owe to the mathematical *theory of games* the insight that decisions can be made under any of three sets of conditions: conditions of certainty, conditions of uncertainty, and conditions of risk. In *conditions of certainty* each action has one predictable outcome; in *conditions of uncertainty* each action may have more than one outcome but their relative probabilities are unknown; in *conditions of risk* each action may have more than one outcome but their relative probabilities are known. Decisions made under conditions of certainty are so rare in foreign policy that they are analytically insignificant. Decisions made under known conditions of uncertainty do not occur in governments of rational individuals. Almost all foreign policy decisions taken by states, therefore, are made under conditions of risk.

Risk in this sense has almost the same meaning as in the "cost/risk calculation," and for the same reason: Any foreign policy decision is made in a context of incomplete information because the built-in time lag between event and decision makes it futile for policymakers to wait until they have complete facts. They must act on the information available to them and arrange their decisions so as to reduce the risk to a minimum.

The inadequacy of information available to policymakers manifests itself in either of two ways: They may not have enough data, or they may have too much. In the first instance they lack one or several crucial pieces of information that will enable them to construct a meaningful and valid decision. If data are unavailable or if they cannot wait for more complete information, they fill the gaps with estimates, extrapolations, or assumptions, and go ahead anyway. In the second situation, they have the information they need but it lies buried under mountains of extraneous and only mildly relevant data. Because of time pressures or because they lack immediately applicable criteria of relevance, the decision makers find themselves little better off than they would have been without the elaborate accumulation of unsifted information.

Under the heading "intelligence," governments today constantly exert themselves to improve both the quantity and usefulness of the information upon which they must base their decisions. As more areas of human life and action become relevant to foreign policy, more kinds of information are gathered and funneled into the decision-making apparatus of each government. Once swept into the analytical net, the information is digested, evaluated, correlated, and distributed to all decision makers whose responsibilities make these data useful and necessary to them. Those officials who consume the end-product of this information-gathering and disseminating network are known in the United States as the "intelligence community."

The purpose of this greater emphasis on information is to reduce the risk factor in decisions—that is, to minimize the extent to which the outcomes of any action are unknown and to amplify what is known of the probability of their occurence. This may be classified conceptually as a "search for certainty" in policymaking, but of course the realistic goal is much more modest. Any effective substitution of knowledge or informed insight for pure guesswork in foreign policy decisions is a net gain, and every state is convinced that enough improvement is possible to justify a major effort.

The Pressure of Time

Still another factor that materially affects foreign policy decisions is the simple phenomenon of time. Modern technology has speeded up the pace of world politics. With improvements in transportation and communication, events occur more rapidly than in the past, and their outcomes reach the decision maker in a much shorter time. This combination of forces cruelly burdens the policymaker's task. Responsible officials lack the time needed to analyze situations, compare alternatives, and make choices. They can deal with most issues only in a summary (and therefore usually routine and unimaginative) fashion. The best they can ordinarily do is conserve their analytical skills for the really important questions, but even in this modest and creditable effort they face difficulties. So pressed for time are they that a crucial issue—if it is in any way difficult to identify—often slips by as "just another problem."

In an attempt to cope with a larger and more rapidly moving flow of business, many governments have expanded their policy-making organizations. This has proved to be a self-defeating expedient, because the rigidity of bureaucracy has more than offset the gain in work force commitment. Lateral communication within the bureaucratic structure and the need for "clearances and concurrences" often slows down decision making unbearably and deprives it of focus and force.

An unfortunate consequence of the pace at which most foreign policy decision makers drive themselves (or are driven) is the disappearance of reflective thought in a climate of tension. With no time to "waste in just thinking," officials lose a quality of perceptiveness and flexibility ordinarily considered an advantage for a policymaker. Individuals under pressure tend to make decisions that will clear their desks for the next problem. Being prudent, they prefer to make minimum commitments and extremely cautious responses, to follow precedent closely, and to interpret their controlling directives as narrowly as possible. A harried official always prefers giving a no answer to a yes, for the former not only spares the individual responsibility for a decision that might later prove unwise, but also obviates the necessity of opening up entirely new areas of analysis and decision for which the individual feels there is little time.

National Style

Decision makers in any state are materially affected by what is called "national style": the prevailing tradition and self-image of a society that predisposes its officials to perform their duties and make their decisions in a way considered unique and peculiarly appropriate. "Style" as a concept is much more useful, as well as being much easier to defend, than the once-popular idea of "national character." Although it is unreasonable to expect an entire people to conform to a given character, the bulk of a society will in their individual personalities reflect a certain stereotype.

National style is important in shaping decisions because of its effects on the analytical pattern of the decision makers. Decision makers are unconscious of the extent to which they partake of a larger code of appropriate and socially sanctioned behavior as they grapple with their special problems, but only hopelessly alienated (and therefore largely ineffective) public servants could dissociate themselves completely from their societies. A common style of analysis and decision forms one of the real elements of cohesiveness in all reasonably well-integrated government structures.

The relevance of notions of style to decisions may be suggested by some examples. In Great Britain, for instance, the idea of "muddling through"—a conspicuous reluctance to relate immediate choices overtly to long-range purposes—gives British policy a remarkable resilience and adaptability that has long been the envy of other states. Russia's obsession with secrecy is a stylistic trait that long antedates the Bolshevik

Revolution. China's proclivity for suspicion is revealed in a policy style of centrism—maintenance of distance from others. The Third World requirements for new roles displays a policy style of protest. The French concern with "honor" and "glory" is far more than the mere symbolic and ritualistic matter it is for most other states; to France it is part of the national self-image and is taken very seriously. The style of the United States has long dictated casting international issues in moral terms and viewing foreign policy as a series of crises broken by random intervals of relaxation.

These tricks of national style cannot help but modify the decisional dynamic each government demonstrates. Considerations of style help explain both deep animosities and close associations between pairs of states, as well as many otherwise perplexing patterns of interaction. We cannot expect the United States to act with a Russian concern for secrecy, nor can the Soviet Union conceive policy along any crisis-relaxation continuum. We would not expect that the maintenance of close and satisfactory relations between two such different styles would be an easy matter, completely aside from any differences in ideology and forms of government that might exist.

Commitments and Precedents

Last on our list of factors influencing decision, but frequently of controlling importance to the policymaker, is the structure of already existing commitments and precedents within which the decision maker must act. No policy decision is ever made in vacuo at a given moment in time. Each is affected to a great degree by many earlier decisions and directed by the national interest. The state as a whole, the policy-making apparatus, and the individual decision maker are all in different ways bound by the remote or immediate past.

One important type of commitment that affects decisions is that made to a state's own public opinion. We have noted its effect in our discussion of consensus. A second includes all the understandings, arrangements, alliances, and other fixed relationships a state has developed with its fellows. A decision violating any of these, or even changing one in any significant degree, would cause a perceptible response and cause many new problems. Ordinarily, therefore, any such initiative is avoided except in clearly unavoidable cases. A third type of commitment is perhaps less obvious: Long-standing hostilities and disagreements with other states also function as fixed factors and materially affect decisions.

This latter category merits a final word. Since major policy undertakings today require extensive "programming" and long-term implementation, a deep-seated conflict among states (such as the

Arab-Israeli imbroglio) rapidly assumes an unspoken institutional character. Any radical improvements in relations would, in strict decisional terms, present almost as critical a problem as would a major crisis. Once such a conflict has become one of the "givens" of a state's international position, that government's decision makers naturally assume the indefinite prolongation of the controversy to be preferable to almost any modification in its conditions.

Recommended Readings

ACHESON, DEAN. *Present at the Creation: My Years in the State Department.* New York: W. W. Norton & Co., 1969.

ALLISON, GRAHAM T. *Essence of Decision.* Boston: Little, Brown and Co., 1971.

BALL, GEORGE W. *Diplomacy for a Crowded World.* Boston: Little, Brown and Co., 1977.

BRECHER, MICHAEL, *The Foreign Policy System of Israel: Setting, Images, Process.* New Haven: Yale University Press, 1972.

CRABB, CECIL V., JR. *American Foreign Policy in the Nuclear Age* (3rd ed.). New York: Harper & Row, 1972.

DESTLER, I. M. *Presidents, Bureaucrats, and Foreign Policy.* Princeton, N.J.: Princeton University Press, 1972.

HALPERIN, MORTON. *Bureaucratic Politics and Foreign Policy.* Washington, D.C.: Brookings Institution, 1974.

HUNTINGTON, SAMUEL P. *Soldier and the State.* New York: Random House, 1964.

KENNAN, GEORGE F. *Memoirs, 1950–1963.* Boston: Little, Brown and Co., 1972.

KENNEDY, ROBERT F. *Thirteen Days: A Memoir of the Cuban Missile Crisis.* New York: W. W. Norton & Co., 1969.

MACRIDIS, ROY C., ed. *Foreign Policy in World Politics* (5th ed.). Englewood Cliffs, N.J.: Prentice-Hall, 1976.

MUGHISUDDIN, MOHAMMED, ed. *Foreign Policy Making in the Middle East.* New York: Frederick A. Praeger, 1977.

ROSENAU, JAMES N. *The Scientific Study of Foreign Policy.* New York: Free Press, 1971.

SAPIN, BURTON M. *The Making of United States Foreign Policy.* Washington, D.C.: Brookings Institution, 1966.

ULAM, ADAM, *Expansion and Coexistence: Soviet Foreign Policy, 1917–1973* (2nd ed.). New York: Frederick A. Praeger, 1974.

Capability in Action

3

An old saw that says a great deal about the nature of foreign policy and the dynamics of interstate relations is, "A state does what it can and suffers what it must." A state's range of action is limited both by definition and in fact. The objectives it selects, and the tactics it adopts in order to achieve them, can never be any more than functions of its overall capacity for action in a given situation. The tension inherent in the contrast of absolute ends and sharply circumscribed means, as we noted earlier, makes policymaking a constant process of compromise and adjustment.

The nature and extent of the state's capacity to achieve its ends is closely allied to state purpose. We have said that a state in any situation attempts to get as much as it can of what it wants. At this point we are therefore interested in how a state estimates how much it can get in a given context, how these estimates find their way into policy decisions, and what factors and elements in a state's position contribute positively or negatively to its ability to achieve at least minimum satisfaction. We shall discuss such matters in this chapter under the overall heading of "state capability."

The Concept of "Capability"
Definition

The broadest and most useful definition describes a state's *capability* as capacity to affect changes in the global environment in its own interest. This does not include all the actions a state may be in a position to take, but only those deemed advantageous to itself. The capability to change the environment in a way inimical or irrelevant to state purposes is regarded as exterior to capability. The concept draws its validity from certain operating assumptions about the nature of foreign policy, and is therefore meaningless except with reference to already postulated purposes.

Change in environmental conditions is obviously the core of the concept's rationale. By means of its capability a state "does what it can"; under circumstances beyond its capability it "suffers what it must." "Change" is to be understood in the broadest sense—in terms of situational relationships that are different than they would have been without application of the state's capability—and the concept therefore includes neutralization of forces as well as positive results. A state makes its intentions effective in the real world by means of its capability.

The concept of capability is thus a shorthand reference to the "means" aspect of the ends-means continuum in foreign policy. The policymaker cannot afford vagueness. However generally the notion may be conceived and discussed in the abstract, capability judgments in foreign policy are useful only when made in highly concrete, specific, and immediate terms.

The Function of Capability

Capability redefines itself to some extent when it is actively committed to the service of state objectives. In the global system, a state can achieve its purposes only by gaining the assent of its fellows. In the absence of an effective international governing body, ratification of state decision depends upon an informal and unstable mechanism of consensus. The entire structure of state interaction stems from this basic operating requirement.

The assent of other states may be stated or tacit, voluntary, uninvolved, or grudging. It may be extended after a relatively simple process of explanation and persuasion, or only after a struggle of will and power. Regardless of its source, nature, extent, or durability, this consensus alone makes possible the accomplishment of a national objective. A state's foreign policy is directed and its capability is committed to the winning of this consent.

We may thus consider the operational function of state capability to be the engineering of an adequate international consensus. Almost any aspect of the policy process can be viewed in these terms. An "open course of action" is actually a series of moves a state feels it can make without running into an effective international veto. The achievement of an objective is really the creation of a favorable state of affairs which other states are willing to accept. Policymaking is really a judgment about how much effort the state must make to gain sufficient assent or acquiescence from other states involved in the situation. Conceiving capability as the measure of a state's ability to command and win agreement with its purposes gives focus and point to the concept and highlights the way in which it is actually used in policymaking.

Influence and Coercion in Capability

A state's ability to persuade other states to agree to its designs is demonstrated in two different ways. A policymaker may be able to obtain the consent of another government in an atmosphere of agreement. Consent may be given freely for any of a variety of reasons: The other state may approve of the projected action, it may be neutral or uninvolved in the question, or its disagreement may be so small as to be negligible. More commonly, the desired approval may be forthcoming after some measure of positive inducement: the promise of direct benefit, a modification of policy in another area, or some other quid pro quo. In any of these instances, absence of open conflict and mutual adjustment of positions is the significant dimension. The aspect of capability involved here is that of *influence:* The state is able to gain adequate consensus by various persuasive and/or harmonizing devices without calling into question issues of force or power.

When consent must be won for policy purposes in a context of conflict and disagreement between states, another dimension of capability becomes operative—*coercion*. This is the province of the "power struggle," as each state attempts to bend the other to its will. The forms of coercion are almost infinite, ranging from the mildest argument through a long threat-pressure continuum to physical force, the ultimate coercive method. At whatever level coercion is employed, its purpose is always the same. In the words of the classic definition of war, it is "to break the enemy's will to resist" so as to secure an agreement.

Influence and coercion are equally genuine and efficacious manifestations of state capability. Since conflict is a more exciting and newsworthy climate of human relationships than is harmony, the coercive aspect usually receives greater attention, and is often mistaken for the entirety of the phenomenon. Yet operationally, policymakers spend a vast majority of their time and effort manipulating such influence as they may possess and resorting to coercion only as a last resort. It costs less to win consensus by influence. Fewer undesirable after-effects are produced, and the results tend to be longer lasting. Policymakers with only coercive forms of capability available to them are indeed unfortunate. Their choice of policies is sharply limited by the relatively high cost that any coercive procedure will entail.

Capability and "Power"

Overemphasizing the role of coercion has led to the substantial discrediting of the once widely held concept of "power." Although it is possible to define and use the term *power* much as we are using *capability* in this chapter, *power* has come to symbolize the capacity of a state to coerce others or to avoid coercion by them. Such an emphasis on coercion leads to a concentration on the most obvious form of coercive capacity—military force. A construct of world politics grounded on "power" runs the risk of overemphasizing a victor and a vanquished in every international confrontation of will and strength. In the vocabulary of the mathematical theory of games, world politics is thus conceived as a "zero-sum" game: One player can win only to the extent that other player(s) lose.

This is simply not the way world politics usually proceeds. Although the values states seek may be mutually exclusive and their prosecution possible only in an atmosphere of conflict, even this does not make all relationships coercive. The values may instead overlap or coincide, making conflict and disagreement irrelevant to the establishment of necessary equilibrium. A simplistic "power theory" of world politics ignores far too many aspects of the actual relations of states to be a reliable guide.

The concept of "power" contains another built-in conceptual trap. Capability is always the ability to do something—to act purposefully in an actual situation. Power should mean this also; in popular political discourse, however, power often becomes a status to which states aspire and which a chosen few achieve. Unsophisticated observers speak of a "powerful" state in the abstract, regardless of how much that state can actually do in immediate action situations. The concept of capability preserves the necessary connection with policy and action that a careless use of "power" often overlooks. It is for that reason that we use the former term in this book to refer to states' overall capacity to act.

Capability Judgments in Foreign Policy

Having outlined some of the ingredients in the concept of capability, we turn next to a brief analysis of how capability is used in policymaking.

What Is a Capability Judgment?

A *capability judgment* made in a policy context is no more than an analysis of the opportunities and limitations implicit in the operational environment of the state concerned. Its end result is the formulation of a range of possible actions by the state—insofar as the analyzing policymakers can identify it. The key idea in any capability judgment is *possibility*. Capability provides the state with the resources of action, but in no other way predisposes the state to act in any particular way among those alternatives possible. The choice among alternatives is a value choice; capability judgments do no more than spell out the viable alternatives.

Thus a capability judgment is a special form of situational analysis. The policy context dictates the specific elements of capability that enter into the analysis, while the capability judgment establishes the parameters within which the operational decision will eventually be made. It is obvious that no sane policymakers will attempt a policy that requires an effort beyond their state's capability.

Judging the State's Own Capability

Policymakers must be fully informed about the several things they can do in the situation before they adopt a course of action. They must know what part of their state's total resources is available to them in the particular situation. They may be (and usually are) restricted by the fact that much of the state's capability is already invested in other commitments, and also by policy decisions that limit them to certain forms of action. (For example, military power may not be available, but they may use all the propaganda and economic measures they wish.) They must also have attempted to predict the consequences of applying any of the available forms of capability.

This process, carried out to whatever necessary and appropriate level of detail, leads to an appreciation of the policymakers' span of meaningful choices. On the basis of this judgment they proceed to apply the criterion of desirability to the several courses of action they have formulated, and to select one of them as policy.

Modern governments are acutely sensitive to the concept of capability and make such a massive effort to keep up to date on the choices they have open at any time that policymakers rarely find it necessary to go through the entire analytical operation sketched above. Usually they have at their fingertips generalized formulations of state capability applicable to detailed situations. Yet the essentials of the process remain the same, regardless of how extensively it may become institutionalized.

Capability Judgments of Other States

Capability judgments are really exercises in the determination of relationships. No capability judgment is of real use except in comparison with judgments of the capabilities of other states. Governments spend at least as much time and effort in attempting to judge the capabilities of other states as of their own.

It is critical to strategists to have an appreciation of the range of action open to other states, particularly those with which they are directly involved at the moment. If they can sense the parameters of action accepted by their opposite numbers in the other government, they will have a great advantage in developing their own policy. As a result, the major focus of political or "strategic" intelligence work in contemporary world politics is devoted to the development of elaborate formulations of the capabilities of all other states.

The method of reaching a capability judgment about another state is not radically different in nature from that used on one's own, but is of course a more difficult task. Information on which the judgment is based is much more fragmentary and difficult to obtain, since no state is eager to have any other gain complete insight into its own capabilities. Even more perplexing is the problem posed by differences in analytical points of view. Capability analysis, in spite of its total emphasis on possibilities, still requires interpretation and evaluation of data, and no two states interpret facts in quite the same way. For capability judgments to be of maximum use in devising strategy and tactics, therefore, a state must somehow also determine how other states' policymakers view their own situations.

Factors in Capability Analysis

Capability analysis, we have concluded, is a crucial step in policymaking. We have also sketched out the essentials of the approach to reaching capability judgments. It is now appropriate for us to review the factors that enter into these analyses.

Analytical Point of View

Perhaps the most important element in capability analysis is the point of view adopted by the analyst. Since a capability judgment is an estimate of the opportunities and limitations intrinsic to the decisional milieu, there is inevitably a gap between the environment as the analyst interprets it and as it exists in reality. Policymakers, subject to all the perceptual and behavioral limitations of any human beings, must act on the milieu as they perceive it, in full knowledge that many factors of the situation are unknown to them and will serve to modify and possibly upset whatever capability judgments they may make. We have already noted the impact of this element of unpredictability on policymaking as leading to caution and tentativeness in commitment and to a strong preference for a sizeable margin of error in any decision.

Any "outside" capability analyst—anyone who makes estimates without bearing responsibility for official action—necessarily has a different point of view from that of an official. Such an analyst may know many things that the official does not, and may be free from the institutional and social biases that complicate the decision-making process. Freedom from the burden of facing consequences of decision may well induce a greater measure of optimism and a willingness to bear greater risk than is normally characteristic of an insider. The "grandstand quarterback" of foreign policy, whether student, journalist, politician, or concerned citizen, can never more than approximate the special analytical point of view of the responsible decision maker wrestling with questions of capability.

The Policy Context

The next factor in capability analysis that merits attention has been alluded to several times previously. Capability is only a useful concept, and capability judgments can only be made meaningfully, in terms of a specific set of policies under analysis and evaluation. It is nonsense to speak of "capability" in the abstract as long as we grant that states move and act in world politics to some purpose. The policy assumptions underlying a capability analysis may frequently be left implicit or phrased as contingencies; this in no way frees the analysis from its policy roots. Even the most ephemeral policy assumptions may serve as the basis for capability analysis.

Capability judgments made without reference to a policy context lend themselves to semimystical deterministic manipulation. The various deterministically oriented "theories" or "laws" of world politics tend to find their empiric root in one of the physical "foundations" of national strength. Geographers, demographers, military scholars, experts on raw materials, industrial resources and agricultural economists, and other specialists have all at some time developed a single-factor theory of capability and politics that purported to forecast the future of international relationships. None of these formulations has been able to explain more than a fraction of the totality of interstate maneuvering, and none has escaped the necessity of allowing for the supremacy of the policy considerations of policymakers and governments.

The Situational Base

If capability makes sense only in terms of a policy context, it is also true that the concept is useful only within a specific situation. This is partly because the "open courses of action" and "opportunities and limitations" regarding capability exist only within a concrete context. The measure of the state's ability to influence or coerce agreement is also a function of the particular situation in which it is operating.

Specifically, a state never has more than a fraction of its total theoretical or actual capability available for its immediate purpose. An overall "favorable" capability position—a relatively large sphere of freedom of action within a state's general policy—may not translate into an equivalently high range of capability in a particular situation. A small and ordinarily weak state may, in an appropriate situation, have greater capability not only to influence a larger one but also to coerce it.

Certain forms of capability, whether influential or coercive, are appropriate to the peculiarities of any situation, while others are irrelevant. The actual capability a state enjoys in a situation is determined by which of its available forms of action are effective in dealing with that situation in view of the policy the state is pursuing at the moment. In this way the actual outcome of most international confrontations—especially those cast in an atmosphere of disagreement and attempted coercion—tends to be less a reflection of any generalized "power" relationship than a function of time, place, and the policies being carried out by the respective states.

Relativity of Capability

Capability is, as we have observed, a concept of relativity in two different ways. In the first instance, a judgment is made of the state's capacity to act in behalf of an already selected objective. Second, any capability judgment is actually a judgment of the state's capacity to act in comparison with the capabilities of other states.

There is only one rational answer to the question, "How much capability does a state need?" "Enough." The criterion of any contingency planning is "adequacy"—sufficient capability to fulfill the anticipated needs of policy. There is no advantage in amassing action capacity beyond what a state sees itself as likely to need, with a generous overallowance for analytical error and unpredictable quirks of fate. Development of capability which has no policy relevance is merely an international political example of "conspicuous consumption."

Regardless of what a state may be able to do in a situation, its net capability is zero if other states can cancel or neutralize each of its moves.

On the other hand, even a narrow range of action may be enough to give the state absolute capability if other states are relatively less well-off. Capability analysis focuses not so much on absolute levels of environmental change as on whatever margin of operational superiority one state may enjoy over another. This is particularly pertinent in questions of military confrontations today. Several states have the "capability" to destroy each other with thermonuclear weapons. Since none is able to focus its absolute military strength to gain a strategic advantage, the massive military machines of contemporary superpowers are, for operational and policy purposes, irrelevant in terms of functional capability.

Capability: A Dynamism

Capability is a highly dynamic concept. Making a capability judgment involves correlating a broad variety of factors within a state with an international situation, all elements of which are moving at different speeds. Any final conclusion about relative capabilities, no matter how up-to-date the information on which it is based, is obsolete by the time of its formulation. To make such an analysis applicable to an existing situation, it is necessary for a policymaker to predict future trends and variables, both in his own state and with regard to all others involved.

In theory, any single capability analysis should serve as the basis for only one action decision. Any later consideration of the same situation would require a new calculation of the relative status of all the states concerned. Literal adherence to this principle would render decision making almost impossible; most governments merely adjust a generalized capability formulation with such additional data as they may have available, and then proceed to a new decision. Even this partial recalculation suggests the transitory character of the ingredients of a capability comparison and the constant necessity of keeping it up to date.

Elements and Factors of Capability

Even after stressing that capability is a relative concept, that as an absolute "objective" formulation it suffers from a certain unreality and a lack of usefulness, we must admit that it is necessary and desirable to make at least a rough catalogue of the elements and factors in a state's position that contribute to its capacity to act effectively. What follows may be thought of as a kind of checklist that indicates the disparate sources from which a state may, in a particular situation, draw resources with which to support its policy. By no means should it lead to absolute operational conclusions about the "strength" or "power" of any state.

The Major Categories

The "elements and factors" of capability are usually broken down into two broad categories for convenience of discussion, although the classification is a rough one. Any overprecise conclusions based on the differences between categories will be at best questionable, and possibly in error. With this warning in mind, we may generalize that the capability of a state comes partially from tangible sources and partially from intangible ones.

Tangible factors are listed in various ways. Here we include five categories: (1) geographic position; (2) population and work force; (3) resource endowment; (4) industrial and agricultural productive capacity; and (5) military power. Each of these is obviously capable of further subdivision; their use in an actual capability analysis requires that they be broken down into greater detail.

The intangible factors we use here are four in number: (1) political, economic, and social structure; (2) educational and technical level; (3) national morale; and (4) international strategic position. As was the case with the tangible factors, these four as named are extremely broad and necessarily vague, and they must be given specific content and applicability if they are to be meaningfully used.

A quick comparison of the two lists leads to the conclusion that the so-called tangibles each has a generous measure of intangibility about it, while the intangibles all have certain aspects of tangibility. The major dimension used in analysis of the tangible factors is that of *quantity*—as modified by such notions as availability, convertibility, and substitutability. The significant dimension in the intangibles is *quality*—estimated not only in terms of "excellence," but also by such criteria as appropriateness and relevance. The analyst *measures* the tangible factors but *evaluates* the intangibles; the quality factor built into the intangibles has a great influence upon the effectiveness with which the tangibles are employed.

Thus a capability analysis logically begins with the most obvious physical factors, such as geography, that are not only the most easily measured, but also have the slowest rates of change. It proceeds through the less obviously concrete (and thus more dynamic) factors, and ultimately comes to rest at the opposite pole of intangibility, where there is little empirical data on which to rely but a rapid rate of change and evolution with which to cope.

The Tangibles

1. GEOGRAPHY. Geographic factors enter into state capability in a number of ways. Among the more immediately remarkable are such characteristics as the size of a state (which is either an advantage, a handicap, or a neutral factor, depending on the policy being pursued), its shape, topography, location, and climate. More subtle geographic influences include the nature of the state's frontiers, its neighbors, its insular, peninsular, littoral, or landlocked condition, its internal penetrability, and the distribution of its population over the landscape. None of these factors affect any state in the same way, yet any capability analysis, either overall or specific, must take into account such geographic factors, which are relatively fixed conditions of state existence.

Various theories of geographic determinism have plagued students for many years. An elaborate theory of civilization can be grounded on climatological data; an insular position is claimed to "destine" a state (like Britain or Japan) for maritime greatness. The most inclusive deterministic interpretation of geography is found in the several theories of "geopolitics," an approach built on perhaps the most fundamental geographic fact of all—the arrangement of land and water on the face of the globe. One nineteenth-century school of thought found mastery of the seas the key to world power because of the critical role of seaborne commerce and military power. This doctrine was replaced by the "heartland" theory identified with the British Sir Halford Mackinder and the Nazi German Karl Haushofer in the 1920s and 1930s. In the latter doctrine, land power was held to be supreme, and the "heartland" of the "world island"—roughly coterminous with the territory of Soviet Europe—was declared the one unassailable power base for world conquest.

Both the sea power and the "heartland" theories demonstrate the danger of drawing conclusions of inevitability from geographic facts, since each was in turn outdated and invalidated by changing technology. Sea power was overtaken by land power with the advent of the internal-combustion engine; the "heartland" lost its immunity with the appearance of intercontinental ballistic missiles and other sophisticated weapons-delivery systems that overcome historical geographic barriers. Geography is neutral in its basic effect on state policy; it may be a handicap or an advantage depending on the purposes to which policy is committed.

2. POPULATION AND WORK FORCE. A second tangible factor of immediate relevance is population and work force. The basic datum is the gross number of human beings the state incorporates. On the assumption that other things are equal, greater population means greater capability to perform more tasks at a higher level of effectiveness. But

other things are seldom equal; population data must be qualified by such factors as age distribution, sex distribution, and spatial dispersion. For military purposes, as an example, a population clustering heavily in the upper age groups or with an imbalance of females may make less of a contribution than might be estimated from its size alone.

Population is perhaps a less meaningful notion for purposes of capability analysis than is "manpower," that portion of the population available for broadly defined foreign policy purposes. All individuals who are politically useless, as well as those needed simply to keep the society functional (such as food producers), must be subtracted from the gross total. The result is the work force quotient that, with appropriate direction, leadership, and administration, can be used to contribute to the military, productive, and political capability of the state.

Capability estimates involving work force, especially when any but the briefest time spans are concerned, must take into account trends of evolution and development within the population. A comparison of birth and death rates, for example, will suggest such insights as the net growth rate and trends in age levels and life expectancy. It is possible, over a fairly long period, for government action to bring about perceptible change in population trends by the encouragement of early marriage and large families. France is today the outstanding example of a state that has done this successfully.

3. NATURAL RESOURCES. The third more or less quantifiable element of capability is natural resources, which include the state's natural endowment and those additional reserves it can control. Natural resources are both agricultural (mainly food and fiber) and mineral. The latter category has been crucial since the Industrial Revolution, as industrial processes have contributed so many new forms of capability to states. In this sense, mineral resources include energy sources (coal, petroleum, wood), the metals of ferrous metallurgy (iron ore and the various metals involved in steelmaking), nonferrous metals, and metallic minerals.

Resource endowments clearly are limiting factors on capability; no state can function at a level beyond that permitted by its resources. But the rigid raw material theory of world politics, popular several decades ago, has few adherents today. Development of synthetics and other new industrial processes, elaboration of stockpiling techniques, and the unexpectedly high capacity of embattled populations to endure chronic shortages have all served to liberate states from the more rigid absolutes of the theory. Today an analyst may draw only the most general capability conclusions (with only peripheral relevance to immediate policy situations) from resource data.

4. INDUSTRIAL AND AGRICULTURAL PRODUCTIVITY. In

70 THE ACTORS

one sense, industrial and agricultural productivity as a capability factor is a function of the two preceding factors of work force and resources. That is, production is the application of human effort to the transformation of resources from raw materials into finished products. Thus the level of industrial and agricultural production is determined in part by the initial resource endowment, and in part by the amount and quality of work force committed to the task.

Production levels are obviously of more immediate relevance to capability than are resource potentials; whatever is produced is available for utilization. Sheer amounts of production, however, or even a less specific concept such as "productivity," are of only limited relevance to immediate capability judgments. Production takes many forms, and only a portion of the total output has any but the most general political applicability. The crucial capability factor involved in production is best suggested by asking: "How much are we producing of what we need at the moment?" Once more we see the critical part played by the policy context of capability.

Particularly relevant in dealing with productivity are such modifying considerations as availability, convertibility of facilities, and "lead time." Since capability judgments normally involve some attempt to estimate future requirements and capacities, these "quality" interpretations of productivity provide estimates of what the state might be doing at some point in the future. Estimates of the ability of the state to increase its politically significant production must take into account the willingness of the population to undergo relative hardship, since increased productive capability involves some deprivation of the civilian-consumption sector of the economy.

5. MILITARY POWER. The most obvious—and the most relativistic—of the tangible factors of capability is military power. Capability judgments must pay deep attention to military factors, and are frequently based on them. It is by military means that states take overt action at the highest level of intensity. Military means are used to achieve final solutions in international politics. The military element in capability is obviously central to all estimates.

Such being the case, it is no wonder that a great deal more effort has been lavished on the development of doctrines and techniques for estimation of military factors than has been spent on any other elements of capability. Analysis and evaluation of the several variables that enter into a state's military capability have been raised to a fine art in almost all states.

As with all the other tangible factors, the initial consideration is one of size: How large is the military establishment in terms of troop force?

A second criterion is that of equipment and arms: How up-to-date and sophisticated are they, and what is the state's capacity to produce more? Third, inquiry is made into deployment—involving (1) the relative allocation of men and material among the various arms and services and (2) the pattern of their placement within the state's territory and (sometimes) its overseas bases. Finally, the full military capability of a state is comprehensible only in terms of whatever strategic and tactical doctrines are in control at the time of the analysis; these principles will govern the way in which the armed forces are actually used in support of state purposes.

As we shall see in later chapters, in no area is there a greater danger of making absolute capability judgments. There is a consoling but deceptive objectivity and clarity about raw troop force and equipment figures that often leads analysts into unsound, absolute conclusions. This difficulty has been compounded by the development of modern weapons and military techniques. What really counts in military capability is the military margin of superiority that may exist between two states, not the absolute level of military power either may have mobilized. Switzerland, it is sometimes said, is a pygmy to France but a giant to Liechtenstein.

The Intangibles

1. POLITICAL, ECONOMIC, AND SOCIAL STRUCTURE. We have pointed out that the tangible elements of capability tend to be measured, whereas the intangibles are evaluated. In approaching the intangibles, the analyst is not seeking a quantitative finding so much as trying to establish the extent to which the phenomena being studied contributes to or detracts from the state's effectiveness in a specific situation.

This becomes obvious when we examine the first in our list of intangibles—the political, economic, and social structure of a state. The efficient capability analyst should be free from any stereotyped prejudices concerning the intrinsic superiority of any one political, economic, or social system. Instead, the analyst must apply the yardstick of efficiency: Considering the mission which the state under analysis has set for itself, do these three structures represent the best possible way of mobilizing the state's effort? Does the political system, for example, provide for both efficient administration and a workable rapport with mass consensus, or is there sufficient disaffection to constitute a drag on governmental effectiveness? Does the economic system reduce waste, lost motion, uneconomic production, and inefficiency to the practical minimum, or are many opportunities for a rationalized productive system lost? Is the society integrated and coordinated and thus capable of unified effort, or is it split apart so that internal tensions dilute the state's international effort?

72 THE ACTORS

These and analogous questions ultimately produce an overall verdict on the general subject of how the state organizes itself for international action, and their answers constitute a significant if imprecise factor in its overall capability.

2. EDUCATIONAL AND TECHNOLOGICAL LEVEL. In a technological and scientific age, another societal characteristic that bears directly upon capability is the educational and technological level of the state. Industrial productivity, military effectiveness, and simple social cohesiveness are all major functions of the extent to which education and technical facility are dispersed within the society. Level of education is one of the major qualitative modifiers of any quantitative finding regarding work force.

Fundamental to the matter of educational and technological level is the simple question of literacy. No state can muster a significant national effort if reading and writing, the communication skills, are mysteries to the bulk or even a significant minority of its people. For reasons of both effective consensus building and efficient administration, a literate population is a necessity if a state is to play a meaningful international role; the massive efforts made by such states as China and India to bring minimal literacy to their people underscores its importance.

A second, almost as crucial, basic element in capability is what we might call *tool skill,* which means orientation toward and facility in the employment of the tools and techniques of modern industrial civilization. This involves emotional adjustment and acculturation as much as the actual learning of skills and procedures. Unless a people are familiar with the subtle ramifications of an industrial system, they will waste a good deal of effort in making the machinery work. Extensive training and inculcation of the necessary discipline are prerequisites to effective tool skill.

The factors of literacy and tool skill are characteristics of the mass of a population. A third factor—and in many ways as crucial an element in a state's educational and technological level—is the quality of the higher stratum of educated specialists. Does the state have enough specialists of the right sort? Is their training and level of performance adequate to the demands the state will make of them? Is the overall standard of scholarly, scientific, and technological effort advancing, declining, or merely static? These and related questions may, even in short-run situations (such as a "crash" program of weapons development), be the real determinant of the state's working range of capability.

3. NATIONAL MORALE. Among the difficult factors to measure, yet one of the few constant determinants of capability, is the elusive notion of national morale. We use this term here to describe the mass

state of mind in a country, with particular reference to how far the society feels itself committed to the government's policy.

A state has high morale when the government feels itself supported by an active, well-informed, articulate, and involved consensus. Such a condition requires that politically self-conscious people constitute the bulk of the society, that these individuals be convinced that the government's foreign policy enterprises are derived from the prevailing mass values of the society, and that the consensus include a favorable vote of confidence in the capacity of the policymakers to meet and overcome challenges implicit in the policy.

Thus national morale has a direct effect on the vigor and human dynamics with which officials mobilize and employ the tangible factors in capability. Widespread apathy toward foreign policy restricts the range of decision, and active disagreement within the body politic virtually paralyzes the government. In this sense, morale involves not only the affirmative characteristics of zest, dedication, and confidence, but also such negative elements as discipline and the capacity to endure stress, disappointment, and temporary failure.

If national morale is so shaky as to raise doubts about the endurability of the consensus on which decision makers must rely, improvement of morale becomes a primary charge on the government. What strategies the government may employ depend upon its judgment of the nature of the deficiencies and peculiar dynamics of the society and its controlling values. It may choose to frighten its people or seek to encourage them; it may become more generous with information and explanation, or control tightly the flow of communication to the public. It may increase the pace of stimulation of the public psyche, or it may deliberately minimize tension. Whatever the devices adopted, however, its policy must remain largely in suspension until its morale goals are achieved.

4. INTERNATIONAL STRATEGIC POSITION. The final element of capability—the state's international strategic position—brings us almost full circle, since it is the general strategic role played by a state in world politics that raises issues of capability in the first place. We have stressed that capability is comprehensible only in a specific policy context. Now we conclude that the state's own policy and strategy contain factors that contribute to its working capability.

This is most apparent in terms of the state's need for the support of other states in the service of its own policy. Its effective capability vis-à-vis its actual or potential associates is reduced exactly to the extent to which it feels it needs allies; it must so conduct itself as to establish or maintain the desired cooperative relationship. Were it following a different policy, it would not require this particular alliance pattern and would have a greater freedom of choice and action in these areas.

A second manifestation is derived from the state's interpretation of its position in the world. If the state feels itself under great and constant danger, it will obviously devote a much greater share of its available capability to defense of its home territory, leaving a restricted margin available for affirmative action on the world stage. Any revision in a state's estimate of the threats it faces automatically affects its capability in other areas. A judgment that the threat has grown less frees the state for more extensive action elsewhere; if the threat is deemed to have become greater, adequate responsive action normally calls for contraction of effort at other points.

In a peculiar and paradoxical way, the very objectives a state selects for itself, and the way it interprets the situation in which it must operate, have a major influence on its capability to achieve those objectives and to function in the situation. A state's international strategic position is to a large measure determined by itself; a state is to a great extent the architect of its own capability.

No more graphic proof could be advanced of the relativistic and policy-grounded nature of the concept of capability. The universe of the policymaker and the capability analyst is largely of their own making. The judgments and decisions they make are expressions of their interpretations of the reality of their world. It should not be surprising that their conclusions about the ability of their state to achieve its purposes are so directly derived from their formulations of the nature of the problems they face.

Recommended Readings

BARNET, RICHARD J. *The Giants: Russia and the United States.* New York: Simon & Schuster, 1977.

———. *The Roots of War.* New York: Penguin Books, 1973.

BLAIR, JOHN M. *The Control of Oil.* New York: Pantheon Books, 1977.

BRZEZINSKI, ZBIGNIEW, and SAMUEL P. HUNTINGTON. *Political Power: USA—USSR.* New York: Penguin Books, 1977.

CAMPBELL, ROBERT W. *The Soviet-Type Economies: Performance and Evaluation* (3rd ed.). Boston: Houghton Mifflin Co., 1974.

DE JOUVENEL, BERTRAND. *Power: Its Nature and History of Its Growth.* Boston: Beacon Press, 1962.

HEISS, KLAUSS, KLAUS KNORR, and OSKAR MORGENSTERN. *Long Term Projections of*

Power: Political, Economic and Military Forecasting. Cambridge, Mass.: Ballinger Publishing Co., 1973.

KNORR, KLAUS E. *Military Power and Potential.* Lexington, Mass.: D. C. Heath and Co., 1970.

_____. *Power and Wealth: The Political Economics of International Power.* New York: Basic Books, 1973.

LASSWELL, HAROLD D., et al. *A Study of Power.* New York: Free Press, 1950.

MOUZON, OLIN T. *International Resources and National Policy.* New York: Harper & Row, 1959.

OSGOOD, ROBERT E., and ROBERT W. TUCKER. *Force, Order, and Justice.* Baltimore: Johns Hopkins Press, 1967.

RUSSELL, BERTRAND R. *Power: A New Social Analysis.* New York: Barnes & Noble, 1962.

SPROUT, HAROLD, and MARGARET SPROUT. *Toward a Politics of the Planet Earth.* New York: Van Nostrand Reinhold Co., 1971.

SINGER, MARSHALL R. *Weak States in a World of Powers.* New York: Free Press, 1972.

TOFFLER, ALVIN. *The Eco-Spasm Report.* New York: Bantam Books, 1975.

The Implementing of Decisions

4

After policymakers have stipulated the objective they will seek and determine their capabilities for action within the particular situation, they next turn to the selection of the appropriate means of implementing their decisions. We have already suggested that they have a considerable range of choice in selecting detailed procedures, and that they attempt to develop a course of action which will carry them to the goal they have adopted. In this chapter we shall examine and characterize categories of state techniques, the four general channels through which the policymaker may act in world politics. We shall not attempt to elaborate a complete catalogue of state procedures in policy implementation, since these are infinite in number and largely dependent upon random and unique factors in the situation.

First, we ought to make one basic point that will be implicit in all our subsequent discussion. Although this chapter concentrates on the various ways states may act, action of any sort is not a necessary consequence of a policy decision. The net result of the elaborate analytical process outlined in Chapter 2 may be a decision not to act at all. While it is true that inaction is a form of action and proceeds (or should proceed) from the same intellectual process that action does, the strategy of inaction obviously raises fewer questions of implementation. For our purposes, we should always keep in mind in our consideration of state techniques that a state decision to act represents a deliberate choice of action over inaction in the particular context.

If a state decides to act, the nature of the state system opens four possible channels for the application of its strength. The first of the four different sets of techniques is political in nature, and its most conspicuous manifestation is the device of diplomacy. The second is economic, probably the most varied and complex of the four in its richness of artifice and stratagem. Third in the list are psychological techniques, of which propaganda and its operational derivatives are examples. Finally there are military techniques, ranging from nonviolent use of armed force to open warfare.

In pure theory, a state may place its entire reliance in a particular situation upon any single one of these generalized techniques. More commonly, however, states develop an approach based on a "mix" of techniques designed to produce the greatest effect. It is axiomatic that a policymaker may develop combinations of techniques in perfect analytical and operational freedom; the only "correct" technique is that one that best achieves the purpose of the state.

A state attempts to preserve flexibility with the implementation of policy. It is thus most important that any operational commitment permit intensification, reduction, modification, or even abandonment if circumstances should dictate. The need for such flexibility has been redoubled as modern technology has led to the drastic reduction of available action time.

Political Techniques: Diplomacy

In one sense all foreign policy techniques are, or ought to be, political. No matter what a state may do in the execution of its purposes, its orientation and goals are always political in that they seek the maximization of its value system. Yet in practice the word *political* is applied more narrowly to those methods that involve direct government-to-government relations. The contacts that governments have with each other and the manner in which this intercourse is carried on are generally subsumed under the name of *diplomacy*.

The Nature of Diplomacy

Diplomacy, as a technique of state action, is essentially a process whereby communications from one government go directly into the decision-making apparatus of another. It is the one direct technique of state action, in that a state exerts its diplomatic power directly upon the crucial personnel of the other government or governments. If the operational purpose of a state's policy is to secure the agreement of other states to its designs, it is only by diplomatic means that such assent can be formally registered and communicated. In this sense, diplomacy is the central technique of foreign policy.

Diplomacy is both a full-fledged technique in its own right and the instrument by which other techniques are often transmitted. A state can act diplomatically in a purely political context, using only the methods and resources of diplomacy, or it may implement economic, psychological, or even military action by diplomatic maneuvering. Although the operating requirements of pure diplomacy and what we might call "mixed" diplomacy differ to some extent, their fundamental rationale remains essentially the same.

The actual procedures of diplomacy are many, ranging from such highly formal devices as notes, aides-memoires, and communiqués to more informal and almost casual conversations. At bottom, diplomacy is a method of negotiating between sovereignties, and although the elaborate ritual and protocol that surround the practice may sometimes seem pretentious and time consuming, their roots lie in the nature of the task. By diplomatic means a state transmits its position on an issue to another state and receives the other state's response. Whatever changes may take place in the respective positions are registered diplomatically, and the eventual elaboration of whatever relationship develops also lies in the hands of diplomats.

The Functions of Diplomacy

We can distinguish several distinct functions of diplomacy. Which of these the working diplomat may be called upon to perform depends on the nature of the policy his government is following.

First, diplomacy is to a major extent a technique of *coercion*. Coercive moves made by other means are communicated diplomatically, and diplomacy itself can be used to exert pressure. In many cases, rupture of diplomatic relations has a coercive element, as does exclusion of the target state from international conferences or oganizations. Coercion may also be applied in negotiation by an ultimatum, by the establishment of a rigid time limit for the conclusion of an arrangement, or by the registration of a formal or informal protest or complaint. In the past few decades, "pragmatic" dictators have added an element of psychological coercion to diplomacy by eliminating the courtesy and good manners traditional to the art and conducting relationships in an atmosphere of vilification and intense emotion. This procedure has had its undeniable advantages.

Second, diplomacy is a technique of *persuasion*. Advancing arguments and proffering a quid pro quo, both persuasive devices, are within the exclusive province of diplomatic technique. In terms of our discussion of the forms of capability, diplomacy is the most frequently used and best suited of all techniques for application of the influence component of state capability. While the distinction between coercion and persuasion is often vague, and the two approaches frequently blend into one another, there is a real difference in both motivation and atmosphere, and most diplomatic initiatives are at least initially cast in a persuasive form.

Third, diplomacy is uniquely a procedure of *adjustment.* It is admirably suited to the task of enabling two states to modify their positions on an issue in order to reach a stable relationship. Its directness of communication, its potentially noncoercive nature, and its subtlety and flexibility all contribute to its usefulness. States may prosecute their differences and intensify their conflicts by a great variety of methods, but they may reduce tensions between themselves only by diplomatic means. However, the adjustment function of diplomacy is effective only if both parties are amenable to negotiation; nothing can overcome a state's unwillingness to change a policy.

Finally, diplomacy is a technique for reaching *agreement;* indeed, it has been said that diplomacy is the art of negotiating written agreements. Formal written agreements are the most binding structures on international commitment offered by world politics, and they can be brought into existence only by diplomatic procedures. We must note that agreement may involve coercion, persuasion, or adjustment, and that no agreement is possible unless both parties wish it. On the other hand, even a strong interest in formalizing an understanding would be pointless if instruments and procedures for reaching one were not available. Here diplomacy comes usefully into its own.

Success and Failure in Diplomacy

What are the characteristics of good diplomacy? More directly, what are the marks of the policy of a state that is making good use of diplomatic techniques? Conversely, what is wrong with the normal practice of diplomacy in the contemporary world that has given the diplomat such a small role in the conduct of world politics?

There is little disagreement about the requirements for success in diplomacy. The essentials of the diplomatic art have been well known for centuries, and the actual practice of its masters furnish us with clear guidelines. We may here reduce the vast literature into four basic operative requirements.

1. *The diplomat must have a clear understanding of the situation.* This requires sensitivity to the forces at work in the problem area and clarity of one's own purposes and the ultimate implications of one's policy with respect to long-range goals. A diplomat must also have a clear understanding of the points of view, interests, and goals of other states, because without such empathy one will be virtually powerless.
2. *The diplomat must be fully aware of one's real capability.* This requires the diplomat's appreciation of how much coercive capacity one's govern-

ment will support one with, and how much influence one may enjoy at that particular moment. A diplomat dare not attempt initiatives that lie beyond one's capability, nor be content with less than full exploitation of the resources appropriate to one's objectives.
3. *The diplomat's approach must be flexible.* This requires preparation for unforeseen developments or for withstanding the consequences of analytical error by having some alternate policies and approaches in reserve, by having an unpublicized "fallback" position available, and by being consistently eclectic in method. A diplomat distinguishes as much as possible between abstract "principle" and concrete interest, and remains firmly committed to the latter while being quite flexible on the former.
4. *The diplomat is eager to compromise within limits of nonessentiality.* A clear priority system is essential to a diplomat because only in this way can a determination be made of which issues are subject to bargaining and which are not. Priorities also suggest quantitative criteria as a guide in determining how a compromise may be made without giving away matters of importance in return for lesser concessions. In theory, a good diplomat should always be willing to give up a position of lower priority to secure one of higher rank; although subject to drastic modification in practice, this rule does have great importance in diplomatic maneuvering. The criterion of a good diplomatic bargain is less how much is given up than how much is won, for only the prize can determine whether the price was too high.

Diplomacy in the contemporary era has not proved able to cope adequately with the dilemmas of politics. Its inadequacy has been so obvious that some critics have been moved to speculate on "the end of traditional diplomacy." In practice, since the end of World War II, the four roles we have formulated have been honored more often in the breach than in the observance. Situations are analyzed far too often in ideological and nationalistic terms, and too seldom realistically. It is currently unfashionable to admit that one's opponent has any point of view, let alone one meriting consideration. Capability factors are grossly misinterpreted, especially in the military realm. Flexibility, thanks to ideology and nationalism, is usually a lost cause, and compromise is normally rejected as striking a bargain with sin.

In these circumstances diplomacy cannot flourish, and current practice has involved either ill-concealed and blatant attempts at coercion or nonpurposive propaganda. Real negotiation, persuasion, and adjustment of positions culminating in agreement have been accidental phenomena instead of the normal procedures of states in the system. Deep popular involvement in foreign policy by means of absolutist and emotional sloganizing, common in both large and small states, has seriously impeded the force of diplomacy by depriving it of the necessary "elbow room" in which to maneuver.

Some recent hopeful signs, however, augur a revival of diplomatic activity in the true sense. The height of the Cold War era was marked by constant advocacy of absolute solutions to problems. More than three decades of struggle have had their effect; absolutist positions are advanced less seriously, and responsible and increasingly prudent governments are willing to entertain the possibility of partial solutions. With this frame of mind becoming more common, the opportunity for diplomacy to work its harmonizing and adjusting effect becomes brighter. The future will undoubtedly see greater reliance on diplomacy and possibly a more favorable record of its success.

Economic Techniques: The Carrot and the Stick

Economic techniques of state action are as old as the state system itself, but their full flower dates only from the Industrial Revolution. The increasing complexity of modern economic and industrial life has made the states of the world to a large degree mutually interdependent; this reciprocal involvement serves to open a broad range of action possibilities to states. Various sorts of international economic action aimed at the achievement of political goals have become a part of foreign policy for all states.

The Rationale of Economic Methods

Probably the most obvious characteristic of economic techniques is their bewildering diversity. Almost any aspect of economic life can, with sufficient ingenuity on the part of policymakers, be turned into a tool of state action. However, certain generalizations are possible concerning the rationale of economic methods in foreign policy.

First, economic techniques are indirect in their application, in contrast to the directness intrinsic to diplomacy. Their immediate target is not the decision-making apparatus of the other state, but rather the totality of that state's society. The consent sought for is supposed to flow from internal pressures of that society upon its government rather than from any direct action by the initiating state. It can be thus said that economic techniques are designed to force the hand of the other government and to urge or coerce it to accede to the wishes of the first state.

Second, as the title of this section indicates, economic methods are two sided, in that they may be either coercive or persuasive in intent. A coercive economic move is one that, in general or specific terms, threatens the target state with deprivation or impoverishment unless it submits.

A persuasive move holds out the bait of economic reward or advantage in return for satisfactory modification of a target state's behavior. A single economic maneuver may frequently partake of both intents, threatening economic damage if no agreement is forthcoming but simultaneously promising rewards for acquiescence. Such ambivalence is usually thought of as ideal.

Third, economic techniques are almost entirely creatures of the particular situation, the effectiveness of any such device being completely dependent upon the nature of economic relations between the states involved. A state with no economic leverage on another would simply be ignored or ridiculed if it threatened economic reprisal to an unacceptable policy. Therefore, maximum use of economic instruments is reserved to those few states with widespread economic influence or to those controlling crucial economic goods or services. An otherwise weak state controlling huge oil reserves, for example, has a considerable range of capability made possible by its atypical and accidental economic situation.

Fourth, economic techniques are productive of generous amounts of resentment, resistance, and retaliation by the target state. Coercive economic moves obviously create hostility, since no people can stolidly accept either the threat or actuality of economic deprivation. Even persuasive and advantageous economic policies engender almost as much enmity among recipient peoples, on the grounds that it is humiliating and status-destroying to submit to bribery and blackmail for policy reasons. Much of the call in the Third World for "foreign aid without strings" flows from this orientation.

Fifth, as a result, economic techniques by themselves have a limited range of effectiveness. Strategists take account of resistance to economic pressures and discount accordingly the return expected from their use. As a rule, economic techniques today are rarely used alone. A persuasive economic policy is usually linked with extensive propaganda and diplomatic initiatives, while coercive programs are accompanied by a strong diplomatic line and frequently by military pressures of various sorts.

Persuasive Economic Techniques

Under the conditions of contemporary world politics, certain persuasive economic techniques have proved useful and appropriate. Probably the best known is "foreign aid": the direct grant or favorable loan of either cash, credits, or goods to other countries. These may be "economic" in nature and consist of foodstuffs, capital goods, or consumer products. The early years of the Cold War placed a high premium on "military" aid, including all types of military material and what the United

States called "defense support" in the form of economic aid committed to military purposes.

A second technique, of great importance since the emergence of the Third World, is development assistance, through which developed states assist less-developed countries in building productive plants and fostering a higher standard of living for their people. Originally undertaken in a Cold War context, development assistance has proved to be so expensive, so long lasting, and so unproductive of Cold War advantage that its leading practitioners have reduced it to a minimum. The results of development assistance have not been advantageous to the Third World either.

Third, much effort has gone into the use of trade and investment policy as a technique of state action. Bilateral trade agreements and international investment are familiar features of world politics today; most of them have clear political overtones, and some—particularly those between a large and powerful state and a smaller one—formalize the exchange of economic advantage for political rewards and investment. In recent years, another aspect of trade policy has appeared: the creation of trading blocs and the extension of an invitation to join such a group as a form of persuasion to political cooperation. So powerful has this lure been that Western European states have been tempted to abandon traditional political rivalries in order to secure the economic rewards of membership.

Closely linked with trade agreements are the many kinds of moves possible in the area of currency stabilization and control. This technique was quite common in the early postwar period, when currencies throughout the world were unstable and in need of assistance from those few states with adequate reserves. Current widespread stability has served to minimize the effect of this technique, although one peculiar anomaly exists: The United States, once the financial pillar of the entire world, has for several years been suffering a balance-of-payment deficit. Today, the United States is subject to the policy influence of the currency stabilization drive utilized by its erstwhile clients in Europe.

Coercive Economic Techniques

Coercive economic techniques are limited in number and variety only by the imagination of the implementing state within the political and economic situation. Here we do no more than attempt a rough classification.

The first type we may call restrictions on economic relations, which include the whole apparatus of currency control, export licenses and quotas, tariffs and nontariff barriers, foreign exchange blocking and control, and freezing of credits. The intent of all of these is to ensure that economic relations continue in a way favorable to the dominant state. The implication of these restrictions is that an improvement in political relations would have immediate economic consequences.

More overtly coercive is the outright interruption of economic relations, notably trade and investment. If the target state is sufficiently dependent on trade and investment with the dominant state, interruption will cause serious hardship and impel the victim toward reestablishment of normal patterns at a political price. Interruption of relations may be effective when the powerful state is a critical supplier of certain categories of capital and goods, or when it is a major market for the products of a single-commodity agricultural economy. Such a boycott is perhaps the most infuriating of all economic practices; since it usually leads to strong pressures for retaliation, it is seldom employed, and then only under especially favorable circumstances.

A special type of coercion stems from the cancellation or suspension of a program of capital investment or economic aid. Recipient states become accustomed to a steady flow of assistance once such a program is established. Their dependence upon continuation of capital flow or aid thus makes them vulnerable to the pressures that develop if the regular supply is interrupted. Again, this technique is most valuable when the coerced state is completely at the mercy of the state extending aid. If the former can actually do without the assistance, or if it should develop another source of capital or aid, then the net results of the effort may well be zero or even a minus factor.

There remains a collection of coercive economic steps that do not readily lend themselves to classification. These are markedly dependent for their effect on almost accidental situational elements, and their impact tends to be random and almost unpredictable. They include such trading practices as dumping, such politicoeconomic moves as preemptive purchase of raw materials (sometimes for the purpose of depriving another country of these supplies), such manipulative tricks as unilateral currency devaluation or barter trade agreements, and nationalization or expropriation of foreign property.

Conclusions on Economic Techniques

The most significant conclusion about economic techniques is that, because of both the unpredictability of their results and their detrimental effect on relations, they are of only limited and special usefulness by themselves.

A second conclusion, however, is that, under appropriate circumstances, economic techniques may have an effect at once devastating and controlling. Coercion in economic terms may cause hostility, but it may also move its victim to rapid and extensive policy revision. At the persuasive end of the spectrum, an imaginatively conceived and skillfully presented program has often earned major political dividends in a noncontroversial climate. Discrimination in the use of economic techniques, adequate understanding of the operative factors in a situation, and a refusal to adhere only to a particular technique all contribute to the overall usefulness of these techniques.

Third, economic techniques are of less value in short-term situations than over a longer period of time. To attempt to extract short-run political gain from application of a single economic device is frequently to court disappointment; seldom is a target state so tightly caught as to be obliged to respond politically in a single dimension to an economic initiative. Over longer time spans, however, the correct economic policies may well develop a pool of consent (or at least reduce barriers of disagreement) that will ultimately prove of major value. This caution has been violated consistently by both major powers during the Cold War era, with predictably frustrating results.

Psychological Techniques: Propaganda and Culture

Psychological techniques, aimed at the mass psyches of relatively large bodies of people, are also indirect means of state action. Thanks to improvement in the art and science of mass communication, propaganda and culture have become major elements in state capability and constitute in themselves a significant area of political action.

The Nature of Propaganda

Propaganda has been defined in many ways, but all definitions agree that, operationally, it consists of messages in a context of action; that is, the purpose of communication is to inspire the audience to act in a particular way. From the propagandist's point of view, however, this generalized concept breaks down into two subcategories. Some propaganda is basically a problem in audience conditioning, designed to increase both audience size and its sympathetic receptivity, while the remainder is directly action centered with the goal of persuading the audience to act in certain specified ways. Both forms have an important place in policy implementation.

Propaganda as a Foreign Policy Tool

We should distinguish among the four distinct "audiences" to which the foreign policy propagandist speaks. The first is the propagandist's own people, whose morale and dedication require that they be kept adequately informed, inspired, and indoctrinated. The second is the populace of those states associated with or friendly and cooperative to the propagandizing state. These also need to have policy explained in such a way as to impress them with the necessity of remaining true to their allegiance. The third is the audience formed by those who are neutral toward the propagandist's policy. Newly important today, they may be won to the state, or at least be prevented from active opposition, by a well-conceived program of information. Finally, there is an audience composed of the people of states hostile or in opposition to the propagandist. Propaganda in this context seeks to reduce their support of their own official policy and perhaps to loosen their bonds of loyalty.

We have spoken of "audiences" in terms of "people" because propaganda is largely a mass phenomenon. Decision-making personnel are normally too committed and too sophisticated to be particularly amenable to propaganda from abroad. Most mass communicators believe that they obtain the greatest results for a given effort by aiming at the broadest possible audience, and the record of their accomplishments in world politics confirms this judgment.

The great bulk of the propaganda messages put out by states are aimed at audience conditioning and sympathy building, a focus which is today called "image projection": The state seeks to be viewed in a favorable light by its several audiences. Direct calls to action are relatively few, partly because of the remote likelihood of their being heeded except in special circumstances, and partly because of the ease with which they can be neutralized by domestic counterpropaganda.

Therefore, most foreign policy propaganda is auxiliary to diplomatic efforts, and propaganda is seldom the single dimension in which a state acts. Effective propaganda may increase the policy impact of diplomatic, economic, or even military moves, but it can rarely accomplish a specific end by itself. It is crucial, therefore, that propaganda be rooted directly in the state's on-going policy and that major efforts be made to maintain consistency of word with action.

A factor seriously inhibiting propaganda today is the fact that virtually everybody is using it. With each audience bombarded by messages and appeals from every point of the compass, and with almost every policy point of view receiving eloquent and repeated expression, the listener has difficulty in formulating a clear impression by which to be guided. The listener is likely to select from the welter of propaganda those messages and appeals which are already familiar and simply ignore the remainder. Thus the policy impact of propaganda is seriously reduced, since it has relatively little influence on established patterns of behavior and response. This helps explain the great emphasis on audience building displayed by so many propagandizing states.

The Role of Subversion

Although subversion—the attempts of a state to overthrow or weaken another by means of internal agitation and conspiracy—is a direct-action technique in its own right, it is included in this discussion of psychological techniques for a special reason. Crucial to a state's establishment and implementation of a subversive activity is the psychological problems of destroying the loyalty that binds citizens to their government. Their loyalty must be replaced in turn by a willingness to follow the commands of an alien and hostile state.

Subversion is an old technique, but it has been raised to the highest peak in the contemporary era. This has been due in part to the development of modern ideologies—nationalism, imperialism, communism, fascism, and anticolonialism—and in part to the improvements in communication that have made it possible for a government to control a subversive movement (or many subversive movements) from a great distance. However, more important than either of these in explaining the rise of subversion as a technique is the fact that the present age is one of great social disaffection, change, and revolution. When a state develops substantial internal divisions and deep animosities, the potential for subversion is heightened. Protagonists of change can often capitalize on such internal cleavages by enlisting key leaders and groups to prosecute their own purposes under the sponsorship of a foreign government.

In theory, subversion is a technique of revolution, the ultimate purpose of which is complete overthrow of the government and its replacement by the revolutionary group. As a technique of foreign policy, however, it is valuable even at a much more restrained level. Organized subversion can deepen divisions within a society to the extent that the government's integrity is compromised, its vitality weakened, and the course of its foreign policy altered in favor of the intervening state.

Subversion is a technique of opportunity, usable only in those special circumstances when the target is vulnerable. Societies in which disaffection is minimal may be annoyed but never inhibited by subversion. States with revolutionary policy can exploit popular discontent successfully, since they have appeal to individuals and groups seeking self-determination or liberation; the activities of the Soviet KGB are a case in point. States pursuing a stabilizing and mollifying status quo policy utilize subversion to ensure the existence of favorable regimes; the activities of the American CIA serves as a useful illustration.

Cultural Techniques in Foreign Policy

A special development in the field of psychological action is the "cultural offensive." Using the standardized techniques of public relations, states in recent years have undertaken active international promotion of their culture patterns beyond their borders. Aided markedly by advances in mass communication, nearly every government today seeks to "put its best foot forward" culturally through a vigorous advertising campaign aimed at a global audience.

The operational demands of propaganda partially explain the cultural attack on mass consciousness. A favorable cultural image of a state and its government might well lead an audience to listen approvingly to policy positions expounded by that same government. But there is a more far-reaching rationale to cultural techniques. Culture patterns—whether economic, social, esthetic, or political—are manifestations of the basic value system of a society. Winning favorable response from other states to certain cultural symbols is a major step toward winning acceptance of the fundamental values on which they are based. Since foreign policy is at bottom an exercise in value maximization, it can be argued that in one sense cultural techniques are a form of direct state action on behalf of national objectives.

Cultural Imperialism

Cultural programs have become so powerful that cultural imperialism poses a serious threat to weaker states. Cultural imperialism is an attitude of cultural superiority and of insensitivity to other cultures and world views, almost always allied to superior political, economic and military power, and possessing superior technology. It favors and reenforces one set of cultural values and styles over others and produces a displacement of the cultures of weaker communities by the values selected and imposed by the dominant culture. The process of cultural imperialism is carried through the use of mass media and educational systems, as well as the control of the symbols of legitimacy and status, to substitute one set of cultural values and styles with another.

In the present global system, cultural imperialism assumes that there is high, middle, and low culture, and especially that high culture is derived from the Renaissance and Enlightenment of Western European Culture—and is automatically superior. It asserts that literacy, abstracting, generalizing, analytic culture represents a higher form of truth than oral, folk, anecdotal cultures. Ethical and religious superiority as embodied in one cultural expression are identified with the dominant culture.

Finally, cultural imperialism displays an incapacity to imagine the experience of a person from another culture. This is accompanied by the inability to understand the experience and manifestation or interpretation of that experience of another person in another culture except in one's own terms. It results in the denial of the validity and value of the experience and cultural manifestations thereof of persons outside of one's own cultural expressions.

Military Techniques: War and Its Approximations

We come now to the fourth and final set of techniques of state action—military capability and the role of force. We should establish our logical base by pointing out something of a paradox. In logic and in the practice of statecraft, there is no substantive difference between military techniques and any others. War is thus "normal" in interstate relations, since the criterion of appropriateness governing use of military power is exactly the same as that used in any other policy decision. Yet policymakers have always recognized that the use of military techniques is predictably more costly and more dangerous than other ways of acting and have normally considered military techniques a last resort, to be used only if lesser measures prove inadequate for attaining a necessary objective. The great technological revolution in warfare has sharpened the impact of this dilemma. Today, one of the more hotly debated theoretical issues, as well as one of the most pressing practical problems of policymaking, is that of the utility of military power—offensive, defensive, and deterrent—in foreign policy.

War in Foreign Policy Calculations

The phrase *military techniques* really refers to some sort of application of military power, the ultimate being actual conduct of war. Reconciling policy considerations with the threat, initiation, conduct, or avoidance of war has long been one of the major concerns of the policymaker.

It is important that we keep in mind that employment of military power is a means to a policy end, not an end in itself; "victory" is a technique and not a goal. The object of the exercise of military power is exactly the same as that of any other type of state action: achievement of enough consent by other states to permit attainment of the preselected objective. The extent to which military power is used in active pursuit of policy goals is determined initially by the value placed on the objective and by the amount of resistance the state expects to meet. The objective of combat—the manipulation and application of military force—is to "break the enemy's will to resist"—not necessarily, it should be noted, the *capacity* to resist.

Resort to military techniques is derived from the same type of cost/risk calculation that precedes any policy decision. Although there is a significant difference in an ultimate decision for war, the difference is less one of quality than of quantity. Costs in war are obviously much higher, since they must be measured to a great extent in human life. The risk factor demands greater odds in favor of success because the price of failure in war is much higher than in any other policy enterprise. Thus cost factors demand that war be reserved for purposes great enough to justify the inevitable expenditure.

In principle, therefore, the use, as policy tools, of military techniques that may culminate in war demands that the magnitude of the force and violence be in reasonably accurate relationship to the worth of the objective and appropriate to the extent and nature of the resistance to be met. It is this concept of the role of violence—phrased by Montesquieu as doing no more damage to the enemy than is absolutely necessary to the attainment of one's purposes—upon which the state system is founded, and it is in this way that war figures in the policy judgments of states.

Technology, Nationalism, and War

Two of the great historical forces of modern times have seriously complicated the role of war in statecraft. The first is technology, which has made possible new horizons in weaponry and expanded incalculably the ability of states to inflict damage on each other. The second is modern nationalism, which has involved entire populations in warfare and largely dissipated the ability of governments to control the magnitude of their military effort. Technology and nationalism have made war a struggle between peoples rather than between states. The objectives of war have become the total submission or utter destruction of the enemy, rather than the lesser purpose of winning assent to a particular policy.

The world has entered the era of "total war," a situation divorced from single-policy objectives which is instead a simple if desperate matter of survival. Under contemporary combat conditions, a total war cannot be considered a rational application of capability to foreign policy (although conflicts on levels below the "total nuclear war" stage may be). Total war represents a catastrophic breakdown in the international political process, while limited wars, internal wars, proxy wars, and the use of threat and bluff may all signal that the system is operating with some prospect of resolution short of annihilation.

The Appropriateness of War

The policymakers of today, knowing that the use of military techniques will trigger extreme nationalist emotions in their people and open themselves and their states to the possibility of attack by the most horrible of new weapons, are cruelly inhibited in their policy choices. While in theory policymakers are free as ever to resort to techniques leading to war, the logic of the cost/risk continuum is inexorable and frustrating to them.

With war certain to cost far more than it ever has before, the number of objectives for which such an expenditure is justifiable has shrunk alarmingly; prolongation of a list of such goals past the initial entry of national survival has become extremely difficult. By the same token, if any war in which the policymakers become engaged is potentially a war of survival, risk factors assume a new relevance. The odds they must have in their favor before risking combat have climbed almost to the absolute, for their enemies are just as likely to assume that the struggle is total, and therefore commit their ultimate capacities in their own defense. Total war can knowingly be unleashed only by a state that has a "first-strike" capability and minimum vulnerability to whatever retaliatory capacity the enemy may possess, either before or after the initial onslaught. Attainment of such dominance in the contemporary world is effectively beyond the capacity of any state.

Nevertheless, war, total or otherwise, has not become impossible, since either an irrational distortion of reality or a serious analytical error could lead a government to take the risk. What has happened is that war, particularly total war, has become inappropriate to foreign policy conceived and implemented in a climate of calculation, prudence, and rationality. This situation, so disruptive of many operating assumptions of world politics, has engaged the attention of scholars and policymakers ever since the dawn of the nuclear age. A considerable body of speculation and doctrine has been concerned with the implications of modern warfare for the future of foreign policy and world politics. We shall be examining these contentions in some detail in Chapter 9, but may anticipate the conclusion we reach there, at least in general terms: There is a persuasive case to be made for the continued relevance of military considerations to world politics, but the ubiquitous factors of cost and risk have served to deter states, particularly nuclear powers, from venturing too far into the dangerous waters of open warfare. The American frustration in Vietnam has illustrated this situation.

Military Techniques Short of War

The role of military techniques in policy implementation has by no means been confined to actual warfare. As a matter of fact, military factors short of combat have long been an ingredient in the normal conduct of foreign policy by all states.

Relative military rank of states has been one of the fundamental structural elements in the state system. The relations of any two states in time of "peace" have long been materially affected and often dominated by their respective military postures, due in part to the direct impact of military differentials that always involve a subtle or blatant threat to the weaker states. As long as a state retained the right and capability to back its demands by military force, a weaker state was obliged to include this consideration in its situational context and to guide itself by a quantitative and qualitative evaluation of the likelihood of this threat becoming a reality. Even more importantly, military differentials had a crucial status-conferring effect. Something very much like a class system gave form to the global scene, as great military powers, medium military powers, and weak military powers developed standardized relations to one another, with differing rank, role, and status in world affairs. It is impossible to overestimate the historic impact of this factor.

But both the element of threat and the element of status (perhaps most usefully conceived as the institutionalized reflection of threat) depended for their energizing effect upon the credibility of the military means. The threat of military power could influence a weaker state only if that government believed that the more powerful state was willing to risk the commitment of force and was also in a position to use that force meaningfully. The status reward of military capability—by no means entirely inoperative today—also flowed indirectly from the credibility of military superiority. As soon as smaller states came to realize this paradox —that the more military capability major states acquired in the nuclear age, the less real opportunity they had to use it, and the less interested they were in committing themselves to its use—credibility began to erode. Threats lost their compelling character, and status began to be dissipated as well.

This revaluation of the real role of military techniques in foreign policy has gone so far that some analysts contend that the world has had its hands tied in a military sense, and has entered the era of the "tyranny of the weak." Others (including ourselves) argue that we have at least left the era of the "monopoly of the strong." If the purpose of high capability is to broaden the area of freedom of choice enjoyed by a state, then the greatest measure of such freedom is enjoyed by states almost entirely devoid of military power, while those governments with the largest establishments discover that their freedom is drastically circumscribed by the very existence of their military machines. In practice, therefore, the strength of the powerless and the weakness of the powerful limits the choice of military techniques.

If this conclusion regarding the place of military techniques reflects a fundamental change in the nature of state relationships rather than a temporary distortion of regular patterns, the global political system will inevitably undergo far-reaching modification. The military channel of action is historically not only the ultimate lever of states but is essential to the operation of orderly relationships within the traditional system. If, however, either technological or conceptual progress results in a recapture of the controlling place of military factors, the system will find it possible to stabilize itself again.

Recommended Readings

AGEE, PHILIP. *Inside the Company: CIA Diary.* New York: Stonehill Publishing Co., 1975.

BARNET, RICHARD. *The Roots of War.* New York: Penguin Books, 1973.

BLACK, CYRIL E., and THOMAS P. THORTON. *Communism and Revolution: The Strategic Uses of Political Violence.* Princeton, N.J.: Princeton University Press, 1964.

ELLUL, JACQUES. *Propaganda: The Formation of Man's Attitudes.* New York: Random House, 1973.

GEORGE, ALEXANDER L. *Propaganda Analysis: A Study of Influences Made from Nazi Propaganda in World War II* (repr. ed.). Westport, Conn.: Greenwood, 1973 (original printing, 1959).

GRIFFITH, SAMUEL B. *Mao Tse-tung on Guerrilla Warfare* (rev. ed.). Garden City, N.Y.: Doubleday & Co., 1978.

JACKSON, W. A., and MARWYN S. SAMUELS, eds. *Politics and Geographic Relationships.* Englewood Cliffs, N.J.: Prentice-Hall, 1971.

JERVIS, ROBERT. *Perception and Misperception in International Politics.* Princeton, N.J.: Princeton University Press, 1976.

LIDDELL, HART, and H. BASIL. *Strategy* (2nd rev. ed.). New York: Frederick A. Praeger, 1967.

MARCHETTI, V., and JOHN D. MARKS. *The CIA and the Cult of Intelligence.* New York: Dell, 1974.

MARTIN, LESLIE, ed. *Propaganda in International Affairs.* Philadelphia: Philadelphia Academy of Political and Social Science, 1971.

NICHOLSON, HAROLD. *Diplomacy* (3rd ed.). London: Oxford University Press, 1963.

SNEEP, FRANK. *Decent Interval.* New York: Random House, 1977.

STOESSINGER, JOHN G. *Why Nations Go to War.* New York: St. Martin's Press, 1974.

WEISSMAN, STEVE. *The Trojan Horse: A Radical Look at Foreign Aid* (rev. ed.). Palo Alto, Calif.: Ramparts Press, 1975.

WHITE, JOHN. *The Politics of Foreign Aid.* New York: St. Martin's Press, 1974.

II

THE GLOBAL POLITICAL SYSTEM: ACTORS AND THEIR RELATIONS

Ideas and Patterns of Global Politics

5

The second part of this book is devoted to the global system: those more or less regularized patterns of relationships formed by the contacts of states and other actors with each other. Our focus will continue to be political, in that we are most concerned with those relationships of actors that stem from their respective attempts at value maximization. World politics results from the actions and interactions of the foreign policies of actors. These initiative, responsive, ameliorative, combative, and compensatory forms of actors' behavior demonstrate sufficient regularity to form what we call here the global system.

The System of States

The global system is a special type of "social system," an arrangement created when a number of operating units—states or nonstate actors—so regularize and pattern their relationships with one another that system-centered behavior becomes to a large extent predictable. The states of the world are the principal operating units. In this case, something like three centuries of experience has brought such a degree of regularity to the structure and dynamics of their relations that the general shape of international behavior is very orderly. It is with this concept that we begin our discussion.

The Characteristics of the System

Although it can be included within the general definition of a social system, the global system has a number of characteristics that mark it as distinctive and unique. It is this measure of difference that lends world politics its distinguishing characteristics.

First, world politics goes on within a *system,* and not within a *society* or a *community.* Although writers are frequently moved to discuss the "community of nations," or the "society of states," such terms must be considered metaphors rather than accurate reflections of reality. An indispensable element in either a society or a community is acceptance of a common set of goals for social action and a common value consensus. The global system has neither common values nor any mutual goal other than survival within the system. No state feels responsibility to anyone or anything outside itself. Society or community feeling is impossible without a common loyalty.

The global system therefore lacks the essential aspects of a more highly organized and articulated community: a controlling moral consensus, a socially sanctioned code of behavior that prohibits behavior destructive of good order and demands other behavior as socially necessary, and an institutional structure to implement the moral consensus and enforce the behavior code. Instead, the global system gains its form and energy from a much more rudimentary set of controls, particularly a calculating kind of prudence that we have already characterized as "strategic" and a thrust to maintain and preserve the system in its essentials as preferable to any other basis of organization, either more or less restrictive.

The operating assumptions of the global system may be classified as those of a semiorganized anarchy. Certain anarchic presumptions—those concerning the free will of the individual state, the right of the state to choose any goal it wishes and take any appropriate implementing action, and the resolution of conflicts of interest in terms of the relative strength of the disputing parties—are absolutely controlling. The principle of sovereignty, if taken literally, permits none but an anarchic base for political action among states. Granted, to a certain extent a state's policy in world affairs is always rooted in the possible necessity of the state's being thrown entirely upon its own resources, with every other state's hand turned against it, and it is common for the rhetoric of statecraft to evoke images of the individual state bravely making its way against the active or passive opposition of the remainder of the system. Yet the logic of anarchy is surprisingly unreliable as a basis for predicting the outcome of state relations in the real world. Policymakers have made considerable progress in softening and diverting the more onerous consequences of the relatively underorganized global system.

This is due in part to the strong tendency of policymakers to prefer an expediential to an absolute formulation of both goals and tactics. We already know how willing policymakers are to settle for half a loaf in foreign policy, especially as the consequences of failure in an all-out effort become more awesome. But the regularities of world politics are also due in large part to the impact of habit and inertia; policymakers no less than ordinary individuals are prisoners of their own past action patterns. The influence of custom and standardized practice has been almost uniformly on the side of stabilization and regularization in the relationships of sovereignties. Today, although the anarchy of world politics is conceptually as obvious as ever, the global system is more elaborately and tightly organized than is generally appreciated.

The State in the System

The individual state, viewing itself as a functional unit within the global system, is a solitary, self-contained, and self-justifying entity. It draws its motivations for action from within itself, feels itself obligated to no other state, is prepared to devote its own resources to the satisfaction of its needs, and is ready to enjoy the rewards or suffer the consequences of its actions. It judges all situations and the actions of all other states by the single criterion of its controlling version of interest, and acquires enemies or friends and acts cooperatively or controversially in response to its internal evaluation of the ebb and flow of political action.

This emphasis on the internalized mission and function of the state in the system reflects the dominant note in the reality of world politics. The state is theoretically a free agent and attempts to achieve as close an approximation of this freedom as possible. Nonidentification of the political unit with the larger community and the greater operational freedom from restraint enjoyed by the state mark the difference of world politics from other forms of social action.

It has been argued, by Machiavelli and his later disciples, that the state's control over its own international role is so complete that it is the architect of its own moral code. In these terms the only "good" the state serves—the supreme value of foreign policy—is the accomplishment of its own ends. Although it is in one sense circular reasoning and not especially useful as a criterion for determining ultimate moral questions, the notion of "reason of state" is of great value in formulating and executing foreign policy. Whatever the state decides to do in world politics is transformed by the very fact of decision into a moral goal. Qualms of conscience need never trouble the working policymakers, for if they conclude that something is demanded by the national interest, it automatically becomes moral and good. Success in achieving an objective, regardless of other factors, is in itself a "good" thing, while failure is intrinsically immoral and therefore reprehensible.

Thus the motive force of the global system does not flow from any centralized source but from each state itself. The "climate" of world politics—the general atmosphere within which relations are conducted and which is subject to change over time—is neither a cosmic force nor an accident of history, but stems from the prevailing patterns of assumptions and actions accepted by the dominant states of the system. Any basic change in the system will find its initial expression in modifications in the way states conceive of their international roles.

The Interstate Relationship

These operational postulates govern the approach of states to one another. We have already mentioned that states, lacking any consensual base, must develop their respective postures on a purely ad hoc basis. Initial stages of any new interstate relationship are always tentative and probing, as each seeks to discover the nature and extent of the involvement of its own interest with the interests of all the others. Only after each state has determined the essential ingredients of the evolving relationship does it feel free to elaborate and exploit a strategy.

The relations of any two states within any situation can be located somewhere along a continuum ranging from total agreement to total hostility, the determining factor being the extent to which the respective interests coincide or conflict. In one sense, therefore, the outcome of any particular collision between states can be termed inevitable. Each has a predetermined notion of interest, and the forces liberated by the interaction of these notions determine the shape of the relationship with almost mathematical precision.

Two further points should be made in this connection. First, inevitability develops after the respective notions of interest are determined; each state has complete freedom until then to formulate its interest as it may please. Thus, because the states set their own goals, the relationship is under complete control at one stage, although almost entirely beyond manipulation after the critical point of goal-setting. Second, the degree to which interests clash does not dictate the level of hostility or tension at which the disagreement is prosecuted. The magnitude of an area of disagreement merely outlines the arena of conflict; whether the conflict is fought at a high level, a low level, or allowed to lie virtually dormant depends upon further policy decisions by the governments involved.

We have already discovered that this primacy of interest in the calculations of policymakers has made strategy and policy a cautious business. With no certain foreknowledge of how other states will react to a given stimulus, a government in order to be safe must assume the worst—any other state is capable of becoming its enemy at any time and for causes, in the last analysis, beyond its own control. The potentiality of total opposition in any interstate relationship materially affects the substance and formulation of policy.

The Pole of Order and the Pole of Disorder

The state system is perpetually torn between the attractions of what we might symbolically call the pole of order and the pole of disorder. Conceptually and logically, the system postulates disorder so complete and controlling as to reduce world politics to a law-of-the-jungle war of all against all. Operationally, although violent outbreaks of disorder and open physical conflict may be "normal," they are also relatively infrequent. States spend a much larger proportion of their effort in prosecuting their ends in a context of order and restraint than they do in any type of open conflict.

The order-disorder dichotomy tends to stabilize the norm of international political interaction somewhere between the poles because of dynamic equilibrium. At times, pressures leading toward disorder may become relatively more powerful than countervailing tendencies, and the system may head toward breakdown. Disorder has taken over twice within the twentieth century, during World Wars I and II. Normally, however, the closer toward open disorder the system drifts, the more powerful becomes the urge toward reestablishment of order, and equilibrium is likely to be restored. In the same way, there is such a thing as too much order in the system, in the sense that many states feel that an overstabilized set of relationships might deprive them of the freedom of decision and action they feel is intrinsic to sovereign status. An excess of stability may well trigger disorderly forces within the system into deliberate attempts to gain elbow room.

Equality and Inequality in Global Politics

One of the paradoxical aspects of world politics is the constant tension between the claims of states to substantial equality and the practical fact of their actual inequality. Both equality and inequality are manifested concretely in the conduct of the relations of states. Both affect the way peoples and governments view the world and the tasks they attempt to accomplish in their foreign policies. Since states do exist simultaneously on the planes of conceptual equality and operational inequality, we must understand the implications of either factor and the significant relations between them if we are to gain a grasp of the realities of world politics.

The Law and the Myth of Sovereignty

Equality of states as a characteristic of world politics has its roots in one of the basic concepts of the entire study of political science—sovereignty. From both the legal and mythical consequences of sovereignty flow many fundamentals of world politics.

Sovereignty is legally a key characteristic of a state: To be accepted as a state, a political society must have within itself a supreme lawgiving authority with the power to issue commands from which there is no rightful appeal. The concept was born during the formative era of the modern state, and today does no more than state a truism. No one would quarrel with the necessity of having a central source of political and legal authority within a state.

Difficulty arose when this internalized idea of considerable utility was applied to interstate relations. What in law and in logic could be the appropriate relationship between two sovereign states, each incorporating an alleged supreme authority which recognized no superior? No relationship except complete legal and status equality was conceivable. It is on this basis that international law, the body of jurisprudence that regulates the relationships of sovereignties, is built.

Accordingly, sovereignty in international relations and law has come to stipulate the absolute and perfect legal equality of all states. None may rightfully dictate to another; each is declared the equal of all others in status, dignity, and honor. All of the protocol and procedure of formal international intercourse pays respect to this symbolism of sovereign equality; even the Charter of the United Nations states that "the Organization is based on the principle of the sovereign equality of all its Members."

Legal sovereignty was given added dimension with the birth of modern nationalism. As popular self-consciousness evolved into intensive nationalist identification, the doctrine of sovereignty, with its insistence that all states are equal and independent, became of great value in molding nation-states. From this has developed the contemporary myth of sovereignty.

Nationalism demands that the nation-state be at least symbolically free from responsibility to external authority. The "national will" is sacred and not to be tampered with, while the symbols of national identity —the flag, the uniform, the historical monuments—acquire overtones of mystical sanctity. Any impairment of sovereignty is to be resisted as a major patriotic duty.

Thus the myth of sovereignty and the concept of nationalism, both grounded in a formalized concept of state equality, unite to reinforce the anarchistic tendencies of the state system. The insistence that the state cannot be controlled by any larger community has contributed to the instability of world politics. Operationally, the incapacity of the conceptual state to accept coercion (for to do so would deny the equality and independence of states) has made it necessary for all international arrangements to be ratified by the (free or forced) consent of the participating states. So long as states consent formally, the integrity of sovereign equality is preserved at least in a formal sense.

The Political Inequality of States

Sovereignty as law and concept is a reality of contemporary political life, so it does little good to argue (as devoted protagonists of international organization and world government frequently do) that the doctrine of sovereignty is "invalid." The persistence of states in acting as if sovereignty were a reality gives the doctrine great political significance. But another equally stark fact must be faced: The conceptual equality of states exists alongside an absolute inequality in political competence. States are completely equal in their right and capacity to develop ego-images, select goals, and adopt action strategies, but they are inequal in their competence to fulfill their purposes. Either in absolute terms or with reference to a particular situational setting, no two states are ever equal in capability and must adapt their behavior to the verdicts of comparative strength.

This political inequality, long recognized as dominant within the state system, is most clearly seen in the surprisingly formalized horizontal stratification of states into great powers, medium powers, and small powers. Great powers are those few states whose capabilities are sufficiently large to permit them to establish and implement a totality of interest; in other words, a great power asserts the political right to interfere in and be consulted with regard to the resolution of any issue anywhere in the world at any time. A medium power is treated with a modest degree of formal deference by great powers, but is expected to confine its concerns to matters geographically or politically closer to home. A small power is permitted to exist but cannot ordinarily maintain an interest in opposition to either larger type; the conditions of its political activity are imposed upon it by the decisions of more powerful states.

In political terms, there are an infinity of gradations and discriminations of rank, power, and status. One of the most trying tasks of policymakers is to conduct relationships so as to preserve the useful fictions of legal equality while making certain that the political solutions accurately reflect the controlling inequality. We already know that the favored device of accomplishment of this purpose is the technique of consent.

The Trend Toward Greater Inequality

The gap between the mystique of state equality and the reality of political inequality is not decreasing, but instead is growing greater. The increasingly greater capability conferred by modern technology on industrial states, contrasted with the birth of so many new, less-developed, and unstable states, has vastly extended the spectrum of inequality. The powerful, both absolutely and relatively, are far more powerful, while the weak are relatively much weaker than ever before. In such a general context, to speak of the "sovereign equality" of the members of the United Nations is meaningless.

To some extent, however, the growing disparity between equality and inequality has been mitigated by certain other factors. Politically relevant forms of capability have changed drastically under postwar conditions; for example, military differentials are no longer so absolute an element of inequality. Such universally relevant international entities as the United Nations have also provided a way in which aggregates of strength can be constructed by small states. By the creation of a sufficiently impressive bloc, they can go far to offset the political dominance of larger states.

But these measures can only soften the inexorable advance of inequality. There is ample evidence today that popular leaders and professional policymakers are beginning to question the rationale of a political system that assumes equality among states and yet attempts to function with such disparity among its members. Whether the familiar political system can survive such a widespread contradiction is one of the major issues of the contemporary era.

Power Politics

The controlling dynamic of the state system has long been known as "power politics." This term, brought into English as a translation of the German *Machtpolitik,* has both a pejorative and a purely descriptive use. It may be used to characterize the relationships of states as being governed almost entirely by force or threat, without any consideration of right and justice. This meaning is perhaps closest to the sense of the original German word. Since our purpose here, however, is less to condemn power politics than to understand a process, we shall confine our use of the term to its purely descriptive sense. *Power politics* in the discussion that follows simply characterizes the way in which the global political process actually works.

The Assumptions of Power Politics

Our discussion of the state system and the respective roles of equality and inequality in the relations of states pointed out the underpinnings of the doctrines of power politics. Given the doctrinal and operating fundamentals of the nation-state, a political system including all states can develop in only one way. Power politics rests on a set of assumptions that are consciously accepted and deliberately implemented by all governments. (1) *There are no absolutes of right or justice in the relations of states.* Each state is the judge of the correctness of its own actions, and world politics goes on in a climate of moral relativism. (2) *The only collective value shared by all participants is the desirability of preservation of the system.* Except for the common concern not to destroy the system and its members, states are conceived as being entirely on their own. (3) *Self-help is the rule of action.* Lacking common values, the system cannot boast institutions and mechanisms of collective action. Individual states must therefore enforce their own rights and can count on support from no external source. (4) *Each state has only as many rights as it can enforce itself.* The state, thrust on its own resources, is obliged to content itself with such rewards as its strength and the wit of its leaders can extract from the system. (5) *The relations of states are determined not by the application of any general principles, but by the expediential interaction of their respective capabilities.* This is the crux of "power politics": Considerations of "power" (capability) govern the outcome of state contacts. (6) *Operationally, therefore, factors of power determine questions of right.* In this sense, might (broadly interpreted) actually makes right.

We can see the extent to which these organizing and operating assumptions flow logically from the postulates about the nature of the sovereign nation-state. If the test of any institution is whether it is appropriate to its social situation and effective in solving its problems, these assumptions—seldom verbalized by policymakers as baldly as we have stated them, but always sedulously adhered to in the practice of statecraft—establish an admirably effective institutional structure for the conduct of world politics.

Of course, the validity of these assumptions depends ultimately upon the extent to which the phenomenon of power or capability can be meaningfully quantified. Such a relativistic and purportedly value-free system of regulating a set of relationships demands the existence of a completely objective and universally accepted arbitrating apparatus. Power has played this role for centuries. The generally blurred appearance of the global system today is partially due to the diminished skill of policymakers in clarifying and quantifying the several categories of power. As a result, many of these assumptions are under serious fire.

Power Status in World Politics

The process of power politics became formalized as a basis for state interaction only when status configurations reflecting the power and strength (actual, potential, or formal) of states were crystallized into institutional form. The social system of world politics has traditionally been sharply stratified, because the three "classes" of states—great powers, medium powers, and small powers—have structured the entire political process. Essential to a working class system is a full appreciation by each class of its relative place in the system and a recognition of the peculiar roles of all other classes. In this regard the global system qualifies as a fully developed class society.

To continue our analogy, the relatively small group of great powers has, throughout history, insisted on their right to regulate all matters within the system in their individual and group interest. For many years the study of world politics actually involved no more than analysis of relations among a cluster of between four and eight major states. So great was their influence and so complete their collective monopoly over the relevant instruments of coercion that these few states repeatedly demonstrated their capacity to police all international relationships.

Membership in the elite inner circle of states was not the result of any mathematical calculation of power components, but rather a function of international practice and consensus. Certain "qualified" states were taken into the group by joint agreement, frequently registered in a major international conference culminating in a reordering peace treaty—such as the Peace of Westphalia (1648), the Treaty of Utrecht (1713), the work of the Congress of Vienna (1815), and the several peace treaties known as the Peace of Paris at the end of World War I (1919). Each of these epoch-making (and epoch-ending) instruments brought erstwhile outsiders into the group of great powers and also temporarily or permanently expelled certain states.

We have already indicated the chief reward of great power status: the implicit right (rooted in action capability) of the state to extend its interest as far as it wishes and to act in support of this interest. Great powers have always asserted that no question is inherently out of their province, and insist on being consulted on the ultimate disposition of any problem in which they may care to involve themselves. The fact that they may override longer-lived and deeper-rooted interests of lesser states is regarded as irrelevant, although some doctrinal efforts have been made toward formulating principles of an alleged "responsibility of power" that would authorize formal, universally accepted great power intervention anywhere.

The consensual base of great power status is clearly shown by the periodic appearance of states that are given membership in the circle for various political reasons, but which in fact lack a large reservoir of action capability. Spain, for example, was kept in the great power class long after its effective role had been extinguished in the seventeenth century. Italy was given courtesy membership after its unification in 1870. France and (Nationalist) China were included at United States insistence in the immediate aftermath of World War II. Such states may enjoy great prestige among lesser powers, but their actual influence on the deliberations of the inner circle is usually minimal.

The global system gives formal recognition to the controlling place of great power status through the mechanism of the "concert of power" —formal assemblies of leading states which attempt to arrange a set of relationships to their mutual satisfaction. In the past this has been most apparent at major peace conferences, such as the Congress of Vienna, and at periodic gatherings for the resolution of particular problems, such as the Congress of Verona (1822) and the Congress of Berlin (1878). Since 1945, the "concert of power" has had a dual aspect; the conference of opportunity continues in the form of the "Conference of Foreign Ministers" of the great powers, while permanent concern activity is made possible in the Security Council of the United Nations.

Less need be said of the two lower-status groups. The values of great power status tend to be automatically accepted by all states, so each smaller state seeks to act as much as possible like a great power. Each seeks as broad an international role as it can effectuate; each is active in augmenting its limited store of status and deference. Both classes (medium or small powers) contain an infinity of gradations, and something like an international pecking order is the norm. So dominant is the role of great powers, however, that these distinctions flow less from analyses and judgments made by lesser powers themselves than from (sometimes almost casual) discriminatory evaluations made by the elite states.

Patterns of Power Politics

Within the general characteristics of the power political system we can distinguish four clear patterns of relationships that have recurred frequently and are operative today. Two of these patterns involve only the great powers, two also involve the smaller powers, and each relates to the general area of great power—small power relationships.

The first pattern develops when the great powers are in substantial agreement about the existing shape of their own relationships within the entire spectrum of issues. Such a situation occurs only when the entire group—or all but a fraction of the membership—is, in terms of the prevailing situation, committed to a generalized status quo orientation.

Great power agreement results in the combined force of the concert being exerted upon the arena of world politics and the almost inevitable control of world politics by the leading states. A notable historical example of this pattern is provided by the course of affairs in Europe between 1815 and (roughly) 1848. The recent detente between the United States and the Soviet Union is a close approximation of this pattern.

The second pattern is the converse of the first in that the great powers, instead of agreeing on the preferable state of relationships, split into hostile and competing camps. This situation normally develops when revisionist points of view take control of a sizable slice of the total power represented by the group of major states. The dominant dimension of struggle is between status quo and revisionist policies. When major states fall out, the overall control of the elite group on world affairs inevitably diminishes, since the break in their common front and the dynamism that characterizes a great power struggle offer opportunities for small states and coalitions to act effectively. The neatest example of such a pattern is the Cold War era that split the great powers between 1947 and the early 1960s.

The third pattern arises when the smaller states of the world (including both medium and small powers) develop a common interest, point of view, and overall strategy to govern their responses to major states. This is a relatively recent development in world politics, made possible only by the appearance of the United Nations as an international actor that derives its motive force from its many small members. Under appropriate conditions—notably the military balance of terror that inhibits great power use of armed force—this pattern has surprisingly great scope. Contemporary world politics, especially the rise in importance of the General Assembly of the United Nations, the increasing initiative of Third World states and cartelization, is a clear demonstration of the pattern.

The fourth pattern, consisting of small state disorganization, lack of communication, and incipient or actual mutual hostility, is historically far more common. In this pattern each small state is subject to isolation and pressure from predatory medium or great powers, irrespective of the state of unanimity of the elite group itself. This tendency of the more numerous but less well-organized medium and small powers to break into uncoordinated fragments has simplified the controlling and dominating mission of the great powers.

One final point about these patterns should be made. Either the first or the second pattern may be controlling the relations of the great powers, while either the third or the fourth may be controlling the status of the remainder of the states. Whichever pair (one or two, plus three or four) is simultaneously functional determines the general shape of international power relations at any particular moment in history.

The Regularities of Global Politics

The anarchy of the global system, at least in concept, contains the constant potential of explosion. Managing the affairs of states in a lawless environment requires the development and application of a variety of relatively unstructured but very pervasive principles of action. These regularities of world politics function to control the external manifestations of power in the order, and to regulate by limiting the effect of power differentials among states. Acceptance of one or another of these patterns by the controlling consensus of states is reflected in their policies. Self-preservation in a context of change is the controlling motivation for the willingness of states to submit to a regularized structuring of their overall responses.

Patterns of Equilibrium of Power

If we assume that the normal tendency of state relationships is to seek equilibrium, we may classify the equilibrium patterns of politics and power as a threefold system. Our first type is characterized by widespread dispersal of action capability among the states of the system; this pattern has long been known as "the multiple balance of power," and received its most explicit institutionalization in the classic European system of the seventeenth through nineteenth centuries. The second pattern is marked by concentration of power on a bipolar basis around two great powers. This is the predominant pattern of the post-1945 world, and it usually is identified as a "simple balance of power." Finally, there is the pattern of integrated power radiating from a single central point, like spokes of a wheel. Although this has never been realized since the decay of the Roman Empire, the League of Nations and the United Nations represent attempts at its achievement in the modern world.

The multiple-balance system, based on a concentration of power in individual states, is uncentralized. The simple balance is in one sense a midpoint in that the number of poles of concentration is reduced to two. The integrated system theoretically does away with dispersed power and replaces it with an integrated power structure.

Multiple Balance of Power

The multiple balance was the controlling pattern of interstate relations throughout the seventeenth, eighteenth, nineteenth, and early twentieth centuries. The global system during this period was characterized by a multiplicity of great powers—at least five at any time—dominating the course of world politics.

In a multiple-balance system the great powers act so as to complement each other and—sometimes intentionally but more often instinctively—maximize the prospects of their survival as individual states and the durability of the system. This system demands an implicit agreement to respect each other's existence and sphere of interests, and to confine disagreements to issues considered marginal. Coalition formation is normal, as is the tendency for these action groupings to balance each other. Any reduction or (to a lesser extent) increase in the number of great powers is considered undesirable, since either modification runs the risk of upsetting whatever stability the system may boast. No great power in a multiple system, therefore, should seriously plan to eliminate another.

World War I signaled the final breakdown of the multiple-balance system. Several profound historic trends, imperfectly understood at the time, had undermined the operative conditions essential to the perpetuation of the tidy world of an earlier period. The emergence of Germany and Italy dramatically increased the number of great powers, while the two new major states energetically pressed for the expansion of the system to include their own interests. The end of imperialist expansion terminated the digressive effect of colonial conquest and again focused great power interests on each other. Britain lost the freedom of action it had once enjoyed as the self-conscious "holder of the balance," and found itself drifting into opposition with Germany and a blurred but binding affiliation with the Franco-Russian alliance. And the ramshackle empire of Austria-Hungary could no longer function meaningfully as a great power. After 1907, the inner political world of the great powers had become almost bipolar as two rigid blocs confronted each other in a situation permitting no real maneuver. The concept of "balance" had become irrelevant to world politics.

Simple Balance of Power

Bipolarization of power between the United States and the USSR, due in part to historical accident in the World War II era but also the result of deliberate policy choices by both sides, has characterized world politics since 1945. In this simple balance (simple in its structure, but difficult and dangerous to operate), alignments shift around the poles of the two major powers, and all states draw their international orientation from the general configurations of strength. Movement and change in a tight bipolar system is minimized, since the rationale of great power policy is to reduce world politics to a concentration on the single issue of the bipolar struggle. The simple balance, therefore, is reminiscent of a seesaw in contrast to the multiple balance of a chandelier.

Integration of Power

Intergration of power is best represented in political terms by the classic concept of collective security, exemplified today by the United Nations. Collective security is simply a system to make real the idea of "one for all and all for one."

The obligations of collective security are spelled out in Articles 39 through 51 of the Charter of the United Nations. The "teeth" of these provisions are found in Article 42:

> [The Security Council] may take such action by air, sea, or land forces as may be necessary to maintain or restore international peace and security. Such action may include demonstrations, blockades and other operations by air, sea, or land forces of Members of the United Nations.

The "other operations" obviously include military action under United Nations' direction, first implemented in Korea and later in the Suez Canal Zone, and in the Congo (Zaire), and in Lebanon.

Collective security and integration of power have never been real successes in the contemporary world. Pending the transfer of state sovereignty to a single world government of some sort, collective security may function only upon the basis of a massive consensus among the world's leading powers. So long as the political world remains divided into hostile camps, collective security demands the impossible, for the system was never designed to restrain part of the community on behalf of the remainder. Its rationale demands that any potential aggressor be an outcast, with every government's hand turned against that government the moment the peaceful climate of the relationships become threatened by violation. Thus collective security is a viable pattern only when the vast preponderance of action capability is in the hands of states with a deep interest in the preservation of at least the essentials of the status quo. A significant revisionist faction among the major states renders the idea inapplicable. It is in no sense pessimistic to insist that the contemporary world is favorably disposed to the policies of revisionism, and therefore true integration of power is not a real prospect in the foreseeable future.

Methods of the Balance of Power

We can identify seven different techniques employed by states to maintain or rectify a balance of power: intervention, compensation, buffer zones, divide and rule, spheres of influence, armaments, and alliances.

1. INTERVENTION. This is the interference by one state in the internal affairs of another, and may assume either defensive or offensive forms. Defensive intervention aims at the preservation of a particular regime or system; offensive intervention is directed at altering such a system.

Defensive intervention is based on the assumption that a state, particularly a great power, cannot permit the balance of power to be materially changed to its disadvantage by another state's change of government or policy. Examples of defensive intervention are numerous in contemporary world politics: Allied intervention in Russia (1918) to maintain the pre-Bolshevik regime; Soviet intervention in Hungary (1956) to protect the Kadar government; American intervention in Lebanon (1958) in support of the Shamoun administration; Indian intervention in Bangladesh (1971) to protect the government; and Syrian intervention in Lebanon (1976) in support of the Lebanese government.

Offensive intervention is expansive and is primarily manifested by penetration. Its purpose is to bring about a change of policy or government in another state, or, if necessary, to eliminate its independence completely. The manner in which both Italy and Germany became united in the second half of the nineteenth century represents offensive intervention employed by Prussia and Piedmont, respectively. The establishment of Communist governments in Eastern Europe following World War II illustrates Russian offensive intervention, while the old American custom of "dollar diplomacy" is still another example of this form of intervention in Latin America.

2. COMPENSATION. This involves giving a state the equivalent of the territory of which it is deprived or the equal of what is given to other states. This usually applies only to victorious states and their allies; defeated states customarily lose territory without compensation. Peace treaties normally result in territorial changes which reflect the principle of compensation. This was the spirit of the territorial settlements embodied in the peace treaties that followed World War I and World War II.

The basic assumption underlying compensation is that one state resents seeing another state increase its power without obtaining a compensating aggrandizement of its own, a principle that characterized the approach of the great powers toward the partitioning of Africa and the Far East during the second half of the nineteenth century. It was an insistence on compensation that made Mussolini actively join the side of the Axis after the fall of France; he refused to permit Hitler to settle Europe's future without deriving benefits for Italy. The assignment of mandated areas to France and Great Britain following World War I and the authorization of the United Nations trust territories following World War II are more recent examples.

3. A BUFFER ZONE. This is a small power situated between two or more great powers. It may also be a relatively weak state located between the spheres of interest of great powers. The assumption underlying this technique is that it is in the interests of each of the great powers to prevent the other from controlling the buffer zone. Each competing power seeks to preserve the integrity of the small state in the middle as preferable to its falling prey to the other.

Switzerland and Belgium have long been considered buffer zones between Germany and France. During the latter part of the nineteenth century, Afghanistan was a buffer zone between the British Empire and Russia, and the Spanish colonies in Africa played the same role between the colonial empires of France and Britain. At present, we can classify Austria as a buffer zone between the Eastern and Western spheres of influence in Europe, and Nepal a buffer zone between India and Communist China.

4. "DIVIDE AND RULE." This means that a great power follows the policy of dividing its opponents and competitors into hostile camps, or at least heightens their disunity. The principal assumption underlying this principle is that disunity and partition will keep the competitor weak.

The principle of divide and rule has been the traditional policy of France toward Germany. The present policy of the Soviet Union in regard to Europe represents another example of the divide-and-rule formula.

5. THE SPHERE OF INFLUENCE. This is a device by which competing great powers delineate their areas of hegemony. Each of the great powers concerned undertakes to respect the others' power rights in its own zone, assuming that in this manner disputes between great powers can be minimized. North Africa was considered a French sphere of influence from the later nineteenth century until only a few years ago, while Egypt and the Sudan became British spheres of influence after 1882. The Balkans are presently regarded as belonging to the Russian sphere of influence, while parts of Latin America are considered in the American sphere of influence.

6. ARMAMENTS. These are the principal means by which a great power tries to maintain and reestablish a balance of power in its favor. The underlying assumption is that a greater quality and quantity of armaments maximizes the capabilities of a state for attack and deterrence.

114 THE GLOBAL POLITICAL SYSTEM

Hence, the inevitable corollary of the armaments race is a spiraling burden of military preparedness consuming an ever-greater portion of the budgets of states.

7. ALLIANCES. These are the most important manifestations of the methods of balancing power. An alliance is an agreement between two or more states for the defensive or aggressive purposes of its members against a state or states outside the alliance. Leading contemporary alliances include the North Atlantic Treaty Organization, the Warsaw Pact, the Rio Pact, and the Central Treaty Organization.

Alliances are an essential function of the balance of power within the global system. They are grounded in the belief that through alliances a state can increase its own power, either by adding power from other states or by withholding the power of other states from its competitors. Alliances are dynamic; their changing patterns are not stimulated by principle, but reflect the circumstances of expediency as viewed by the state concerned. Common interests are the primary considerations in the establishment of alliances between states, with the alliances themselves defining the general policies and concrete measures serving these interest. Although the interests which unite states in an alliance against an opponent are typically explicit, the policies to be pursued and the objectives to be sought are less precise.

Alliances may be regarded as essential methods in the regulatory process of world politics. They are important instruments in the adaptation of the nation-state to the global system, and help to fill the gap between the ideals of organization and the realities of quasi-anarchy in the system. Alliances also contribute to divisiveness in world politics by casting interstate relations into rigid grouping.

Recommended Readings

BELOFF, MAX. *The Balance of Power.* Montreal: McGill University Press, 1967.

CASSIRER, ERNST. *The Myth of the State.* New Haven: Yale University Press, 1946.

CLAUDE, INIS L., JR. *Power and International Relations.* New York: Random House, 1962.

COX, RICHARD H., ed. *The State in International Relations.* San Francisco, Calif.: Chandler Publishing Co., 1965.

DEHIO, LUDWIG. *The Precarious Balance.* New York: Alfred A. Knopf, 1962.

GULICK, EDWARD V. *Europe's Classical Balance of Power: A Case History of the Theory and Practice of One of the Greatest Concepts of European Statecraft.* New York: W. W. Norton & Co., 1967.

HERZ, JOHN. *International Politics in the Atomic Age.* New York: Columbia University Press, 1959.

KRADER, LAWRENCE. *The Formation of the State.* Englewood Cliffs, N.J.: Prentice-Hall, 1968.

LASKI, HAROLD J. *Authority in the Modern State* (repr. ed.). Hamden, Conn.: Shoe String, 1968 (original printing, 1919).

MACBRIDGE, ROGER LEA. *Treaties Versus the Constitution.* Caldwell, Idaho: Caxton Printers, 1955.

MERIAM, CHARLES E. *History of the Theory of Sovereignty Since Rousseau.* New York: Columbia University Press, 1928.

NIEBUHR, REINHOLD. *The Structure of Nations and Empires.* New York: Charles Scribner's Sons, 1959.

SCHUMPETER, J. *Imperialism and Social Classes.* New York: Meridian Books, 1955.

STOESSINGER, JOHN G. *Nations in Darkness: China, Russia and America* (2nd ed.). New York: Random House, 1975.

WIGHT, MARTIN. *Power Politics.* London: Royal Institute of International Affairs, 1949.

New Conditions of Global Politics

6

The international political system, incorporating the historically validated ideas and patterns that we have just examined, has in this generation come into conjunction with modern technology. The several revolutions of the contemporary era—in transportation, communication, energy, production, weapons, and space—have all had their direct effect on the actors as well as the environment. The conditions of global politics today are radically different from those of even a half-century ago. Many of the tensions of present world politics come from the inevitable frustrating effort to fit the contemporary environment into traditional political categories.

Today the states of the world function within a global political system. In analytical terms, the frontier of traditional international politics has disappeared. Every explosion of political, economic, or social force within this global system inevitably radiates to all portions of our planet. No part of the earth's surface can be classified as politically undesirable or strategically unimportant. Every state is in some way relevant to every other state.

The States of the World

One manifestation of the new dimensions of world politics is the great change in the number and nature of participants in the process.

Despite the contentious chicken-and-egg quality to the debate, the environment shapes actors as much as actors shape the environment. Thus there are significant reasons for a descriptive analysis of the operating environment. When instead we stress the prime importance of actors, we limit our understanding of the environment: we come to believe that the political environment is not *cause* but *effect*. Political actors, not unlike organisms, thrive in certain environments and decline or expire in others. Emphasis on the actor—invariably the state—manipulating and dominating the environment has reduced a *dynamic* concept into a *static* one. Actors have come and gone. New ones are emerging. But we are insensitive to these vicissitudes by failing to stress that environment is the arbiter of these developments.

By stressing the nature of this environment—that is, the breakdown of distance, technological diffusions, expanding communication grids, and changing belief systems and forms of human organization—we can appreciate what kinds of actors we would expect such an environment could support. Thus we reduce the conceptual limitations imposed by stressing actors. A treatment of the environment helps us appreciate changes in the system and understand the potential of the environment to generate new actors.

The traditional international system, with its international relations and international politics, has been replaced by a global system characterized by transnational relations—relations among states as well as non-state actors—and the politics of transnational exchange. With the members of the global political system so different, it is no wonder that the process has been greatly modified.

The Contemporary Global System

The total number of national actors (states) in world politics has nearly tripled since the end of World War II. When the United Nations was established in 1945, its membership included 51 states; more than 30 years later membership had risen to 150. This increase in number is further highlighted by the current geographic distribution of membership. In 1945, the United Nations had 19 members from Central and South America, 19 from Europe and other Western areas, 9 from Asia, and 4 from Africa. The number of Central and South American and other American states remained unchanged until Jamaica, Trinidad-Tobago, Guyana, Barbados, Grenada, and the Bahamas became independent in the 1960s and the '70s, while the states of Europe and the West have increased to 34. In contrast, the number of African states has increased to 51 and those of Asia to 38. Together, the states of Africa and Asia constitute nearly two-thirds of present membership. The vast majority of the new members have been former colonies of Western powers.

Thus the system which was once a purely Western cultural pattern has been altered by non-Western or Third World peoples and their value structures. This great shift in the background and general orientation of the bulk of participants in world politics has had a number of immediate consequences for the system. Consensus on many issues is more difficult to obtain than it was when states shared a common moral and historical orientation. The new states arrive at world politics with a point of view different from that of the older states, and they apply different criteria of judgment and evaluation. The resulting communication between old and new states thus has been marked by suspicion, misunderstanding, and confusion of motivations. A new force—Third World nationalism, usually expressing itself in the form of anticolonialism or antiimperialism—has come to play a major determining role in the course of political life. Many of the new states look upon their former colonial masters as natural enemies and press their case against imperialism almost as a matter of principle. The older states with a history of rule over alien peoples are almost morally and intellectually powerless against this onslaught. The dawn of political consciousness in many once-somnolent peoples has shown them the startling contrast between their familiar way of life and the much higher standard long enjoyed by older states. They have pressed their governments to win by international action what they feel to be their just share of the good things of life. This familiar "revolution of rising expectations" is a direct consequence of the broader membership in the global system. The older and better-established members of the system have been obliged to broaden their own political horizons to take account of the new conditions of world politics. Not only have they been required to extend their interests to include many once-neglected areas of the world, but they also have been constrained to deal with a broad range of substantive problems (e.g., basic human needs, ethnicity, terrorism, human rights) that rest outside the traditional context of international politics.

Origins of the Nation-State System

Social behavior is related to our basic biological needs. Historical example suggests that while individuals have organized in a variety of ways, the reasons for grouping together have remained relatively constant—search for food, shelter, and protection. A variety of personal motives—fear, hunger, anxiety, and drives for recognition, power, or material gain—may be factors that affect the way in which individuals organize.

More importantly, though, the way individuals organize presupposes a type of value system. Even if our basic needs—food, protection, and shelter—do not shift, our values and our belief systems change and subsequently the social/political order alters. When a political system does not adjust to changes in the value system or to new technology, it is forced to adjust to new conditions. When we valued kinship and community most, individuals grouped in tribes; when we valued religion most, we lived in Christendom or Dar al-Islam;* and, when we valued land, property, and political freedom, we embraced the nation-state system. When the system of political organization has not reflected the shared values of the community, the system has changed.

The first form of political organization was the tribe. In the Middle East, the indispensable conditions for the permanent settlement of the nomadic gatherers and hunters of the Neolithic period—food, water, and building materials—were provided by the Nile Valley and the region between the upper waters of the Tigris and the Euphrates Rivers in what is now Iraq. Ties based on family and kinship were then formalized. The cohesion in these small bands of people were reinforced by mutually perceived fear. These tribes were nomadic partly because they were confronted periodically by more powerful tribes. One small tribe might come into contact with another tribe and they would have to either fight for the territory or flee. The tribe was a small social group that could move with facility and protect itself. In other words, the functions of the tribe—providing security, access to food supplies, and a sense of community—are not dissimilar to the functions of the modern state.

Eventually individuals began to settle into river valleys and other fertile regions and subsequently they developed agriculture and domesticated animals. Nomadic tribes began to form villages around their cultivated land. Kinship no longer was the singular tie that held human communities together. The village, as a method of organization, reflected increased concern with territory. It was the result, too, of increased population and new technological discoveries. The tribe simply could not serve as an adequate means of organization in this changed environment. Villages began to unite or to associate with one another, especially as labor became more specialized. In Greece, for example, villages would group around a common myth or religion. Shared value systems is an element that increasingly contributes to social cohesion. In what became known as the city-state, the society constructed temples for religious worship as well as fortifications for defense against enemies.

Organizations are complex and adaptable creatures that often outlive their purposes and begin to take on a function of their own from the time of their inception. Such is the case in the Holy Roman Empire, and such is the case in the nation-state system. The papal state, an outgrowth of the preceding city-state system, was said to be ordained by God by those in seats of authority and power. However, this world view was altered by the discoveries of Copernicus and Kepler. Religious determinism and domination no longer served its intended purpose as a mech-

---

* The Abode of Islam, a term designating the Islamic Order.

anism to preserve authority. Thus this shift in values, in shared perceptions of a world unit, resulted in the burial of the antiquated form of organization—but only after it fought for hundreds of years to survive.

The nation-state as a form of sociopolitical organization is the fusion of two separate components, the nation and the state. The nation is a group of people who choose to identify themselves as a unique group—who usually speak a common language, usually share a common race, culture, and historical tradition, and usually inhabit land that is contiguous. The state is a system of centralized organization encompassing territory.

The conscious choice of the individual to identify with a larger whole is the basis of national identity. In some cases the people of a nation may be bound together and identify with one another as part of a larger whole through a shared language. For example, most members of the "French" nation speak French. On the other hand, members of the "Chinese" or "Han" nation speak many different languages but are bound together through racial similarities and shared historical tradition. Generally as well, people who consider themselves to be a nation live in close proximity to one another, although some "nations" such as the nation of Jews are scattered around the world. An ideal nation would be made up of people with the same racial characteristics, culture, language, and historical tradition who inhabited a part of the globe that no other nation could infiltrate.

It is obvious that the ideal nation occurs rarely in history. One factor (language, culture, etc.) typically plays a greater role than any other in determining whether or not people consider themselves part of the greater whole. What makes a nation is the perception of the individual that one or another grouping of people is more or less similar to the individual and hence is deserving of one's allegience.

The state is a construct of the human mind, a tool to be used by individuals to fulfill their basic needs and wants. A state is not territory, it is not people, although without these two components there is no state. The state is the methods and institutions by which land and people are organized to attain certain goals. The state is supreme within the territory it encompasses. That is, no other state impinges upon the right of another state within the state's territory.

The ideal state also occurs infrequently in history. The supremacy of the state within the boundaries that delineate its jurisdiction is often called into question through the actions of other states within its territorial jurisdiction. Intervention by one state in another state's affairs diminishes the supremacy of the state in which the intervention takes place. The ideal state would have perfect and complete control over all that takes place within its borders and would have a completely free hand in external relations. Thus the ideal nation and the ideal state rarely occur in history.

Imperfect nations and imperfect states do not combine to produce perfect nation-states. The boundaries of a nation and a state are not necessarily coterminous, and indeed usually are not. States can encompass many nations (for example, the USSR and India). States can cut across nations (for example, Iran and Iraq's boundary cuts the Kurdish nation in half). States may be a collection of many nations, none of which is exclusively contained within the boundaries of the state (for example, Zaire and Angola). Disregarding the ambiguities of the nation and the state and their infrequent coterminality, the nation-state has been *the* organizing concept of the traditional international system until very recently.

The Rise and Decline of the Traditional International System

Most of the distempers of the global order today are due to this one overpowering fact: The technological and political developments of the past two decades have created a set of entirely new conditions. Policymakers, however, have not yet succeeded in adjusting to this new global system. The premises on which the classic doctrines of statecraft were founded have been largely invalidated. Machiavelli and Clausewitz have so little to say to us today because the kind of world they knew no longer exists. The state that defines its purpose in the old terms and seeks its goals by the old methods must reconcile itself to living indefinitely with frustration. It is no wonder today that international problems are only postponed but never solved.

The Old International Order

What is the nature of the new global order? We may characterize it as a pluralistic one with a crude but vital form of international democracy, as contrasted with the essentially aristocratic state systems it is replacing. "Democracy," in this sense, refers only to relations between and among *states*, not necessarily to any internal political arrangements. States approach each other differently today than they used to. In the past they pursued their destinies and resolved their differences within a rigid and hierarchial social system. Today they function within a flexible and egalitarian one. To look at the world from this general orientation results in a drastically different interpretation of trends and events.

We may make fruitful use of historical analogy. At the height of the feudal system during the fifteenth century, society was rigidly stratified. Individuals knew their place, their superiors, and their obligations to them. The key to the whole society was the status of the nobility. Sharply differentiated by privilege from the other orders, they nevertheless gave the entire system its dominant tone. Acutely sensitive to matters of rank, status, and honor as symbols of their greater intrinsic worth, they guarded their right to defend their own interests and were proud of the status symbol of their class: the sword. Although prone to quarrel among themselves, they were unanimous in denying all protests from the lower orders and stood shoulder to shoulder to the last against threats from below.

What doomed feudalism, aristocracy, and the sword was, of course, the invention of the crossbow and the later introduction of gunpowder. When yeomen developed the weaponry to crush aristocratic pretensions to superiority and aggresive monarchs used this power to consolidate their regimes, the whole social fabric fell apart. Skill with sword was the class mark of the aristocrat. It was thus not only humiliating for aristocrats to be transfixed by a crossbow shaft or hit with a musket, it was frequently fatal. It made no difference whether the enemy was a bourgeois or a peasant; the aristocrat was dead all the same. The national state that followed feudalism was royal rather than aristocratic and depended for its survival on bourgeois-financed peasant armies. The final victory of the farmers and the townspeople over the baron was signaled by the English Revolution in the seventeenth century and the French Revolution in the eighteenth.

It was during the climax of the era of absolute monarchs, however, that the state system was born at the Peace of Westphalia in 1648. The new generation of royal sovereigns, in abasing their fractious nobility, had transferred to their own persons the ritual of intrinsic superiority they had stripped from their barons. We know this today as the "divine right of kings." They carried into their dealings with each other—the primitive form of what became international relations—the identical aristocratic code that had flourished under feudalism, garnished first by the legal paraphernalia of sovereignty and later by the mystique of nationalism. From that era until very recently, the traditional international system has never departed from its initial orientation to the rules and practices of feudal aristocracy.

The Emerging System

The order of power worked so well for three hundred years that no one thought it really necessary to introduce any modifications in it. Each technological development was incorporated into the system without altering its basic design. Governments practiced the rules of survival within its terms. Proposals for change found hard going, as practical policymakers consistently preferred the shortcomings of the familiar to the unknown dangers of a new set of techniques. Problems, after all, reached solutions that were at least tolerable, the costs of doing international business were kept within reasonable limits, and familiarity with the mechanisms of power bred, if not contempt, at least confidence and skill.

Nevertheless, since World War II something has obviously been wrong, and especially so during the last few years. The old order and its configurations of traditional forms of power have been unable to deal with the issues of the contemporary world. Stalemate has become the usual fate of any problem that becomes entangled in the net of great-power relations. States, apparently bereft of their capacity to achieve their own fulfillment, yet retain the ability to frustrate each other. Although everyone has been trapped in this dilemma, it has been the erstwhile major powers, deprived of their dominance, who have found the situation most exasperating. Power relations have become a monumental exercise in futility, and policymaking flounders in a vacuum.

Once again we may usefully turn to the history of feudalism in our search for an insight into what has happened to international relations. Technological advance, in the form of the crossbow and the musket, ended the reign of the aristocrat by making the terms of combat too expensive for an aristocrat's limited resources. At the same time, a dynamic egalitarianism was rising that challenged the static belief structure of the stratified feudal system and prepared the way for the eventual victory of democracy. The historical parallel with the present is striking.

Technology has made the terms of combat as heavily disadvantageous to the aristocrats of the traditional international system as they have long been to smaller states. The traditional international system is feeling the immediate consequences of the obsolescence of the central motivating force. The revolt of the Third World and the entry of dozens of new and small states into active participation in world politics reminds us strongly of the sudden eruption of the bourgeoisie into postfeudal politics. Like their middle-class predecessors, the new states find the long-sanctified aristocratic values of international life largely irrelevant to their own concerns. They demand recognition, satisfaction, and justice from an order that has long slighted them as virtual nonentities.

We are saying here that the old international system is dying because of two intersecting and mutually reinforcing historic trends. First, war as traditionally conceived is no longer a useful means of implementing policy, thus contributing to the rapid decay in the position of the former leaders. Second, a new force is moving to take the dominant place once occupied by great-power military strength: the egalitarian and transforming urge of the new states who look on the old aristocrats as their natural enemies and who are frankly seeking a drastic reordering in international relations.

Diversity and Integration

As long as power in the international order was confined to a limited number of European and Western states, there was no need for any supranational authority to regulate the relations of states. The balance of power, as practiced by the policymakers of Europe, served to stabilize the traditional international political process. Since the effectiveness of the balance of power depended on an unequal distribution of power among states, the services of Great Britain, as the self-conscious holder and wielder of the balance, were required most of the time.

The new dimensions of global politics have given rise to a drastic modification of the traditional patterns of power distribution. The conditions underlying the old system have disappeared, and the devolution of power since the Industrial Revolution has created an entirely new situation. Three current trends merit separate mention. First, the number of national actors in world politics has increased. The number of independent states has tripled since World War II, from about 55 to roughly 165 today, an increase almost entirely in the category of small and medium states.* Second, the number of *essential* national actors has actually decreased. During World War II there were eight essential national actors (great powers)—the United States, the Soviet Union, the United Kingdom, France, Italy, Germany, China, and Japan. Today the number has been reduced to two unmistakable superpowers, the United States and the USSR, while China, the United Kingdom, France, Japan, and Germany occupy important yet secondary positions. The number of great powers in the world today, however, is the smallest it has been since the beginning of the nation-state system. And third, the differentials between categories of national actors are becoming wider, due to differences in industrial, political, and military conditions rooted in the newer aspects of technology. Barring some reversal of trends, many experts fear the indefinite prolongation of this evolution, with important consequences for the future of world politics.

These trends, operating within the more intimate global environment created by technology, have had a significant dual effect. First, they have led to concentration of the visible forms of power within the major political blocs that dominate contemporary world affairs. These rigid groupings, expressing in their most intense form the traditional values of the nation-state system, emphasize the diversity on which the political approach of states to one another has long been based. Second, the integration of power demanded by the newer questions facing the system has received its institutionalization in the form of a recent phenomenon:

---

* This figure includes states that are not members of the United Nations.

the international actors epitomized by the United Nations and other international organizations such as the specialized agencies, regional actors exemplified by the European Community, bloc actors such as the Warsaw Pact, transnational actors such as multinational corporations, ethnic nations, terrorist groups, and nongovernmental organizations actors such as Amnesty International. The struggle between diversity and integration, although as old as political life itself, has acquired a new and portentous dimension. The traditional system and the new system as ways of organizing power stand in direct confrontation.

Nonstate Actors in Global Politics

Actors and institutions usually develop as responses to compelling societal needs within any given historical period. Hence the compulsion to satisfy unprecedented needs, generated largely by the technological revolution, has given rise to nonstate actors and institutions in world politics whose function has been to deal with systemwide or regionally defined issues. Some of these issues had heretofore been considered only by states acting unilaterally. The experience of two world wars, the increasing vulnerability of the national actor (with the resultant inability to guarantee national security), and the recognition that economic and social instability produces political instability, which may in turn threaten general systemic instability, have combined to produce an accelerated growth in internationalism and transnationalism. The new institutions which manifest the international and transnational trends have at least minimally assumed the role of actors themselves. The bounds of action permitted these actors, however, are determined by the collectivity of national actors comprising each institution in the case of international actors and nongovernmental organizations or the mother country in the case of transnational actors, and these bounds are usually situationally determined. The interests of the members and the issues of the moment determine the extent to which the new institutions can act in the global system.

The term *international actors* refers to institutions whose structure, composition, and interests transcend national boundaries but whose membership is composed of states. There are three major types. *Bloc actors* are groups of states that share certain controlling political and/or security interests, and usually a common orientation in their foreign policy objectives. The *international organizations* are actors which comprise within their respective structures almost all the existing members of the global system. These actors take the form of general or specialized international organizations (a general organization incorporates all aspects of international life, whereas a specialized organization is restricted and incorporates only a few). *Regional actors* are associations of states sharing common interests that are more inclusive than the mere political and/or security interests of blocs, yet less comprehensive than the interests of an international organization. Membership usually follows a geographic rationale. Like the international organization actor, regional actors may be either general or specialized in terms of the problems, issues, and interests which are considered.

Bloc Actors

Bloc actors are not completely new phenomena in world politics. By virtue of the technological revolution, ideological competition, and the emergence of a large number of economically and socially underdeveloped and politically incompetent entities as independent states, they have become more common and on occasion more cohesive. Today, most of the essential national actors in world politics are more or less bound into two blocs by means of alliances. Each bloc is led by a dominant essential national actor (the United States and the Soviet Union, respectively) and comprises a number of middle and small powers which act in conjunction with their respective leaders on many issues. These alliances are not as monolithic or cohesive as they were in the immediate postwar period, since their cohesion is directly proportional to the consensus produced by the situation and issue of the moment. In other words, alliances today are much more fluid and, according to some, in a state of decay and increasing irrelevance, as middle and small powers grow reluctant to focus their foreign policy within the restricting context of alliance or bloc policy. Intrabloc conflict has become increasingly important in contemporary world politics, inasmuch as national actors outside the bloc are often compelled to formulate foreign policy toward factions within each of the blocs.

The identity and integrity of each bloc depends on the ability of the dominant essential actor to preserve its capacity as the leading producer of all those things—materials, money, moral stimulus, and leadership—thought necessary to the vital interest of all other members of the bloc. This is not a simple matter of the bloc leader exercising internal hegemony over its minor associates. Each of the essential actors makes great commitments to the other members, but this protection is reciprocal. Even relatively small and weak bloc members contribute in some measure to the overall viability of the grouping.

The foreign policy tasks of the United States and the Soviet Union have become more complex as the range of their bloc interest has expanded. Each bloc has attempted to extend its span of effective action to whatever area of the world in which it might wish to operate. Interbloc conflict, familiar to the history and logic of the traditionally structured Western state system, has in recent years come forcibly into contact with the emerging, newly sensitive, and operationally viable non-Western world.

The new states, most of which came on the world scene after the major blocs had been institutionalized, have reacted by resisting affiliation with either and by developing a variety of workable definitions of nonalignment. Although admittedly imprecise, this idea unquestionably reflects both the instinctive leanings of many Third World states and the practical range of possibilities open to them in the pattern of interbloc relations. This range is increased as the fluidity of the major blocs grows and as opposing factions within the major bloc become more manifest.

So consistent has been the reaction of the bulk of emerging states to the massive confrontation of the two groupings that today it is common to speak of a nonaligned or Third World. While this is an overstatement (as is the popular term *Afro-Asian bloc*)—since the nonaligned group displays neither the relatively high degree of integration nor the policy consensus that marks a genuine bloc actor—it is undeniable that, on issues separating the United States and the USSR, the otherwise incongruous nonaligned states have frequently been able to form a common front in opposition to the attempt of bloc leaders to universalize their dispute. More recently, Third World states have developed a new pattern of affiliation along a North-South division, the North being the industrialized states.

International Organizations

The conditions that have given rise to the evolution of blocs have also contributed to the creation of the most inclusive institutional form: international organizations with both specialized and general competence. International organizations with general competence, defined as having the capacity to consider all aspects of the global system (political security, economic, social, and humanitarian), have included the League of Nations and the United Nations. International organizations with specialized competence are usually restricted to consideration of selected economic or social concerns. The essence of the international organization in world politics is that it acts in the global system in the name of all members of the system, subject to the authority granted by the membership. It is armed at any moment with whatever measure of effective systemwide consensus is available, and performs restrictive, ameliorative, or affirmative functions as the case may dictate.

THE LEAGUE OF NATIONS. The League of Nations, founded as

part of the peace settlement after World War I, was the first serious attempt to create an international organization. Although the total membership ultimately included the majority of national actors then active, significant absences in the membership virtually doomed it to ineffectiveness. The United States never became a member, and never during the League's brief history were all the other great powers members at the same time. After a hectic period of prosperity in the mid-1920s, the League fell apart under the successive shocks of the Depression of 1929, the Japanese invasion of Manchuria in 1931, the rise of Hitler, Italy's aggression in Ethiopia, the Spanish Civil War, and the Russo-Finnish War of 1939–40. It went out of formal existence in 1946 when its property and personnel were transferred to the United Nations.

The League of Nations may have been premature, because the machinery for responding to these crises was certainly available. Either the members of the League elected not to use the machinery or were incompetent to do so, indicating that the system had not developed to the point where such a sophisticated tool could be utilized.

THE UNITED NATIONS. World War II stimulated the establishment of the United Nations. The real history of the U.N. begins with the London Declaration of January 1941, the Atlantic Charter of 1942, and the Moscow Conference of October 1943. Churchill, Roosevelt, and Stalin, during the Teheran Conference of 1943, strongly supported the movement. In the Dumbarton Oaks Conference between August and October 1944, the governments of the United States, Great Britain, the Soviet Union, and China drew up the blueprint for what later became the Charter of the United Nations. At the Yalta Conference in February 1945, the United States, Britain, and the USSR agreed to a conference (the United Nations Conference of International Organization) designed to draft the Charter of the United Nations. The San Francisco Conference met between April and June 1945, with fifty-one states attending. In October 1945, the United Nations was officially established.

The declared purposes of the United Nations are to maintain international peace and security, to develop friendly relations among states based on respect, equal rights, and self-determination of peoples, to cooperate in solving economic, social, cultural, and humanitarian global problems, and to promote respect for fundamental freedoms and human rights.

The United Nations has a number of operational principles set forth in its Charter:

   1. The sovereign equality of all its members is assumed, at least theoretically.

2. Members are to fulfill in good faith the obligations they have assumed under the Charter.
3. Members are to settle their disputes by peaceful means and refrain from the threat or use of force.
4. Members are to give every assistance to the United Nations and refrain from giving assistance to belligerent states.
5. The United Nations is not to intervene in matters essentially within the domestic jurisdiction of member states.

The United Nations is different from the League of Nations in a number of respects, the most important being that the essential national actors of the global system are all members. The United Nations has developed a more elaborate organizational structure and hence is better equipped than the League to carry out its functions.

It is composed of six principal organs which operate through a number of committees, commissions, and boards. They are the General Assembly, the Security Council, the Economic and Social Council, the Trusteeship Council, the International Court of Justice, and the Secretariat.

THE SPECIALIZED AGENCIES. The development of the United Nations has stimulated the growth of international actors operating in the form of specialized agencies—multilateral institutions to assist the United Nations in carrying out the economic and social stipulations of its Charter. The specialized agencies have emerged in functional response to the new technical, economic, social, and humanitarian conditions of the international system. The Economic and Social Council (a "principal organ" of the United Nations) is responsible for their coordination.

There are now fourteen specialized agencies. Three were established before World War II: The International Telecommunication Union (ITU) and the Universal Postal Union (UPU) were founded in the latter part of the nineteenth century, whereas the International Labor Organization (ILO) developed with the League of Nations. The remaining eleven agencies, products of World War II and the United Nations, include the International Bank for Reconstruction and Development (IBRD), the International Monetary Fund (IMF), the International Finance Corporation (IFC), the International Development Association (IDA), the Food and Agricultural Organization (FAO), the United Nations Education, Scientific, and Cultural Organization (UNESCO), the World Health Organization (WHO), the International Civil Aviation Organization (ICAO), the World Meteorological Organization (WMO), the Intergovernmental Maritime Consultative Organization (IMCO), the World Intellectual Property Organization (WIPO), and the International Fund for Agricultural Development (IFAD). There are two semiautonomous authorities which are responsible directly to the UN General Assembly: the General Agreement on Tariffs and Trade (GATT), established in 1948, and the International Atomic Energy Agency (IAEA), established in 1957.

Regional Actors

There are two types of regional actors (regional organizations) operating in the global system—general regional actors and specialized regional actors, of which the latter deal with specific economic and technical matters. The distinction between the two categories is determined by differences in competence or purpose and scope of activities.

General regional actors are more inclusive in membership. Their range of interests tends to be broader and less sharply defined than that of the regional actors for specific technical and economic cooperation. They are associations of states with a community of interest. There are three general regional organizations which have been institutionalized into formal organizations: the Organization of African Unity, the League of Arab States, and the Organization of American States. Such associations as the British Commonwealth of Nations and the French Community do not have the structure or competence to be considered formal organizations, but may be more akin to bloc actors.

Regional actors for specific technical and economic cooperation are more exclusive in membership. Their interests are limited to economic, social, and technical matters. A successful example of this type of regional actor is the European Community.

In 1951, France, West Germany, Italy, Belgium, the Netherlands, and Luxembourg signed the draft treaty of the European Coal and Steel Community (ECSC), thereby establishing the first European organization with a structure extending beyond the state. Since the launching of European integration by the Coal and Steel Community, the six participating members have formed two other bodies: the European Atomic Energy Community (EURATOM) and the European Economic Community (EEC or the Common Market), the latter formed in 1958. These three organizations (ECSC, EURATOM, and EEC) are described as the European Community. The original membership was expanded to include the United Kingdom, Ireland, and Denmark. Greece, Spain, and Portugal are awaiting membership.

Regional actors have appeared in response to the need for units of action larger than the nation-state but short of the full range of universalism. Their usefulness depends in great measure upon whether the problems they face can actually be solved on a regional basis. Because of their smaller and generally more cohesive membership, regional actors have proved to be more effective action organizations than has the United Nations.

Transnational Actors

The term *transnational actors* refers to organizations whose structure, composition, and interests transcend national boundaries and whose membership is not composed of states. There are three distinguishable types—multinational corporations, ethnic nations, and terrorist groups. These transnational actors have developed in response to the changing conditions of world politics during the third quarter of the twentieth century.

MULTINATIONAL CORPORATIONS. Multinational corporations (MNCs) are commercial enterprises which produce and market in several countries under central direction. The growth of these commercial enterprises is a distinct trend with important implications for contemporary and future world politics. At the present time, about one-sixth of the gross world product is produced by MNCs—and this proportion is forecast to exceed one-half by the end of this century. There is hardly a country that is not affected by the capital movement and technological transfer generated by the multinationals. These MNCs are unique instrumentalities of the industrial states, particularly the United States, whose multinational investments account for nearly three-fourths of the world's total and whose aggregate overseas earnings are the equivalent of the world's third largest gross national product. Additionally, MNCs operate as independent actors for the home countries.

Investment is an instrument by which allocation of wealth, power, and prestige is determined, hence affecting the pattern of stratification in the global system. In terms of scope and implications, the phenomenon of the MNCs rivals traditional economic transactions between states due to the size and geographical spread of multinationals and the diversity of their activities and objectives. These actors are as yet not subject to regulation and control by a single authority. While MNCs' operations are global, their interests are corporate.

ETHNIC NATIONS. The significance of ethnic nations as transnational actors lies in the growing tendency of individuals who reject identification with their nation-state in favor of separate political status. The transformation of ethnic discontent into ethnic nationalism, as in the case of the Basques and the Kurds, has made its mark on the internal and external policies of states in a persistent and meaningful fashion. Out of an estimated 164 disturbances of significant violence within states between 1958 and May 1966, a mere fifteen were military conflicts involving two or more states. The most significant violence which has taken place since 1945 has been rooted in ethnic and racial disputes which have demonstrated a "spillover" effect in world politics. The legitimacy of the modern nation-state is at stake in the struggle to overcome a challenge to its supremacy rooted in primordial concepts of "blood and land."

TERRORIST GROUPS. Terrorism, due to its diffuse and individualistic nature, does not lend itself to a single definition. Grave ambiguities arise at the outer fringes of any distinctions made between terrorism and seemingly separate phenomena. Terrorists use violence or the threat of violence for political objectives. They are motivated and sustained by deep feelings of frustration seated in perceptions of profound social, economic, and political inequities. While the causes of frustration may vary from case to case, these general factors are causes of terrorism. Not only are terrorists motivated by similar frustrations, but the methods they use to vent their frustrations are similar. Terrorist groups, whether the Japanese Red Army or the Black September group, are forced by considerations of reality to pursue a strategy of a small group against a larger group. The tactics that can be employed by terrorists also are limited to a few major classifications: killings, bombings, kidnapping, and sabotage.

Nongovernmental Organizations (NGOs)

The term *nongovernmental organization* (NGO) is defined by the Economic and Social Council (ECOSOC) of the United Nations as any international organization which is not established by intergovernmental agreement and which enjoys a consultative status with ECOSOC. NGOs accept individual members or persons designated by government authorities, provided that such membership does not interfere with the free expression of views of the organizations. International Associations, itself an NGO, has set criteria which have been endorsed by both the United Nations and the Economic and Social Council. These criteria assert that the aims of NGOs must be genuinely international in character, that membership should include individuals or groups from at least three countries, that the organization must provide for a formal structure, that there should be designated intervals of headquarters and officers among the various member states, and that substantial contributions to the budget must come from at least three countries.

Nongovernmental organizations have grown rapidly since World War II, from less than a thousand to over three thousand at the present time. An NGO such as the International Cooperative Alliance has a membership over 200 million people; the World Federation of Trade Unions has a membership over 125 million, and the World Federation of Democratic Youth has over 100 million. The membership of these NGOs as well as others extends to all but a handful of states in the global system. Other important NGOs include Amnesty International, focussing on human rights, and organizations ranging from religious concerns to medical, literary, and a thousand and one interests, including the International Society for the Protection of Animals.

Nongovernmental organizations perform diverse functions, all of which are nonprofit and service-oriented. Accordingly, NGOs enjoy international legal status, in fact if not in theory, and exert influence on the conduct of world politics. However, NGOs do not have the stature of other actors in the global system. They do not possess the power of national actors, the clout of international actors, the economic influence of multinational corporations, or the dramatic appeal of ethnics or terrorists. Nevertheless, NGOs play an important role in world politics.

Recommended Readings

CALVOCORESSI, PETER. *International Politics Since 1945.* New York: Frederick A. Praeger, 1968.

CARR, EDWARD H. *Twenty Years' Crisis, 1919–1939: An Introduction to the Study of International Relations* (2nd ed.). New York: St. Martin's Press, 1956.

CLAUDE, INIS L. JR. *Swords Into Plowshares* (4th ed.). New York: Random House, 1971.

FLIES, PETER J. *International Relations in the Bipolar World.* New York: Random House, 1968.

GOODMAN, ELLIOT. *The Fate of the Atlantic Community.* New York: Frederick A. Praeger, 1975.

KEOHANE, ROBERT, and JOSEPH S. NYE, JR., eds. *Transnational Relations and World Politics.* Cambridge: Harvard University Press, 1973.

KIRGIS, F., JR. *International Organizations in Their Local Setting: Documents, Comments and Questions.* St. Paul, Minn.: West Publishing Co., 1977.

LADOR-LEDERER, J. J. *International Non-Governmental Organizations and Economic Entities: A Study in Autonomous Organization and Ius Gentium.* Leiden: A. W. Fijthoff, 1963.

MACDONALD, ROBERT. *The League of Arab States: A Study in the Dynamics of Regional Organization.* Princeton, N.J.: Princeton University Press, 1965.

MANGONE, GERALD. *A Short History of International Organization* (repr. ed.). Westport, Conn.: Greenwood, 1975 (original printing, 1954).

MANSBACH, RICHARD, YALE FERGUSON, and DONALD LAMPERT. *The Web of World Politics: Non State Actors in the Global System.* Englewood Cliffs, N.J.: Prentice-Hall, 1976.

NORTHEDGE, F., and M. GRIEVE. *A Hundred Years of International Relations.* New York: Frederick A. Praeger, 1971.

PAXTON, JOHN. *The Developing Common Market: The Structure of the EEC in Theory and in Practice, 1957–1976* (3rd ed.). Boulder, Colo.: Westview Press, 1976.

ROSECRANCE, RICHARD. *Action and Reaction in World Politics: International Systems in Perspective* (repr. ed.). Westport, Conn.: Greenwood, 1977 (original printing, 1963).

STOESSINGER, JOHN G. *The United Nations and the Superpowers.* New York: Random House, 1965.

Conflict and Adjustment

7

Politics viewed as the pursuit of the common good as understood by a given community underlies the conduct of the relationships of states. The controlling idea of the common good energizes the formulation of aims and objectives which, for all their shifting and changing qualities, mark evolving stages in the pursuit of the ideal. Every attempt to organize the global system is in this sense a response to the urge to attain the common good.

In world politics, however, states are concerned with practicalities. Absolute ends are less immediately germane than relative means, so conscious search for the common good is reduced to a secondary place in the global system. The unequal distribution of power and the mystique of sovereignty make the world order relatively unresponsive to ideas of the public well-being on any basis transcending the state.

This emphasis on state-centered common good has immediate consequences for the process of dynamics and change in the global system. No community of interests exists that is sufficient to control all members. Any change in relationships is as likely to be the result of conflict as of peaceful adjustment; in fact, conflict of some form is quantitatively the more usual atmosphere of change and realignment in world politics.

The Nature Of Conflict

Competition, whether actual, seeming, or potential, is a normal relationship between states, as a result of the growth of the state system. International conflict has become an intermittent but inevitable feature of world politics.

The Sources of Conflict

The state system is inherently competitive, since it is based on an ego-centered concept of state destiny—an aspiration to preserve and increase the power and stature of a state relative to those of all of its fellows. When a state insists upon universal recognition of its political independence and freedom of choice and action, it finds itself in a dilemma. It must grant every other state the same freedom and independence, yet it cannot really trust anyone but itself. The state must seek salvation by its own efforts and maintain a guarded attitude toward every other state. Absolute security is possible only if the state controls more power than the remainder of the world combined. When one state makes even slight progress toward this objective, however, all other states feel less secure and are impelled to seek some corresponding advantage to rectify the balance.

The logic of this paradox derives from the fact that a state's political decisions are always based on its priorities of objectives and interests. The interdependence of states exercises a pacifying influence in world politics only so far as political conflicts remain limited. The needs of interdependence, however, are virtually powerless to disarm political antagonisms that are already consolidated.

The absolute character of national policy interests and objectives reinforces the tendency toward interstate conflict. While states can generally achieve limited objectives that are spelled out in concrete terms, pursuit of an absolute objective tends to involve the state in continuous struggle. Enhancement of prestige, aggrandizement of power, and promotion of ideology are common examples of absolute objectives which attract opposition and conflict because of their lack of rational content and clearly defined limits. On the other hand, unilateral defense of territorial integrity and of political independence, even though they are themselves concrete, have on occasion been conceived in such absolute terms as to bring on intense conflict.

Types of Conflict

There are two broad categories of international conflict, with the criterion of classification being the principal technique utilized. Nonviolent conflict involves the use of diplomacy, pacific methods of settlement, or forcible procedures short of war as means of prosecuting national purposes in a climate of disagreement. In violent conflict, major reliance by contending parties is placed upon military measures and wars.

VIOLENT CONFLICT IN WORLD POLITICS. War, a condition

in which two or more states carry on a conflict by armed force, is a common form of violent international conflict. War is, of course, a legal status as well as a means of executing policy, but its policy relevance is much greater.

Since the sixteenth century the devastation of war has grown as weapons increased in effectiveness and new theories of warfare were developed. Today entire populations are personally involved and identified with military operations as combatants, targets, or producers. The objectives of war are now usually formulated in terms of one state gaining an absolute triumph over another. The once-limited conduct of warfare has become universal in scale, and great powers, forces, and ideas are hopelessly caught up in it.

Wars do not usually arise out of disputes concerning the respective rights of the belligerents, but spring instead from conflicts of interest. States' motives in war are entirely political, even though a legal discussion of "rights" and "justice" often furnishes the pretext for violence. Many causes of war have been isolated by scholars, but rather than enumerate them here we will simply state a generalization: Since war is rooted in the global system, any specific war is more a product of the general dynamic of that system than it is of the unique circumstances out of which the conflict has grown.

NONVIOLENT CONFLICT IN WORLD POLITICS. In essence, the difference between nonviolent and violent conflict is of degree rather than kind. Nonviolent conflict has the same rationale as war, with the single exception that the states involved conclude that cost and risk factors as related to the worth of the disputed objective demand that the struggle be prosecuted at a lower level of intensity and commitment. Otherwise, both the purpose and conduct of the conflict is governed by the same principles of strategy and tactics that control the most violent warfare.

As a rule, states accept nonviolent conflict as routine but look on violent conflict as exceptional. The overall costs of nonviolent conflict are always less than those of a war, at least within similar time spans. By the same token, the penalty for defeat in a nonviolent struggle is almost always less than that demanded by a military victor.

VIOLENT AND NONVIOLENT CONFLICT: PROBLEM OF DISTINCTION. Before the advent of twentieth-century military technology, the distinction between violent and nonviolent forms of conflict was relatively clear and unambiguous. A state of war was recognizable militarily, politically, and legally. The devastating nature of modern military technology is blurring the traditional contrast between the two types of conflict, which had formerly been marked by qualitative and quantitative distinctions of a legal and military character. In part, this reflects a response to what has been termed the "technical surprise" of modern weaponry (initially experienced in World War I), in which the means of warfare have far outdistanced rationally conceived ends. Military means, once they are employed, tend to force a reappraisal of ends: The warring parties want to ensure that the objectives of conflict appear justifiable and proportional to their physical and emotional commitment.

This traditional view of the conflict ends-means relationship has been transcended through the threat of escalation into mutually destructive nuclear war. Therefore, total warfare has been discarded as an acceptable option, and more ambiguous and less overtly provocative forms have taken its place. In this sense, unconventional warfare and limited warfare represent a return to the familiar Clausewitz doctrine that war represents a continuation of diplomacy by other means. Although the post-World War II experience with conflicts of this order would seem to validate such a conclusion, it is equally clear that conflict and war have taken on special meanings unknown to their eighteenth- or nineteenth-century predecessors.

The difference lies in part in the more modest nature of political objectives (as distinct from goals) for which states are apparently willing to commit military forces, and the diminished relative magnitude of the forces actually employed in support of these objectives. Each of these affects and is affected by the other. Thus violent conflict is limited (both as to means and ends) in a way unknown even to the eighteenth century. Such an assertion does not imply that this condition of conflict could not be changed and escalated through miscalculation, desperation, or reckless aggression. However, the post-World War II experience of violent conflict, actual and potential, has resulted in an awareness of the inescapable dangers of nuclear conflict, with a mutual if tacit willingness to control the means and ends (objectives) of military and political policy within a framework of tolerance so that world politics can be pursued in a modified, though relatively traditional, manner.

The return to modified traditional forms of violent conflict is largely dependent upon the continuing credibility of the threat of nuclear destruction. Should this threat subside markedly, or should peoples and decision makers become conditioned to its presence and immune to its demands, it is possible that the level of permissible conflict might be raised. This would close the gap between limited warfare as a condition and nuclear warfare as a possibility in the spectrum of violent conflict.

Objectives of Conflict

We can distinguish analytically between two major categories of conflict objectives. The first, *balancing-objective* conflict, is typical in a relatively fluid international situation characterized by wide dispersal of power and the operations of a multiple-balance system. Under such circumstances, the participants in an interstate conflict primarily seek restoration of a disturbed equilibrium. The range of choice open to all parties is narrow, and their efforts tend to be concentrated upon a single object of controversy substantially independent of their relations in other policy areas. *Hegemonic-objective* conflict, on the other hand, has a goal of domination rather than balance. The disputing parties are less concerned with specific objectives than with the establishment of a clear margin of superiority over the other in a very broad range of issues. In other words, balancing-objective conflict concerns itself primarily with a particular set of relationships in the real world, while the controversy over particulars in hegemonic-objective conflict is only symptomatic of much deeper maladjustments in the political approach of the involved states.

Balancing-objective conflicts assume many forms, since they stem from the essential requirements of the global system for simultaneous dynamism and equilibrium. Among the broadest categories are the clash of expansionist politics, the revisionist-status quo confrontation, disputes between aroused nationalisms, conflicts growing out of history, and a variety of racial, religious, social, and cultural involvements. Hegemonic-objective conflict has only one real form, although it is almost infinite in its manifestations.

Balancing-Objective Conflict

EXPANSIONIST POLICIES. The form of conflict that arises from a collision between two or more states that are following policies of expansion or revision is the most dynamic and potentially dangerous. Such states are usually driven by such strong motivations as prestige, acquisition of raw materials, new markets, cheap labor, military bases, or various internal pressures. When a revisionist policy encounters resistance, the government will usually increase its own pressure. When two such states conflict, the dispute is marked by a rapid increase in the power each commits to its objective and the rapid development of crises. Furthermore, because of the internal and international pressure, revisionist states find it difficult to reverse policies short of their ultimate objective.

Imperialism and the colonial methods in which it is expressed are a common historical example of conflict of expanding policies. The traditional methods of expansion underwent steady decline beginning with the first half of the twentieth century. Half a century later the great colonial empires were dissolving. But new types of expansionism are developing in the forms of various dependencies (economic or military). and satellite states. *Economic dependencies* are nominally independent states whose major economic activities are heavily under the control or influence of a great power, while military dependencies are independent states whose foreign policies are in varying degrees under the influence of a more powerful state. Conflicts growing from these relationships are prone to be both intense and prolonged.

REVISIONISM VERSUS STATUS QUO. A frequently recurring form of conflict arises from a situation in which a policy of expansion collides with the interests of a passive, status quo state. The distinction between this type of conflict and the first is important. In expansionism, the motives of the contending states, both seeking expansion in their span of control, are basically identical. In the type we discuss here, the objectives of the contending states are complementary. The revisionist state seeks to take away from the passive state a particular object of advantage. The latter, seeking nothing, tries to retain what it already has.

The revisionist state always takes the initiative in this form of conflict. It seeks through any appropriate means to detach the passive state from its control. The status quo state confines its strategic actions to defensive measures, countering each affirmative step of the revisionist state. On occasion, however, it may assume a tactical initiative.

CONFLICT OF NATIONALISM. Many of the areas of tension in contemporary world politics are characterized by a battle of embittered or exaggerated nationalist attitudes. An aroused nationalistic group becomes heedless of the regularities of world politics and uninformed about the subtler details of the policy of either its own government or the government of its enemy. When mass emotions are aroused in a particular state, great pressures are brought upon the government to take forceful measures against the offender. The other state is impelled to react in a similar manner, and a web of conflict is woven from which both states find it difficult to extricate themselves.

Another example of nationalist conflict is furnished by colonial revolutions and their aftermath. No subject people can become free of alien control without first developing a keen sense of nationalistic particularism and making the achievement of independence a primary objective. When independence is gained, whatever hatreds evolved through the struggle for self-determination continue and form a significant part of the policy of the new state toward the former colonial master.

Still another source out of which nationalist conflict grows is the clash of expanding great power nationalisms. When a people with a "universalist" outlook live in a state having great power resources, a powerful dynamic element is injected into world politics. When two such states exist simultaneously, a serious and long-lasting conflict develops. This was the case of French and British nationalism in the Napoleonic era. The rival nationalisms today are the Russian and the American.

CONFLICT OF HISTORICAL EXPERIENCE. The foreign policies of many states are characterized by nationalist animosities nourished by a long history. Even though the origins of these hatreds are often veiled in obscurity, the concerned peoples may come to see them as a familiar and expected part of the way their government formulates its foreign policies. While these animosities lie dormant for long periods, they often flare up at critical moments. Familiar examples of such historical animosities are the Russo-German, the Franco-German, and the Greco-Turkish nationalist hatreds. Some of these, of course, slowly recede in the face of changed circumstances.

CONFLICT OF RACIAL, RELIGIOUS, SOCIAL, AND CULTURAL ISSUES. In these forms of conflict the specific issues themselves seem trivial, yet they are symbolic of deeper ideological differences. Compromise is usually difficult, since in the minds of the people it would involve making concessions upon points of fundamental moral significance. Examples of such conflicts are the racial issue in South Africa and the religious split between Muslims and Hindus in India and Pakistan.

Hegemonic-Objective Conflict

Hegemonic-objective conflict has become synonymous with the power struggle between the United States and the Soviet Union in the era of the Cold War and after. In this struggle a single broad purpose underlies an entire family of conflict issues. The crisis points of these issues lie in those areas where the main opposing forces are in direct contact. In its military aspect this type of conflict takes the form of a tireless race for allies, raw materials, military bases, and armaments; in political terms it requires a constant search for "victory"; in psychic terms it calls for the pursuit of absolute hegemony over the adversary.

At present, on the periphery of the Eastern and Western camps, great power competition multiplies the zones of possible friction. Calculated pressures are heightened or relaxed according to circumstances and are aimed less at winning a premature decision than at testing resistance and asserting the prestige and image of either party.

On the ideological plane, hegemonic-objective struggle gives rise to an enterprise of subversion which finds expression in a crusade by zealots. The mobilization of minds and psychological warfare support the political-military effort. This form of tension leads to the centralization of governmental power in both major states and thrives on what becomes a conventionally high level of mass emotional stress. It produces generalized anxiety, is prolific of myths, and generates self-justifying theorems that equate national objectives with the imperatives of an absolute ideology. The themes of provocation and inequality, developed with a rhythm of increasing "power," energize continued action and reaction in a climate of crisis.

Hegemonic-objective conflict requires long-term planning and must reckon with time. Given the present balance of forces, the more sensitive both sides are to the risk of total war, the greater the corresponding tendency for American-Soviet competition to establish itself as a way of life and to develop fixed patterns and practices.

The Tactics of Conflict

Certain elements of the intellectual process involved in conducting international conflict can usefully be reviewed here. At bottom, there are three sorts of decisions required of a policymaker in the course of a struggle with another state: (1) when to begin the active phase of the conflict; (2) how to conduct his own part of the dispute; and (3) when to break off the controversy and resume normal relations.

The decision concerning the moment of beginning the active struggle is usually made by the state with the greater involvement of interest or the greater pressure for action. Once the crucial overt act has been performed, a certain power of decision remains with the second state, since it is not obliged to respond unless it wishes to. If the original provocation was above the threshold of tolerability, some conflict-oriented response is almost automatic. Lesser initiatives may often be ignored unless escalated or repeated. This general principle is more applicable to nonviolent moves than to military attack, since modern nationalistic states react without hesitation to direct military onslaught.

After being launched on open conflict, each side has further tactical decisions, depending on whether its approach is basically balancing or hegemonic. If initial considerations of intensity become relevant, how deeply will either side commit itself to this particular quarrel? Next, various operational decisions must be made. Will the state attempt to work changes in the general situational environment, or will its effort be expended in attempting to preserve the status quo? Will neutralizing policies—if they are adopted—be in the form of direct head-to-head counters to initiatives from the other state, or will they be indirect counteroffensives? Will a defensive strategy remain defensive throughout the struggle, or will success lead to a magnification of objectives and acceptance of an unforeseen offensive program? Many such questions relate directly to how the state chooses to formulate policy and doctrine for the conflict.

Ending a conflict is frequently more difficult than beginning one. In principle, a state may escape from a dispute on any of four grounds: (1) achievement of its objective; (2) negotiation of an acceptable compromise that gives it adequate if incomplete satisfaction in return for its effort and involvement; (3) abandonment of the conflict as inevitably inconclusive; or (4) complete defeat. The first and fourth reasons are self-evident if the objective is explicit and the cost/risk factors kept well in mind. An acceptable compromise is often the most useful avenue of escape, but it is feasible only if both sides are fully aware of their respective notions of acceptability and their minimum requirements coincide. An inconclusive breakoff, usually occurring only if both sides decide that their objectives are beyond reach at a bearable cost and risk, is seldom made explicit; a broken-off conflict most often lapses quietly without fanfare or formal registry.

The Adjustment of Conflict

The existence of conflict in the global system requires that states develop techniques for the adjustment and settlement of their disputes. The choice of a particular method and its ultimate success or failure depends upon the purpose, skill, and interests of the contending parties.

Not every conflict or disagreement between states needs to be formally adjusted or settled. Many disputes settle themselves, particularly if they are left alone. However, when popular passions become increasingly inflamed, especially when the object of the conflict is a matter of great importance to the disputing states, a formal adjustment may become the only viable alternative to violence. Acceptable solutions to the more pressing and important disputes are usually the most difficult to find, because of the danger that both sides may have hopelessly involved their prestige. Unless both sides are able to preserve their self-respect, the substantive core of the problem may be beyond reach.

The methods developed over the centuries for the adjustment and settlement of international conflict may be classified into three general categories: methods of pacific settlement, coercive procedures short of war, and forcible procedures through war. Each of these has its strengths and weaknesses.

Pacific Settlement

The methods of pacific settlement make available a variety of peaceful substitutes for violence. In general terms, they may be classified as diplomatic-political or judicial.

DIPLOMATIC AND POLITICAL METHODS. Diplomatic and political methods of adjusting conflict do not result in final judgments which the disputing states are obligated to accept. Hence they are described as nondecisional or nonbinding. Settlement rests on mutual agreement, usually based on substantive compromise. Political disputes involving value judgments of environmental factors are particularly susceptible to diplomatic procedures.

Diplomatic methods of settlement can be attempted through direct negotiations, good offices, mediation, inquiry, and conciliation.

Direct negotiation may take the form of bilateral or multilateral diplomacy. Such negotiations may be conducted between heads of state (as in the presently common personal or summit diplomacy), directly through ambassadors and other accredited diplomats of the concerned parties, or through an international conference.

Good offices is the name given to a semidiplomatic contact through the intervention of a third party (a state, an international organization, or a prominent individual). It is frequently resorted to when the disputing parties have become deadlocked in their diplomatic negotiations. A third state offers its services as a go-between to expedite contacts between the disputants. Although negotiations proceed through the third party, this party is not empowered to suggest a solution, nor does it participate directly in the negotiations. Good offices, once accepted, usually lead to mediation. A famous example of good offices was the role played by President Theodore Roosevelt at the conclusion of the Russo-Japanese war in 1905.

Mediation is a procedure by which, in addition to providing good offices, a third party participates actively in the negotiations. It tries to reconcile the opposite claims and to appease mutual resentments developed by the contending parties. The mediator may not impose its own solutions on the dispute, but is expected to take a strong initiative in proposing formulas. The role of Dr. Ralph Bunche as United Nations mediator during the Arab-Israeli war in 1948 is a famous modern instance of the use of this technique.

Inquiry designates the settlement of a dispute through establishment of a commission of inquiry. Such a group, consisting of an equal number of members from each of the disputing parties plus one or more from a third state or states, acts to facilitate solution of the conflict. Article 33 of the Charter of the United Nations authorizes the organization to create such a commission when appropriate.

The commission of inquiry does no more than determine the facts of a dispute by means of impartial investigation. The theory of inquiry is based upon two assumptions. The first is that a basic obstacle to peaceful settlement is the difficulty of establishing a statement of facts to which both parties agree. Second, this difficulty perpetuates itself by allowing passions to be aroused which obstruct agreement between the parties on points of principle.

An example of this form of settlement was the Commission of Inquiry which convened in Paris in 1905 to deal with the Anglo-Russian dispute over the action of a Russian fleet firing on English fishermen in the North Sea. The commission's report of the facts led to speedy settlement of the controversy.

Conciliation is a procedure that combines inquiry and mediation. An individual or a commission (structured much like a commission of inquiry) may perform the functions of conciliation. Its functions thus extend to both determination of facts and presentation of formal recommendations for settlement.

Conciliation multiplies the pacifying effects of both mediation and inquiry in the settlement of troublesome disputes. It is the most formalized of the diplomatic and political methods of settling international conflicts. It is particularly useful for serious political disputes, since its flexibility makes it more adaptable to varying circumstances than more rigid judicial or legislative procedures. Its object is always peace by compromise, not justice by law. The United Nations has used several conciliation commissions since 1945.

It must be pointed out that neither inquiry nor conciliation provides a means of settling conflict unless the solution worked out is acceptable to the disputing parties. Usually the contending parties will agree to such a solution only when they are persuaded that it offers them enough to justify breaking off the struggle.

JUDICIAL METHODS. Judicial methods of settlement are an attempt to regularize the terms and procedures which form the basis of the disposal of disputes. The two judicial procedures are arbitration and adjudication. Solutions are reached on the basis of law—and in some cases equity—but they explicitly exclude political compromise, since only legal disputes can be judicially resolved. The awards of arbitration and the decisions of an international court are binding on the disputing parties, and hence these procedures are described as decisional or binding.

Arbitration is accomplished either by an ad hoc tribunal or by the

Permanent Court of Arbitration at The Hague. Adjudication today is the exclusive province of the International Court of Justice, an organ of the United Nations. With few relatively unimportant exceptions, submission of a dispute to either judicial procedure is a voluntary act of the states involved.

Judicial methods of settling disputes have certain advantages over any diplomatic method. Probably most important is that the conflict is taken almost entirely out of the hands of the disputing parties, thus avoiding prestige problems which might impede a settlement. The conflict is disposed of by reference to standards common to both parties and external to the dispute. Judicial settlement may depoliticize a dispute more completely than diplomatic methods of settlement, since it implies voluntary renunciation by the parties of their individual powers of decision and submission to the impersonal criteria of law.

On the other hand, judicial settlement of disputes presents certain disadvantages. Relatively few of the important issues of world politics can be usefully cast in terms of a controversy that can be settled in a court of law. The more crucial the conflict is to the parties, the greater the likelihood that neither will be anxious for a settlement by any outside agency.

Arbitration may be defined as the settlement of international disputes through judges chosen by the parties. The first Hague Conference in 1899 established the Permanent Court of Arbitration. Since then this court has become the principal instrument of international arbitration. The Permanent Court consists of a panel of judges, four appointed for six-year terms by each member state.

Disputing parties wishing to use the Permanent Court of Arbitration must first negotiate an instrument called the *compromis d'arbitrage*. This agreement spells out the procedures the tribunal will follow and the rules of law to be applied. Each party then selects two judges from the panel, only one of whom can be its own national. These four judges choose a fifth member, called the "umpire." In their deliberations, the arbitrators can utilize only the rules of law which the contending states have agreed on in the *compromis*.

Adjudication has come to designate the settlement of an international dispute by the International Court of Justice of the United Nations. The court, established in 1945 as a successor to the Permanent Court of International Justice set up by the League of Nations, is also headquartered at The Hague. It consists of fifteen judges elected concurrently by the Security Council and the General Assembly of the United Nations for a term of nine years. Decisions of the court can be based on either law or the principle of *ex aequo et bono* (equity and justice).

All members of the United Nations are automatically parties to the statute of the International Court of Justice. In practice, however, states are not compelled to submit their disputes to the court, particularly since each state may qualify its adherence to the court's statute. A state not belonging to the United Nations may adhere to the court on conditions to be determined by the General Assembly on recommendation of the Security Council.

States which are parties to the court's statute may at any time declare that they recognize as compulsory, ipso facto and without special agreement, in relation to any state accepting the same obligation, the jurisdiction of the court in all legal disputes concerning (1) interpretations of a treaty; (2) any question of international law; (3) the existence of any fact, which, if established, would constitute a breach of international obligation; and (4) the nature or extent of the reparation to be made for breach of an international obligation. States which thus choose to accept this compulsory jurisdiction may do so either unconditionally, on a basis of reciprocity, or for only a certain time.

The functions of arbitration and adjudication as methods of settling international conflict are narrow. Obstacles to the broadening of these functions spring directly from the nature of the state system and the eminently political character of the relations it engenders. Settlement of disputes between states is never comparable to settlement of disputes between individual persons.

For individuals, judicial settlement is the impersonal application of law, an expression of inculcated discipline embracing virtually the whole of social relations. This predisposes individuals to limit their claims to what is legally defensible and to formulate them in legal terms. The global system incorporates neither a hierarchic order embracing the totality of state interests and values nor a single central power system that can control the play of competing forces. Law is therefore only peripheral to the real disputes of states and can have no more than a random effect on their settlement.

Coercive Procedures Short of War

States turn to coercive but nonviolent methods of settling a dispute if pacific procedures fail to produce satisfaction. Most of these devices, although expressed in the mechanics of the diplomatic process, have their ultimate coercive effect in the psychological realm.

Among the leading nonviolent coercive techniques are the recall of diplomats, expulsion of diplomats of the other state, denial of recognition, rupture of diplomatic relations, and suspension of treaty obligations. Somewhat more obviously "unfriendly" (in the legal sense) is the class of actions involving "force short of war": blockade, boycott, embargo, reprisal, and retorsion (a technically complex form of retaliation).

Forcible Procedures: The Role of War

The last resort of world politics, the final and unanswerable device for producing solutions to conflict, has always been the organized application of violence in the form of war. A nonregulatory social structure like the global system can have no final arbiter in a clash of wills except violence. The evolution of the international political process has resulted in a well-defined place for the institution of war. Policymakers have assumed a generic relationship between the dynamics of force and political antagonisms of states, and the interdependence of war and politics implies the rationality of force. Force was creative because it could be employed to resolve outstanding political issues between states. The scope and function of wars lent credence to the assumption that force and politics complement one another.

War is a distinct way of prosecuting conflict, not a special category of conflict. The disagreement between states that gives rise to armed combat lies in the policies or nationalist identifications of the adversaries, and the decision to fight is based on expedience. The principles of tactics that govern other types of conflict apply to war as well. For example, it is especially important to know when to initiate war, how to fight it, and when to stop.

Wars, like any other form of conflict, may be either balancing-objective or hegemonic-objective. In other words, a war may either be fought "according to the rules" and thus honor the controlling equilibrium, or it may threaten to destroy that system by altering relationships drastically and permanently. The balancing-objective form of war is known today as "limited" war, while the hegemonic-objective type is "total" war.

Limited war—the form of war made classic by centuries of examples —is conceptually a method within the family of familiar policy techniques: a single enterprise aimed at achieving a single objective. The amount of violence employed is calculated to inflict no more damage than is necessary to gain "victory" in the form of that objective. The end of such a war is theoretically marked by reestablishment of normal relations between the former enemies after political readjustments have been made.

Such wars are supposed to culminate in a negotiated peace. Both sides, having fought their campaigns with partial commitments of power, thus retain bargaining capability when the struggle ends. The terms of peace reflect the continuing power relationship between them, as modified by the verdict of the battlefield.

The Relationship of Force and Political Conflict Resolution

Radical changes in the quality of force and the nature of conflict account for the fact that political antagonists no longer go to war in the same way or for the same reasons. Nationalism and technology—the two forces that have had a devastating effect on so much of world politics—have transformed the sophisticated notion of war as a regulating and adjusting device into a much simpler yet much more deadly form of action. While war was previously defined as the establishment of a balance, nationalism redefined war as the attainment of hegemony. Technology made it possible for wars to become struggles of annihilation between peoples rather than the resolution of single-issue disputes between states.

The Changing Nature of Force

Discrimination in the use of force in total war has become extremely difficult. Greater military efficiency may be achieved by the new weapons of wholesale slaughter, so real victory must be total. The only conceivable forms of defeat are either utter destruction or abject submission in order to avoid such pulverization. No lesser margin of superiority will induce a people to surrender to a loathed enemy as long as they possess the capacity to fight on.

In logic, therefore, the only possible solutions of total war are absolute verdicts of dominance and submission. In the traditional course of world politics, questions demanding absolute answers have been relatively uncommon and dangerous, in that the consequences of a hegemonic decision are unpredictable. The so-called military dilemma of the contemporary era flows from the difficulty facing policymakers in developing a clear political (dispute-settling or objective-gaining) role for modern warfare.

It is incorrect to argue that total war cannot render a political decision; decisions are possible even in a thermonuclear war. But total war cannot provide the broad spectrum of possible outcomes that simpler warfare made available. It is inconceivable, for example, that anything resembling the traditional form of negotiated peace could emerge from a war initiated by a massive nuclear exchange. Solutions by total war are inevitably extreme. Only two political outcomes are possible from an all-out struggle between nuclear powers. Such a war will either run its full course and result in the collapse, capitulation, or obliteration of one belligerent and a claim of victory for the other, or it will be abandoned by both as inconclusive and mutually devastating. An expensive and dangerous method that can produce only absolute answers or none at all is of only limited political usefulness. War is in no sense a widely applicable method of resolving conflict today.

The Changing Nature of Conflict

The nature of post-1945 political conflict has been analyzed on several levels. Some political theorists argue that the transition from the rational norms of the Enlightenment to the ideological forms of Communism, Fascism, or totalitarianism have torn the global system into irreconcilable camps. Divergences among these camps cannot be smoothed over by any conventional modes of statecraft, including force. Others have said, in a related vein, that the "anomic" condition of twentieth-century individuals has rendered them vulnerable to irreconcilable "isms." Twentieth-century individuals are true believers who express themselves with selfish and irrational abandon on the international stage.

Such theses of present international political conflict fail to make the connection between their alleged causal factors, ideologies, and true believers, on the one hand, and—governments on the other. Governments—not "isms" or true believers—are the immediate sources of international political conflicts and governments are not controlled by principles although they use them as justification.

A more cogent analysis of the nature of present international conflict can be made by noting the interdependence of domestic and foreign policies of many governments. It is apparent that many governments now predicate their internal legitimacy—the maintenance of which is the primary goal of all governments—on the performance of external policies. The implication of this observation for the relationship of force to political conflict resolution in the present global system is evident. Since many governments justify their existence by reference to foreign policy commitments, these policies must be maintained despite forceful reversals. For a government to renounce its fundamental policies after military defeat would be to undermine its own internal legitimacy at the time of its gravest weakness. Hence, for many states, foreign policy is the dogmatic pursuit of fixed goals.

International antagonisms generated by these rigid and often irreconcilable foreign policies are not susceptible to political accommodation. Since only total defeat of a government's antagonist can allow it to terminate many frozen lines of policy, international conflicts—except in cases of total defeat of the enemy—remain unmoved by the dynamics of force. This phenomenon is illustrated by the political conflicts outstanding between the Arab states and Israel and between North and South Korea.

Primarily because of the interdependence of domestic legitimacy and international commitments, many present-day international political issues are not resolved at all. Such political issues in diverse regions of the globe defy the assumptions of traditional and limited war theorists who implied that force is a creative instrument for political conflict resolution. They also defy the assumptions of those who believed that with the advent of the atomic bomb, the "unthinkable" nature of force would abolish wars in the modern world.

Due to the imperatives of internal legitimacy, many governments are engaged in conflicts which will terminate only with annihilation of the governments which oppose them. It is unfortunate that the norms of political conflict of one antagonist become socialized dialectically by other antagonists, and that these norms soon come to be accepted as operational principles by many governments in the global system.

Recommended Readings

ARON, RAYMOND. *The Great Debate: Theories of Nuclear Strategy.* Garden City, N.Y.: Doubleday & Company, 1965.

BOULDING, KENNETH. *Conflict and Defense: A General Theory.* New York: Harper & Row, 1962.

BUTTERWORTH, ROBERT, and MARGARET SCRANTON. *Managing Interstate Conflict, 1945–74: Data with Synopses.* Pittsburgh: University of Pittsburgh Press, 1976.

CARLSTON, KENNETH S. *The Process of International Arbitration* (repr. ed.). Westport, Conn.: Greenwood, 1972 (original printing, 1946).

CONN, PAUL H. *Conflict and Decision Making.* New York: Harper & Row, 1971.

FISHER, ROGER. *International Conflict for Beginners.* New York: Harper & Row, 1970.

FROMM, ERIC. *The Anatomy of Human Destructiveness.* New York: Holt, Rinehart, and Winston, 1973.

GALTUNG, JOHAN. *Peace, War, and Defense.* Copenhagen: Ejlers, 1976.

GAMBLE, JOHN, and DANA FISCHER. *The International Court of Justice.* Lexington, Mass.: Lexington Books, 1976.

HOFFMAN, STANLEY. *The State of War: Essays on the Theory and Practice of International Politics.* New York: Frederick A. Praeger, 1965.

IKLE, FRED C. *How Nations Negotiate* (repr. ed.). Millwood, N.Y.: Kraus Reprints, 1976 (original printing, 1964).

LORENZ, KONRAD. *On Aggression.* New York: Harcourt Brace Jovanovich, 1963.

RUMMEL, RUDOLPH J. *Understanding Conflict and War.* New York: Sage, 1975.

SALTER, LEONARD M. *Resolution of International Conflict.* New York: Vintage Press, 1967.

SCHELLING, THOMAS C. *The Strategy of Conflict.* Cambridge: Harvard University Press, 1960.
SPIEGEL, STEVEN L., and KENNETH WALTZ, eds. *Conflict in World Politics.* Cambridge, Mass.: Winthrop Publishers, 1971.

Limitations on State Action

8

In spite of the deceptively simple logic of sovereignty that defines the absolute power of the state as complete freedom of state choice, the global system could not survive unless states accepted and acted upon a well-understood set of restraints. The limitations on state action, acknowledged by all governments as the price they pay for the continued viability of the global system, are only partially formalized. They rest to a large extent upon tacit agreement and the force of practice. To ignore these considerations, or to deduce a mechanistic doctrine of blind power as the energizing factor in world politics, is to condemn oneself to system building in a vacuum. The limitations on freedom of the state and other actors in world politics are not only as intrinsically important as that freedom itself, but also serve to give it form and direction.

In this chapter we shall examine three families of restraints that in some measure inhibit the choices that states make. Initially we shall consider the extent to which states are restrained by the teachings of morality. We shall next examine the role of international law in narrowing human choice in foreign policy to those actions that are legally sanctioned. Finally, we shall briefly review the effect of the policymaker's code of prudence in world politics. Although this three-category list is by no means exhaustive, each restraint acts in its own fashion to reduce the effective range of state action beyond the implications of pure theory.

Morality as a Limitation:
What is a Moral Consensus?

The state is composed of human beings, all of whom accept and act upon a set of moral principles. All human action may be judged with varying degrees of accuracy and relevance in moral terms. These two factors—the moral base of government action in the global system and the application of norms of morality to the behavior of states—constitute the basic elements of any discussion of morality as a limitation on international political action.

The Moral Problem in International Politics

Central to this perplexing issue is the intrinsic morality of the state and the relative claims that public purpose and private morality make on the consciences of individuals. The foreign policy of any national state has no necessary connection with any absolute or universal moral code. Whether the state is viewed as an amoral agent destined to function in an order beyond and irrelevant to moral codes, or as the architect of moral principles that are higher and more binding on individuals than private ethics, the result is the same.

As long as politics and private morality are kept separate, such a duality raises few problems other than abstract ones. The moral issue becomes pertinent, however, when commands of the state to the individual represent a direct contradiction of what that individual has been taught to regard as right and good. The classic instance is the taking of human life. The Ten Commandments stipulate that "Thou shalt not kill," but killing enemies of the state on command of one's government is an act of highest patriotism.

Regrettably, states have not felt seriously inhibited by this contradiction. Nationalist codes either emphasize that ordinary moral scruples do not apply to public purposes, or else assert that killing, stealing, or lying on behalf of the state are in themselves moral acts. Somewhat more sophisticated versions of these arguments suggest that moral principles might apply in ordinary circumstances, but the demonic nature of the enemy and the special sacredness of the national mission are ample reasons for individuals to suppress any personal qualms.

Theologians, philosophers, and psychologists of all kinds have grappled with the problem of reconciling the requirements of foreign policy with the absolutes of personal morality, or at least reducing the clash between them to a bearable level. The public may be told that, since the human being is inherently sinful, we should not worry about committing what we might consider immoral acts for public reasons—a sufficiently worthy end justifies any expedient means. Morality and conscience are no more than semisuppressed guilt feelings, runs another argument, and "mental health" is attained by cheerful support of political leadership and performance of whatever tasks are assigned to the citizen.

The ingenuity of these arguments has not relieved us from our essential dilemma. Traditional morality contradicts the pretensions of the state at many points, and no completely satisfying rationale of reconciliation can be found. The enormity of the world crisis and the cataclysmic strategies adopted by many states have sharpened this acute sense of moral crisis.

The Rupture of the Moral Consensus

The problem of moral consensus, always inherent in world politics, has been exaggerated by the development trends of the state system in the past two centuries. Modern world politics was born in Europe in the aftermath of the universal moral code of the Middle Ages. The monarchs who played the game in its early stages operated within a clear moral consensus and a full set of principles of action. But by 1815, Czar Alexander's "Holy Alliance," which proposed joint action by the rulers of Europe in a spirit of Christian brotherhood, was startlingly inappropriate.

The moral consensus that served to restrain world politics in the seventeenth and eighteenth centuries no longer exists, due to two related historic forces—nationalism and universal ideology. Modern nationalism, born in the era of the French Revolution, replaced "mankind" or "Christendom" as the supreme moral unit with the concept of the "nation." The national group was invested with the special moral superiority and sacred mission that had formerly been widely dispersed. From this atomization of a once-universal moral code came an aggregation of differing political moralities, all phrased in absolute terms but each incorporating a distinct national point of view on questions of good and evil. All contemporary universal ideologies stem from a particular world view, and all are much more sweeping interpretations of human action than are nationalist interpretations—but their effect is even more divisive. While nationalism proceeds from a moral base, it includes a generous admixture of crass and concrete calculation. Modern ideologies, however, fit all human experience within a moralistic framework and base their action programs on inflexible ideas about the moral nature of human beings.

Therefore, two additional sets of moral codes currently vie with traditional morality for the allegiance of individuals. Nationalist morality and ideological morality often join forces—as in the case of Communist states—but as often they conflict. Religious principles with clear universalist implications are commonly modified, stretched, or even perverted to serve one of the newer moralities. The political consequences of this moral pluralism are obvious.

No state admits publicly that its policy has any but a moral base. Political conflict between mature states has an inescapable, if futile, moral dimension, as both sets of participants insist that their goals are the achievement of the highest good. However, only rarely does a moral argument advanced by one side receive even a hearing, let alone acceptance, by the other. World order today is suffering not from too few moral referents, but from too many.

Morality and Foreign Policy

The ubiquity of moral discourse has an immediate effect on the choices made by states. Decision making goes on in a social context, a large portion of which flows from the moral orientation of the society. The objectives of policy are derived from social values with a self-evident moral basis. A moral code generates a world view, a way of observing, classifying, and giving meaning to phenomena in the real world. Thus what we have called situational analysis is obviously limited by the prevailing moral predispositions of the society. The tactics of policy are clearly affected by social considerations of what public actions are right (permissible) and wrong (prohibited). At every turn, internal morality guides and inhibits the policymaker.

If policy is developed by individuals who take note of the consensus, and if it is consistent with public interpretations of absolute good, its implementation is greatly strengthened. Any contradiction of mass moral expectations raises the prospect of internal divisions or reduced public vigor and zeal. Such matters as nuclear testing, espionage, strategic bombardment, and compromise bargaining with Communists have spawned serious moral problems for Americans in the past few years.

Morality, Interest, and Power

Two conceptual distinctions have plagued the discussion and analysis of moral issues in world politics. The first is the distinction between morality and national interest, the second between morality and power. Although these conflicts are far too complex to detail or solve here, some observations seem suitable.

The alleged clash between morality and national interest would appear to be false, since there is no reason why the teachings of any moral code and the formulation of any state's national interest should conflict. National interest is based on a controlling value system. If a state chooses to make advancement of moral principles its highest political value, this does not make its national interest any less valid a criterion. Those who profess to discover such a contradiction are often in reality pressing a particular policy in the face of opposition and—especially in the United States—are convinced that they can strengthen their case by discrediting "idealists" who advance moral principles in support of different policy prescriptions than their own.

Morality and power constitute a more formidable contrast. Power in this sense is understood to be brute force, often alleged to reflect humankind's inherent sinfulness. This formulation of power deprives power of moral neutrality and its instrumental character and elevates it to a positive factor in a moral equation. A state, it is alleged, can be either moral and therefore ineffective in a power-dominated world, or powerful and effective. Such an embrace of power is a compromise with strict morality, to be justified only on the basis of the duality of human beings. Because absolute moral solutions cannot be found in an amoral (often immoral) system, individuals are urged, even if sometimes regretfully, to set aside strict moral principles in the interest of effective use of power.

Analytically, this position is illogical and indefensible, there being no reason to equate power with force or to strip it of moral content. A state is concerned with winning international consensus in support of its purposes. It is not difficult to cite many examples of cases in which moral principles have proved important to the achievement of that consent. In this sense, morality becomes a part of power—or more accurately, of capability. The role of morality in strengthening or weakening a state's international competence is therefore a function of particular situations and not subject to generalizations.

The distinction between morality and power is not meaningful either as a basis for calculating capability or as a pretext for suspending individual moral scruples. Power may be used for immoral or moral purposes. Morality may be exterior to capability or one of its key components. Lack of agreement on moral standards in world politics does not free us from our responsibility to remain moral beings, even when considering questions of foreign policy. Power and morality are concepts that belong in different analytical frames of reference and cannot be joined in any prescriptive way.

The Rise of International Morality

A dream that has energized the efforts of many would-be reformers of world politics is that of a rebirth of an international moral consensus. If some way could be discovered to recreate the common moral ground rules that governed the course of world politics prior to the birth of modern nationalism, the political system and humankind itself would be enormously better off. The danger that differing but equally passionate moral outlooks might precipitate catastrophe would be sharply reduced, and the possibilities for finding common ground for mutually acceptable solutions to important problems would be correspondingly increased. Some such idea of what was called in the nineteenth century a "natural harmony of interest" among human beings motivated much of the effort that culminated first in the League of Nations and later in the United Nations.

An international moral consensus is a prerequisite to an orderly and stabilized world. More efficient international organizations and safer world politics will remain illusory hopes so long as the human species, bound into a constricted political space by a one-way technology, continues to break into quarrelsome and mutually exclusive factions on moral issues. We must reach some agreement on our basic moral terms of reference before there can be any significant improvement in the tension climate of world affairs.

Put this way, the proposition has been traditionally felt to be self-canceling. A world divided into a set of sovereign states, each busily perfecting and promoting its own nationalistic morality, has long been held incapable of mustering adequate agreement to permit formulation of "international morality." Ideologies, cutting across national and ethical lines, provide a broader base of moral action than state morality, but ideological conflict represents movement away from consensus rather than toward it. The failure of Woodrow Wilson's dream of the "Parliament of Man," as epitomized in the League of Nations and the deep and bitter divisions of the Cold War era, seems conclusive proof of the unattainability of international moral consensus.

But recent developments throw doubt on this long-standing generalization. The technology that has made war so destructive has also brought states into closer physical contact with each other. Especially in the United Nations, but in all manner of conferences, meetings, and assemblies, individuals and governments are jointly exploring the larger issues of the age and discovering, often to their surprise, that their moral judgments are astonishingly similar. From this new awareness of their common interest in a single destiny has emerged the beginnings of a true international morality.

Its root is, of course, expedience—the urge to survive in a planet of great danger. No moral code makes a senseless death morally justifiable, and sanity argues that the continued existence of the human species is a highly desirable goal. Sheer biological survival is not, however, the crux of this moral outlook. If individuals are to die, they insist that they die for a *cause* which is in some way advanced or defended by death. The new morality is slowly proceeding beyond this fundamental moral judgment to develop a more elaborate rationale on which to base state behavior in a less political world.

Any international morality must inevitably weaken the narrow bonds of nationalism. Although this is still a highly nationalistic age, the character of mass national identifications is perceptibly changing. In some areas a clear decline has set in, in others nationalism is still seeking a new direction, and in still others it continues to seek larger units of loyalty. Only a few states espouse the old, militant, integrating impact of nationalism. Similarly, the decline in the impact of ideologies on the behavior patterns of average citizens, detectable only in recent years, is a hopeful sign.

The Restraining Effect of Moral Consensus

The new force of international morality—a force that is as yet peripheral—is given form by means of an international consensus. Whether expressed formally in the General Assembly of the United Nations or informally by the intangible of "world opinion," collective moral judgment is now a situational factor that policymakers must take into account.

International moral restraint is, of course, powerless to prevent a great power from taking a single overt step or even from launching a particular policy. It probably never will be an instrument for casting an effective vote on a unique event. Its role up to the present has been to help condition the climate of decision for both large and small states by developing clearer and more restrictive limits within which the state system can move. Nor is it likely that its negative restraining function will ever be overtaken in importance by a positive and goal-postulating role. Morality may define the permissible for states, but not the mandatory.

However, the logic of technology and the evolving mutual awareness of individuals have combined to make moral judgments again relevant to the course of world politics. The recognition of mutual vulnerability has created a newly born international criterion of evaluation available to individuals everywhere. Its usefulness so far, although admittedly limited, argues for its continued and more extensive application. Morality, international as well as internal, will continue to be a limitation on state action, difficult to define but impossible to ignore.

International Law

Whether international law is "law" in the true sense has been a subject of constant debate among jurists. Certain theoretical aspects of the nature of law must be understood in order to grasp the significance of this problem.

Law in the abstract suggests a fixed relationship between or among certain entities. Two types of law may be distinguished in terms of their subjects: natural law (in the sense of law of nature) and human law. Natural law is the law of natural causes of human or nonhuman phenomena and thus contains no element of volition. In human relations, however, volition is omnipresent. Human law covers the relations among persons or groups governed by rules to which the subjects have explicitly or tacitly agreed to conform, subject to official demands for obedience. Human law rests ultimately on agreement.

International law is a branch of human law. In spite of the concept of sovereignty, the global system is generally regarded by all its members as having a legal base resting on the consent (theoretically explicit) of all states bound by the law. International law is a product of the operation of the global system. Its growth is almost accidental in that it seldom is the result of deliberate planning, but instead develops slowly from international practice. A rule has often attained near-maturity before policymakers appreciate that there has been an addition to the total body of the law.

Probably the greatest inspiration for the continued historical growth of international law has been the demands of states for reciprocity, uniformity, and equality of treatment. In world practice this demand approximates the ideal of "justice," in that each state expects its due from the law. The legal rights a state may enjoy (apart from the freedom of action to influence or coerce other states) depend upon the willingness of other states to recognize these rights in practice. The divergence between this idea of justice and the working principles of international intercourse may be bridged only by effective application of the rule of consent.

The Subject Matter of International Law

The considerable dimensions of international law can be reduced to three general areas: the acquisition and meaning of statehood, the rules and procedures of peaceful international intercourse, and the rules and procedures of war.

THE LAW OF STATEHOOD. This deals with the legal personality of the state and its rights, duties, and privileges. It covers such subjects as assumption of statehood through recognition, state succession, and loss of international personality. It delineates the methods of acquiring and losing territory, and defines the status of equality of states and the responsibility of a state for events on its territory and actions by its nationals abroad. It defines national territorial jurisdiction over air, land, and sea. It also covers state jurisdiction over persons, including the broad ground of nationality, citizenship, and the rights of resident or transitory aliens in its territory.

THE RULES AND PROCEDURES OF PEACEFUL INTERNATIONAL INTERCOURSE. These include the law of diplomacy, the law of treaties, and the law of pacific settlement of international disputes. The law of diplomacy prescribes the powers and privileges of diplomats and establishes the protocol affecting the conduct of diplomatic business. The law of treaties, one of the most important aspects of international law, designates the methods of negotiation, tests of validity, rules of interpretation, and processes of termination of a treaty. The law regulating the pacific settlement of international disputes controls the various procedures utilized to settle international conflicts short of war and the rights of the parties in such procedures.

THE LAW OF WAR. This deals initially with the legal concepts of belligerency and neutrality. In traditional international law, belligerency grants a state many legal rights it does not enjoy when at peace, while depriving it of others. It also requires a state to obey the laws governing the conduct of warfare. Neutrality confers certain special rights upon a neutral state, such as the maximum immunity practicable from the effects of the war. In return, it imposes certain obligations on the neutral state, such as abstention from specific unneutral acts and preservation of strict impartiality. In addition, the law of war covers rules for the conduct of warfare relating to attacks on general populations and treatment of prisoners of war, prohibition of certain weapons, and similar matters.

Political Conception of International Law

International law reveals most sharply the contrast between domestic and global political systems. The legal order in the global system is decentralized, resting upon the reciprocal discharge of functions by national states which are technically equal. In a national system the legal order includes a centralized hierarchy of institutionalized decision makers, ranging from the minor political official to the head of a state. They are two completely different orders.

State officials acknowledge the obligatory character of international law as a body of rules, but reserve to themselves determination of the rules, how they apply to specific situations, and the nature of their administration. Such a decentralized system is not utterly chaotic, and state officials do not have unlimited discretion to act arbitrarily. They are deterred from doing so by a number of considerations: the general need for order and stability, the reciprocal advantage of many rules, and the desire not to offend other states for a variety of reasons, including the possibility of incurring various sanctions.

Law and its political institutions reflect the ideological and normative order of the society in which they operate. Law can exist only in a society. There is no law in a community without norms. Law is effective in a society only when its positive laws (commands issued by officials) correspond to its "living" laws: customs, traditions, and experience.

During medieval and early modern times many jurists advanced a theory of natural law which was intrinsic in God and nature and was discoverable by human reason. We see today, however, that the idea of natural law which was advanced in their writings was almost entirely a historical development with origins in Greco-Roman philosophy and jurisprudence and in Christian ethics. It was influential in the era of the "medieval synthesis," helping to provide a common moral, religious, and philosophical basis for a unified society. The increasing extension of international contacts to non-European cultures has made this concept of natural law, rooted as it was in European philosophical, legal and religious principles, no longer valid as a basis for the evolution of a universal international law.

Beginning in the sixteenth century, various schools of thought regarding the nature of international law gradually developed and are yet discernible today.

The *naturalists* hold that natural law is the one and only legal system governing states. They argue that natural law comes to humanity through human reason and the nature of the human being. Law in this way cannot be derived from the consent of its subjects, but rather is the supreme command of a super-human authority, often explicitly divine in nature. Custom has thus no legal force, and treaties are binding only because of their basis in natural law.

The *positivists* originated in the eighteenth century but did not become conspicuous until the nineteenth. The positivists emphasize the role of consent as the source of international law. They believe that whatever dictates of natural law are not incorporated in practice by the overt consent of human beings are binding only upon their individual consciences. "Natural law" to them is no more than a set of moral principles external to real law.

The *eclectics* contend that the sources of international law are both natural and consent. The school appeared as early as the seventeenth century and is probably the dominant group today.

International law undoubtedly functions as a regulatory and limiting mechanism in world politics, but only in an intermittent and partially effective fashion. In large measure this incomplete effect is due to certain key characteristics of international law as a legal system.

First, its exact content is and will probably continue to be indeterminate, since states define their legal rights and duties themselves with a sharp eye to their own interests. Second, international law is still largely a self-help system and is thus not enforced in the fashion of municipal law by a socially sanctioned international institution. Third, obedience to law is in legal theory a voluntary act on the part of any state, for any stronger doctrine would do irreparable damage to the foundationstone of sovereignty. Fourth, international law is an incomplete system with many aspects of interstate life clearly beyond the scope of the law. The political judgments of states are generally regarded as beyond legal restraint.

In spite of these shortcomings, however, the great bulk of normal and routine international and transnational relations takes place within the framework of principles of international law. Such key notions as the rights and duties of states, the conduct of diplomacy, and the negotiation, ratification, and application of treaties have been all brought solidly under legal control. In general, we may conclude that procedural law is very well established in the relations of states, but that substantive law (that part of law that gives concrete content to abstract matters of right) is still amorphous. It is at the latter point that international law begins most obviously to fail as a regulatory technique.

International law, like world politics, emphasizes self-help and the unilateral enforcement of legal rights. The global order does not provide automatic and effective social sanctions for the principles of law which it identifies. Yet it is a mistake to conclude that there are no sanctions at all to contribute to the enforcement of the legal rights of states.

The greatest sanction of all, the one that led to the birth of the legal order in the first place and has constantly stimulated its growth, is expediency. An international legal code exists because states find it more rewarding to develop and apply generalized legal rules to their relations than to live always in a condition of unregulated anarchy. States, in other words, are impelled toward obedience to the law because the positive advantages of obedience are usually considered to be relatively greater than those arising from disobedience.

A second category of sanction is inertia, or habit. Long-standing legal procedures have become so well established in state practice that conformity to them is usually a matter of unthinking but conditioned response. The possibility of disobedience simply does not become one of the realistic action alternatives considered by the policymaker.

Finally, as at least a semicoercive sanction today we may cite here the international consensual apparatus referred to earlier in this chapter. We must of course be on our guard not to overestimate the effect or the extent of world public opinion, but we must also be most careful not to underestimate it. A legal sanction, after all, is primarily a method of securing obedience to law rather than of punishing disobedience, and it is undeniable today that the only occasionally articulated demand of much of humankind for greater order in world relations has resulted in much greater attention to legal niceties by all types of governments. State decisions to "bow" to world opinion on legal issues may be based on expedience rather than principle, but the effect is the same: a greater conformity of state behavior with the rule of law. This is in essence the function of all sanctions.

Third World Attitudes toward International Law

The emergence of Third World states has had an undeniable, though not easily measurable, impact on international law. Their interpretation of international legal norms differs from traditional Western views and expresses the need for change. They consider many of the rules of international law inconsistent with their conditions, concerns, and aspirations.

Third World states acknowledge the binding force of international law, all of them having invoked its norms in disputes with other states and in debates in international organizations. However, Third World leaders stress the need for further development of international law to reflect their values and interests in such areas as nationalization, investment, resources, territorial rights, the law of the sea and treaties.

A generally accepted "international standard" in traditional international law governs state responsibility for the treatment of aliens, as regards both their person and their property. In the case of a state's expropriation or nationalization of alien property on its soil, the international standard has required payment of "prompt, adequate, and effective" compensation. The Western states uphold this traditional standard, whereas the Third World favors the doctrine of "equality of treatment," providing for compensation to aliens in accordance with the local laws of the expropriating state.

With regard to the law of the sea, most of the Third World states are against the traditional doctrine of the three-mile offshore territorial sea boundary which is still upheld by the leading maritime powers of the West. At the 1958 and 1960 Geneva Conferences on the Law of the Sea, coalitions of most of the non-Western states with the Soviet bloc frustrated the prospects for reaffirmation of the three-mile limit. At the sixth session of the Third United Nations Conference on the Law of the Sea held in Mexico in 1977, Third World states demanded that an international authority under the aegis of the United Nations be the exclusive agency allowed to exploit mineral resources in the deep seabed area. The United States, on the other hand, wanted to create a dual- or parallel-access system that would allow any state or private corporation access to deep seabed minerals. This and other items such as the width of the territorial sea (whether it should be three or twelve nautical miles), a two-hundred-mile economic resource zone, and protection of the marine environment remain unresolved issues.

In the law of treaties, the Third World states have tended to oppose the "unanimity doctrine" of the admissibility and effect of reservations to multilateral conventions. They show preference for the Pan American Rule, developed by the Latin American states, in accordance with which the reserving state becomes a party to the treaty with respect to other parties that do not object to the reservation.

On the issues of sovereign immunity, Third World states favor the "restrictive" doctrine (the view that a state is not entitled to immunity from suit in the courts of another state with regard to claims arising out of its commercial activities). This view is gaining increasing support in Western Europe and the United States. The Soviet Union, on the other hand, upholds the "absolute" immunity doctrine.

Assertions that Third World states are not bound by old norms do not imply wholesale rejection of traditional international law. Rather, they must be regarded as an expression of the resentment still felt by these states over their colonial past, and as an assertion of their sovereignty and equality. They also serve to remind the older states that the views of the newcomers are not to be disregarded in the formulation and further development of international law. There is resentment among Third World leaders against what appears to them a double standard—reliance by the developed states on the arrangement obtained by force or pressure during the colonial era, and their simultaneous denial of the lawfulness of the use of force by Third World states to uproot these fruits of past aggressions. In the attempt to provide legal justification for their efforts to change the status quo, Third World states rely increasingly on the argument that "unequal" treaties imposed by duress are invalid.

It must be stated, however, that sovereign states' concern for equality is not limited to Third World states. This principle has been enshrined in such documents as the United Nations Charter and the final act of the Conference on Security and Cooperation in Europe—the Helsinki Agreement of August 1975 (Articles I and VIII).

Not unlike some of the developed states, Third World countries are cautious about the compulsory jurisdiction of the International Court of Justice under the optional clause of Article 35 of the court's statute. This may stem from fear that the court might apply norms of international law rejected by Third World states, or might uphold the legal rights of developed states against attempts to change the status quo inherited from the colonial era. There have been, moreover, very few African and Asian judges on the court.

Recent Trends in International Law

Contemporary trends in international law demonstrate a closer link with world politics. It has proved impossible to adjust life to law, so the controlling emphasis is upon the adjustment of law to life. International law of the nineteenth and earlier centuries assumed above all the sovereignty of states. Its object was not to eliminate war, but to restrict it in time, place, and method, and hence establish an equilibrium of power. Twentieth-century international law has acquired the goal of establishing an equilibrium of justice and assumes the interdependence of states and the integration of power.

The technological revolution has produced both positive and negative effects on international law. Progressive development of the positivist view, which heightened the role of power by making it more difficult to subject states to rules of law, secularized the entire concept of international law and weakened its moral foundations. Law in a power-oriented society maintains the supremacy of force and hierarchies established on the basis of power and gives legal respectability and sanctity to the system. Many new states which have gained their independence in recent years do not share in the historic tradition of international law. Hence, they are not inclined to limit their claims to what is legally defensible under the old system, a system that they feel is biased in favor of older, more developed, and more powerful states. In this sense, modern trends already have begun to weaken the universality of law.

On the other hand, the logic of the technological revolution and its by-products compel states to establish a better balance between law and politics in order to form a more cohesive global system. International law today is formulating these demands in terms of new standards of justice. The relationship between international law and the dynamics of the global system is more apparent today than at any time in history. Law and social organization operate upon each other reciprocally: Law sets limits to the structure, functions, and effectiveness of a social system, while the organizational dynamics of a society control the development, formulation, and application of legal rules. Modern technology, by clarifying this two-way relationship and demonstrating the necessity for greater cohesiveness in the global order, emerges as a positive force for the elaborations of international law. A more effective legal system in international and transnational relations will automatically result from an increasingly integrated if not interdependent global system.

The Calculus of Prudence in Statecraft

Our analysis of the foreign policy process in Part I pointed out that strategy in foreign policy or in war is a very conservative enterprise. The unknowns of cost and risk in an intrinsically unstable action system combine to inhibit decision and limit implementation. Under such circumstances, perhaps the most powerful and certainly the most widely applicable restraint on state freedom of choice is the code of prudence that governs rational policymaking.

Rationality and Prudence in Statecraft

Operationally, there is no reason why all policymakers should be sane. A lunatic, if capable of issuing coherent orders, would be as qualified to operate the controls of government as a philosopher-king. But sanity and rationality are assumed to be requisite qualities in a foreign policymaker because only individuals marked by these traits can anticipate the probable results of their actions and govern their decisions in response to these calculations. The rational policymaker is the prudent one.

An analytical and rational approach to foreign policy must be marked by caution because of a number of factors already discussed, including incompleteness of information, possibility of accident or pure chance, and perverseness of the human personality. If every decision takes account of these limitations on the accuracy and validity of choice, a generous margin of error is inevitably built into policy. Game theory teaches that the primary responsibility of the player is to ensure that player's continued participation in the game. No more graphic summary could be made of the task of the player who invests one's state's survival in one's ability to match strategies with fellow policymakers.

The Role of Probability

Policymaking requires the application of probability theory. Every policymaker accepts that nothing in world politics is either inevitable or impossible—or at least that the determination of inevitabilities or impossibilities is beyond the scope of his analytical techniques. A policymaker is therefore forced to determine the relative probability of the various possible outcomes of each problem faced. Action decisions are based upon the greater probability of one outcome, with the necessary margin for error provided by the conclusion as to how much more probable one alternative is than others.

One psychiatric interpretation of this situation asserts that to ignore

168   **THE GLOBAL POLITICAL SYSTEM**

relative *probabilities* and instead become fixated on *possibilities* is a mark of paranoia. A policymaker may on occasion (as did Adolph Hitler in trusting to his "intuition" that the Nazi armies would defeat the Soviet forces in World War II) conclude that a certain eventuality is cosmically inevitable—and pay for one's error with one's head. Much more common, however, is the opposite error: to conclude that a desired result is impossible, and thereby miss a real opportunity for meaningful action. Whether or not policymakers who commit these blunders are actually paranoid, they are certainly performing at a level far below the optimum, and their respective states bear the cost of their failures.

The Virtues of Half a Loaf

Prudential calculation is also apparent in policymakers' strong preference for partial successes achieved at minimum risk rather than all-or-nothing choices. With continued survival as the prime consideration in statecraft, rational policymakers strive to gain such prizes as can be won without endangering their self-preservation or security. This has contributed to what we have noted as a characteristic pattern of interstate conflict: the struggle for small victories with only partial commitments of capability. Each state involved in such a contest can accept defeat with only minimum disturbance, since it knows in advance that even the most unfavorable outcome will leave it in a viable position for further action.

The cost/risk calculation requires that analysts never give themselves the benefit of any major doubts and that they be prepared to pay the maximum probable cost for their objectives. Since the individual decision maker has only a limited ability to reduce cost factors in a situation over which there is only minimal control, the only way of avoiding an unfavorable cost/risk computation is by scaling down one's objective to an affordable level. Once again, prudence dictates restraint on decision.

The Relativism of Decision

Absolute calculations and absolute decisions have no place in rational policymaking. A high degree of relativity in all phases of decision and action is a characteristic of the skillful and successful policymaker.

Success is the only absolute criterion of value in foreign policy. A foreign policy is "good" or "bad" only to the extent that the state moves toward its objectives and in behalf of its national interest. Since the objectives themselves, and even definitions of national interest, change in response to shifts in mass preferences and situational dynamics, policymaking is a constant exercise in relating many variables to one another.

There is no room for fixed and absolute generalizations about the nature of the political world, the nature of the problems facing the state, or the substance or methods of the responses the state must make.

If all policymakers were equally prudent, world politics would never reach the boiling point. But history points out many overoptimistic leaders who misread the probabilities of a situation, as well as some who were persuaded that they had the key to the final significance of history and could reshape human destiny. The global system could tolerate such leaders in a simpler day, when failure was confined to the offending state.

Today, however, humankind is the loser each time imprudence takes command of the policy machine of a state. The best most of us can hope for is that prudence will continue to shackle the hand of recklessness and adventure. The stakes are too high to permit any but the cautious to play the game of survival in an age of thermonuclear bombs.

Recommended Readings

AMACHER, RYAN C., and RICHARD JAMES SWEENEY. *The Law of the Sea: U.S. Interests and Alternatives.* Washington, D.C.: American Enterprise Institute for Public Policy Research, 1976.

BENNETT, JOHN. *Foreign Policy in Christian Perspective.* New York: Charles Scribner's Sons, 1966.

BRIERLY, J. L. *The Law of Nations: An Introduction to the International Law of Peace* (6th ed.). Oxford: Clarendon Press, 1963.

BUTTERFIELD, HERBERT. *Christianity, Diplomacy, and War.* New York: Abingdon-Cokesbury Press, 1953.

CLARK, GRENVILLE, and L. B. SOHN, eds. *World Peace Through World Law* (5th ed.). Cambridge: Harvard University Press, 1975.

CORBETT, PERCY E. *Law and Society in the Relations of States.* New York: Harcourt, Brace & World, 1951.

FALK, RICHARD A., and WOLFRAM F. HANRIEDER. *International Law and Organization.* Philadelphia: J. B. Lippincott Co., 1968.

FRIEDMAN, WOLFGANG. *The Changing Structure of International Law.* New York: Columbia University Press, 1964.

GAMBLE, JOHN, JR. *Marine Policy: A Comparative Approach.* Lexington, Mass.: Lexington Books, 1977.

HOLLICK, ANN L., and ROBERT E. OSGOOD. *New Era of Ocean Politics.* Baltimore: Johns Hopkins Press, 1974.

JACKSON, JOHN. *Legal Problems on International Economic Relations: Cases, Materials, and Text on the National and International Regulation of Transnational Economic Relations.* St. Paul, Minn.: West Publishing Co., 1972.

KELSEN, HANS. *Principles of International Law* (2nd ed.). New York: Holt, Rinehart & Winston, 1966.

Kish, John. *The Law of International Spaces.* Leiden: Sijhoff, 1973.
Niebuhr, Reinhold. *Moral Man and Immoral Society.* New York: Charles Scribner's Sons, 1960.
Nussbaum, A. *Concise History of the Law of Nations* (rev. ed.). New York: Macmillan Co., 1947.
Schwarzenberger, Georg. *The Dynamics of International Law.* Milton, England: Oxon Professional Books. 1976.
Thompson, Kenneth. *Political Realism and the Crisis of World Politics* (repr. ed.). Port Washington, N.Y.: Kennikat, 1971 (original printing, 1960).
Von Glahn, Gerhard. *Law Among Nations* (3rd ed.). New York: Macmillan Co., 1976.
Wright, Quincy, *Contemporary International Law* (rev. ed.). New York: Random House, 1961.

III

THE SUBSTANCE OF GLOBAL POLITICS: MAJOR ISSUES OF OUR AGE

War
and
Arms Control

9

In Parts I and II, we analyzed the rationale of foreign policy as conceived and executed by individual states and examined the general characteristics of the global political system within which actors move. One primary consideration has affected everything we said in both discussions: Under the standardized condition of interstate life, it is impossible for a state to operate and for the system to function except if the state can resort to physical coercion or violence as most clearly expressed in war. We cannot avoid the analytical and practical centrality of military judgments. The system as we know it today is postulated on the right and capacity of states to work their will by force if they so desire.

However, the nature of world politics has undergone a dramatic transition. Foreign policies, particularly those of major powers, do not receive the vigorous and powerful implementation one would expect. Interstate disputes seldom reach the resolution in power terms that the system would seem to demand. Small states display relatively greater choice of action, while great powers cast about (with indifferent success) for ways to make their supposed dominance again a reality. To a great extent the political world has been, if not turned completely upside down, at least knocked off balance.

The major reason for this unprecedented state of affairs is that new theories of warfare and the weapons that have given birth to these theories have radically altered the traditional conceptions of interstate political relations. Policymakers of the major powers wrestle with the problem of fitting modern military doctrines and techniques within the framework of foreign policy and world politics. They have not yet succeeded. The old ways of war are outmoded, and the new warfare has not yet found its political niche. Paralleling the difficulty in defining the relationship between military power and political consequence has been the increasing incidence of conflict used to achieve change within states. If any development of the fourth quarter of the twentieth century approximates the traditional role of force as a coercive agent of change, it is its use by competing groups *within* states as much as across international boundaries. Internal conflicts have placed greater emphasis upon the political effects of military action than upon the military outcomes per se, a development which has further obscured the conventional relationship between military and political objectives as observed by the major powers.

In this chapter we shall examine the nature of the military dilemma, in terms of both its own components and its impact on the political process. Recent years have seen a great increase in emphasis given to military matters in the study and teaching of world politics. While this chapter can only skim the surface of the vast subject of military science, it is designed to acquaint the reader with at least the basic vocabulary of contemporary military discussion and to relate these concepts to the larger context of world political affairs.

Total War and the State System

What have been the specific effects of total war upon the state system? How has the possibility of general nuclear warfare affected the general pattern of world politics? We have already answered both questions in general terms, but certain basic considerations merit further attention.

The Possibility of Catastrophe

War became a normal aspect of world politics because it provided a final answer to problems *within the system itself.* That is, war balanced the political process without endangering it. Even World War II, with all its destructive and disruptive results, nevertheless ended with a recognizable political system still in existence. General nuclear war, however, raises the grim possibility of destruction of the political system and perhaps of technologically advanced societies.

Advocating resolution of an international dispute using a technique that might completely destroy humanity is like recommending decapitation as a cure for headaches. No purely political goal is so important that it justifies risking survival. Considerations of risk—even assuming an optimistic cost calculation—thus seem absolutely to rule out a decision for total war. This has been the factor restraining all policymakers who have faced the choice since the dawn of the nuclear era.

Prior to the development of today's massive nuclear arsenals, analysts speculated that total war might not obliterate humanity or the monuments to our civilization, but rather that industrial society could achieve relatively rapid recovery from a thermonuclear holocaust. Given the destructive power associated with modern nuclear weapons and the effects that such weapons would have on urban, industrialized societies, no government has been willing to gamble its existence (and that of the entire world) on the validity of these hypotheses. The possibility of catastrophe and the inestimable costs of general nuclear war loom large in all military calculations today.

The Invalidation of "Victory"

With the constant possibility of utter debacle, and with the certainty of monumental devastation no matter what the course of the war, the classic military objective of "victory" has been substantially stripped of meaning. Victory in battle has always meant submission of the enemy; victory in war has always meant achievement of the positive or negative goal for which war was fought. These classifications are almost meaningless with respect to present-day total war.

The destructiveness of thermonuclear war is beyond belief. If one state loses 75 percent of its people and 90 percent of its productive capacity, will the survivors be consoled by realizing that the enemy lost 85 percent of its people and all its productive capacity? Will victory in such a case be sweet or—in the words of a leading theorist of nuclear war—"will the living envy the dead?"

Victory in total war is a notion without content, a fact that exercises an inhibiting effect. The development of secure, invulnerable strategic weapons systems such as missile-firing submarines has all but eliminated the prospect of destroying in one blow an enemy's capacity to retaliate. Since even a retaliatory blow would wreak havoc on the attacker's society, there is no advantage (and hence no incentive) to launch a surprise first nuclear strike. With no likelihood of bringing about a real triumph, a policymaker's urge to begin combat never grows very strong. Total war is unthinkable for any rational decision maker; without victory to give it point, it finds no political justification today.

The Rethinking of Political Values

The motive force of world politics has long depended on the primacy of political values over all competing notions of good. Citizens were expected to support the state's efforts at whatever cost to themselves, even to sacrificing their lives. Now that total war may have lost its point, the justification for patriotic death is no longer self-evident. Additionally, as we have already discussed, the traditional concept of victory is no longer applicable. To be sure, there are levels of conflict below total war which might be waged, but they would be limited wars, fought for limited objectives. It will be increasingly difficult for states to inspire their citizens to make the ultimate sacrifice for "limited" results.

Revaluation of the conditions under which such demands might be made has led to a serious rethinking of political views. Many once-self-evident truths about the purpose of foreign policy are undergoing reanalysis, and drastically different answers are being advanced to old questions. Some observers are suggesting that the content of political life needs overhauling in order to make it more directly responsible to individual needs and aspirations. Such a trend could conceivably sweep away many of the underpinnings of traditional world politics. Internal wars, "proxy" wars, and well-circumscribed wars between "minipowers" employing conventional weapons remain exceptions to this evolution of political values. In these conflicts patriotic death has lost neither its meaning nor its allure. People, even states, have demonstrated that they remain quite willing to sacrifice themselves for political, religious, or social goals. Conflicts of this kind, usually labeled "limited wars," are limited only in the eyes of the major nuclear powers; to small states and to countries in the throes of revolution, these wars are *absolute*. In this sense, such low-level conflicts, and their persistence in the nuclear age, have restored the efficacy of war as an instrument of political policy, even if as a mutation of the pre-World War II variety. But the invalidation of "victory" in total war between major powers leads inevitably to a rethinking of the political values that underlie considering the use of force a legitimate and viable policy alternative.

The Disappearance of Decision

With war no longer a good foreign policy investment, the state system is deprived of its only effective method of reaching a clear decision in a direct confrontation between states. Smaller states, although not risking nuclear incineration if they fight, operate in an environment severely constrained by the probability of great power intervention and the fear of consequent expansion to total war. States repeatedly become involved in positions from which only a successful war could extricate them, but inhibitions on warfare prevent them from taking the critical step. Unable to go forward and unwilling to retreat, the contestants remain locked in an uneasy stalemate, and issues remain unresolved. In "microwars" between or within small states, great powers, spurred by fears of the ultimate confrontation, have usually intervened prior to the achievement of a permanent political or military resolution. Although the small states have fought, the issues have tended to remain undecided.

World politics since the end of World War II has seen a succession of great power issues strained to the breaking point and then remain hanging. Cultural lag prevents most states from recognizing and acting on the implication of this loss of decision capability in the system. They persist in embarking on policies whose full fruition might require war, and express baffled annoyance when they feel themselves trapped. Some smaller states, recognizing both the opportunities and limitations inherent in such an era, have had great success in pursuing active policies cast in a frame of implementation that excluded high probability of war. With increasing frequency, they have enlarged that frame of execution to include war itself.

Decision by Consensus

With war stripped of its role as last resort, some effective substitute is necessary if the global political system is to maintain stability. The most broadly applicable alternative to war has been the institutionalization of consensus. Speaking primarily through the General Assembly of the United Nations, but on occasion through special conferences or other ad hoc instrumentalities, a cohesive and articulate body of supranational consensus has sometimes exercised a controlling effect on crisis situations. If international consensus is developed, displacing military power as final arbiter, the global political system will be vastly different than it has been for three centuries.

Political Effects of the New Warfare

We have considered some of the effects of total war on the operation of the state system. Equally important to an understanding of the impact of military technology are its influences on policymakers.

The "Balance of Terror"

Probably the most important consideration affecting foreign policy decisions by both large and small states is the so-called balance of terror. This situation stems from the present distribution of military capability in the world: Two great states have built up arsenals of new weapons that far outclass all other states, yet each remains incapable of mounting adequate superiority over the other. This allocation of military power inhibits everyone to the same extent, if not in exactly the same way.

Since each of the great powers is unable to contemplate unleashing war on the other, both the United States and the USSR have a vested interest in avoiding war. There is little philanthropy or charity in this self-restraint, only elementary calculations of the prospects for survival on the cost/risk scale.

Furthermore, neither is safe in making indiscriminate use of its great military power against lesser states. A large proportion of the smaller powers are under the protection of one or the other of the giants, and any overt pressure on these proxies or "demiproxies" could bring their great power patron into the dispute.

Although the concept of neutrality has changed, and the post-World War II notion of Cold War has become an oversimplified anachronism, small nonaligned states are as well protected as when their status was preserved by the Cold War counterweights of the major bloc leaders. However, the prevalence of internal conflicts, externally supported in many cases by major powers or their proxies, has encouraged great power counteractivity in these nonaligned states and in inevitable political-military polarization of the particular regions. If the polarization continues, spurred by the seemingly irreversible trend toward internal violence, the concepts of neutrality and nonalignment in the old Cold War context will probably disappear altogether. Any attempt by either ideological camp to exert military coercion on almost any neutral would provoke a reaction from the opposing bloc and once again polarize the military situation.

If the nuclear giants are inhibited by the balance of terror, so are the smaller states. Neither nuclear leader can view calmly an outbreak of war anywhere, so both deny smaller powers the capability to reach decisions using the violence which they themselves are denied. Their reasons for preferring peace are the same as those governing their direct confrontation: A war which cannot be won, or in which the prospects of real victory are remote and difficult to visualize, is of no value to them. A small war may spread and involve either or both in massive risk for small possible profit. Even here the influence of the nuclear standoff is paradoxical, since control of conflict may require the active great power intervention the nuclear nations seek to avoid.

The small war belligerents have exploited the freedom afforded by this dilemma. When the superpowers have chosen restraint, combat has been pursued to exhaustion or completion. When some intervention has been exercised, the small states have skillfully manipulated their bargaining position between the powers. The significant dual developments of great power preoccupation with conflict control and the demise of the bipolar system have afforded the small powers an unexpected amount of freedom in employment of military force. Thus it may be said that modern weaponry, as long as it remains narrowly distributed, is a poor way to fight a war but a remarkably effective device for preventing one. The continuing proliferation of nuclear weapons promises to upset commonly accepted views about their deterrent effects. New nuclear states such as Great Britain, the People's Republic of China, and France, although attaining only a marginal edge in military "power" vis-à-vis the United States and the Soviet Union, have greatly enhanced their prestige and created serious political repercussions within their military blocs and geographic regions. This lesson is not lost upon other states with the means of purchasing nuclear technology, and is a variable in recent trends in nuclear proliferation.

Such nonnuclear states as West Germany and Japan, potentially facing an intransigent nuclear-armed opponent, have deliberately retained the technological options necessary to achieve nuclear capability at manageable cost within a relatively short period of time. The acquisition of nuclear capability by India demonstrates that the allure of becoming a nuclear power is strong among the less-developed countries of the world. A number of these states—Pakistan, Brazil, South Korea, Egypt, and Iran, for example—seem capable of producing nuclear weapons without undue economic dislocations.

Whatever the reasons states seek nuclear arms, the uncertainties of nuclear proliferation and its strategic consequences will probably continue. As ownership of nuclear weapons expands, the mathematical probability of their use increases. The political and military pressures demanding their use are not as great, but still quite as predictable. Whether these influences will be balanced by the deterrent effect of the "balance of terror" and the responsibile awareness of "nuclearhood" remains a major uncertainty in the late-twentieth-century nuclear environment.

The Declining Credibility of Military Force

The balance of terror not only makes war irrelevant to policy, but also deprives military power of much of its credibility as a coercive or persuasive technique in the course of ordinary political confrontation. The *credibility* of the threat of violence as a tool of policy is no more than a partial function of the threat. Of even greater importance today is the *likelihood* of its being made a reality. The sheer enormity of contemporary threats, especially mounted by nuclear states, is greater than at any earlier period of history. Their impact on affairs, however, is almost negligible, since it is so unlikely that the threatening state will make good its menace.

We see the consequences of this development at every turn. The fear of escalation to nuclear war influences the superpowers to make every effort to avoid direct confrontation. Threats of dire consequences made by nuclear states against lesser opponents lack credibility and are therefore simply not viable instruments of policy. Even in great power confrontations, the nuclear giants search for conventional military forces to implement a "nuclear" strategy that they are neither spiritually nor politically prepared to use. Among nonnuclear powers, where more traditional calculations might be expected to hold sway, the variety of restraints render once-dominant military superiorities less forceful. Ironically, however, stability on the nuclear level may lead to instability on the conventional level. The lack of utility of nuclear force means that the use of conventional force may become more likely. The balance of terror renders a nuclear response to provocation unthinkable. Therefore, the use of conventional force to achieve certain goals is indeed possible. As the nuclear powers and their proxies have become accustomed to the environment of possible mutual annihilation, they have edged with increasing temerity away from the view that the use of military force is restricted to either total war or complete abstinence. They have begun to operate once again in the gradations of force between the poles.

The End of Status

The declining credibility of military power has threatened to erode (but not eliminate) the status system that regulates the relations of states. The old classification of states into categories of rank and privilege based upon their respective military capabilities has been substantially invalidated. Great powers could not receive deference if they could not act in the way expected of great powers.

States of all military levels approach each other on a basis of theoretical status equality. The deference and privilege enjoyed by each in a particular relationship is a function of the specific situation and their respective range of capabilities, and cannot be inferred in advance from any generalized characteristics or self-image. The essence of a status or class system is a fixed stratification of groups, and military capacity long functioned as the determinant of a state's level. No universally accepted criterion of rank has arisen to replace military power, although economic power may be a more relevant measure of influence than traditional calculations of military might. Militarily inferior states such as Japan and the members of the Organization of Petroleum Exporting Countries (OPEC) wield much more international clout than their limited military forces would indicate. The burgeoning number of newly independent states in the past two decades has rendered the global social system more fluid and less structured today than it has been since its inception. There are no habitual "leaders," no "inner circle" of dominant powers that consistently give shape to the patterns of world politics—except insofar as the nuclear states can keep attention riveted on themselves by virtue of the destructive capacity they control.

The Utility of Military Force Today

Are we arguing that military force and the institution of organized armed conflict has lost all relevance to contemporary world politics? In strict conceptual terms, the temptation to adopt that position is strong, but a glance at the real world suggests that military power retains much of its capacity to render a decision in an increasing number of special cases. A brief catalogue of these instances will not only measure the relevance of war today, but also highlight some salient characteristics of the contemporary political world.

The first present-day situation in which military force is useful is one in which a leader of a major bloc uses armed force to subdue a rebellious or recalcitrant military dependency. Classic instances were Soviet intervention in Hungary in 1956 and in Czechoslovakia in 1968. With the threat of violent intervention thus made credible armed forces may be used by the bloc leaders to coerce maverick satellites, with the contingent mission of reinforcing indigenous bloc forces if violence flares. The rigidity of the bloc's international position effectively inhibits the likelihood of an attempt at interference from any outside source, specifically from the other bloc.

The worldwide competition between the superpowers has led to the development of "proxy" relationships whereby a smaller state is supported in its efforts by one of the major powers. Consequently, a new range of "proxy wars" has materialized. Proxy-patron relationships have assumed a surprising degree of complexity and unpredictability on all levels.

Probably the most conspicuous example of one form of this device was the extensive Chinese and Soviet support given North Korea during the Korean War of 1950–1953. The pattern there of proxy versus great power multilateral force was altered by the appearance of Mainland Chinese "volunteers" who fought a large part of the battle.

The Indo-Pakistani wars of 1965 and 1971 also demonstrate the complex and confusing nature of proxy relationships. The United States was caught in a conflict where both combatants were proxies, while the USSR was supporting a demiproxy, India, against a strategically important neighbor, Pakistan, which was backed by the Chinese. Under such confusing circumstances, the haste of the great powers to achieve some kind of peace is understandable.

The Arab-Israeli conflicts of 1967 and 1973 illustrate yet another kind of proxy war, but one on three levels, where one bloc leader, the United States, played patron to segments of both sides. The United States resisted the Soviet drive to polarize the region into Arab-USSR and American-Israeli blocs by keeping a foot in both camps—supporting moderate Arabs while also sending massive amounts of aid to Israel. The increasingly close relationship between the United States and Egypt in the mid-1970s indicated that the United States would become even more committed to both sides, since it could not lend support to Egypt without corresponding assurances of Israeli security. The peril inherent in assisting two proxy states which are themselves antagonists was demonstrated in 1977 when Somalia expelled the Soviets because of continuing Soviet support of Ethiopia, with whom Somalia was in conflict over the Ogaden region.

The emergence of wars of national liberation in the less-developed states has lent still another aspect to the texture of proxy wars in this decade. They have provided ideological justification as well as practical opportunities to play out the great power conflicts through proxies in the Third World. Involvements in recent years have included Soviet-Chinese support of the Pathet Lao in Laos, the MPLA in Angola, the FLN rebels in Algeria, and the Viet Cong in Vietnam.

Vietnam illustrates the dynamic quality of these conflicts. Their character changes as the great power proxy relationships shift. From its origins as a civil-internal guerrilla war with outside support originating in both blocs, it evolved, with the massive U.S. assistance that triggered USSR-North Vietnamese reaction, into an international war much like the Korean conflict. The relationship of the combatants, with a major power fighting a proxy of another, and the nature of the fighting were very similar to the earlier Asian conflict. Thus the conflict moved from the guerrilla-internal war side of the spectrum toward conventional war-direct great power involvement, a development which illustrated that great powers will engage in "limited" conventional military actions in the nuclear age.

Another example of the use of military force which may become more prevalent, especially if major power intervention in "small wars" persists in being as unsatisfactory as the U.S. experience in Vietnam, is in conventional combat between small states. Wars in sub-Saharan Africa or South and Latin America may not invite great power participation because the costs outweigh the benefits of their intervening. Mutual indifference will also deter interference, although political and military developments, possibly instigated by a third power, may change the calculations of the major powers. Intervention in these cases would not be unlike proxy war situations. Great powers may also refrain from intervening in small state wars because they fear escalation to the nuclear level, although this constraint seems less compelling now than a decade ago.

Significantly, modern experience has indicated that military power may be used to obtain political decisions by groups of small states acting under authority given by the United Nations or regional organizations.

Examples of where United Nations troops have been used successfully are in the Sinai following the 1973 Middle East War and on Cyprus following the Greek-Turkish dispute in 1974. However, a realistic appraisal of U.N. peacekeeping in the nuclear age would conclude that little can be done in the face of great power intransigence.

Despite the instances listed above, however, the range of effective military action to influence behavior in the interstate system is quite narrow. At the superpower level, the problem of relating contemporary military capability to foreign policy objectives will continue to defy solution until military specialists and political leaders learn more about the implications of modern technology as applied to war. Smaller powers are also faced with the problem of understanding and handling the use of military force within an uncertain and dynamic great power milieu which provides no safe or predictable frame of reference for their operations.

New Doctrines and the Military Dilemma

We must not suppose that military experts have remained suspended in bemusement at the massive effect of the new technology of warfare on their profession. On the contrary, military and civilian analysts in all countries have been devoting great effort to coming to terms with the changed conditions of war. Out of this enterprise have come a great number of new doctrines and concepts, covering a broad gamut of situations, but analogous in their attempt to develop an intellectual base for warfare in the modern world.

The Importance of Military Doctrine

The scope of modern warfare is so vast and its instruments so complex that it would be impossible to conduct a campaign without a doctrine governing the military process. A military doctrine spells out a series of assumptions about the nature and conditions of combat and the calculations controlling its initiation, prosecution, and termination. Military doctrine also resolves in advance the dilemmas inherent in battlefield operations: the relative importance of conserving materiel compared with conserving life, the respective roles of position and maneuver, the concept of "firepower" as opposed to that of occupation of territory, and so on. Military doctrine, by developing a mental framework within which operational decisions can be made, makes the task of modern commanders manageable.

Military doctrine occupies a central place in the capability judgments of a state. Since it governs the makeup of the military machine, the principles that will affect its employment, and the point of view and professional orientation of its officer corps, doctrine is one of the filters through which raw military potential must pass before a sophisticated evaluation can be made of a state's real military capacity. American military doctrine has always emphasized firepower and maneuvering as the ingredients of victory, and has always argued that the offensive is both less costly and more productive than a defensive posture. Preservation of manpower has always ranked higher than that of materiel. The maintenance at all times of a force ready to fight is another standard American tenet, although one developed only since World War II. These principles contrast with the relatively low rank given by Chinese military thought to the conservation of life, and the emphasis on small-group irregular tactics developed by Mao Tse-tung. Soviet doctrine emphasizes massed firepower and places less emphasis on maneuvering and mobility. All of these considerations (to which analogues could be found in military doctrines of all states) have a significant effect on the way the state's armed forces are constructed and used. They are important to both the foreign policy planner contemplating military action and the policymaker evaluating the potential of another state.

The Doctrinal Crisis: Is This a New Era?

The great crisis currently facing scholars of military doctrine involves an estimate of the impact of the new technology on the classic principles of warfare. Do these rules of strategy and tactics—evolved over the centuries and absorbing earlier technological advances from the bow and arrow to the tank, the "blockbuster" aerial bomb, and the technique of "vertical envelopment" by airborne forces—still apply in the era of thermonuclear warheads on intercontinental ballistic missiles? One school of thought argues that changes in warfare are entirely quantitative and not qualitative, and that the historic doctrines of warfare need only adapt to new conditions. Another group contends that modern weaponry has changed the meaning of warfare, and entirely new concepts are needed before men can exploit this as-yet-untried range of capability.

Traditionalists argue that the new weapons are no more than advanced versions of classic types. A thermonuclear bomb has the explosive potential of 50 million tons of TNT. Although a frightening figure, this comparison suggests that it would be possible to duplicate the blast of a hydrogen bomb by traditional means. Missiles are no more than improved delivery systems; the entire history of warfare involves gradual advance in delivery techniques, from the individual footsoldier carrying his spear, through rifleman, cavalryman, tanker, airplane pilot, and now the missile operator. Each advance, although not eliminating the human element, has involved increases in both the speed and reliability of the delivery of a weapon to its target. Thus, the argument goes, there is no conceptual difference between the doctrines of Caesar's legions and those of contemporary ICBM squadrons—only the technical details of mobilizing and employing the individuals and material are new.

The opposite position stems from the belief that destructive capabilities, such as those of hydrogen bombs and delivery systems using precision guidance and multiple independently targetable warheads, have made a travesty of the established doctrines of warfare. Not only have modern weapons endangered the survival of the political system that they are supposed to regulate, but they have also made war a cruel deception and a recipe for holocaust.

Advocates of new doctrines go in two different directions from this basic premise. One school contends that a new theory of total war must be developed, founded on principles different from historic practice and emphasizing the major characteristics of the new weapons: destructiveness and rapidity of delivery. The other group contends that war has been rendered obsolete, and that the principal military mission of the future will be to prevent recurrence of combat rather than to win a war.

The doctrinal dispute wages unabated, and policymakers remain suspended between passivity and recklessness while the experts wrangle. There seems little likelihood that any normally prudent policymakers will take the risk intrinsic to modern war until they have resolved the doctrinal dilemma to their own satisfaction. So long as military specialists continue to deepen the gaps between the several schools of thought, the use of armed force on an organized basis by any major state remains only a remote possibility.

Doctrines of Total War

DETERRENCE. Deterrence—the capacity of modern weapons to dissuade another state from initiating warfare—is one of the pervasive doctrines of the new military era. This notion has always been part of military lore, but the peculiar qualities of the new techniques make deterrence more significant than ever before.

Much thought has gone into the ramifications of the deterrent mission of modern military establishments. The development of massive nuclear arsenals by both major powers led to the acceptance of "nuclear parity," whereby each side recognized that any attempt to achieve nuclear superiority would result only in a reescalation of the arms race. Deterrence came to be based on "assured destruction," the premise that a state's retaliatory capacity should be sufficient such that, regardless of the damage inflicted by a first strike, the enemy would immediately receive an unacceptable amount of return damage to its cities, industrial capacity, and clusters of population. This "countervalue" theory has been supplemented by the "counterforce" concept that bases deterrence on the development of capability sufficiently well aimed to destroy the enemy's military capacity while leaving cities and population relatively intact. In practice, all states with adequate productive capability have attempted a policy that partakes of both capabilities. The ultimate deterrent, regardless of the counterforce-countervalue mix, remains the ability of a state to assure an unacceptable level of damage to another state's society.

Deterrence is the mission for which modern weapons are extremely appropriate. Their indiscriminate and uncertain effect, and the fact that the "new generation" of weaponry has never been used in combat, make policymakers extremely cautious and susceptible to being deterred. It is paradoxical that such refined and sophisticated military technology has proved best suited for making war an unwise gamble, rather than for winning it.

THE NATURE OF RESPONSE. Conceptually part of the deterrent policy, but a considerable doctrinal issue in itself, is the question of the response a state should take to a military-political provocation. As in deterrence, several different approaches have been proposed. We shall look at the way the controversy has developed in the United States, although all major states are seized by the issue.

An early school of thought favored "instantaneous response," more popularly known as "massive retaliation." Americans advancing this argument contended that any direct Soviet-American armed conflict was inevitably a total war, and urged that whatever strategic advantage lay in the first strike should be retained by the United States. The theory of response, therefore, was that the moment a Soviet provocation crossed the threshold of tolerability, the full weight of American nuclear capability was to be unleashed on the entire spectrum of targets in the USSR. The advocates of this doctrine insisted that it not only insured the optimum basis for accepting total war, but also contributed to the efficacy of deterrence. No aggressor, certain that total war would result, would risk breaching an admittedly unclear measure of tolerance.

When the policy of massive retaliation was espoused in the mid-1950s, the United States possessed the ability to destroy the military forces of the USSR with little likelihood of serious retaliatory damage. The rapid growth of Soviet strategic nuclear power undermined the assumptions of massive retaliation. The balance of terror meant that the threat of massive retaliation was to some degree reciprocal. Therefore, the United States could not massively retaliate in any general or large-scale war without risking enormous damage at home from Soviet strategic forces.

A second major implication of the balance of terror was that strategic nuclear forces were much less credible in the deterrence of local aggression. Critics of massive retaliation argued that the threat was not effective in deterring local or limited war because it was not believable. As a result of such criticisms, a more sophisticated position known generally as "flexible response" has been developed. Its basic rationale is that the United States should not commit itself to an all-out immediate response to a challenge, but should allow itself a "pause for decision" before taking action, and then respond only at a level adequate to neutralize the immediate threat. Responsibility for escalating the conflict will rest upon the enemy, and the United States will be free from the danger of initiating an unnecessary total war.

American policy, long officially committed to instantaneous response, has shifted to a version of flexible response, with a wide range of force capabilities that provide multiple response options across the force continuum. Although this was hailed as a basic doctrinal overhaul, the United States still overtly retains the right to initiate nuclear warfare in the event of an unbearable but nonnuclear provocation from the Soviet Union. This proviso, built into the doctrine, furnishes the doctrinal and tactical link between past and present policy.

LIMITED NUCLEAR OPTIONS. Mutual invulnerability of weapons systems and the low probability of success have, in the eyes of many, stabilized the nuclear deterrence environment. The United States has developed increasingly invulnerable retaliatory weapons systems such as the Trident nuclear missile submarine and the cruise missile. The USSR has also developed weapons systems with low vulnerabilities, giving it essentially the same second-strike destructive capability as the United States. Since an attacker would be destroyed regardless of the size of the attack, there is no advantage, and hence no incentive, to launch a first strike. Since the United States is strategically more interested in deterrence than in initiating war, it must maintain great retaliatory capability and yet avoid increasing tension and the probability of war. However, if deterrence fails, it must be capable of successfully conducting and limiting the war that has been forced upon it.

In the mid-1970s, the United States promulgated a new American doctrine of limited nuclear options. In order to limit the chance of uncontrolled escalation if war occurred, the United States introduced flexibility into its nuclear employment planning by incorporating the capability to react in a selective and controlled way against enemy military targets. Such a capability, it is argued, would enable the United States to tailor its strategic response to the nature of the provocation rather than being forced to choose between responding massively against enemy cities or doing nothing. Since there is great uncertainty about how a nuclear war might start, responses should be available to deal with a wide range of possibilities.

Opponents of limited nuclear options claim that as nuclear war becomes more manageable, it also becomes more likely. A policy of "limiting" a nuclear response might mean that the horrors of nuclear weapons would become obscured. The ability to destroy only military targets, sparing population centers, seems to lower the cost of nuclear war, and the psychological barriers inhibiting policymakers from employing nuclear weapons might be weakened. Further, leaders might believe that a limited response could be controlled, implying a degree of precision that belies the traditional notions of nuclear retaliation.

Nevertheless, as the major powers have accepted the states of nuclear parity, they have come to view additional weapons systems and upgraded capabilities in terms of war fighting and war termination, should deterrence fail. While it is hardly an enjoyable prospect, the fact remains that analysis of such an event requires deliberate and thoughtful treatment prior to its occurrence if the pressures for escalation to general nuclear war are to be avoided.

DEFENSE AND SURVIVAL. Estimates of the casualities that would be produced by a nuclear attack on an urbanized state are uncertain—since no one knows what would actually happen—but all are terribly high. Concern over the prohibitive cost in human life has produced considerable studies of civil defense prospects for national survival after a major blow.

The discussions cluster around two major points. One concerns the defensive measures civilian populations might take, including evacuation, shelter, permanent underground installations, and fallout and radiation protection. The entire subject suffers from a number of conceptual and practical difficulties: Since there is no reliable experience on which to build, the extent to which the theorists and responsible officials are themselves persuaded of the utility of their measures is debatable, and public fatalism and widespread apathy reflect a profound belief that initiation of nuclear war is simply the end of everything. No major state has more than scratched the surface in the field of passive defense, although the Soviet Union has a much more substantive program than does the United States.

Theorists of recuperation also have little evidence to support their dogmas. Their usual criterion is the rapidity with which the attacked state might be expected to restore its productive plant to preattack levels, and estimates vary according to the optimism of analysts and their evaluations of their opponent's strategy. Only a few theorists have addressed the question of human response to a destructive attack and inquired into the extent to which battered survivors would perform public reconstruction after their private lives had been shattered. It is generally agreed that a nuclear onslaught would destroy political democracy and individual freedom. How would a population accustomed to an open society respond to the imposition of an authoritarian regime in the midst of smoking ruins and wholesale death?

The size and destructive capability of modern nuclear arsenals have muted discussion of defense, survival, and reconstruction. The concept of assured destruction seems to have resigned the populations of the world to their fate as nuclear hostages. Until a credible defense system seems possible, initiation of total war will remain a risk of unpredictable dimension.

Doctrines of Limited War

We have scrutinized the doctrines advanced and developed by theorists of total war. However, since war continues at the nonnuclear level, it is obvious that the balance of terror and reciprocal deterrence have not eliminated warfare that is less than total. Limited war doctrines acknowledge the deterrent power of nuclear weapons, but challenge their universal effectiveness. That is, nuclear weapons may deter a *nuclear* attack, but they are not credible deterrents against relatively minor provocations. Such challenges can best be met by conventional responses, with the ensuing conflicts fought to a political decision without escalating into apocalyptic conflagration.

What does the concept of "limited war" mean in a nuclear age? To say that all wars short of general nuclear war are limited may be accurate, but analytically unsatisfactory. What distinguishes limited war from total war? Limited war involves an important kind and degree of restraint—deliberate restraint. This deliberate restraint can be thought of in terms of limitations—limitations on *objectives* and limitations on *means.*

When the power available to one or both contenders is physically limitless, there must be a degree of self-restraint imposed on political objectives. An attempt to obtain total victory might force the conflict across a threshold beyond which the costs to both contenders vastly exceed the potential gains to either. In limited war, therefore, the extremes of the possible-outcome continuum (total victory and total defeat) become practically irrelevant. Both contenders must be willing to tolerate an outcome neither had foreseen, and in which the objectives of both are achieved imperfectly or not at all. Successful limitation thus paradoxically presumes a relatively high degree of cooperation between the belligerents. The losing side must avoid expanding its wartime objectives and hence its military operations. The pressures for escalation operate on both sides. Limitation is, then, a cooperative process.

CONVENTIONAL WAR. The most common formulation of the limited war position is cast in terms of "conventional war"—war fought with high-explosive rather than nuclear weapons. The traditional division between conventional war and nuclear war is blurred by the introduction of "tactical" nuclear warheads, some with yields in the high-explosive range. Debate persists over the advisability of employing any nuclear weapons, even in a limited role. Most analysts agree that when the nuclear "firebreak" is crossed, the complex relationship among the stationing of the tactical systems, their ranges, their basic nature (aircraft, artillery, missile), and the strategies under which they are employed may lead to a rapid self-propelling jump to total war. Contrary arguments are possible, but the great uncertainties associated with the introduction of tactical nuclear weapons to the battlefield generally exclude them from the range of attractive military options in "limited war," and they have been relegated to a deterrent role (as in Europe) or to the status of additional help if deterrence fails. This argument suggests that the balance of deterrence is absolute, and that conventional and traditional military calculations can proceed almost as if nuclear weapons had never been invented. Indeed, as we discussed above, some analysts believe that nuclear parity has increased rather than decreased the credibility and utility of conventional war.

Conventional warriors in the Western world have pressed their case with skill and determination, but the Soviet line has not been encouraging to their position. Soviet pronouncements have suggested that Moscow feels that any direct Soviet-Western conflict would escalate into all-out nuclear exchange, and that conventional military doctrines cannot provide any rationale for such a struggle. It is possible that this Soviet position is part of Moscow's own deterrent strategy, and perhaps the limited war theorists are correct. In the face of such a grim warning, however, few Western leaders are willing to gamble survival on their ability to keep an open clash with Moscow from becoming a total war.

The record of the Cold War period indicates that the West can meet Communists on the battlefield without the war becoming total, as shown by the experiences of Korea, Vietnam, and other crises. However, since limited war means limiting political objectives, a war between nuclear powers can be kept at a subnuclear level only if each side recognizes the imperative requirement for self-restraint and limits its objectives accordingly. The lesson was learned in Korea and relearned (with variations) in Vietnam. The Vietnam War demonstrated the use of military power to gain military and political objectives but, as we shall see, represented the inappropriate application of a limited war strategy in a revolutionary war environment.

REVOLUTIONARY WAR. Revolutionary war has become an increasingly frequent phenomenon during the latter part of the twentieth century. The causes of revolutionary war are varied but usually stem from economic, social, racial, religious, or colonial dissatisfactions. Since nuclear deterrence has little impact on the initiation and prosecution of revolutionary war, such wars may become the most prevalent setting for the use of military force in the last quarter of the century.

The U.S. involvement in Vietnam focused attention on the nature of revolutionary conflict and the role of military force in a counterrevolutionary environment. As a form of strategy, counterinsurgency is applicable only in those special situations where the basic ingredients are present: a population alienated from its government and gripped by widespread disaffection, and a government that lacks energy and efficiency in dealing with both the guerrilla threat and the social-economic-political conditions that spawned the revolution in the first place. It is of limited relevance to those states, including most leaders of the Western bloc, whose interest lies less in overturning governments and promoting revolution than in stabilizing and harmonizing relationships. Counterrevolutionary activity—strategically a doctrine of defense rather than attack—has an unquestionable military dimension, but just as the revolution has its roots in social unrest, so campaigns against guerrillas must be based on social reform, and use military operations as a fringe effort rather than as their ideological and operational center. Military force in a revolutionary war must be used to achieve political ends.

The failure of U.S. policy in Vietnam was ultimately based on the misconception that the war could be prosecuted using a strategy of limited war wherein the application of military force would bring the Viet Cong and North Vietnamese to negotiate a tolerable outcome. American objectives, limited from the start, became increasingly more limited under domestic and international pressure, whereas the objectives of the revolutionaries were total—reunification of all Vietnam under the leadership of the North. The use of military force may be necessary in a revolutionary war, but only vigorous political action by the existing government to address the cause of the revolution will ultimately succeed.

The Arms Race, Arms Control, and Transfers

With the logic of military action so open to question under contemporary conditions, it is not surprising that states have been pursuing the issue of securing some release from the grim pressure of potential destruction.

Two interacting political trends have accompanied the doctrinal and conceptual discussion of military matters since the dawn of the nuclear era. The major military powers have embarked on a massive arms race conducted primarily in the categories of new weapons and delivery systems. At the same time, significant efforts have been made to discover workable formulas for arms reduction, arms control, and—at least in principle—eventual total disarmament.

Each of these enterprises is really an almost instinctive attempt by governments to develop a larger margin of relative security in a world grown more dangerous. Both are understandable and merit sympathetic analysis, yet each tends to cancel out the other and leave the system as it would have been. Neither the arms race nor disarmament has made the world any more secure.

The Arms Race

The arms race between the Soviet bloc and the Western bloc, essentially a technical rather than a military contest, has been in effect for more than two decades. Each side seeks advances in quality as well as quantity of weapons. The major categories of effort include the increase in explosive "yield" of large nuclear bombs, the miniaturization of nuclear warheads for tactical purposes, the improvement of delivery systems—primarily in longer-range and more accurate missiles—and the development of multiple independently targetable reentry vehicles (MIRVs).

The rationale of the arms race is devastatingly simple. Although military theorists question whether either side can ever gain a meaningful advantage, neither dares to relax its effort lest the other succeed in achieving a technological and military breakthrough. Each new move brings its inevitable countermove, which in turn triggers another step, and so on.

Ample military and scientific arguments exist to justify indefinite prolongation of the race. There is much that the experts can accomplish in the improvement of old weapons and the development of newer and more sophisticated devices, so in this sense the arms race is actually a productive enterprise. In addition, every new move that makes weapons more effective and war more horrible also augments the deterrent effect of military power. A persuasive case can even be made for the arms race as a force for peace, in that it progressively narrows the range of military action enjoyed by states.

Yet there would seem to be a point of vanishing returns. When each side has developed a truly finite deterrent (possessing the capacity to destroy the other completely), any further refinement becomes merely "conspicuous consumption." The stakes become no more than prestige, with faint possibility of achieving any meaningful psychological advantage over the other contestant. However, as in the antiballistic missile (ABM) debate, there has occasionally risen a technological possibility which threatens to upset the precarious balance. In this case, there was danger that one major power, the Soviet Union, could so degrade the assured destruction capability of the other that mutual deterrence would be eroded to the point of dangerous instability. Part of the debate revolved around which measures to take—offensive or defensive—if the Soviet ABM was indeed effective. It was apparently technologically feasible to overwhelm the ABM offensively (through pure saturation and sophisticated tactics), possibly restoring the deterrent balance, but at the great additional cost always attending massive increases in total weapons systems. This grim prospect of a costly arms spiral upward with no prospective increase in security convinced the major powers that they should explore new ways to limit the arms race.

Strategic Arms Limitation

In May 1972, after some thirty months of negotiation, the first significant agreement on levels of nuclear armament was finalized by the United States and the Soviet Union in the form of a Strategic Arms Limitation Agreement containing an ABM Treaty and an Interim Agreement on offensive weapons.

The ABM Treaty, the tenure of which is indefinite, limited each signatory to the development of 200 of its ABMs in two equal fields. The treaty also established a number of prohibitions against qualitative improvements in ABM capabilities by banning space- and sea-based systems. In a 1974 amendment to the ABM Treaty, the United States and the Soviet Union agreed to limit ABM deployment to 100 missiles in one site. In 1976 the United States closed its operative site, while the Soviet Union continued to maintain a limited ABM capability around Moscow.

The Interim Agreement on the Limitation of Strategic Arms was an attempt to freeze certain aspects of the offensive weapons competition between the United States and USSR for a five-year period. The Interim Agreement dealt with intercontinental ballistic missiles (ICBMs) and submarine-launched ballistic missiles (SLBMs). It did not deal with manned bombers, tactical nuclear weapons, or intermediate-range missiles. A Protocol to the Interim Agreement translated certain provisions of the document into concrete figures, setting numerical limits on numbers of ICBMs and SLBMs. Although the Interim Agreement expired in October 1977, both sides pledged to abide by its provisions pending the outcome of negotiations for a second Strategic Arms Limitation Talks (SALT II) accord. Based on an agreement "in principle" signed at Vladivostok in

1974, the two sides continued trying to reach agreement to limit the numbers of all offensive strategic nuclear weapons and delivery vehicles. The arms control process has been complicated by the development of new strategic systems such as the American cruise missile and a new generation of Soviet heavy ICBMs. However, since SALT had become an important symbol of superpower cooperation, it appears that there would be a new agreement.

The Future of Arms Control

A dismal page in the history of world politics between 1945 and 1963 was the utter failure of any attempts to reach an agreement on arms reduction or arms control. All the abortive projects, different only in detail, shared the same fate. Plans were advanced for elimination of nuclear weapons, reduction of conventional armaments, cessation of nuclear testing, and various inspection schemes to reduce the probability of cheating or surprise attack. All came to inglorious ends, and the arms race appeared to have been accepted by the major powers as an acceptable substitute for arms control. Yet both East and West had embraced the principle that general and complete disarmament, except for international security forces, was the goal for which all must strive. Progress was halted, not on matters of principle, but on the nature and sequence of steps to be taken to achieve the eventual end. Each side had an initial sine qua non on which it has insisted in full knowledge that the other would reject it: the USSR demanded nuclear parity and abolition of nuclear weapons by treaty before it would consider any implementing steps, while the United States demanded full acceptance of a "control and inspection" system as a prerequisite to any consideration of the substance of disarmament. No negotiations were able to pass over this initial hurdle, and all broke off in mutual recriminations. The Soviets claimed American concern with inspection was a cloak for espionage, while the United States found the Soviet attempt to forbid use of nuclear weapons in war a sinister plot to undermine American security. With the advent of Soviet nuclear weapons parity and the celebrated political "detente," both sides have been able to overlook prior objections and initiate some encouraging steps toward arms control accommodation. These steps include the Nuclear Test Ban Treaty (1963), a treaty barring the interjection of nuclear weapons into outer space, signed in 1966; the Nuclear Non-Proliferation Treaty of 1968; the Sea Bed Treaty of 1972, which prohibits weapons on the ocean floor: the Threshold Test Ban Treaty (1974), limiting the size of nuclear explosions to 150 kilotons; and the SALT I Agreement, discussed above.

Arms control negotiations conducted in 1978 included the efforts for a followup on the Strategic Arms Limitation Agreement, Mutual and Balanced Force Reduction talks designed to reduce force levels in central Europe, attempts to limit the level of military presence in the Indian Ocean, and preliminary consultations on a comprehensive test ban agreement to eliminate all nuclear explosions, for both military and peaceful purposes.

The lengthening list of arms control agreements and negotiations, however heartening, does not mean that the threat of nuclear war has been eliminated. Technological advances in weapons systems have multiplied the destructive power of each superpower's nuclear arsenal even as agreements designed to limit them have been instituted. States do not sign arms control agreements for altruistic or humanitarian purposes; they must serve the national interest. However, such agreements can reduce the probability of war by reducing tensions or limiting the levels of armaments. They will serve as a valuable instrument in developing an environment in which the threat of nuclear destruction is not the preeminent fact of international life and in moving toward the eventual demise of the "balance of terror."

The Role of Political Decision

The root of the difficulty in reaching agreement about disarmament lies in the political preconceptions each side has brought to the analysis of issues of arms control. So long as both camps feel their security is better served by a continuing arms race, disarmament will remain an ephemeral goal. So long as both prefer the great but familiar risks of open conflict to the unknown dangers of living under military wraps in an untried and possibly entrapping control system, there is not enough appeal in the new to justify abandonment of the old. So long as the shadow of the Cold War persists, arms reduction (which would inevitably tend to stabilize relations) is of limited political value.

Disarmament, like the arms race, is much more a political than a military and technical question. The arms race is not a *cause* of the tension between East and West. Thus arms control itself will not ease conditions. The Cold War period had been a political exercise, and the recent thaw has demanded new political judgments as well. Only when Moscow and Washington both conclude that their need for military defense systems has decreased will further realistic disarmament discussions be possible. Only the future can state with certainty whether the tensions of the age will permit such a reassessment of the political situation. No one now alive knows if humankind has enough time to devise an escape from the military dilemma in which it has placed itself.

Arms Transfers

Arms transfers between supplier and recipient governments has become a major contentious issue within the present global system. By any reasonable standard of measurement, the great powers, particularly the United States, are the leading suppliers of military equipment to less developed countries. During fiscal year 1978, for example, the United States will enter into agreements to supply more than $13 billion of such equipment. This will bring to more than $120 billion the total American arms transfers to other countries since 1950.

Most independent states have some kind of armed forces to ensure internal order, territorial integrity, and national dignity. Whether new or old, superpower or ministate, few states judge themselves able to maintain only a constabulary rather than a military establishment. In 1977, the military expenditures of 142 countries amounted to approximately $400 billion. Most of these countries have no arms industry, or at best a rudimentary one, and must acquire military equipment from other more industrialized states on a cash, credit, or grant basis. Basic issues for the United States, are where it should apply military equipment, type of equipment it should supply and in which instances it should exercise restraint in selling weapons of war.

Arms transfers occur through training, technology, and actual sale of military equipments. The United States provides economic supporting assistance in order to reduce the budgetary burden associated with purchases of new arms or training of military personnel. Arms transfers are motivated by profit, minimizing research and development costs, and security considerations.

Recommended Readings

ARON, RAYMOND. *On War.* New York: W. W. Norton & Co., 1968.

BRODIE, BERNARD. *Strategy in the Missile Age* (rev. ed.). Princeton, N.J.: Princeton University Press, 1971.

BULL, HEDLEY. *The Control of the Arms Race.* New York: Frederick A. Praeger, 1965.

CLAUSEWITZ, KARL VON, ed. *On War.* Princeton, N.J.: Princeton University Press, 1976.

FARLEY, PHILIP J. et al. *Arms Across the Sea.* Washington, D.C. The Brookings Institution, 1978.

KAHAN, JEROME H. *Security in the Nuclear Age: Developing U.S. Strategic Arms Policy.* Washington, D.C. The Brookings Institution, 1975.

KAHN, HERMAN. *On Thermonuclear War* (2nd ed.). New York: Free Press, 1969.

KISSINGER, HENRY A. *Nuclear Weapons and Foreign Policy.* New York: W. W. Norton & Co., 1969.

KNORR, KLAUS, ed. *Historical Dimensions of National Security Problems.* Lawrence: University Press of Kansas, 1976.

LONG, FRANKLIN A., and GEORGE W. RATHJENS, eds. *Arms, Defense Policy, and Arms Control.* New York: W. W. Norton & Co., 1976.

MARTIN, LAWRENCE. *Arms and Strategy.* New York: David McKay Co., 1973.

NEWHOUSE, JOHN. *Cold Dawn: The Story of SALT.* New York: Holt, Rinehart & Winston, 1973.

RUSSELL, BERTRAND. *Common Sense and Nuclear Warfare.* New York: AMS Press, 1974, repr. 1959.

SAMPSON, ANTHONY. *The Arms Bazaar: From Lebanon to Lockheed.* New York: Viking Press, 1977.

SCHELLING, THOMAS C. *Arms and Influence* (repr. ed.). Westport, Conn.: Greenwood, 1976 (original printing, 1966).

SNYDER, GLENN H. *Deterrence and Defense: Toward a Theory of National Security.* Princeton, N.J.: Princeton University Press, 1961.

WALTZ, KENNETH N. *Man, the State, and War.* New York: Columbia University Press, 1959.

WRIGHT, QUINCY. *A Study of War* (2nd ed.) (2 volumes). Chicago: Chicago University Press, 1965.

YORK, HERBERT F. *Race to Oblivion.* New York: Simon and Schuster, 1970.

Ideology, Nationalism, and Prestige

10

One of the features of contemporary world politics that distinguishes it from the "classic" pattern of an earlier era is the manipulation of mass beliefs and popular ideas by decision makers. The emergence of mass movements of vast size and irresistible force has diluted the once-exclusive control of foreign policy exercised by highly skilled elites. Careful strategic calculations are now explained in simplistic formulations of international reality, their relevance in no way mitigating the militancy with which they are defended. Mass as well as individual ways of thinking are manipuated by the national and international political process.

Ideology and World Politics

In a manner unknown to history since the great shocks of the Renaissance, the Reformation, and the Industrial Revolution washed away the underpinnings of the unified society of the Middle Ages, individuals have turned to all-encompassing belief systems to explain reality. In contrast to the *rational person* who was the ideal of the eighteenth century and the *optimistic person* who characterized the nineteenth, the present century has at its center the *"true believer."* Individuals adrift in a universe that grows more difficult to comprehend and cope with every day increasingly find relief and comfort in systematic, comprehensive systems of belief.

This tendency, running through the entire fabric of social life, is sharply reinforced in matters concerning world politics. The world has grown uncomfortably smaller, and national groups everywhere have been wrenched from a cultural isolation that had endured in some cases for centuries. However, the great increase in the number of global problems demanding solution has been accompanied by a marked decrease in the probability of their solution. Faced with an agonizing dilemma of impossible choices, entire societies have fled from the reality of coexistence (in its non-Communist and literal sense) to the refuge in an ideological utopia. Present-day states have given the conduct of international political relations a measure of tension, danger, and potential explosiveness that has no parallel in history. The secular rationalism of contemporary ideologies has moved beliefs from the realm of religion to the arena of politics.

Ideology also thrives in an environment of limited resources and choices for action, while pragmatism, the opposite side of ideology, characterizes societies with abundant resources. Thus, ideology functions to manipulate scarcity. This accounts for the popularity of radical ideologies in the poorer states of the Third World. Conversely, richer states mold ideologies that justify and legitimize their control of power and wealth. Max Weber studied the simultaneous rise of Protestantism and Capitalism in the Western world and concluded that the two mutually reinforced each other. The capitalist mentality successfully solidified the Protestant ideology, and the Protestant ideology provided rationale for the possession of wealth and power—it was ordained by God.

Because ideologies represent material positions, they are bound to clash. The self-righteous protection of an ideology is logical because the ideology symbolizes a personal and collective life style. Any threat to the ideology is taken as a direct attack on personal life style. The death of an ideology is seen as the death of self.

Ideologies, then, depend primarily on the wealth of a state, and there is a link between the level of technology and the success of a belief system. The ideological conflicts that may rage in the coming decades are bound to be shaped by the commodities that will be prized and sought after: food, energy, technology, liberty, and quality of life style.

In the aftermath of the World War II apocalypse, ideology became unfashionable, as evidenced by popularity of Judith Shklar's *After Utopia: The Decline of Political Faith* and Daniel Bell's *End of Ideology*. We must remember, though, that while some ideologies may die, from their ashes new ones are born. Still other ideologies may adapt, mutate, or otherwise change. Certainly the American system was altered by the socialism of the Great Depression. Marxism was modified by Lenin.

The Nature of Ideology

The term *ideology* was initially used when French revolutionaries wanted France to be governed by the principles of the French Revolution. Today, an ideology may be defined as a self-contained and self-justifying belief system that incorporates an overall world view and provides a basis for explaining all of reality. Beginning with certain postulates about the nature and role of the individual, it develops from these a theory of human history, a moral code, a sense of mission, and a program for action. All ideologies purport to embody absolute truth, reinforced with certain supernatural (or superhuman) justification. Adherence to the system is thus both a rational and a moral act, and disagreement is not only error but sin.

Ideologies are not new in world politics. Every system of government and every national group has at some time found it expedient to ground its international conduct on what it conceived as eternal verities. But the *mass movement,* defined here as an ideology with implications of social action which gathers sufficient adherents to become a real force, is a contemporary political phenomenon. Ideological formulations of international issues color the bulk of today's confrontations of states.

An ideological approach to world political problems displays certain marked characteristics. Ideology leads inescapably to the formulation of problems in moral terms. An international dispute thus becomes a clash between good and evil with the stakes never less than absolute vindication or total defeat. Ideological controversy (which is inevitable in any contact between states embodying total belief systems) is not susceptible to compromise or accommodation. No ideology permits bargaining with evil. Ideologically oriented policy can never "succeed" in the sense that strategic calculations can be crowned with success. States cannot kill ideas, only people; wiping out a population in no way destroys their unpopular beliefs.

Ideology and Foreign Policy

Ideologies have served historically to fill the needs of individuals usually by attempting to bridge the gap between the prevailing limits of reason and the psychological needs of individuals within a society. Although often beginning modestly, they tend to grow all encompassing and soon claim for themselves universal truth. Ideologies also show a propensity for becoming outmoded, going through stages of messianism, corruption, misuse, and eventually—as circumstances change—meaninglessness. They often lead to the generation of their antithesis. Ideological conflict, if disaster is to be avoided, requires that militancy be replaced by toleration, and hostility by mutual respect.

The role of ideology in world politics—how ideology affects foreign policy and the resulting implications for international relations—has become an increasingly important subject. This issue has been magnified by the challenge of present-day ideological formulations of world politics. One important question concerns whether a government's foreign policy is formulated according to dogmatic ideological tenets, or whether it follows the traditional method of realistic appraisal of concrete situations within the context of its individual national interests and the relevant information available concerning those situations.

Another question involves the overlap of theory and reality. Is there not a mixture of both ideology and realistic appraisal, although in varying degrees, in the formulation of foreign policy by almost all states? Every state is equipped with a priority system for the determination of foreign policy goals and tactics. There are certain levels of action in which either ideology or realism is predominant, and between these two extremes some sort of balance is achieved. There is, however, no fixed relationship that can be postulated; rather, ideology and realistic appraisal meet in each distinct situation of foreign policy, with different degrees of emphasis. In this context, ideology plays the smallest role in situations where choices are most restricted, but becomes increasingly effective when there is greater freedom of choice of alternative action possibilities. In attempting to discover which tendency—ideology or realistic appraisal— operates more strongly, it must be remembered that a state can remain consistent with its ideological tenets even though its actions appear strikingly at variance with its stated purposes.

What evidence is there for continuity of purpose? How may we determine to what extent ideology conditions foreign policy decisions? One must infer a state's intent from the content of a whole series of actions, and allow for a possible discrepancy between what is said and what is done. We cannot draw accurate conclusions from a series of statements, since verbal consistency does not necessarily imply consistency in action. There must be a connection, however, between ideology and action. The nature of the state dictates that its actions implement its real purposes, but not necessarily a verbalized ideology. The possible relevance of verbalizations cannot be completely discounted, but their importance depends upon whether actions bear them out.

The conflict is therefore between the systematic world view imposed by an ideological approach to action and the uneven, incomplete, and paradoxical fashion in which the real world impinges upon a state. Ideology and national interest both have their roots in a system of values, but they differ in how they dictate action. Ideological formulations make generous use of concepts of inevitability or impossibility, and lead to one-dimensional foreign policy thinking. A pragmatic national interest is fixed only in its (possibily utopian) view of the future, and is infinitely flexible in its intermediate goals and objectives and in the tactics adopted for their achievement.

Ideology may, of course, become the basis for formulating national interest and long-range goals. If these aspirations are deeply rooted in the social dynamic of a people, and if the government is adept at tactics, a successful foreign policy is possible. But if ideology intrudes into situational analysis and state action is made dependent on imperatives of belief, statecraft in the classic sense is left helpless.

Ideology: Myth and Reality

Individuals relate themselves to the facts of life by creating myths, which simultaneously shield them from the realities of social life and make those realities comprehensible to them. Political society is invariably validated by myth. Even such theorists as Hobbes and Locke, who appeal to reason for a basis of political society, posit such notions as "rational man" and "natural right."

The individual realizes that life without purpose adds up to nothing —it cannot be measured. Involvement in political society provides one measure of personal failures and achievements. Such political action expresses the human strategy, which subordinates reality to higher human priorities and goals. It also represents the human project, designed to give purpose and meaning to life. This is one way individuals refuse to accept reality. Determined to impose a new reality upon the earth, they are suspended between perpetual aspirations and perpetual frustrations.

International political life in the twentieth century reveals a discordant pluralism totally unsupported by a transcendent myth. Successful political action in such a world demands a convincing ideology, but the issue is not whether ideology is predicated upon myth, nor whether myth and reality are identical. An object is real in a given context only when it functions in that context. The myth of Pegasus had an operational reality in the Golden Age, but not in the modern concept of objective reality. Beauty exists in the public context of nature; art and heroes exist in the public context of history. In other words, contemporaneity begets reality; what exists in the present situation is real.

Myth is creative of reality when it becomes the substance of consensus in a given society. It is delusive when it confounds appearance with reality. Myths remain relevant until environmental change demolishes their institutional structures. Stripped of its supporting myth, the structure is vulnerable to revolutionary pressure—a new myth will eventually appear on the horizon. Potent as myths are in creating reality, however, they cannot form the exclusive or quasi-exclusive basis of behavior in world politics.

Ideological Formulations in World Politics

The post-World War II era marked a challenge to the traditional criteria and concepts of the classic international system. New formulations arose to compete with the time-honored precepts of statecraft. Their advocates sought, with varying success, to apply them in a nontraditional world. We may view these as ideologies, each seeking an appropriately changed situation in which to be applied.

By 1950, three such ideologies had found more or less precise expression, and their subsequent interplay has given the postwar world its definitive coloration and shape. Since any ideology other than simple nihilism must incorporate a utopian vision of perfect order, these doctrines may be initially compared in terms of the ideal each considered itself to be serving.

The first was, of course, the world view of Communism. Its utopian vision was of a classless and therefore stateless society where individuals would live in relatively unfettered community. Its operational emphasis was (and remains) protection of existing Communist beachheads in the world and, at a somewhat lower priority level, extension of Communist influence by persuasion, subversion, and war. Purporting to be "scientific," its perfect world order was postulated as attainable, feasible, and inevitable.

The second great utopia was projected by the United States. American doctrine envisages a world organized under law into a peaceful and harmonious society of states, where individual and group obligation to humankind placed limits on the freedom of states—a translation into world political terms of the familiar domestic political philosophy of Americans. Committed ideologically to free will and personal responsibility for action, the United States could not predict the inevitable realization of its dream, only its possibility.

The final ideology was the nonalignment of the anticolonial world, eventually given many specific forms but first verbalized clearly by independent India. Its utopia was a world almost entirely nonpolitical, in which distinctions among states were obliterated in favor of global cooperative efforts to elevate the material misery of the human race. In practice, this meant secession from the familiar problems of world affairs and continued emphasis on issues of development, race, and cultural diversity in the name of a higher morality.

From each of these utopian postures were derived formulations of the minimum requirements necessary for a believing state compelled to exist in a nonideal world. To Communists these included prevention of any hostile coalition strong enough to menace existing Communist systems and preservation of sufficient instability and tension in the non-

Communist world to permit continued expansion of Communist power. For Americans the requirements included adequate stability in the world to give existing mechanisms of international organization a chance to survive and grow, while at the same time preserving the uniquely favorable position enjoyed by the United States. Nonalignment requirements were somewhat more numerous, beginning with the simple idea of early liquidation of colonialism and extending to establishment of inhibitions and limitations on all major states by international mechanisms. The nonaligned wished "a plague on both your houses" to the superpowers, but generalized the curse to include all aspirants to high status and a broad sphere of power in the global system.

Out of the clash of these requirements has come the subject matter of world politics since 1945. The Cold War itself, especially in its acute phase, brought the minimum demands of the United States and the Soviet Union into close and often irreconcilable juxtaposition. Only in the latter years of the struggle (since approximately 1955) did the hostility between Moscow and Washington become restrained as the Third World demanded and received a hearing from both sides.

The Soviet Approach to the World: A Form of Communism

How does the Soviet Union approach the world? What are its operative assumptions? How does it construct its own mission? Through what sort of intellectual filter do Soviet decision makers see the outside world?

The Soviet Union, thanks to its official ideology and one-sided propaganda attack on domestic consensus, has a unified verbal answer to these and all related questions. Marxism and its later derivations profess to unlock the riddle of history and to enable true believers to understand the basic nature of world relations. The verbalized Soviet approach to the world has since 1917 been that of orthodox (as of any given moment) Communist theory.

The Soviet Union sees itself ideologically as a revolutionary power committed to the destruction of existing institutions and patterns and their replacement by an entirely new order. Such an approach necessitates the assumption that all existing international arrangements are inherently temporary (except those already under Soviet control) and subject to change by Soviet initiatives. Any understanding or agreement with non-Communist powers is by definition tentative and designed only to serve a long-range strategic purpose. Conflict is to be protracted indefinitely until victory crowns the entire effort and utopia becomes a fact.

A distinct evolution is apparent in the Soviet attitude. Beginning from a position of a great psychic and physical insecurity, Kremlin leadership felt obliged to strike a continuously militant pose and to fight with words battles they were incapable of prosecuting in action. As the processes of history have subtly modified the nature and expanded the dimension of the world role played by Moscow, and as the Kremlin itself has gained in self-confidence and prestige, the necessity for extreme positions and flamboyant language has gradually disappeared. Moscow's interest in preaching the message of revolution is reduced exactly to the extent to which it is acquiring a stake in the existing order. Far from being a revolutionary and radical force in world affairs, contemporary Soviet policy is more like the nineteenth-century ideal of a great power functioning within the European concert—the *arriviste* is being won over by the Establishment. It is a sardonic coincidence that this in-group is losing its status and its power to control events just as it is expanding its ranks to include the Soviet Union.

The United States Approach to the World: A Form of Democracy

The American approach to the world is the result of a peculiar mixture of vigorous tradition and accidental historical circumstance. There are three important identifiable ingredients among the basic assumptions about world politics upon which the United States rests its strategic concept: (1) the historic American theory of international relations; (2) the new sense of national importance and mission that came with victory in World War II and the role of leadership that the country was forced to play in its aftermath; and (3) hopefully to be thought of as a dimension of continuous expansion, a greater degree of realistic understanding of the nature of the global system in the twentieth century. Each makes its own contribution to the conceptual framework of American strategy.

American culture portrays world politics as taking place within a universal system and order governed by and amenable to both logic and morality. Individuals who operate the controls of government are rational and moral creatures; the purpose of world politics is advancement of the common interests of humankind, to be achieved through cooperative action by all states and the solution of "problems" as they arise. Peace marked by amicable resolution of differences and a steady stream of formal (i.e., legal) agreements on particular issues is the normal condition of the world. War is abnormal, the result of the unpredictable appearance of individuals or groups who insist upon immoral and illegal behavior. As an abnormal system, war is outside world politics proper.

The task of the state caught in a war is to end it as soon as possible, punish those responsible, and "get back to business" with minimum loss of time.

Although never put so baldly as we have summarized it here, this ideal has energized American action for a century and a half. This was the image of utopia—strengthened by institutions for both affirmative cooperative behavior and the punishment of evildoers—for which the Wilsonians fought so bitterly and so long. It still affects the conceptual and the operational atmosphere in which American policy is decided, and remains in some form as a recognizable key ingredient in the American self-image. Any more elaborate or sophisticated strategic interpretation must build upon these principles if its advocates wish it to gain public acceptance and support.

The second element in the American world view is the new sense of historical importance with which the postwar generation has been forced to come to terms. Up through World War II, Americans were permitted by history and their own code to conceive of themselves as virtually nonparticipating observers of the world political process, dealing with an intrinsically corrupt system at arm's length and trapped into direct involvement only on widely separated occasions. The country's normal world mission was to act as a moral example. When events conspired to draw the United States into the thick of battle, the national purpose was to set things right, to provide others with a more reliable guide to future action by institutional change, and then to retire gracefully to lofty observation of the eccentricities of world politics. All of this philosophy was swept away by World War II, the birth of the nuclear age, and the appearance of the Cold War.

Once the most reluctant of dragons, America moved within a relatively few months between mid-1947 and early 1949 into complete acceptance of a starring role. Virtues were discovered in living under the inscrutable gaze of history. The phrase "responsibilities of world leadership" fell increasingly from American lips, and with each hearing became more palatable. Today Americans enjoy their key position as one of the arbiters of humankind's fate, even though they may occasionally betray a nostalgic yearning for the days of happy irresponsibility. The thought that some portion of the earth for which the United States has assumed primary responsibility—such as Western Europe—might wish to throw off American sponsorship and strike out on its own causes serious tremors in American political and strategic circles. The American public is convinced that the United States will eventually play the largest single role in giving the world its definitive shape.

Finally, the gradually increasing realism of American thinking about world affairs should be mentioned. What we called the "American theory" of international relations was, at least until World War II, accepted less as a utopian dream than as a serious description of world politics, an illusion that had survived almost undisturbed all the shocks of the twentieth century up to 1939. The searing experience of World War II, however, began the eye-opening process reinforced by the two decades of the Cold War.

Let us indicate briefly the major elements in the new realism. First, the United States is less inclined in the fourth quarter of the twentieth century than it was in the 1950s to seek absolute solutions to problems, or even to formulate issues in simple black-and-white terms. Second, Americans now appreciate the irrelevancy (or at least the frequent inapplicability) of private morality to the behavior of states. Third, there is reduced acceptance in American policy of the constant alternation of crisis and relaxation and a correspondingly greater search for a significant dimension of positive and affirmative action. Finally, the distinction-blurring concept of "mankind" has been replaced to a great extent by a more sharply focused and clearly rationalized idea of American interest as the controlling criterion of purpose.

These disparate elements combine to produce a reasonably clear and workable world view for the use of American strategists. The United States now conceives of the international system as unstable but capable of being stabilized, as disorderly but capable of order, and as potentially warlike but capable of being structured on a continuing basis of peace. The image of the world adopted by the United States thus contains its own built-in action imperatives: The United States, by the definition of the problem it faces, is obliged to seek a solution.

The controlling impulse of American strategy is the creation of a peaceful, orderly, and stable world—a translation into operational terms of the prevailing national myth. Although popular treatments of the subject emphasize that achievement of American ends would benefit the entire human race, in reality the motivations underlying such a formula are the most practical American strategists can discover. A world such as this would be one in which American security risks were reduced almost to the vanishing point, American economic and status-prestige concerns received full satisfaction, and the final vindication of American doctrines about the individual and society would be complete.

Third World Approach to the World

Though Third World approaches are diverse in form, and offer no uniform blueprint for world revolution, they stress a common theme—it is nationalistic, antihierarchic, and socialistic. Third World nationalisms range from tribal factionalism to pan-African Nationalism. It is seen by some as a means of recapturing past glories, while others emphasize the immediate and future problems of building modern societies. It seeks to demonstrate that emerging Third World states will take their rightful place in the world, despite the old Western claim that they are incapable of doing so, and will overcome the inferiority forced on them in the white-dominated Western world. This imposed inferiority has left a deep emotional scar, causing Third World leaders repeatedly to assert their nationalism in order to prove their viability and dignity.

In their colonial past, many of the new states were denied racial equality and national political freedom. Rebellion against this enforced inferiority and the drive for acceptance and racial equality developed into revolutionary urgings. Nonwhite, non-Western, and non-Establishment characteristics were proclaimed to be the framework of a unique personality of which its possessors should be proud. What began as an attempt to give the Third World a sense of personal worth and self-respect rapidly changed into a reaction to white and Western domination which could easily be distorted into Third World racism.

It is here that the concept of antihierarchy is realized. As the basic ingredient of nationalism, antihierarchy serves two primary functions: It provides the unity and support for a successful liberation movement in areas still under great power domination, and it provides the commonly perceived threat which is invoked to preserve both their domestic and international positions.

Proceeding from the premise that equates Establishment-West-white supremacy and capitalism, many Third World leaders see these interests continuing in a postindependence attempt to exert de facto political control by economic means. They see the independence and progress of their new states threatened by covert foreign economic domination, which is denounced as the direct cause of the immediate failures of the postindependence period.

Third World universal predicament is mass poverty. A lack of appropriate skills and managerial talents, inordinate income differentials, and the desire to overcome a Marxian, colonial self-image are the intertwined problems of these societies. Many Third World leaders believe that socialism is the only answer to the need for a moral and just social order. Human dignity, social justice, and equality of opportunity are promoted as the highest social values.

The Third World views the global system differently from both American democracy and Soviet communism. Throughout their modern history, many of the new states have been victims of great power rivalries. The disparate strands of their foreign policies derive from several basic assumptions: Neocolonialism or neoimperialism poses the principal threat to their existence; American-Soviet confrontation is merely a struggle for power and domination of smaller states; and the bipolar international system does not accommodate their interests and objectives.

From these basic attitudes, the Third World states have come to place great stress on international organization. They feel that the United Nations should exert a strong influence in settling international disputes, even among great powers. International organizations become vehicles for increasing the political power and influence of traditionally insignificant states, which are attempting literally to force the great powers to pay them heed.

Accordingly, Third World states have adopted a strategy of nonalignment, in order to transcend the present ideological split. As translated from precept to practice, nonalignment is designed to serve specific functions—to reconcile between national sovereignty and the requirements of security; to harmonize between political independence and economic dependence to maintain and enhance national solidarity; to maximize foreign policy alternatives and power in world politics. Nonalignment plays another role for these states, one which is derived from domestic political considerations: it acts as a rallying point to mobilize widespread support behind governmental actions vis-à-vis the external world. The states are caught in the middle of domestic factional struggles among groups which are closely identified with the values of the Western tradition, ultranationalists whose response to the outside world may border on racism, and quasi-Marxists, neocolonialists, or socialists inclined toward emulation of Soviet or Chinese models.

To preserve an already tenuous and strained national unity, create a national consciousness, and progress toward promised development, Third World leaders must pursue policies which will satisfy everyone. Nonalignment seems to offer the possibility of avoiding the disasters of civil war or domination by the superpowers. An assertive foreign policy and a demonstration of willingness to support, cooperate with, and receive aide from both blocs are attempts to satisfy the domestic factions in the interest of unity.

In 1955 India, Burma, Ceylon, Indonesia, and Pakistan invited twenty-seven heads of government to a conference of nonaligned states in Bandung, Indonesia. From 1955 to 1961, President Tito of Yugoslavia worked actively with Third World leaders—Nehru of India, Nasser of Egypt, Nkrumah of Ghana, and Sukarno of Indonesia—to promote nonalignment. The result was the first Conference of Heads of State or Government of the nonaligned countries that convened in Belgrade in 1961 and was attended by twenty-five members and three observers. Since that time the nonaligned movement has broadened its base of support. The 1964 Cairo summit was attended by forty-seven full members and twelve observers, the 1970 Lusaka summit by fifty-three full members and twelve observers, the 1973 Algiers summit by seventy-five full members and twenty-eight observers, the 1976 Ghana summit by eighty-six full members and observers, and the 1978 Belgrade foreign minister's conference by eighty-five full members and observers.

Nationalism: Old and New

Nationalism is the common sentiment of feeling of solidarity which transforms a people into a nationality and expresses itself in an attitude which assigns the collective activity of the state a high (frequently the highest) place in the hierarchy of social value. Nationalism is one of the absolutely controlling phenomena of world politics today, as it has been since the French Revolution. It grows from a variety of sources. Some of the more obvious factors that impel individuals to join with others in a national group include a common language, religion, historical background, cultural tradition, and racial background. Several of these may interact in subtle ways to reinforce a cohesive tendency in a people. The nationalist ethos is best expressed in the broadly based and deeply felt philosophy of political, economic, and social life that becomes the operational creed of the state. It is also reflected in a complex variety of symbols: external enemies, myths, heroes, history, and folklore.

Traditional European Nationalism

Rudimentary forms of nationalism can be traced to the states of antiquity. Ancient peoples commonly considered themselves divinely chosen and believed that their gods were the sworn foes of other states. Regarding themselves as greatly superior in all aspects to the rest of humankind, they viewed others as approaching excellence in proportion to their acceptance of the particular values of the state.

Development of the European state system and the expansion of Western civilization gradually brought into sharp focus the effects of nationalism on world politics. The Hundred Years' War (1337–1451) between France and England may be considered the beginning of modern nationalism. The initial foundations for the union of Normans and Saxons into Englishmen were laid down in England during the twelfth and thirteenth centuries, to be fully achieved by the middle of the fourteenth century. In France, an elementary form of French national consciousness first appeared during the Hundred Years' War. The French, however, lacked the more elaborate political institutions of the English, and the development of full national identity was slower in France than in Britain. By the seventeenth century, England and France had become nation-states in almost a contemporary sense, to be followed shortly by Sweden, Holland, Spain, and Denmark.

The unifying influence in nationalism, which initially brought order and stability within the national state, ultimately promoted a highly diverse community of sovereign states. During the early stages of its growth, nationalism promised peace, order, and justice predicated on the fulfillment of national aspirations. The paradox of nationalist logic, however, was highlighted after the middle of the eighteenth century. Since then it has functioned more as a force of disintegration and fragmentation than of unity.

The development of world politics since the middle of the eighteenth century furnishes much evidence of how difficult it is to promote nationalism without aggravating the conditions of world order. A people's aspiration to create a nation-state has almost always conflicted with territorial claims of other states. Nationalists, generally not satisfied with internal achievements, tend to seek glory through expansion and empire, whether territorial, economic, or cultural. Furthermore, intense nationalistic identification tends to undermine flexibility in policy and the capacity to compromise in interstate disputes.

The series of major wars that have been waged since 1815—especially World Wars I and II—embodied overt attempts to apply the principles of nationalism. Almost every one was fought by one or more belligerents in the name of national self-determination, and the results of these wars were reflected in peace settlements allegedly predicated upon the same principles. Yet a victory of nationalism, instead of bringing peace and order to world politics, only led to an exchange of the roles of oppressor and oppressed. Far from creating a more stable system, nationalism contributed to the "balkanization" of world order and exaggerated an already strong proclivity to tension.

Unable to cope with its own success, nationalism has not developed into a broad enough political concept to unite political institutions, ideologies, and economic systems in the same way that science and technology have compressed the world. It is eroding both communism and democratic liberalism, and has created a polycentric mosaic in place of these two supranational ideological blocs that emerged following World War II. The ideologies have been transformed from universal political faiths into power techniques to promote the national interests of individual states.

Nationalism in the Third World

The impact of European nationalism on the Third World has been explosive, partially because the environment was peculiarly prepared to respond to the stimulus of these ideas. Since the middle of the nineteenth century, non-Western peoples coming into contact with the expanding West have been searching for some orienting concept upon which to base an adequate response. With their old societal and personal values eroded by the technological transformation everywhere in the less-developed world, these peoples have found in nationalism a method of giving new meaning to their lives.

The non-Western world is finding it necessary to reconcile tradition with the demands of modern thought and life. Success in this effort has been minimal because of the peculiar dimensions of the problem. Non-Western leaders, seeking a sufficient mass revival to produce a political and cultural renaissance, fear massive social or political revolutionary change. Caught between the necessity of doing something and the reluctance to do too much, leadership in the non-Western world faces the danger of fleeing from overcontradiction into moral and intellectual skepticism. Old codes no longer meet the social and political need, but new principles of intellectual life from the West are unpalatable. Lack of sociopolitical change has been the consequence.

A nation-state in the Western sense is difficult to fit within the boundaries of countries of the Third World. These states do not reflect spontaneous political growth, but rather the aftereffects of the division of the world by European colonial powers. In many instances no concept of nationality exists. Communal and tribal loyalties still form the central core of the society. Government is minimal in organization and in effect, and the visible symbols of national identity are few and unimportant.

Thus nationalism in Asia and Africa is often disorganized in its expression. Past glory is evoked at the same time that the people are exhorted to abandon their old ways and join the mainstream of modern life. Withdrawal and pervasive self-expression are equally prominent. The non-Western world wants simultaneously to escape from the "vulgarities" of Western life and to emulate the comforts found there. Nationalism in the new states is more a reflection of culture shock than it is a formalized belief system and a base for governmental action.

Despite these shortcomings, non-Western nationalism evokes a sense of self-respect which was unknown during the colonial period. It stimulates social solidarity and helps create a community to which diverse peoples can claim common loyalty. It is of prime significance when it helps create the national unity of purpose and readiness to sacrifice which is required for development and even survival.

The elites of the nationalist movements, usually products of modernization or militarization, are the mediators between the old and the new. They must set the ends and employ the means of modernization, yet the values and techniques which they have adopted are often inappropriate to the conditions of their societies. More often, the elites are subverting the existing order and society, which they want to change in order to satisfy their own needs. Their desire for change is in part a narrow personal wish, but it is also rooted in their desire to bring to their people the "better life." However, the amount of change needed to arrive at political and cultural awakening necessarily disrupts orderly transition. The endeavor to create a national state through common effort usually runs into traditional patterns which strengthen factionalism and division. Such obstruction of nationalist ideals is often met by the creation by the elites of one-party states which suppress opposition and deal ruthlessly with dissidents and separatists.

The Prestige Race

An era such as the present, marked by great modifications in the conditions of world political life and a drastic recalculation of the ponderables of state capability, gives considerations of prestige a special significance. States normally wish to acquire high prestige. When the coercive component of state capability has a diminished effect in achieving state purposes, the relative role of noncoercive influence cannot help but increase in importance and scope. This is the special province of prestige.

This chapter has considered the ideological formulation in world politics, and the point was made that ideological conflict is no longer a struggle for the achievement of absolute truth, but rather a competition for results, with the prize going to the system that best approximates in reality the utopia promised in its preachments. The antagonists hope that the impression of competence and effectiveness they convey will produce meaningful political results.

What is Prestige?

The initial problem facing states is the augmentation of prestige. The notion of "prestige" has no specific content, and must be given meaning in more precise terms. To be "well thought of," a state must decide the characteristics with which it wishes to be favorably identified. It may elect to acquire prestige by military strength, by a reputation for astute diplomacy, by a high standard of living, by an advanced cultural and/or technological level, or by conspicuous dedication to certain abstract principles, such as freedom or justice. It may even select several of these to make up what we might call a "prestige package." Then the state devotes itself to clarifying this image.

However, another difficulty arises. Not only must a state decide the terms in which it wishes to be judged, it must also persuade other states to apply the same standards. This is a far more complex task, involving identifying the state's actions with the values of the judging state or states. A related problem develops from the differing ways in which high prestige may be demonstrated. Does the state wish to be respected, feared, admired, loved, emulated, or disliked? All are, given appropriate circumstances, equally valid ways of demonstrating high prestige. Which one a state chooses depends in large part upon the policy results it wishes.

The Race for Prestige

The world scene today displays vast competition for prestige. The major powers are involved on a global scale in a massive effort to put their best foot foreward. The states of the Third World, seeking a clearer identity, are actively promoting whatever aspects of their own societies they feel might produce greater respect. The older states of Europe, although increasingly preoccupied with their own problems and consequently less sensitive to worldwide implications of political prestige, are nevertheless constantly alert to the social, psychological, economic, and cultural aspects of European prestige.

At least two troublesome aspects of the prestige race complicate the course of world politics. For many states, the prestige competition is a two-sided game in which one state may gain in prestige only to the extent that its adversaries are humbled. This approach, founded on the idea that the total amount of prestige is finite and that a larger slice for one state means a diminished portion for another, is particularly important in some formulations of the stakes of American-Soviet confrontation. Many Americans, for example, are convinced that each American victory is also a defeat for the USSR, and that every Soviet failure in some way augments America's world image.

The second complication of the prestige race is its inconclusiveness. The relationship between high prestige and the capability of a state to accomplish its stipulated objectives has not yet been clarified. The real "influence" component of prestige is unclear. A suspicion remains that a state's search for international prestige flows from internalized motivations—that a people obsessed with the need for greater world renown is seeking to assuage internal insecurity. If this condition does exist, it makes the prestige race a self-defeating international enterprise. No rewards formulated in the classic framework of world politics can be derived from such a contest.

Recommended Readings

APTER, DAVID E., ed. *Ideology and Discontent.* London: Free Press, 1964.
BELL, DANIEL. *The End of Ideology: On the Exhaustion of Political Ideas in the Fifties.* New York: Free Press, 1965.
COHEN, CARL. *Communism, Fascism, and Democracy* (2nd ed.). New York: Random House, 1972.
CRABB, CECIL V., JR. *The Elephants and the Grass: A Study of Non-Alignment.* New York: Frederick A. Praeger, 1967.
DORE, R. P. "The Prestige Factor in International Relations," *International Affairs* (London), April 1975.
EBENSTEIN, WILLIAM. *Today's Isms: Communism, Fascism, Capitalism, Socialism* (7th ed.). Englewood Cliffs, N.J.: Prentice-Hall, 1973.
FANON, FRANTZ. *The Wretched of the Earth.* New York: Grove Press, 1965.
HAYES, CARLTON J. *The Historical Evolution of Modern Nationalism* (repr. ed.). New York: Russell, 1968 (original printing, 1931).
HOOK, SIDNEY. *Marx and the Marxists.* Princeton, N.J.: D. Van Nostrand Co., 1955.
IKEDA, SHIMBORI, HIDEO IKEDA, TSUYOSHI ISHIDA, and MOTO KONDO. "Measuring a Nation's Prestige," *American Journal of Sociology*, no. 69, July 1963.
MATES, LEO. *Non-Alignment: Theory and Current Policy.* Dobbs Ferry, N.Y.: Oceana Publications, 1972.
SARGENT, LYMAN. *Contemporary Political Ideologies: A Comparative Analysis* (3rd ed.). Homewood, Ill.: Dorsey Press, 1975.
SCHAPRIO, J. SALWYN. *Liberalism: Its Meaning and History.* Princeton, N.J.: D. Van Nostrand Co., 1958.
SHKLAR, JUDITH. *After Utopia: The Decline of Political Faith,* Princeton University Press, Princeton, N.J.: 1969.
SIGMUND, PAUL E., ed. *The Ideologies of the Developing Nations* (2nd rev. ed.). New York: Frederick A. Praeger, 1972.
SINGHAM, A. W., and TRAN VAN DINH. *From Bandung to Colombo.* New York: Third Press Review Books, 1976.

Humankind, Technology and the Ecosystem

11

We live today in a technological age. The assault of human intelligence upon the secrets of the natural world has yielded such spectacular discoveries in the past seven decades that the twentieth century has seen greater changes in the conditions of human existence than have taken place in all previous recorded human history. The technological revolution of this century has had the same direct effect on the politics of states as it has had on every other feature of social interaction. We have already noted the tremendous impact of advanced technology on the theory and practice of warfare, and the extent to which long-standing postulates have undergone systematic revaluation. This development has been paralleled in almost every other dimension of world politics; the very organizing assumptions of state life have been called into question as a result of the new relation between humankind and the ecosystem which consists of the relationship between both living and nonliving entities in the natural world.

In this chapter, we shall examine six of the hundreds of technological developments and resulting conditions that are putting the state system under such strain. This is not to imply that these few are the most important, or that they are unique in their effect. We shall note their general similarities in modifying and perhaps transforming world politics. The tentative conclusions we shall advance at the end of the chapter are applicable to almost any other technological issues.

The six we have selected for brief analysis and evaluation are (1) energy; (2) the conquest of space; (3) the population question (a result of technology rather than a new factor in itself); (4) mass communications; (5) the new patterns in economic production, consumption and distribution; and (6) computers.

Energy

During the last quarter of the twentieth century, energy has become a primary issue in the global system. The drastic increase in the cost of petroleum by The Organization of Petroleum Exporting Countries, (OPEC) combined with the Arab oil embargo in 1973 served to define the limits of the imperium of the industrial states. Traditional energy policies are being reappraised and governments are searching to alter patterns of consumption and to develop alternative sources of energy.

Fossil Fuels

Fossil fuels have been the prime source of energy for the past century: Crude oil, natural gas, and coal have been employed to serve the majority of our needs. The use of these rapidly dwindling resources has proven to be economically inefficient and ecologically harmful. Increasingly, more research and development is geared toward the development of solar energy sources which unlike fossil fuels, are inexhaustible.

It is essential in this connection to distinguish a "shortage" from a "scarcity" of energy. A scarcity refers to a situation whereby the goods in question are available in the marketplace to anyone willing to pay the higher price which their scarcity entails. Although it is doubtful that an actual shortage of fossil energy resources will be encountered in this century, the need to establish alternative energy sources is nonetheless pressing—sources of energy from which all of humankind can benefit, not merely those who are able to pay the ever-rising price of energy from scarce, nonrenewable sources.

Nuclear Energy

The splitting of the atom resulted in the discovery of a new source of energy whose availability is far greater than that of fossil fuels. Without energy, modern industrial civilization would be impossible. The historic Industrial Revolution was grounded upon successful conversion of coal to the production of large amounts of energy in the form of heat. Prior to that time, energy came from natural or human sources in small amounts and with great technical and economic waste of wind, water, and human energy. Coal as an energy source was much more efficient and made large-scale enterprise feasible. Since the dawn of the coal age, we have discovered other energy sources of wide utility, particularly petroleum and hydroelectric power. Modern industry has been built on these three bases.

Developments in weaponry demonstrated that the energy locked in the atomic nucleus also could be liberated. Consequently, the total amount of energy potentially available for human use has increased dramatically, since the raw material of the nuclear reaction is in huge supply. Known uranium resources could last for hundreds of years if the efficient but controversial breeder reactor is widely employed. Supplies of hydrogen for another atomic process called thermonuclear fusion are infinite in relation to human needs, although their use will require significant scientific and engineering advances.

The Second Industrial Revolution

The development of atomic energy is immediately relevant to the pattern of world relationships because it makes possible a "second industrial revolution." States that became industrial giants in the days of coal-iron technology had accidentally been endowed with deposits of these raw materials, of which coal was the more important. Great economic power and world political leadership were built on this base, and states without adequate energy sources were condemned to second or even lower rank. The rise to importance of OPEC illustrates this reality.

Now, however, nuclear energy could equalize the conditions of competition. Nevertheless, the opportunity for the nonindustrial states to skip the coal-oil stage entirely and to move directly into this more advanced technology is compromised by its high capital cost. Already-industrialized states have an advantage in their relatively large supply of scientists, technicians, and production specialists, but this advantage is neither absolutely controlling nor permanent in its effect. Fissionable materials are relatively common, and the total amount necessary for energy production is by no means huge. The new industrial revolution could result in a substantial reordering of the relative production ranking now held by states and will also culminate in a much narrower spread between the top and the bottom.

Nuclear Energy and World Politics

The military uses of nuclear energy have been a factor of division and have intensified competition and tension in the relations of states. While each nuclear power has sought to confine its advances to itself and to monopolize all its rewards, proliferation has occurred through sale or reprocessing. The attempt to develop nuclear energy for nonmilitary purposes on an exclusively national basis has not been a success. International cooperation and conflict in the peaceful uses of nuclear energy have been natural developments for a number of reasons.

First, the theoretical simplicity of the task has not been matched by an equivalent ease in execution. Scientific and technological elaboration of what is already known is an extremely expensive operation. National competition in this area condemns each state to repeat each stage in the process, while cooperation enables all to build on the totality of everyone's findings.

Second, for most effective use, nuclear energy arrangements should be on a larger scale than most smaller states can develop. Cooperation in establishing supranational research-and-development programs could obviously result in dividends beyond the capacity of individual states to muster.

A third factor is the attitude of the scientific community toward itself. Committed by professional ideology to freedom of knowledge and the exchange of ideas and findings in a common pursuit of truth, scientists have formed a powerful pressure group urging governments into cooperative ventures.

Finally, on the one hand public imagination has been captured throughout most of the world by the possibilities of a future made lighter by ample energy supplies, and a considerable degree of public approval greets each new step in its realization. On the other hand, there is also much opposition. Scientists do not know how to dispose of nuclear waste safely.

The two most conspicuous examples of international cooperation in the exploitation of nuclear energy for peaceful purposes have been the International Atomic Energy Agency (IAEA), established in response to American initiatives under the auspices of the United Nations, and the European Atomic Community (EURATOM), set up by the six states of the European Community. These two enterprises provide for joint and cooperative exploitation of the peaceful possibilities of nuclear energy. Up to the present their record of accomplishment is not extensive, but the nature of their task calls for a long period of preparatory work before a few visible results can be followed by an outburst of specific applications. Other cooperative efforts of less impressive scope are in the making as well. It must be pointed out, however, that substantial concern has been raised about the dangers inherent in the proliferation of nuclear technology for peaceful uses. The principal difficulty is that the radioactive material involved in nuclear fission has been diverted into military use.

Solar Energy

Lately, we have come to realize that in reality there is not a scarcity of energy. Vast quantities of renewable, nonpolluting, and cost-free energy fall everyday upon all parts of the earth in the form of solar radiation.

Even fossil fuels, whose quantities are limited, consist of solar energy which was trapped and stored milennia ago by green plants. Both wind and water power derive from the sun's irregular heating of the earth's crust and the evaporation of its bodies of water.

Research into the direct collection, storage and use of this plentiful energy source is proceeding at an accelerated pace. It is now economically feasible to utilize solar energy for hot water; soon it is likely to provide economical space heating and cooling for buildings. By the end of the century, solar researchers predict it will be possible to generate significant amounts of electricity; either directly from the sun, using photovoltaic cells, or indirectly, by harnessing the heat in the oceans and deserts, at prices comparable to or lower than fossil fuel methods. Such considerations may mean that a third, and even more dramatic industrial revolution may result from the wide spread exploitation of this source.

Appropriate Technology

A third industrial revolution would depend upon a variety of technologies, not simply those related to solar energy. The term "appropriate technology" denotes combinations of technological methods, both traditional and innovative which are scaled in size, cost, and degree of complexity to the situations to which they are applied. It is a strategy for the selection and implementation of technological methods that are effectively calibrated to situational needs, resources, and priorities. Thus, in many rural areas of the United States it may be more effective to install a variety of dispersed energy-production devices such as windmills or solar heaters than to build new centralized power plants, no matter what their energy source. In the less-developed countries, programs of industrialization may require construction of large generating facilities, even if fueled by polluting, nonrenewable fossil materials.

The Conquest of Space

The nuclear age dates from 1945, but the age of space has been a reality only since 1957 when—in the course of a massive multistate scientific effort under the auspices of the International Geophysical Year—the Soviet Union launched the first artificial space satellites followed in 1958 by the United States. Since that time, the attempt to gather more scientific information about the reaches of space and to launch vehicles and persons deeper into the universe has become increasingly concentrated. The Soviet Union in 1961, and the United States early in 1962, put human beings into orbit around the earth and brought them back safely. Plans for larger vehicles, longer flights, and eventual manned voyages to the moon and beyond were immediately announced. In view of the rapidity with which the penetration of space has been proceeding, very few nonspecialists are willing to minimize the probabilities that these and even more spectacular steps will be taken as scheduled. So accustomed have individuals become to rapid progress in space exploration that few pause to reflect how recently the entire enterprise began.

The Breakthrough into Space

The birth of the space age was made possible by intensive cooperation among many kinds of scientists and technologists aided by generous appropriations of funds and material by governments on both sides of the Iron Curtain. Physicists, biologists, meteorologists, physiologists, chemists, metallurgists, and dozens of other scientific specialists made direct and indispensable contributions. In addition, every type of engineering and technical skill played a direct part. The two critical areas of technological advance, without which a breakthrough would have been impossible, were the development and refinement of the science of rocketry (especially the development of booster thrust) and the sophistication of metallurgy which, coupled with dramatic advances in pyrotechnics, permitted the construction of space vehicles capable of withstanding the strains of launching and friction of reentry into the earth's atmosphere.

Spectacular landmarks in astronautics include the first satellite, *Sputnik,* launched by the USSR in 1957; successful use of satellites as communications devices by the United States in 1960; successful photography of the hitherto unseen side of the moon and the landing of a rocket on the moon's surface, accomplished by the Soviets in 1960; the first manned orbital flight made by Russia's Yuri Gagarin in 1961; the *Telstar* communication satellite and other orbital breakthroughs in 1962; the Soviet spacecraft *Luna IX*'s first successful semisoft lunar landing with a 220-pound instrument package containing a television transmitter in 1966; and the American *Surveyor 1*'s soft landing on the moon, also in 1966.

Great advances have been made since the launching of the first *Sputnik.* This is evidenced in the *Apollo 11* mission of astronauts actually landing on the surface of the moon in 1969 and the Soviet Zond program which places the USSR within a step from the same accomplishment.

The extent to which persons have already penetrated space, and the justified sense of real accomplishment, should not obscure the fact that, compared with the enormity of the task we have set ourselves, no more than the merest scratch has been made on the surface of space. Space is, of course, an infinite notion. Travel until now has been little more than 250,000 miles out into space, a tiny centimeter in relation to the infinite expanses of the universe. The deepest-ranging probes have gone only a small way into the solar system, with nonhuman piloted vessels having been sent to investigate conditions on Mars and Venus. Beyond lie galaxies and nebulae as yet only dreamed of. We dare not lose sight of the awful immensity of the universe into which we are venturing.

However, a remarkable technical and scientific harvest has already been gathered in the few short years in which space efforts have been progressing. The instruments for further action are either at hand or on the way to development; the extent of knowledge is adequate to support and justify a constant forward movement along this frontier. Interestingly, the two most active areas of scientific and technological progress are those that focus upon the smallest unit of scientific inquiry—the atomic nucleus—and the largest—the cosmos itself. In these two areas the most fundamental questions are leading to extremely interesting and useful answers. It is clear that the immediate goal of the space programs of the 1960s was one of exploration, while aims of the 1970s have been in terms of space utilization, a shift from single-purpose spacecraft to multipurpose space research stations. Previous programs were intended to explore the possibility and capability of people to function in space, while current research is oriented toward study which may not be feasible otherwise because of limitations on earth (gravity etc.). Aside from uses in telecommunications, weather, climate, and land use research, space research will continue to be on a more theoretical plane, as in biology and physics studies. Most of the benefits of space research have arisen when technology that was developed for the program have found other applications—for example, in computer technology (the development of mini- and microcomputers), medicine (improved body-function-monitoring techniques), and in industrial purposes.

The Space Race

It is an interesting commentary on the spirit of the times that the great breakthrough into space has been conceived of as a race between the Soviet Union and the United States. *Sputnik* was a great blow to American pride since the American public had assumed its technological primacy. This led to a strong American reaction. The long-range program leading to manned space flight, was transformed into a battleground of the East-West confrontation. The USSR obviously enjoyed its sudden (perhaps unexpected) reputation for scientific and technological leadership, and accepted the American challenge. The exploration of space was solely a competitive venture until 1975, when the US and the USSR launched a joint mission into space culminating in a link up of the Apollo-Soyuz spacecrafts.

The Soviet Union has had considerable success in maintaining its lead in spectacular breakthroughs. Its most prestigious accomplishments were unquestionably the successful attempt to hit the moon, the trailblazing manned orbital flights, and the soft lunar landing. Yet there is evidence that the United States is well ahead in overall sophistication concerning space and its problems, and that the Soviet Union senses its relative deficiencies in these respects and is interested in changing some of the terms of the contest.

Following the early Russian successes, most Americans succumbed to a "let's catch up" philosophy toward the space race. In spite of American successes in communications and unmanned satellites, this attitude continued into the mid-1960s. When astronaut Edward White took his "walk in space" during the four-day *Gemini 4* flight in June 1965, a public controversy arose and NASA was accused of "prematurely" trying to match a similar Russian feat. The public and the news media still thought of the United States as "closing the gap" in the space race with the Russians.

Political and Military Considerations

The stakes in the space race have been both political and military. The political aspects, clustering about the much-discussed but undefinable rewards in prestige that accrue to the state holding the lead, have been perhaps the more obvious. There is no doubt that Soviet successes have had a profound impact upon mass opinion in much of the less-developed world, and have gone far to destroy the myth of Russian technological backwardness. The widespread dismay and frantic and concerned self-analysis of segments of the American public in the face of Soviet advances have contributed as well to the possibility of a drastic revision of their respective world images.

Yet the political rewards that some pessimists in the West have been prepared to concede to the Soviets as a result of their leadership in space conquest have proved disconcertingly small. There has been some doubt whether prestige in space exploration is a politically negotiable commodity, and about the real extent to which Soviet success has damaged the United States (except possibly in the eyes of Americans themselves). Moscow has obviously enjoyed Washington's discomfiture, but apart from this almost routine behavior, the political consequences of the space race have been either minimal or as yet undiscovered.

The military significance of space achievements has been widely debated by both Eastern and Western observers. Soviet leadership in booster thrust was evidence for a time of a dangerous "missile gap" in Moscow's favor, although this argument was eventually abandoned by both Russians and Americans. Earlier, there was talk about the possibilities of manned "space stations" for reconnaissance and possibly attack purposes, but their real military advantages were difficult to pinpoint. Soviet development of fractional-orbiting vessels capable of delivering nuclear warheads from outer space to a target on earth provides a concrete example of the use of outer space for military purposes. But generally speaking, the level of scientific knowledge (and perhaps the imagination of military leadership) is not yet adequate to capitalize on these considerations. Neither doctrine nor technique is able to explain the full military advantages of a command of outer space.

The radical advances in missiles and rockets which exemplified the space race after 1957, plus the Soviet policy of cutting its military troop force and emphasizing weapons of strategic deterrence, brought on a continuing debate in the United States about force levels and budgets. In an era when evaluation of the real contribution of soldiers and weapons to national security was the most difficult in history, the dispute was inevitably inconclusive (or perhaps indeterminable). Neither the "budgeteers" nor the "security" group had enough concrete data to give their arguments the strength needed to win a consensus.

Cooperation in Space

A countertrend to the space race began to manifest itself during 1961 and 1962—a strong urge toward the cooperative exploration of space without political overtones. Proposals for cooperation had been frequent during earlier stages, but the pressure for political and possibly military advantage had prevented their implementation. Proposals to declare space "out of bounds" to the East-West confrontation, and to share both the costs and the findings of further explorations, were accepted in principle, but considerations of timing, prestige, or national security blunted these preliminary efforts.

The successful accomplishment by the United States of a manned orbital flight early in 1962, however, brought the race to its closest approximation of prestige parity since it began. In his congratulatory message, Premier Khrushchev—in a relatively friendly manner—raised the possibility (originally an American proposal) of the two space leaders developing ways of extensive cooperation in the future penetration of space. American response was affirmative, and negotiations for the formulation of areas and techniques of joint interaction were immediately initiated in a climate of relative goodwill and free exchange.

The apparently sincere acceptance of cooperation in space by the two states which had been competing so grimly was both important in itself and profoundly suggestive. If it were actually institutionalized, one dimension of an exciting but relatively unproductive dispute would be eliminated from the American-Soviet confrontation. Furthermore, cooperation in space would affect the remaining areas of open conflict between the two; it would be difficult to maintain a complete "we or they" approach in a political matter if both sides were working cooperatively on so newsworthy and extensive an enterprise as space exploration.

The test ban treaty in July 1963, which, among other things, banned nuclear testing in outer space, and President Kennedy's revolutionary proposal before the United Nations for joint Soviet-American exploration of the moon, were both indications of the different posture being assumed by the United States. In May 1972 the United States and the Soviet Union signed an agreement to cooperate in the exploration and use of space for peaceful purposes.

The United Nations has been a major forum for discussion and resolution of conflicts of space. In 1963, the General Assembly adopted the nine-point Declaration of Legal Principles Governing the Activities of States in the Exploration and Use of Outer Space. This declaration recognized the "common interest of man" in space activities—exploration and use of space and celestial bodies should be for the benefit of humanity. Outer space and celestial bodies are not subject to national appropriation or claims of sovereignty. All are free for use by all on the basis of equality. States retain ownership of their vehicles and control over their personnel, but astronauts are considered "envoys of mankind," to receive all possible aid in event of emergency. This declaration was expanded upon by the Outer Space Treaty (Treaty on Principles Governing the Activities of States in the Exploration and Use of Outer Space, Including the Moon and Other Celestial Bodies). The latter treaty was signed in January 1967, and is now in force in most of the states of the world.

The area of communication is of the greatest immediate concern in the developing field. In 1962, the United States created the Communications Satellite Corporation (COMSAT), a corporation with stock held by the public and by American communications companies, with several of the directors to be appointed by the president. COMSAT, in turn, is the American representative and the manager of the International Telecommunications Satellite Consortium (INTELSAT), which functions under special and interim agreements to supply some 90 percent of all present international telecommunications traffic through communications satellites. The Soviet bloc has a similar system based on the Soviet Molniya ("lightning") system. Aside from the creation of possible conflicting systems, there is pressure on the United States to grant greater input in management to others in the pact. There is pressure in the United States that COMSAT give up its monopoly. There is potential disagreement over placement of satellites, as some locations are better than others.

There are limits to availability of radio frequencies—the bands are crowded and becoming more so. Finally, there is the potential of the satellite as a propaganda tool in time of war. None of these questions have been significantly addressed.

The Population Problem

Science and technology, joining forces in the fields of public health and preventive medicine, have brought to the world one of its largest contemporary problems: the population question. The number of human beings on earth today is by far the largest in history. One significant study points out that one-third of all the people born in the entire history of the human race are alive today.

Only in the recent past have political leaders become alarmed by the steady acceleration of birth rates in many parts of the world. Now that population has acquired a political dimension, it has become a matter of great concern to many governments. Unfortunately, the degree of awareness of the problem has not been matched by any equivalent growth in facility for dealing with it.

Causes of the Population Problem

The population of less-developed countries has traditionally stabilized at the maximum supportable by local food supplies and prerequisites of living. It has been kept in check by "Malthusian restraints": war, epidemic, famine, and disease. A predominantly youthful population (because of short lifespan), and very high birth and death rates were generally regarded as characteristics in most of the Third World countries.

In the twentieth century, these states began to benefit from public health measures, improved sanitation, and modern medicine. The results have been spectacular. Death rates have dropped at a dramatic rate, primarily in infant mortality and in epidemic diseases breeding in filth, while birth rates have increased. As more infants have survived to become parents, population figures have soared, with the result that population pressures have begun to force the hand of many governments.

There are no absolutes about the problem of population, no magic optimum figure for the human race or any part of it. Population pressure is a relative factor. A society suffers when any increase in its overall population results in a reduction in the amount of goods and services available for any individual. When an increase in the number of mouths to feed means less food for each mouth, a population problem exists. The crisis in some states is almost frightening. For example, the annual increase in population in Egypt and India is greater than that in productivity. Neither state can, by its own efforts, accumulate the surplus capital necessary for the industrial development that offers hope of relief from the maddening pressure of human biology. While real efforts on the part of states with a serious population problem is necessary, they all stand in dire need of external assistance if they are not to suffer serious undernourishment.

A raw statistical analysis of worldwide data would suggest that we do *not* have a population problem as it is defined here (reduction in the amount of goods and services available for any individual). This is because the production of labor in creating goods and services still tends to exceed consumption. As a result, it still "pays" to produce children—they are profitable. What we have is, due to world grain surpluses, the possibility for many governments to avoid disruption of overall development by food shortfalls through grain imports. Cheap grain is available in world markets.

Political, Social, and Economic Effects

The consequences for the states directly affected by the population problem are simple and devastating. Since no government dares plan wholesale starvation for removing the burden of excess population, all must accept the primary responsibility of keeping their citizens alive. But this does not alleviate or even reduce the problem—birth rates remain high and each year the crisis becomes more intense. State plans for long-range development and social stabilization are repeatedly deferred in favor of frenzied annual attempts to ward off famine. Systematic and sensible social planning in such a climate is obviously impossible.

Within the society itself, the constant specter of starvation haunts everyone. Although for centuries this situation was accepted passively, today powerful ferments are at work in once-quiescent societies. There is a movement to demand rapid improvement in the conditions of life. The tenor of political discourse in these societies has grown more extreme as distress augments political self-consciousness. The governments are less willing and able to withstand these pressures, and measures of increasing desperation gain steadily in attractiveness to their beleaguered policymakers.

At this point, the problem becomes pertinent to world politics. Governments under such pressure at home and with so little room to maneuver before their own peoples are neither forces for stability in world politics nor free to make long-term international commitments. A state with accelerated population growth is incipiently revolutionary. The tragedy of this situation is that any such revolution is by its own terms destined to failure. Population pressure cannot be relieved by a change in government. Oversimplified but persuasive "explanations" of the problem, suggesting that the root of national difficulties lies in the machinations of malevolent enemies, may open the door to particularly dangerous international adventures. Several of these have occurred since World War II.

Thus the reproductive habits of individuals in the tropics are of direct relevance to stabilized and industrialized states of the Western world. Population pressure is a major contributing element in the militancy of Third World revolution, and must be faced by the more fortunate peoples as they devise a long-range response to this new challenge. The ultimate destiny of modern civilization may well rest on humankind's success in seeing that all human beings are provided at least a minimally tolerable share of the world's resources.

The minimal international consequences of famines in the African Sahel region and Bangladesh undermine the global implications of local, Malthusian situations. Interdependency has been overemphasized. International concern about Malthusian situations has to be justified on ethical, not prudential, grounds.

Avenues of Solution

It is probably presumptuous to discuss any "solution" to the problem of population. The most we can seriously consider are some possible lines of attack. No quick results can be expected, and the tensions produced by population problems will form part of the context of world politics for a long time. Nevertheless, a combined internal and international approach does offer some promise of eventual relaxation of the impersonal threat of overpopulation.

Internally, there is already some evidence that forthright and courageous leadership of an extensive program of education and preventive techniques can help in reducing birth rates. This is a matter in part of development of a simple and effective contraceptive, and much research and effort has already gone into this task. However, religious and cultural barriers will remain strong even after the requisite medical findings have been made widely available, so the courage and determination of a government become crucial. The only way to develop a viable social structure may be a broadly based campaign to modify traditional social customs. Only exceptionally strong leaders are likely to run such a risk.

Globally, the population problem can best be attacked by development programs inspired and financed by industrialized states. If performed on a sufficiently large scale, avoiding digressive elements of competition and prestige seeking, the vicious circle of an increase in population eating up each year's economic growth might be broken. Only some such effort has any chance of real success over the long term. Short-range techniques merely defer the day of reckoning. This approach does not demand that every overpopulated state immediately undergo industrialization, but that the economic structure be sufficiently rearranged to free the most productive portion of the population from subsistence agriculture. Specialization in a controlled economic system will make it possible for the necessary foodstuffs to be imported from more productive areas.

Population Pressure and the Shape of World Politics

Some ecologists and biologists argue that the pressure of population is the most influential single factor in shaping the future of the human species. In political terms they contend that ideological and nationalistic drives pale in comparison to the frantic search for subsistence by two-thirds of the world population. Unless this challenge is met head on, they contend, a new wave of barbarism will threaten to sweep the planet.

Regardless of how seriously these warnings may be taken, and after a mere cursory examination of population figures, we cannot escape the conclusion that the global system must adjust to this stark phenomenon. Whether it leads to war and destruction or to a new cooperative climate for solving common problems, the rising tide of humanity is a political problem of the first order. We will hear much more of it in the years ahead.

Mass Communication

Mass communication devices and techniques are another entry in the list of technological advances that have gone so far to revolutionize life in the twentieth century. It is now possible for one person to communicate simultaneously with an audience numbered in the tens of millions. Development in 1965 of commercial satellite telecommunications—the Early Bird system and subsequent development with possibilities of direct-broadcast satellites—seems to indicate that an even greater role can be played by the communication media in the future. This capability to affect the emotions and increase the knowledge of vast numbers of people within a short time span has had a profound effect on patterns of social life everywhere. Information, entertainment, intellectual stimulation, and political leadership are all part of the content of the mass media. Anything so powerful in its impact directly affects world politics as well.

Mass Media in World Politics

The primary relevance of mass media to world politics has already been noted in our discussion of propaganda. New techniques of conveying messages to an audience have led to great advances in propaganda effectiveness. We identified four different audiences for national propaganda efforts: the state's own people, the people of its allies, the people of neutral or uninvolved states, and the people of its opponents. In reaching each of these audiences, the propagandist makes extensive use of the mass media.

At home, electronic media (radio and television) are used widely, with applications varying according to the richness of the technical installations and the sophistication of the home audience. Printed and visual media—books, magazines, motion pictures, posters—also play a large role. The problem of access is much more complex when a foreign audience is being approached—the audience is in no sense "captive" and must be reached more circumspectly. Radio is especially valuable, since home radio receivers are common everywhere and the technique of beaming short-wave broadcasts is so well developed. Television is useless without receiving sets, which are few outside the Western world. Printed media and the cinema obtain audiences in foreign countries only by sufferance, and their effect depends upon the delicacy and deftness of their approach rather than the strength of their messages.

Western manipulators of the mass media of communications tend to aim at the largest possible audience, even if this demands a dilution of their message content. Communist mass communicators, however, tend to emphasize impact upon the individual listener more than pervasiveness of reception and risk alienating many members of their audience in the interest of security strong responses from a minority segment.

Today critical communication policy problems confront all states with far-reaching decisions. These decisions will not only affect domestic policies for some time to come, but they may also restructure the coming world order in transnational and global communications.

Image Projection in Foreign Policy

Contemporary concern with matters of prestige and status in world politics has led to a concern with the "image" a state "projects" in the course of carrying out its world role. Each self-conscious state tends to formulate the most desirable ego image, and then seeks to project it and gain its wide acceptance abroad. These images vary widely according to the values each society prizes. One state may project strength, another culture, a third moral integrity, a fourth cunning and resourcefulness, and so on. Dissemination of the controlling image and its manipulation for the state's policy purposes are the major tasks of mass media in foreign affairs.

Image projection is an elusive business even within a homogeneous society with a stable value code and the available resources of the communications industry. In world affairs, the image that one state holds of another is only partially the result of deliberate projection by the government concerned. It is also made up of historic impressions, random and uncontrollable events that come to symbolize the state, "unintentional propaganda" (such as the behavior of tourists and government officials, motion pictures, and so on), and the image of that particular state which other governments, for their own purposes, choose to project. Image projection in this case falls far short of its goal.

National concern with image projection has had a clear impact on the formulation and conduct of foreign policy. Many states insist on adhering to their image in performing the routine and special tasks of foreign policy. A state committed to an image of strength may overlook opportunities for successful compromise. A state conceiving itself as superior in culture may be caught in irrelevant posturing with no policy content. The dangers of "imagery" in foreign policy frequently overshadow whatever gain it may promise. Mass media does not make very effective instruments of foreign policy, as excessive reliance on these devices may well produce more difficulties than they solve.

Destructive and Constructive Applications

The methods of mass communication, like almost any technical skill, are neutral and without policy significance. However, they may be put to destructive and dangerous uses or they may serve constructive ends—the decision is left to responsible policymakers. Examples of both categories abound in the contemporary world.

Destructively (at least potentially), mass media are appropriate for intensifying nationalist hatreds and the tensions component of an international confrontation. By mass methods the people of one state may be worked into a condition of intensive hostility toward another people, and great pressure may be generated. Adamant public positions on crisis issues can be developed, while equally powerful drives for adoption of new policies can be unleashed. Perhaps more significant than any of these is the role of mass media in filtering and interpreting the flow of information received by the audience. Whether acting on its own or as a tool of the government, the mass communication machine in any state is the means whereby individual citizens acquire both factual data and authoritative interpretations of the problems their government faces. The state of mass opinion in a modern society at any particular moment is to a major extent the work of the mass communicators in that society.

The significance of mass communications techniques is the opportunity that they offer governments to monopolize communications in a society. This degree of centralized information generation and diffusion was not possible in the past. In the past, there were storytellers in every town. Now, the state is the only legal storyteller.

Constructively, mass communication media are potentially important to the creation of a global consensus. In today's rapidly moving world, opinion can focus on a particular issue in time to affect its outcome only if the mass media purvey the information widely and quickly enough. Technical execution of the task is relatively simple, in view of the advanced state of the art today. The difficulty is due partly to the national identification of the communicators and to the confusion of motivations and evaluation displayed by these individual practitioners. A cohesive world community is conceivable only if individuals are tied into a single and responsive communications network. This is the great opportunity that lies before today's technologists of message transmission.

Production, Consumption, Distribution

Another technological problem is constituted by great changes in world production, consumption and distribution, of economic goods. Each of these three areas has been affected directly by the technological revolution we have been analyzing throughout this chapter. So vast are the economic implications of modern technology that we can do no more than suggest a few of the leading considerations.

New Production Techniques

Almost every aspect of industrial technology has affected production in a remarkable way. Best known of the new techniques is "automation"—the application of electronic controls and simplified patterns to the production of higher-quality goods by only a fraction of the labor force formerly needed. Even nonautomated industry has been so revolutionized by new techniques that almost any factory built before 1945 is obsolete today. This has been dramatically demonstrated by the industrial success of the war-devastated states of Europe since 1945. Forced to rebuild industrial plants from the ground up, they have been able to incorporate new arrangements and techniques, with a consequent impressive gain in productivity.

The principal result of new production techniques has been a great increase in the capacity of the world economy to produce goods of all sorts. More goods are available for consumption than ever before, and the trend is toward a continuation of the upward spiral of productivity. This phenomenon is independent of any considerations of profit margins, markets, or employment. It is simply a macroeconomic conclusion that the world, viewed as a unit of production, is increasing its gross product at a significant rate. The social and political consequences are functions of decisions made in other contexts, and cannot be inferred from the mere fact of an upward trend in production. It is up to the policymaker of the future to decide how this new abundance can best be put to the improvement of the lot of humanity.

Rising Consumer Expectations

Paralleling the revolution in production technique is an analogous upward curve in the rise of consumerism in the industrial states and more recently in the less-developed countries. Regardless of the standard of living enjoyed by an individual, the urge for consumerism is constant. Although the United States, with its consumption economy of "affluence," has long set the trend for higher standards of living, Western Europe, the Soviet Union, and the semiindustrialized societies in the Middle East, Latin America, North Africa, and Southeast Asia have recently followed suit.

Worldwide interest in consumption of economic goods has placed many governments in a dilemma. Most are committed to collectively phrased nationalist goals whose attainment will call for a significant portion of national production to be committed to the "public sector" of the economy; but a heavy burden of armament and the capital formation prerequisite to industrial development require that individual consumption be limited. However, the increasingly vocal demand of the mass public for more of the better things of life inhibits the vigor with which the government can prosecute the themes of sacrifice and dedication so necessary to public programs. No government has yet found a satisfactory escape from this quandary.

The Problem of Distribution

The state system divides the world into a collection of commonly accepted independent and self-sustaining economies. Some of these are productive of surpluses, while others can do no more than budget deprivation. At the subsistence level, for example, today's food production potential is adequate to feed the entire population of the world; in other words, hunger exists only because of failures of distribution.

How, within the present structure of the world economy, can distribution be rationalized so that increased productivity can be reflected in increased consumption and a richer and better life for everyone? Some of the world's most serious thought has been addressed to this question in the past decade and a half. It is a strange turn of fate that makes some economies suffer from an excess of consumer demand, while a combination of social, economic, and political inhibitions impede the socially and politically useful distribution of needed goods.

However, an international solution to the problem of local Malthusian situations is unrealistic. *If* world production were shared equally among everybody on earth, there would be no starvation. True. *But,* since an international solution is not forthcoming, it behooves us to concentrate, once again, on national development. Indeed, in the 1970s international food aid has been criticized for discouraging local production. Remember that in the nineteenth century capitalist exponents of the laissez-faire school criticized charitable do-gooders for taking away incentives for work. Recent criticism of food aid reiterates this perennial half-truth. International aid *can,* under certain circumstances, discourage national development.

Also, traditional eating habits cause malnutrition in the sense that, for approximately nine cents a day, one could get all the needed nutrients by eating only soybeans, vitamin capsules, etc. But for cultural reasons, people want food to taste good and be socially acceptable.

Political Significance

The political ramifications of these general observations are self-evident. The basic economic issues of production and consumption have been sharpened by the technological breakthroughs of the contemporary era. Politically, the world emphasizes division and separateness; economically, the maximum social advantage is attainable only in a system emphasizing unity and joint action. The economic problems of the contemporary world are insoluble on a state level, except for a few fortunate states of great expanse and rich resource endowment. Perpetuation of the national attack on global economic issues can do no more than buy time, and may possible eventually worsen the problems or intensify differences. Here, as in other areas, no automatic or guaranteed response to the challenge of technology exists. Policymakers will discover new and possibly more rewarding approaches only insofar as they are able to devise new structures for action that leave room for a broader basis of calculation.

Computers

The role of the computer as thinker and decision maker in human affairs and world politics is still being assessed after more than twenty years of study. While computer technology has had a clear and dramatic impact in almost every field of management to which it has been applied, much uncertainty is still encountered in this field. This is in part due to leeriness on the part of many after seeing that computer capabilities have not lived up to previous expectations, partially due to the very subjective nature of the field itself. Finally, the goals themselves are often none too definite.

Computers, with their massive memories, can be used most effectively in two ways—in data storage and manipulation, and in simulations. There is no dispute as to the computer's value in the former, particularly in fields such as intelligence analysis, where the massive amounts of information which must be dealt with make effective manual manipulation impractical, if not inconceivable. (Cryptography—code making and breaking—as it is practiced today is defined in terms of the latest technology available.)

Uncertainty arises in evaluating the effectiveness of conflict simulation, wherein the computer is given a set of circumstances, capabilities, and "rules of play" and asked to act out potential outcomes of a particular situation—for example, the causes of World War I, a potential Mideast war, or a potential land war in Western Europe. While these "games" often give the player or the interpreter a fair idea of relative importance of various factors (supply problems, geographic imperatives), these can only be interpreted in light of the importance that differing factors are given in the game's instructions—as in other computer applications, the output is only as reliable as the input. Also, little allowance is made for the unforeseen. Thus a major problem in postsimulation thinking is that it may narrow thinking a bit much for the planners. None of the "five (or fifty) most likely scenarios" is guaranteed to occur. Input is also often a problem in that cultural prejudice or insensitivity may interfere with accurate representation of motives, interests, and so on. While it is certainly an overstatement to say that the computer and computer thinking got the United States into Vietnam, the United States learned some painful lessons there concerning the limits of the value of computer simulation.

A special problem of computer application to international relations deals not with the uses of the computer itself, but rather with the computer as a factor in international trade, particularly with the Third World. Computer technology would allow these states to skip over considerable portions of industrial development, making it immediately possible for them to become competitive in world markets. This applies not only to management technology, but also to weapons technology. This problem becomes more pressing as technology continues to develop. Many American computer specialists feel that it is best for less-developing countries to gradually progress through the stages of development that the industrial countries have gone through, vis-à-vis computer technology, in order for them to achieve the most satisfactory integration of computers into their societies. This was happening as a matter of course until recently. It could be charged that the West was dumping its "previous-generation" technology on the less-developing countries. However, part of the development of computer technology has been a trend of decreasing costs, which make "current-generation" technology no more expensive than the "previous generation's."

Recommended Readings

BLOOMFIELD, LINCOLN P., ed. *Outer Space: Prospects for Man and Society* (rev. ed.). New York: American Assembly, Columbia University, Frederick A. Praeger, 1968.

BRONOWSKI, JACOB. *The Ascent of Man.* Boston: Little, Brown and Company, 1976.

CHAMBERLAIN, N. *Beyond Malthus: Population and Power.* Englewood Cliffs, N.J.: Prentice-Hall, 1972.

CHOU, MARYLIN, DAVID P. HARMON, JR., HERMAN KAHN, and SYLVAN WITTWER. *World Food Prospects and Agricultural Potential.* New York: Frederick A. Praeger, 1977.

Committee for Economic Development. *Nuclear Energy and National Security.* New York: Committee for Economic Development, 1976.

GERBNER, G. *Communications Technology and Social Policy.* New York: John Wiley & Sons, 1973.

GREEN, DANIEL. *The Politics of Food.* London: Gordon Gemonesi, 1975.

HAYAMI, YUJIRO, and VERNON W. RUTTAN. *Agricultural Development: An International Perspective.* Baltimore: Johns Hopkins Press, 1971.

HAYES, DENIS. *Rays of Hope: The Transition to a Post-Petroleum World.* New York: W.W. Norton, 1977.

KUHN, THOMAS. *The Structure of Scientific Revolutions.* Chicago: University of Chicago Press, 1970.

LOVINS, AMORY. *Soft Energy Paths: Towards a Durable Peace.* Cambridge, Mass.: Ballinger Press, 1977.

MCNAMARA, ROBERT. *Accelerating Population Stabilization Through Social and Economic Progress.* Washington, D.C.: Overseas Development Council, 1977.

PIEL, JOSEPH E., and JOHN G. TRUXAL, eds. *Man and His Technology: Problems and Issues.* New York: McGraw-Hill Book Company, 1973.

SAGAN, CARL, and JEROME AGEL. *The Cosmic Connection: An Extraterrestrial Perspective.* New York: Dell, 1975.

SAMPSON, ANTHONY. *The Seven Sisters: the Great Oil Companies and the World they Made.* New York: Viking Press, 1975.

SCHILLER, H. I. *Mass Communication and Cultural Domination.* White Plains, NY: International Arts and Sciences Press, 1976.

SUSSKIND, CHARLES. *Understanding Technology.* Baltimore: Johns Hopkins Press, 1973.

Interdependence, North-South Relations, and Development

12

For over three hundred years the state has been a viable action unit for the conduct of political relations among peoples. The logic of statehood and the assumptions of the state system were laid down in the Western world in the era before the Industrial Revolution. When this great transformation in the method of production launched the massive reorientation in the conditions of 'human life that still exists today, the incompatibility of the state form with rational economic life for individuals became apparent.

Despite the expectations of individuals everywhere, no state is economically self-sufficient. All are in some measure dependent upon outside sources for some share of their economic goods. Resources are not distributed among states in any recognizable proportion to demand; raw materials inadequately supplied in one state may be in surplus in a neighboring state. States differ in their productive skills and plants, so that many commodities are obtainable advantageously or even exclusively only from certain favored states. Since all people today have economic goals, these differences in physical, political, and human economic circumstances lead to different and often conflicting economic policies by governments.

Interdependence, Integration, and Convergence

Integration

There is a tendency to confuse the two concepts of integration and interdependence. *Integration* is a condition where social, economic, political, and communication systems are technified to the extent that exchange or transaction is the rule. It is underscored by organizational ability and managerial skills. However, the term integration is commonly used to refer to relationships among states which leads to system properties that could be lacking if considered separately, i.e., the process by which two or more actors in the global system form a new set. *Interdependence* is the sharing of sovereignty, responsibility, and decision making. However, the term interdependence is commonly used to refer merely to a state of affairs of mutual dependency, i. e., the condition where any event in the global system affects another part. In our view, interdependence is a political process consciously realized and refers to a structure of relationships; integration is a technical condition.

Integration is usually analyzed within the contexts of functionalism and communication theory. Functionalism, developed by David Mitrany and Ernst Haas, asserts that the national-state cannot respond adequately to the technical, economic, and social challenges of modern society.[1] Mitrany proposes a restructuring of the global system into a horizontal organization consisting of international administrative units instead of a vertical organization based on national hierarchy. Mitrany believes that such a structure would abolish the national distortions between states and eliminate conflict. Sovereignty will lose its meaning, cooperation will increase, and technology will overshadow diplomacy. For Ernst Hass, functional integration is possible only in pluralistic societies where power is not monopolized by a single group but is shared equally by all groups. Political disagreements should not alter the consensus on basic values. A bureaucratization of the decision-making process will facilitate and achieve harmony. Economic integration opens the process for a gradual political integration through centralization of the decision-making process. The result is the creation of a new state. Haas differs with Mitrany on the strategic value of centralized institutions in the integration process.

Karl Deutsch in his work on communication distinguishes between two types of political communities: the pluralist community where groups maintain their autonomy and the complex community where groups enjoy no autonomy.[2] In the complex community groups are swallowed up in a central unit. This type of integration requires common values, perceptions, and traditions. In the pluralist community, integration is achieved through more reduced social conditions. The social values are not contradictory and the perceptions of elites are not harmonized by the common interest. According to Deutsch, pluralist integration is more easy to achieve than complex integration.

---

[1] See David Mitrany, *A Working Peace System* (Chicago: Quandrangle Books, 1966) and Ernst B. Haas, *Beyond the Nation-State: Functionalism and International Organization* (Stanford, Calif.: Stanford University Press, 1964).

[2] See Karl Deutsch, *Political Community at the International Level: Problems of Definition and Measurements* (New York: Doubleday & Co., 1952).

Interdependence

Interdependence carries with it the potential for both conflict and cooperation. Increased mutual vulnerability precipitates moderation and cosmopolitanism. Also, it becomes more difficult to contain the spill over of new science and technology across national boundaries. At the same time, interdependence poses threats to global stability. An incident in a region exporting raw materials could have dramatic consequences in another region. Less mobile elements (i.e., unions, farmers) may defend narrow interests.

Interdependence may consist of the sharing of objectives and aspirations only, as has characterized the political and psychological posture of the United States in recent years. The less-developed countries view interdependence as the sharing of international growth by the industrial states with the Third World. It is the material effects and consequences upon them that characterize their concept of interdependence. Only the European Community has developed an interdependence representing the sharing of responsibility and acting together.

Technological advances have accelerated the processes of integration in the present global system but have not produced structures of global interdependence. The concept of interdependence encounters a tradition of political thought which postulates the logic of international fragmentation, reduces relations among actors to military-strategic global policy, and ideologizes history as a static law of anarchy. Instead of interdependence, the global system is experiencing a diffused web of dependencies.

Convergence Theory

The concept of interdependence, of peace through convergence between diverse actors in the global system, is quite recent. Of course, we can find "great ancestors" of the idea—Alexis de Tocqueville foresaw a common trend toward democracy as a result of industrialization beyond the rivalry of the United States and Russia. Max Weber observed that social systems are "mixed orders" in constant evolution and perpetual change. Thorstein Veblen predicted the growing power, in every industrial society, of a new class of decision makers: the managers. But the contemporary notion of interdependence appears first in the 1950s in the works of economists, sociologists, and political scientists: George Kennan, Walt W. Rostow, Raymond Aron, Jan Tinbergen, and John Kenneth Galbraith in the West and among Marxist writers including Georg Lukacs and Andrei Sakharov. Some of these analysts argue that there is a symbiotic movement, a new mixed system emerging from interaction between economic development techniques and patterns of social organizations. Others assert that there is a transition to a new synthetic system, totally different from its roots.

Pitrim Sorokin tried to determine the sociological similarities between the United States and the Soviet Union.[3] He proposed a convergence toward a mixed sociocultural model, since both capitalism and socialism are defective and cannot bring a better future. The development of relationships between the two societies will differ from the Marxist historical law. The law of progressive social changes leads to the formation of a "hybrid" model, which appears in different fields: natural sciences, techniques, social sciences, philosophy, ethics, education, sports and leisure, arts, religion, family life, sex, economic systems, social relations, and political institutions. Beyond Sorokin's "macrosociological" approach, Jan Tinbergen's "microeconomical" theory classifies and analyzes the tendencies of both systems.[4] In the West, this phenomenon is seen in the growth of every economic sector—the growth of the public sector, the growing budget of government, antitrust measures, comprehensive planning and cost/benefit analysis, and measures against inflation which affect prices, salaries, and state aid. In Marxist societies, it is seen in the specialization in production, new technocracy with managerial skills, income according to productivity, use of monetary indices and capital interest, individual consumption and more meaningful free choices, acknowledgement of international trade, and a certain decentralization and autonomy in the economic decision-making process. Tinbergen concludes that there is a reciprocal imitation. However, he does not select one of the two aspects, Eastern capitalization or Western socialization. Beyond the differences, divergences are not definitive.

Walt W. Rostow asserts that economic development passes through the following stages: traditional society, preconditions for takeoff, takeoff, drive to maturity, and the age of high mass consumption. At the end of those five phases will appear a more humane stage, "beyond consumption." According to Rostow, both the Soviet Union and the United States are in a period of rapid transformation. In fact, there is only a stage difference between the development of Western capitalist and socialist societies. It is a difference in degree and not in kind. The Soviet Union is technically and psychologically ready to enter the mass consumption society.[5] The remaining obstacle is government's decision to spend an increasing part of its budget in defense appropriation and heavy

---

[3] See his books *Russia and the West* (New York: E. P. Dutton, 1950) and *The Basic Trends of Our Time* (New Haven: Yale University Press, 1964).
[4] See his book *Central Planning* (New Haven: Yale University Press, 1964).
[5] See Walt W. Rostow, *The Stages of Economic Growth,* 2nd ed. (Cambridge: Cambridge University Press, 1971).

industry—the goal of the industrial military complex being world supremacy and dominance. This is only a transitional era, however, and the evolution toward mass consumption cannot be stopped indefinitely. The Soviet Union will catch up with the United States in industrial production, and parity will bring a typological conversion in the Soviet Union. Beyond the fifth stage of development, production and diffusion of consumer goods and services with urbanization will characterize the industrial society.

Less ambitious than Rostow, John Kenneth Galbraith analyzes only the actual industrial stages of development.[6] The technological revolution transforms modern societies into affluent societies and affects capitalist as well as socialist societies. The two systems, similar in their technostructures, develop into new industrial state syntheses. The technostructure, a product of business managers and state appointees, provides the absence of conflict between political and economic power if not their harmony. It assures security and growth and technical progress which allow for profit maximization. It also establishes control over production and investments which leads to consumption pragmatism instead of market. Production, capital, and technology are the features of the new industrial state, a result of the evolution of Western and Marxist industrial societies which will converge.

Raymond Aron emphasizes that certain specific patterns are common to all industrial states.[7] He identifies five characteristics of the industrial society: (1) separation between private enterprise and the national economy; (2) division of labor in modern enterprise; (3) accumulation of capital; (4) the vitality of the economy and economic forecasting; and (5) concentration of productive forces in the urban sector. Every industrial society converges toward a new kind of society characterized by social egalitarianism and political participation.

Another sociologist, Reinhard Bendix, compares the effects of industrialization in Great Britain, the United States, and the Soviet Union.[8] He asserts that the evolution of industrial societies is marked by the rise of a new class sharing a common ideology and power. This class is different from the elite of nonindustrial societies in its recruitment, training, and mentality.

Andrei Sakharov emphasizes that social development in the United States and the Soviet Union evolves toward more complex structures and forms of management which will produce a new class of managers whose

---

[6] See his book *The New Industrial State*, 2nd rev. ed. (Boston: Houghton Mifflin Co., 1972).
[7] See his books *The Industrial Society: Three Essays on Ideology and Development* (New York: Frederick A. Praeger, 1967) and *Marxism and Existentialists* (New York: Harper & Row, 1969).
[8] See his book *Work and Authority in Industry* (Berkeley: University of California Press, 1974).

social character will be about the same in both countries.[9] Sakharov foresees four stages of development: (1) political democratization in Marxist societies and the victory of peaceful coexistence in the capitalist countries; (2) transformation of ownership structure in capitalist societies and collaboration with socialist countries under the prudent leadership of the liberal bourgeoisie; (3) collaboration of socialist and capitalist countries to assist the Third World; and (4) scientific and technological revolution within the socialist and capitalist systems which will lead toward the creation of a world government and the disappearance of contradictions between these systems.

This vision of convergence is quite optimistic, anticipating the end of ideology, the meeting of the socialist and capitalist systems, and the appearance of the new person. Other writers, such as Herbert Marcuse, are more pessimistic.[10] Marcuse argues that both socialists and capitalists, through technological progress, will move toward a dehumanization of social relations. He sees future individuals dominated by an antihuman technology.

Convergence theories suffer from at least three weaknesses. First, we cannot be reasonably certain that methods of production and social structures will become closer. There is little evidence to support this proposition. Divergences could also grow. Second, economic convergence does not produce a convergence of political structure. Cultural systems do not give up easily. Finally, there is little guarantee that global convergence will produce world peace. The evolution toward a more homogeneous society does not exclude confrontation. Throughout modern history identical structures have attempted to destroy one another. Unity is not certain to change minds. We can only hope that humanity "beyond convergence" will be more rational than in the presently divided world.

North-South Relations and the New Economic Order

The global system comprises the developed countries (the North), the affluent countries in North America, Western Europe, and Japan which account for about 15 percent of the world population but more than 60 percent of world income, and the less-developed countries (the South), scores of poor countries in Asia, Africa, and Latin America which comprise most of humankind, but possesses little of the earth's bounty. Both

---

[9] See Andrei Sakharov, *Progress, Coexistence, and Intellectual Freedom* (New York: W. W. Norton & Co., 1968); and Morrison Salisbury, *Sakharov Speaks* (New York: Alfred A. Knopf, 1974).
[10] See his book *One Dimensional Man* (Boston: Beacon Press, 1964).

the North and the South conduct economic relations within a framework that is not presently redistributing wealth and is disadvantageous to the South, which remains characterized by underdevelopment and its social consequences. The North and the South advocate development, yet each views the methods to achieve it from different perspectives.

The New International Economic Order?

The North's development strategy consists of improving those sectors of the less-developed countries' economies which concern the raw materials needed for the North's industries and consumption. The developed states generally discourage heavy industry in the less-developed countries that have the potential of competing with the production of manufactures in the North. The developed states protect themselves from competition through the application of quotas, tariffs, and other devices which are monitored by market demand.

The developing countries seek a solution to their plight in the establishment of a new international economic order. They aspire to develop by augmenting their income through exports of raw materials. At the present time, due to the higher remuneration obtained in the export of manufactured products, the less-developed countries are striving to industrialize.

While the North and the South are dependent upon one another, each group's dependence varies in terms of raw materials, manufactured products, capital, technology, industrial capacity, political and military power, and cultural vitality. The North possesses heavy industries, large capital, and military power, but is dependent upon raw materials to fulfill its market demand. Although the South is economically, militarily, politically, and culturally weaker, it can exert substantial leverage through its possession of vital raw materials.

The condition of mutual dependence between the North and the South does not alter the disadvantages experienced by the South in the present international economic order. The position of the less-developed countries may quite often be described as a position of vulnerability rather than dependence. It is a condition of defenselessness. Dependence implies reliance rather than defenselessness. Therefore, the South's advocacy of a new international economic order is due to its vulnerability rather than its dependence upon the North.

Karl Sauvant and Haja Hasempflug provide an excellent summary of the proposals of the less-developed countries in the Paris North-South dialogue to bring about changes in global economic relations as well as the developed countries' reaction to those proposals. These include:

1. Orientation of the international monetary system toward the interests of the developing world.
2. Production cartels along the lines of OPEC.
3. Commodity agreements to regulate prices and quantities.
4. Linkage of export prices in the developing countries to the prices they have to pay for imports (under the general heading of indexation).
5. Extension of preferential treatment in trade.
6. Recognition of developing countries' permanent sovereignty over their natural resources, covering also the issue of exploiting the ocean floor and the related question of territorial waters.
7. Structural policies in the industrial countries to promote the industrial development of the developing nations.
8. Transfer of advanced technology to the developing countries on preferential terms—to some extent without a quid pro quo but with guarantees by governments.[11]

The North regards these demands as far-reaching. The developed countries feel that the proposals of the South would dismantle the market-based global economic system. Exponents of the position of the North argue that the demands of the South would create a severe imbalance in the developed countries, for they would favor countries which are less integrated in the world economy due to their considerable reserves of raw materials.

On the "threatening" proposal of cartels along the lines of OPEC, the argument follows that cartels have a limited exporting power because the developed countries can in most instances use other raw materials (or synthetics) as substitutes. The development of production techniques would reduce the consumption of raw materials and the import of raw materials from countries not members of cartels.

The third proposal, on indexation, also meets the opposition of the North—again for the imbalance it would create: Developed countries with low inflation rates would suffer from the indexation of raw material prices, while countries with high rates of inflation would profit.

The new international economic order as envisaged by the South meets skepticism in the North regarding its effectiveness in bringing about development. It is asserted that its scope will be limited by one very important factor: Over half the raw materials exported in the world come from the industrialized countries of the North. Accordingly, the argument follows, any measure to support prices in the South would benefit the main exporters of raw materials, which ironically have long since reached the development stage.

[11] See Karl Sauvant and Haja Hasempflug, eds., *The New International Economic Order: Confrontation and Cooperation Between North and South* (Boulder: Colorado Westview Press, 1977).

The South's demand for the extension of preferential treatment in trade also faces opposition by the North. The North feels that generalized tariff preferences should be granted slowly and incrementally to avoid social and economic problems in the developed countries. In regard to the proposal of the South to promote industrialization, the North favors industrialization on a sectoral basis, and on a basis not competitive to the industries of the developed countries.

As with industrialization, the transfer of advanced technology also provokes the North's protectionist tendencies. Most of the advanced technology in the South is within the jurisdiction of multinational corporations which monopolize technology in order to promote their economic interests. These MNCs seek to retain control of patents and discourage or exclude competitors. The South obviously desires to gain access to this valuable technology.

On the exploration and exploitation of the ocean floor and the question of territorial waters, the less-developed countries favor a strong international authority capable of allocating and redistributing resources in an equitable manner. The developed countries, which possess the technology to extract these resources, favor a weak international authority, thus ensuring themselves a greater freedom of movement to promote their economic interests.

In conclusion, the developed states see the proposals of the less-developed countries contributing to imbalances within the global system favorable only to the less-developed countries. The developed countries would like to avoid any new forms of disequilibrium and at the same time reduce the gap existing between the less-developed countries.

The North-South Dialogue

The proposals of the South were presented by the less-developed countries in 1974 at the Seventh Special Session of General Assembly of the United Nations. A stalemate still exists in the North-South dialogue, as demonstrated at the 1977 Paris North-South Conference. The South accused the North of not favoring the imports of manufactured products from the less-developed countries. The North's complaints were directed at its area of greatest dependence: energy. The developed states requested consultation on oil pricing and an end to oil indexation. The less-developed countries demanded a larger transfer of real resources, stable and remunerative prices for raw materials, generalized preferences for manufactured exports and more influence in the management of international financial institutions.

Jahangir Amuzegar has provided an insightful analysis of the North-South dialogue.[12] He observes that the Paris conference recorded three results: (1) the North agreed to contribute $1 billion to a Special Action Program to assist low-income countries; (2) the North agreed to finance buffer stocks for certain raw materials exported by the less-developed countries; and (3) the industrial states agreed to increase their volume of development assistance. The North also reached consensus with the South on the importance of energy availability and supply for world economic development, on the principle of international cooperation in marketing and distributing primary commodities, on stressing assistance for infrastructural development in the less-developed countries, and on a number of noncontroversial aspects of private foreign investment such as less-developed countries' access to capital markets.

The province of consensus between North and South, however, excluded the main issues separating them. They could not agree on the relationship between the price of oil and its supply. The issue of raw materials and trade as provided for in the United Nations Conference on Trade & Development Program for Commodities in Nairobi in 1976 and the establishment of the $6 billion Common Fund which the less-developed countries consider central to the new international economic order were left out. The conference could not agree on the issue of debt relief for the most seriously affected states. And lastly, North and South could not reach agreement on measures against inflation.

The present world economic system remains suspended between two development stages—an old one fighting against death and a new one struggling to be born.

Development and Approaches to Development

As with the tension of world politics in the nuclear era, which arose largely from the inevitably frustrating effort to fit the contemporary environment into traditional political categories, the tensions of national politics in the less-developed countries arise from their equally frustrating effort to fit the modern concept of the national-state into their traditional institutions.

[12] See his article "A Requiem for the North-South Conference," *Foreign Affairs*, October 1977, pp. 136–59.

Approaches to Development

Both Western and Communist conceptions of the development process have been ambushed by events in the Third World since 1945. A conceptual crisis accelerated by the declining intensity of the Cold War and the erosion of shared values in industrialized states has even created doubts about the validity of shared visions of the future and the inevitability of progress endorsed by both Marxists and conventional theorists.

Current theories of development, especially the notion of a "revolution of rising expectations" combined with the notion of a "revolutionary vanguard," present serious policy dilemmas for the United States. On the one hand, failure to promote development effectively in a world where communication has raised levels of expectations will guarantee revolution. On the other hand, rapid development will only accelerate revolution. In effect, given the current state of theoretical consensus, reasonable persons can conclude that the only viable policy alternative for the United States would be to promote revolution. It is no accident then, that intellectual consensus in the United States for the International politics of "stability" is in a crisis.

The ebullient optimism which kicked off the 1960s as the "decade of development" has degenerated into theoretical and policy frustration. Some development did, of course, take place. But the optimistic thesis of gradual peaceful change and the rise of social democracy espoused by Western liberals has not been justified. Nor has there been an increasing tempo of revolution held as an article of faith by various Marxist schools of thought. It is true, of course, that the end of the Cold War has contributed to a lowering of the priority of sponsoring development in advanced countries. More recently, the growing world ecological crisis has raised doubts as to the adaptive value of advanced industrialism in its present form, even for advanced states.

Not so long ago, a given state was considered to be underdeveloped if it failed to fit a model structured by Western notions of politics and community: If the state lacked democratic, competitive political parties and a high standard of living, it was by definition underdeveloped. Few scholars gave serious thought to the dynamic nature of the modernization process, and it was generally believed that a people emerging from colonialism would naturally express their independence in a systematic effort to construct a modern state.

This optimistic approach was reflected in the few early postwar analyses of the newly independent states of Asia and Africa. These were largely historical, administrative, and anthropological studies. Historians were generally preoccupied with the origin and evolution of particular states. Political scientists engaged in comparative analyses of newly formed constitutional, electoral, and legislative processes, employing the conceptual scheme of the Western political tradition. Perhaps alone among the social scientists, anthropologists rejected the normative patterns of thought that characterized most of the studies produced in this initial period. As inveterate defenders of everyone's cultural values, anthropologists had always subscribed to a relativistic ethic that opposed imposition of alien rule on weaker societies.

Because the early transitional period in the new states of the Third World was characterized by stubbornly persisting political instability and social discontinuity, early enthusiasm for independence and the happy anticipation of these states evolving along modern democratic lines began to fade. The disappointingly unrestrained revolutionary momentum and turmoil that maintained themselves, instead of the expected development of stable institutions and economic growth, led to a reexamination of prior assumptions. Using such indices as per capita income, literacy rates, and levels of industrialization, economists and sociologists associated political instability with economic backwardness. Some emphasized the need for economic and military assistance to countries threatened by Communist aggression and infiltration. Political scientists often limited their approach to the context of the Cold War. As the U.S.-USSR rivalry intensified, the practice of international development and alternative approaches to the problems of modernization (communist versus democratic) acquired considerable status as important foreign policy issues.

Western social scientists were reluctant to think about the issues of modernization in a meaningful pattern. Having conceived the problem in terms of the unprecedented speed and intensity of social change, they found it difficult to make their assumptions explicit or to relate theory to specific issues. However, the resulting concern with modernization problems, as issues in themselves, had the solutory effect of forcing the social sciences to devise new categories and techniques for analysis of the phenomena of rapid social and political change.

One outgrowth of this trend was a "revolution" *in the social sciences.* The decline of the restrictive normative approach in the social sciences was a postwar development. There was widespread optimism that social science research on development stood on the threshold of considerable achievement. This was a result of the increasing use of comparative analysis techniques and of cross- and interdisciplinary cooperation. To this end, theorists of development began to devote themselves to the broadening of research methodologies and to the construction of developmental theories which produced useful predictive hypotheses. Captivated as they continued to be by the patterns of predictability, political scientists were most ambitious in this area of inquiry. This optimism was also reflected in the more recent growth of functional and behavioral theories which attempt to relate political governmental institutions to other dimensions of the social system. This trend was further manifested in the development of the so-called dynamic theories of the future political evolution of the less-developed countries. Only in this way, it was argued, could knowledge of the modernization process be broadened and valid generalizations be developed.

This combined effort toward a deeper understanding of political development, as contrasted with the exclusively technical problems of economic development, is regarded as one of the most significant advances in social science research on states of the Third World. Resting on the assumption that a significant relationship exists between social, economic, and political development, this approach has been praised for providing the policymaker with a fresh and more realistic method of assessing the long-range problems of development.

Because of the often extreme difficulties encountered by the Third World in building modern, politically viable states out of their traditional societies, the primary importance of political development was recognized as the key to the overall process of modernization. It became generally assumed that political development is a precondition of fully successful economic development. Accordingly, social scientists attempted to analyze the problem systematically by coverging on theoretical and methodological interests. The manner in which political scientists use such concepts as "legitimacy," "stability," "adaption," "articulation," "aggregation," and "integration" in place of "constitutions," "elections," "interest groups," and "legislatures" is indicative of the shift toward functional and behavioral theory.

The behavioralists have sought to integrate the ideas of system, culture, function, structure, and action in a conceptual scheme particularly designed for comparative analysis. This approach is an obvious improvement on the narrower and more provincial studies of political behavior, legislation, and other rituals of democratism. It seeks to identify and analyze the politicocultural systems and subsystems in states of whatever levels of political sophistication. Its method of inquiry, relying on sociological and anthropological theory, rejects the earlier separation of comparative politics into East-West, American, African, Asian, and Middle Eastern area studies. This approach advocates an empirical analysis of political functions and the processes of change and modernization without regard to culture or geographical peculiarities. Because of its more precise analytical framework, the behavioral approach has provided a strengthened conceptual unity in the study of comparative politics. But at the same time, the behavioral approach has minimized the importance of values and goals by placing its primary emphasis on processes. Its methods as yet preclude significant treatment of the subjective dimension of modernization.

It is admitted that behavioral methods of research readily enable political scientists to construct refined inventories, detailed charts, and useful models of the political system. Operationalized concepts yield quantitative data on the national political body and provide a means for testing hypotheses.

But if the problem is to be approached in terms of political structure, no particular model can be claimed to represent a necessary or ideal precondition for economic and social development. Even in the present century, industrialized states have experimented with or accepted divergent governmental institutions. These have ranged from monarchies to multiparty democracies, from oligarchic capitalism to democratic centralism. It has also been argued that the new states may require innovative forms of governmental institutions, perhaps related to their own societal values and traditions.

Analysis of Third World development often assumes that a similar corollary of social and economic conditions among less-developed countries is a discrete mode of political development. Despite the improvement in analytical methods and techniques, the problem is often approached with unconsciously implied normative definitions. The most popular approaches are based on the assumptions that democracy is a symptom of modernity, that it is the ideal form of political development, and that it is a prerequisite of development. But democracy has produced so many hybrids and derivations, and is applied to such a multitude of aphorisms, that it has lost its meaning—unless precisely defined within the organic framework of a given state. Such Western culture-bound definitions and approaches to the problems of political development have not served their purpose well.

The expectations as well as the fears of serious theorists and policymakers during the pre- and immediate postindependence phase of the majority of new states were based on a connection between democratic theory, stability, and modernization. This equation has been articulated in many variations. It generally states that stability plus democratization (broadening the base, interest aggregation, etc.) equals at a minimum the necessary preconditions for political modernization. An equation of this sort has apparently served as a model for many scholars—the assumption being that if one examined a given state against the model, the stage of development could be revealed and point the direction in which further study could proceed.

While this is a useful methodology, it has not proved valuable in understanding the political phenomena of the Third World. Perhaps the most important reason for this was based on the factor that these three concepts (democracy, stability, modernization) are normative in nature and lack precise definition. They are also Western concepts evolved from the political evolution intimately connected with Western states. Since their value to the West is hard to define, the attempt to superimpose these on a framework for Third World studies was doomed to fail from the start.

Beyond Economics toward Adaptation

There is more than one viable human value system. Therefore, no transcultural standard exists with which to judge the relative merits of one system against another. It makes little sense to divide humanity into "traditional" and "modern" cultures. All human cultures are constantly evolving, while none stand still. Furthermore, historical precedents of encounters between developed and less-developed societies illustrate that the less-developed society does not become a carbon copy of the more advanced one, but rather a hybrid society. Since the imported values and techniques do not affect all segments of the less-developed society equally, certain groups—the army and the intelligentsia—are more adaptive. The techniques of cultural innovation designed to oppress or indoctrinate—arms and ideas—are most readily acquired by the elite of the less-developed society.

From the Western culture-centric point of view, Westerners call the struggle of former colonies to emulate the technology, life styles, economic practices, and other characteristic behavior of the West "development" or "modernization," as if Westerners were in a position to judge the adaptive value of other societies when Western culture seems nonadaptive even to Westerners. It is quite conceivable that those societies putting up the greatest resistance to the technocratic mentality may be vindicated by history as having refused to go down a blind alley. We may believe or hope that the present transformation from agriculture to "techniculture" (for want of a better word) now sweeping the planet will eventually produce modes of behavior consistent with the ecology of the earth, but such an outcome is neither inevitable nor self-evident.

The usual focus of the study of development—on the nation-state as the unit of analysis—seems to be parochial. And the usual issues of whether modernization can be achieved on an incremental, nondisruptive, and above all peaceful basis appear to be the height of wishful thinking. The average regime has a life cycle of only a few years or even a few months. One of the oldest regimes—the United States of America—is little more than two hundred years old. The other major complex of issues—concerning which ideology or strategy of development will be adapted—seems to suffer from the same myopia. The state of present knowledge is that any regime which invests heavily in mass education and industrial investment begins to look more like other industrialized states. The process appears to relate more to changing the behavioral repertoire of a culture than to the adaptation of a new political program. Russia began modernization (by emulating European states) with Peter the Great. By the year 1912, five years before its revolution, Russia was already the fourth-ranking industrial power. It may be that former colonies had merely exchanged the forced feeding and indignities associated with being imperial wards for the less direct exploitation implicit in becoming disciples of one developmental model for another. Japan consciously chose to emulate Great Britain in its drive for techniculture. Does anyone seriously think it would have made any difference over the next five hundred years if Japan had instead chosen France or Germany?

The economic standard commonly used as the primary criterion of development is being increasingly questioned by both emerging societies and the West. Radical states such as China, which claims that it is not emulating the West's pattern of growth, view the Western concept of development as a residual form of imperialism and as a cover for a continuing exploitative arrangement between imperial powers and their former colonies. Western ecologists point out that it is per capita gross national product (GNP) and energy consumption in industrial societies—both usually seen as indices of development—rather than overpopulation which are creating a worldwide environmental crisis. Some long-range planners have even begun to talk about advanced societies where declining population, dropping energy consumption, and negative aggregate GNP growth will be viewed as "progressive." On balance, it seems fair to say that most specialists view the emergence of a distinctive literary, legal, administrative, and political subsystem within the Soviet Union as more significant from a developmental point of view than the USSR's rising GNP.

Our view is that *development*, with its connotation of "bigger is better," is a misnomer. A more appropriate term might be *adaptation*—thus an adaptive society would have stability as its ideal rather than uncontrolled growth. It is quite possible that the twenty-first century will find Western extractive industry and pollution as more repellent and blameworthy than either imperialism or racism. We must treat the development process in both normative and moral terms, rather than from the traditional economic viewpoint or the more current, purely formalistic approaches.

Development: Problems and Prospects*

We view development as a historical process through which human beings choose and create their future within the context of their environment to achieve a humane and creative society. It is concerned with the dignity of the individual, a secure level of self-esteem, and the establishment of institutions appropriate for these ends.

Development is a process whose goals are to realize the human potential for total societies and for the total human being and whose success hinges upon the satisfaction of those goals. The most reliable sources of goals common to humanity are the various documents on human rights, including the United Nations' Universal Declaration of Human Rights, International Covenant on Economic, Social, and Cultural Rights, and International Covenant on Civil and Political Rights; Pope Paul's *Pacem et Terris;* and Third World declarations. Obviously these documents reflect the weaknesses and strengths of the United Nations and the historical context and cultural realities of the time.

A *developed* or adaptive country is one where the obstacles to human freedom, community, and creativity have been as nearly eliminated as possible, where the social, economic, political, and cultural institutions support and stimulate freedom, community, and creativity for all persons, where there is a nearly approximated norm of equal dignity and respect for all persons and groups, and where there is a nearly equal and adequate level of living for all persons.

Development goals are the furthest projection of human objectives consisting of hopes and ideals, the components of the ideal society, the best possible society that can be imagined. Development objectives are the concretely defined goals, considered reasonable and realizable within the limits of available technology and resources, that are established as aspirations within the context of an existing situation. Development targets are short-range objectives, usually those that are selected as the target level of a particular program (e.g., to raise the literacy rate from 30 to 70 percent—70 percent would be the immediate development target). Development targets are reliable objectives between existing situations and the development objectives. Development targets and development objectives should be consistent with and build toward the realization of consciously chosen and explicit development goals.

Modernization is the process of adapting technology for the uses of the society and attempting to make that society more rational, efficient, and predictable, especially through the use of comprehensive planning, rational administration, and scientific evaluation. Modernization also carries the connotation of a more productive society, at least in economic

---

* This section has been coauthored by Brady Tyson, The American University, Washington, DC.

terms. Like development, modernization is always at least a partially conscious effort on the part of some, who therefore have a vision or model of what a "modern" society should look like.

Humanization is the process of enlarging and making more equal the dignity, freedom, opportunity for creativity and community, and welfare of individuals in society, as well as the restructuring of the institutions and culture of that society to support these goals. Therefore, modernization plus humanization equals development.

The goals of development can be divided into two broad categories: the human quality of life and the infrastructure of the development process. The human quality and level of life include:

1. *Physical and mental health*—that state of life and consciousness that supports and stimulates the greatest self-knowledge and community knowledge and realization through the maximization of physical and mental energy and creativity and the maximum diminution of physical and mental malfunctions, diseases, and suffering;
2. *Security, dignity, and freedom*—that state of life of the individual and the group that supports and encourages the greatest self- and community realization through the maximum possible reduction of external threats to the integrity of the individual and group;
3. *Education and training*—that quantity and quality of facilities and resources available to individuals and communities to provide the skills necessary for the preservation, enhancement, and continuous re-creation of culture and the development of the talents and skills of the individual and the group to the maximum degree possible;
4. *Culture and leisure*—that quantity and quality of time and cultural opportunities afforded, as well as the facilities and resources, for the group and for individuals, for cultural development and enrichment, for cultural creation, and for group and individual fulfillment.

The infrastructure of the development process includes:

1. *The system of ecosystemic maintenance*—encompassing the conservation of natural resources, avoidance of pollution and waste, and health and safety support;
2. *Social, cultural, educational, and communications support systems*—to enhance the goals of a developed society, to expand the sense of community and human solidarity, and to stimulate cultural creativity and responsibility;
3. *The political system*—the level and quality of participation in setting social, economic, and political guidelines for the society and the group, the level and quality of responsiveness, review, and accountability of the political officials to its society, the efficiency of administration of public programs, and the level and quality of research and planning in the allocation of social resources and values;
4. *The economic system*—the quality and adequacy of research planning in the

use of human and natural resources for purposes of the production of goods and services, efficiency and adequacy of the quantity and quality in the production of goods and services, including working conditions, the distribution system, and the level and quality of accountability of the economic system to the society for its research, planning, efficiency, administration, and allocation of resources.

Otherwise, development threatens to become collectivistic, fascistic, autocratic, and inefficient. In such an environment weapons and armaments become the hallmark of a developed society. The individual becomes a means to an end. Such an idea of development is a libel upon humankind and an insult to its inate nobility.

Recommended Readings

ALMOND, GABRIEL A., and G. B. POWELL, JR. *Comparative Politics: A Development Approach.* Boston: Little, Brown and Co., 1966.

BERGER, PETER. *Pyramids of Sacrifice: Political Ethics and Social Change.* New York: Basic Books, 1975.

CHOUCRI, N., and V. FERRARO. *International Politics of Energy Interdependence.* Lexington, Mass.: Lexington Books, 1976.

ERB, GUY. *Beyond Dependency.* Washington, D.C.: Overseas Development Council, 1975.

GALTUNG, JOHAN, and WIRAK ANDERS. *Human Needs: Human Rights and Theory of Development.* Oslo: Universitetet i Oslo, Profecoratet i Konflick—Og Fredsforskning, 1976.

GOULET, DENIS. *The New Moral Order: Development Ethics and Liberation Theology.* Maryknoll, N.Y.: Orbis Books, 1974.

HAAS, ERNST B. *Beyond the Nation-State: Functionalism and International Organization.* Stanford, Calif.: Stanford University Press, 1964.

UL-HAQ, MAHBUB. *The Third World and the International Economic Order.* Washington, D.C.: Overseas Development Council, 1976.

KEOHANE, R., and J. NYE, JR. *Power and Interdependence.* Boston: Little, Brown and Co., 1977.

LASZLO, ERVIN et al. *Goals for Mankind: A Report to the Club of Rome on the Horizons of Global Community.* New York: E. P. Dutton and Co., 1977.

MALLY, G. *Interdependence: The European-American Connection in the Global Context.* Lexington, Mass.: Lexington Books, 1976.

MITRANY, DAVID. *The Functional Theory of Politics.* New York: St. Martin's Press, 1976.

ROSTOW, WALT W. *The Stages of Economic Growth* (2nd ed.). Cambridge: Cambridge University Press, 1971.

SCHUMACHER, E. F. *Small Is Beautiful: Economics as if People Mattered.* New York: Harper & Row, 1973.

TINBERGEN, JAN. *RIO: Reshaping the International Order.* New York: E. P. Dutton and Co., 1976.

TUCKER, R. *The Inequality of Nations.* New York: Basic Books, 1977.

Multinational Corporations

13

Multinational corporations (MNCs) have become increasingly the focus of interest of the concerns of world politics. In fact, several of the larger MNCs exert more collective influence than all but a handful of states. The patterns of investment and activity of these corporations affect issues of war and peace, intervention and nonintervention, and may even determine the long-term prospects for world economic development. Little is known about decision-making processes and their underlying rationale within and among these new (and not-so-new) corporate endeavors. The applicable tools of inquiry are alien to national intelligence efforts, because they focus on balance sheets, reports of board meetings, and stock market quotations rather than official government white papers or biographies of policymakers. We are not accustomed to thinking of the foreign policy of Standard Oil or General Motors. But decision making by these companies has as much or more impact on global conflict and cooperation as do the foreign policy decisions of states that are receding in significance as actors.

Historical Evolution of Multinational Corporations

The multinational enterprise is not a recent phenomenon. In 1902 F. A. MacKenzie's *The American Invaders* appeared in London, analyzing the impact of American direct investment abroad stimulated by many American companies, among them Otis Elevator, Singer Company, and General Electric. Before the coming of the Industrial Revolution, international

---

This chapter is adapted from A. A. Said and L. R. Simmons, *The New Sovereigns: Multinational Corporations as World Powers* (Englewood Cliffs, N.J.: Prentice-Hall, 1975).

financial institutions flourished in the fourteenth- and fifteenth-century cities of Venice, Barcelona, and Genoa. In 1689 the Bank of Amsterdam was established to finance the explorations of the Dutch East India Company. The French Compagnie d'Occident was created in 1717 to foster trade with the Louisiana territories, and by the nineteenth century the center of banking activity in Europe had moved to Germany, which had established affiliates in South America, the Far East, and Eastern Europe.

Multinational banking saw its golden age in nineteenth-century England, where much of the economic development of the United States (particularly railroads) was subvented from capital originating in London. It was the failure of the British banking house of Baring Brothers that precipitated the first world financial crisis, a consequence of which was the massive depression in the United States in the 1890s.[1]

Another early form of multinational business was the seventeenth-century trading company, which obtained grants from the crowns of Europe to monopolize colonial trade. Such companies were chartered by the competent mercantile powers—England, Holland, Sweden, Denmark, and Spain—and were manipulated as appendages of the political and economic policies of the country that chartered them.

However, it has only been since the end of World War II that the multinational corporation began to emerge as a pervasive force in world politics. Direct investment by a MNC in a state, as distinguished from portfolio investment, has been a conspicuous feature of national development, generally yielding positive results. Since World War II, direct investment in Australia has been the most important source of capital formation in this area. In the 1960s American, British, and Japanese corporations assumed a major role in furnishing technology and capital to exploit the significant mineral discoveries made during these years. The role of direct investment in modernizing industries and stimulating domestic markets has been generally perceived to be beneficial in such diverse countries as Norway in the development of hydroelectric power, South Africa in mining and gold, Canada in oil, natural gas, and minerals, and also Argentina and the United States.

Direct investment in the less-developed countries has been consistently associated with economic imperialism and colonialism. Although both historically and economically there is sufficient basis to draw such conclusions, often a passionate distaste for imperialism has clouded the separate issue of whether or not the colonized state has derived any benefits from the colonizer. The classic instance in this debate is India, where despite the undeniably inhibiting influences of the British pres-

---

[1] See Ralph W. Hidy, *The House of Baring in American Trade and Finance: English Merchant Bankers at Work* (Cambridge: Harvard University Press, 1949).

ence it still seems unlikely that this country could have undergone modernization alone.[2]

But it has only been since the end of World War II that direct investment abroad leaped from $19 billion to $101.9 billion, while foreign private investment in the United States grew from $8.0 billion to $40.3 billion. The annual growth rate in investment has been approximately 10%.[3] Presently the United States has a GNP of approximately $1.85 trillion per year, and 25% of the world's GNP is generated from branches and subsidiaries of United States corporations; 20% of the gross world product is "European or Japanese tinged."[4]

The sales of "foreign-owned" production not only equal the volume of world exports but have been increasing more rapidly. Judd Polk has estimated that if the current rate of growth is maintained, international production would be worth half the value of aggregate GNPs by the end of the century. It is estimated that between 5 and 10% of the total increase in aggregate GNP of the industrial states was a result of direct investment.[5]

The world seems to be moving toward a situation where a major portion of its industrial output will be dominated by several hundred large corporations. The multinational corporation is in an excellent position to facilitate capital transfers between states, stimulate capital formation, and serve as a conduit for the transfer of technology. The emergence of nonsecurity, development-oriented issues has naturally focused on the activities of these economic entities, as a focal point of transnational relations becomes how nations can preserve their political, economic, and cultural identities while still sharing in the benefits of rapid industrial growth.

The majority of the world's multinational corporations are American based; of the 500 largest corporations in the world, 306 are American and 74 are from the countries of the European Economic Community. Nearly half of *Fortune*'s 500 largest corporations had overseas investments totaling $50 billion[6] (although all large American corporations have extensive foreign holdings). Moreover, 187 U.S. multinationals account for

---

[2] Tapan Mukerjee, "Theory of Economic Drain: Impact of British Rule on Indian Economy, 1840–1900," in *Economic Imperialism*, edited by Kenneth E. Boulding and Tapan Mukerjee (Ann Arbor: University of Michigan Press, 1972), p. 2.
[3] David T. Devlin and Frederick Cutler, "The International Investment Position of the United States: Developments in 1968," *Survey of Current Business* 49, no. 11 (October 1969): 23–26.
[4] Sanford Rose, "The Rewarding Strategies of Multinationalism," *Fortune*, September 15, 1968, p. 100.
[5] The annual gross world product is valued at $3 trillion, 15% of which is produced by multinational corporations.
[6] See Raymond Vernon, "Multinational Enterprise and National Sovereignty," *Harvard Law Review* 45 (March-April 1967): 156.

one-third of the sales and one-half of the assets of U.S. enterprises. Sixty percent of the sales of the Parker Pen Company, nearly $75 million, represents foreign business. Parker has plants in Canada, Britain, South Africa, Argentina, Brazil, Colombia, Mexico, Spain, Australia, Rhodesia, and West Germany.

But not all of the largest multinational enterprises are American. For example, Phillips Lamp Works, headquartered in the Netherlands, operates in some 68 countries. Japanese-based multinational corporations have expanded rapidly so that today Japan is the second largest center of multinationals in the world. In 1965 this position was held by Britain (55 companies), but in 1970 the Japanese had 51 companies to Great Britain's 46.[7]

What, however, do these statistics suggest about the MNC as an actor in the contemporary world environment? Is it of political significance that the aggregate sales of General Motors are larger than many states' GNP? Should we inquire how many armed divisions are controlled by General Motors, or does this merely beg the question? Is General Motors a sovereign actor in the global system, or are most multinational corporations merely appendages of states' foreign policies? Is the multinational corporation an independent actor or a reflection? First, let us make an elementary observation. The multinational firm is an actor that possesses considerable influence but little power in the system. Whatever (little) power it exercises exists in the ability to inadvertently trigger global financial crises. Multinational corporations control such vast quantities of money that they can precipitate world monetary crises by moving only a small proportion of their funds from one country to another. A study made at the request of the International Trade Subcommittee of the U.S. Senate Finance Committee estimated that some $268 billion of short-term liquid assets were held at the end of 1971 by "private institutions on the international financial scene" and that the "lion's share" of this money was controlled by American-based multinational corporations and banks. The $268 billion was "more than twice the total of all international reserves held by all central banks and international monetary institutions in the world at the same date."[8] Because of the enormity of the multinationals' assets, only a fraction needs to be moved for a serious crisis to develop. For examples it is certain that these largely American multinational corporations precipitated the devaluation of the American

---

[7] See George Modelski, "Multinational Business: A Global Perspective," *International Studies Quarterly* 16, no. 4 (December 1972): 411.
[8] Committee on Finance, United States Senate, "Implications of Multinational Firms for World Trade and Investment and for U.S. Labor and Trade" (Washington, D.C.: February 1973), pp. 531–46.

dollar in the monetary crisis of March 1973, as speculators unloaded dollars and purchased German marks and Japanese yen.

Why, then do some writers persist in seeing the American multinational corporation as a "tool" of American imperialism when the American MNC can apparently pursue policies quite independent of—and in contradiction to—those of the United States government? Exponents of the radical critique for example, avoid acknowledging this fact because they attempt to explain foreign policy by merely counting a state's capital assets abroad and by dwelling on those sensational episodes when the United States government has putatively intervened in the affairs of a sovereign state on behalf of an American corporation. Thus the multinational corporation is not viewed as an independent actor capable of pursuing objectives incompatible with the United States' national interest but as a reflection of U.S. foreign policy. There are two problems with this analysis. First, it ignores the extremely tenuous relationship that exists between U.S. direct investment abroad and the U.S. GNP. Only in the wisdom of historical retrospect could so fragile a coefficient as the percentage of U.S. GNP invested abroad be seized upon as an index of national behavior.

The second problem is that such a position ignores to a significant degree the relationship American multinational corporations have had with the Soviet Union and the historical role the American business world has assumed in assisting the Soviets with much-needed technology.

Although it is true that the U.S. government has occasionally intervened abroad on behalf of multinational corporations, American business enterprise abroad was often a pretext for the United States to secure its national interest objectives, wholly unrelated to the interests of the business enterprise.

However, the multinational enterprise should not be confused with a corporation like the British East India Co., created as a tool of a specific foreign policy objective. The very existence of the U.S. Trading With the Enemy Act and the possibilities surrounding its invocation are evidence that this conflicting interest is perceived to exist between the business community and the state. It is evident that the U.S. government has had to devise ways to control American business.

Goals of the Multinational Corporations

The classic formulation of the motivations of states is that they seek the accretion of power and the disposal of that power in the service of their perception of security. The classic formulation of corporate motivation is the profit-maximizing model. However, even this model does not furnish an objective norm for corporate behavior but rather establishes the permissible frontiers or limits of corporate behavior beyond which the corporation cannot go. These frontiers suggest that although the profit-maximizing model is by no means an infallible guide to predicting multinational enterprise behavior, it is closer to the mark than other analyses which persist in explaining the behavior of multinational corporations in terms of the political nomenclature associated with the behavioral phenomena of the state. The multinational corporation is not *power-maximizing*. Among the factors that inform the decisions of the multinational corporations to expand are the need to control resources, the saturation of home markets and access to foreign markets, scarcity of production factors at home, and preferential tax treatment in other countries.[9]

The American multinational corporations often seek access to foreign markets to move behind high tariff walls which would make the export of U.S. goods to these states unprofitable. By having direct access to foreign markets, the multinational corporations are better able to guarantee a supply of products to their markets without the threat of such actions as dock strikes. Often less-developed countries insist that factories or refineries be constructed locally as a joint venture. If penetration of the market cannot be accomplished in any other way, then direct investment is the only logical alternative. Where relatively unskilled labor can be combined with sophisticated technologies, a prima facie case has been made for business expansion abroad.

A powerful motive for a U.S. move abroad is when a native corporation has surplus investment funds for which it sees only marginal opportunities in the United States. Japanese multinational concerns have also accelerated direct investment abroad in recent years. The Normura Research Institute has estimated that Japan's direct investment rose by $2.5 billion in the fiscal year ending March 31, 1972—three times the rise of the preceding year.[10] Among the reasons cited for the activity of Japanese multinationals are increased yen revaluation which has made Japanese exports prohibitively expensive, scarcity of land for industries such as aluminum and oil refining, the rise in Japan's labor wages, and the economic advantages of investing in countries with abundant natural resources.

Charles Kindelberger observes that in a world of perfect competition "direct investment cannot exist." Nowhere is this more evident than in the differential rates of taxing multinational enterprise income that

---

[9] See U.S. Department of Commerce, *The Multinational Corporation: Studies on U.S. Foreign Investment* (Washington, D.C.: U.S. Government Printing Office, 1972), pp. 14–16, for a brief analysis.
[10] *New York Times*, April 16, 1973, p. 59.

exists in different states as inducements to multinational firms.[11] (See Table 13-1).

TABLE 13-1   MNC INCOME TAX

Corporation	Global Tax Rate
Singer	38%
Revlon, Inc.	39
Westinghouse Electric Corp.	42
Pfizer Inc.	42
General Electric Co.	43
Union Carbide Corp.	44
ITT	44
Johnson & Johnson	45
IBM	48
General Motors Co.	48
Eastman Kodak Co.	49
Ford Motor Co.	49
Avon Products Inc.	51

Yugoslavia and Australia represent two distinct examples. In 1972 the United States signed an agreement with Yugoslavia to encourage capital investment in joint ventures. The agreement commits the Overseas Private Investment Corporation to provide insurance and financial aid to American investors. The Yugoslav government responded by eliminating requirements for reinvestment of 20% of profits and holding out an attractive tax rate of 35% on earnings. In the less-developed republics of Montenegro and Macedonia the tax rate is maintained at 14% as an inducement to investors. The *New York Times* reports that "Yugoslavia has registered a total of 73 joint ventures so far. Only two foreign companies have chosen to withdraw. . . . The basic interest of the Yugoslavs is that the foreign partner introduce modern technology and that production be oriented toward the export market."[12]

Changes or fluctuations in a state's posture toward the multinational corporations are factors to be weighed in predicting behavior. Often states provide outright subsidies to multinational enterprises, which can reach 40% of the investment, as in Great Britain.

Finally, it cannot be emphasized too strongly that when multinational enterprises decide to invest in a specific state, it is not necessarily in anticipation of a high rate of profit but for the contribution that plant will make to the multinational corporation's worldwide operation. Thus it

---

[11] *Wall Street Journal*, March 12, 1973, p. 6.
[12] *The New York Times*, January 19, 1973, p. 217.

may be that producing an item in country X will contribute to profits made in country Y where the item is combined with other technological resources and where item X could only be produced at a prohibitive price scale. This can lead to what is known as "transfer pricing," whereby the multinational enterprise adjusts its prices on intracompany sales to minimize losses and maximize profits. In this fashion multinational enterprises can seek to take their profits in states with a lower tax rate or avoid the policies of states seeking to prevent the repatriation of profits that might upset their position in the foreign exchange. These by no means exhaust the rationales upon which multinational corporations have relied in their worldwide expansion.

Multinational Corporations and "Nation-States"

The ranking of countries and corporations according to the size of their annual products raises the familiar argument that some multinational enterprises have evolved into powers more formidable than many states (see Table 13-2). The economic dimensions of the multinational enterprise are indeed staggering, as the previous discussion of world production and direct investment has indicated. But how do these statistics lend themselves to the formulation that the sovereignty of the state is being encroached upon and its role as an actor in the global system obscured?

It is important to emphasize that the decline of the significance of the state as the preeminent actor in the global system has more to do with the deemphasis of external security issues in world politics than the growth of the multinational corporation. Similarly, it is paramount that distinctions between such concepts as "power" and "influence" do not become blurred by the blizzard of statistics relating to world aggregate production. In the present global environment, Japan has little power but significant influence, as judged by the stability of the yen in world monetary affairs. Power is the ability, in a specific situation, to translate resources into capability to compel a settlement of an objective conflict on terms favorable to the actor. Israel has considerable power in the Middle East, none in Southeast Asia, but, however, surprising influence among the African states. The multinational enterprise possesses considerable influence in varying parts of the world. But influence is not power, and it is power that inspires the concept of sovereignty in transnational relations.

TABLE 13-2   THE LARGEST NATIONS AND CORPORATIONS, 1975

STATES AND CORPORATIONS	GNP AND SALES (in billions of dollars)
1. United States	1,508.68
2. USSR	665.91
3. Japan	495.18
4. West Germany	408.75
5. France	304.60
6. China	285.96
7. United Kingdom	214.94
8. Italy	164.11
9. Canada	151.73
10. Brazil	107.87
11. Poland	98.97
12. Spain	95.63
13. India	91.81
14. Netherlands	76.34
15. Australia	76.19
16. East Germany	71.25
17. Mexico	71.17
18. Sweden	64.58
19. Belgium	59.44
20. Czechoslovakia	55.04
21. Switzerland	51.51
22. Iran	48.82
23. **Exxon**	**44.86**
24. Argentina	39.81
25. **General Motors**	**35.72**
26. Austria	35.52
27. Denmark	35.03
28. Turkey	34.59
29. South Africa	33.54
30. **Royal Dutch/Shell Group***	**32.10**
31. Yugoslavia	31.64
32. Romania	27.65
33. Venezuela	26.67
34. Norway	26.24
35. Hungary	26.07
36. Saudi Arabia	24.95
37. **Texaco**	**24.59**
38. Indonesia	24.18
39. **Ford**	**24.00**
40. Finland	24.00
41. Nigeria	23.08
42. Greece	21.50
43. **Mobil**	**20.62**
44. **National Iranian Oil***	**18.85**

* Non-American Multinational Corporations

TABLE 13-2 THE LARGEST NATIONS AND CORPORATIONS, 1975–CONTINUED

STATES AND CORPORATIONS	GNP AND SALES (in billions of dollars)
45. South Korea	18.65
46. Bulgaria	17.77
47. **British Petroleum***	**17.28**
48. **Standard Oil of California**	**16.82**
49. Philippines	15.73
50. Portugal	15.04
51. **Unilever***	**15.01**
52. Thailand	14.54
53. New Zealand	14.46
54. **IBM**	**14.43**
55. **Gulf Oil**	**14.26**
56. Iraq	14.26
57. Taiwan	14.21
58. **General Electric**	**13.39**
59. Colombia	13.17
60. Peru	12.52
61. Israel	12.40
62. Libya	12.40
63. Algeria	12.29
64. **Chrysler**	**11.69**
65. Egypt	11.55
66. **ITT**	**11.36**
67. Kuwait	11.28
68. **Philips Gloeilampenfabrieken***	**10.74**
69. **Standard Oil of Indiana**	**9.95**
70. Pakistan	9.83
71. **Cie Francaises Des Petroles***	**9.14**
72. Bangladesh	8.82
73. **Nippon Steel***	**8.79**
74. **August Thyssen-Hutte***	**8.76**
75. Malaysia	8.69
76. **Hoechst***	**8.46**
77. **ENI***	**8.33**
78. **Daimler-Benz***	**8.19**
79. **U.S. Steel**	**8.16**
80. **BASF***	**8.15**
81. **Shell Oil**	**8.14**
82. Chile	8.05
83. Morocco	7.89
84. **Renault***	**7.83**
85. **Siemens***	**7.75**
86. **Volkswagenwerk***	**7.65**
87. Ireland	7.56
88. Hong Kong	7.52

* Non-American Multinational Corporations

TABLE 13-2 THE LARGEST NATIONS AND CORPORATIONS, 1975–CONTINUED

STATES AND CORPORATIONS	GNP AND SALES (in billions of dollars)
89. Cuba	7.43
90. **Atlantic Richfield**	7.30
91. **Continental Oil**	7.25
92. **DuPont**	7.22
93. **Bayer***	7.22
94. **Toyota Motor***	7.19
95. **Elf-Aquitaine***	7.16
96. Puerto Rico	7.10
97. Vietnam	7.10
98. United Arab Emirates	6.87
99. North Korea	6.79
100. **Western Electric**	6.59

* Non-American Multinational Corporations
Note: The model of comparing countries to corporations was developed by Lester R. Brown, *World Without Borders* (New York: Random House, 1972), pp. 214–15. This table was updated by Joel Busch, the coauthor's graduate assistant at the American University, using *World Bank Atlas* and *Fortune* magazine.

The state retains a variety of means in its armamentarium to regulate the activities of the multinational enterprise. The relationship between the multinational enterprise and the state will be formed out of a relative advantage-disadvantage calculus which will vary with each specific situation. Canada, a recipient of an increasing portion of U.S. direct investment, has experienced remarkably little interference with its sovereignty. Professors Litvak and Maule have aptly observed that "in spite of all the research which has been undertaken, there is little concrete evidence of cases involving infringement of Canadian sovereignty.[13] In 1973 the Canadian government proposed to Parliament a revised bill to control foreign investment in Canadian business. The regulations would apply to any takeover by foreigners of a business concern with assets of $250,000 or more or annual reserves of $3 million or more. The bill was designed primarily to cope with U.S. direct investment, which controls two-thirds of all Canadian industries. However, Gerald Regan, premier of Nova Scotia, has articulated opposition to "any interference whatsoever" from the national government, citing his province's 10% unemployment rate.

In Southeast Asia, Japanese direct investment has become an object

[13] Isaiah A. Litvak and Christopher J. Maule, "Foreign Investment in Canada," in *Foreign Investment: The Experience of the Host Countries,* edited by Isaiah A. Litvak and Christopher J. Maule (New York: Praeger Special Studies in International Economics and Development, 1970), p. 99.

of national resentment on the part of host countries, renewing the old detestation of Japanese domination. Japan, which relies upon Indonesia for nickel, copper, timber, and low-pollution oil, has extended more low-interest, long-term loans to that country than to any other Asian state. Indonesia has sought to balance Japanese investment with German, French, and British investment. Japan and Indonesia have split over Indonesian demands for Indonesian-based-and-controlled export industries. At Pomala, the Mitsubishi Corporation agreed to finance a $25 million nickel smelter, but only on condition that the Indonesian state nickel company relinquish its controlling interest. The Indonesian government has threatened three Japanese companies which receive 900,000 tons of bauxite annually from Bintan with the loss of all or part of their concession unless the Japanese invest $415 million in an aluminum smelter and an adjacent hydroelectric complex.[14]

Despite the considerable degree of emotional conflict between MNCs and host countries, there is scant evidence that the MNC has emerged as an arbiter of political affairs. Clearly the most celebrated example of an attempt by a multinational corporation to interfere in the political affairs of a state is the Chile-ITT affair, which indicates that although a multinational enterprise may think political thoughts, it possesses pitifully little influence to effectuate them.

The investigation of the ITT affair by both the United States Senate and the OPIC (Overseas Private Investment Corporation) reveals the extent of ITT's unconscionable scheme. However, in spite of the legal suits brought by ITT-controlled Kennecott Copper against three important copper users in Rome, Milan, and Brescia as well as in Sweden, France, and West Germany, Chile was able to sell its 1973 copper output. The coup against the Allende government in 1973 by the Chilean armed forces was a response to a complex internal political struggle and CIA subversion and less to ITT influence.

The ITT affair should not obscure the fact that Latin American governments have moved freely to nationalize and expropriate American multinational corporations. Peru expropriated the International Petroleum Company and W. R. Grace Company. Bolivia expropriated the Gulf Oil Company, and in Chile the Ford Motor Company and Bethlehem Steel Corporation were forced to terminate their operations.

Although it is clear that the MNC has rarely conceived of itself as a political actor, or that when it has the limitations of its influence have been surprising, it is equally clear that its impact on the economic affairs of states has grown steadily, creating a special interest in its transactions with the less-developed countries. Much of the thinking and analysis of

[14] *Washington Post*, March 2, 1973.

the relationship between the multinational corporation and the less-developed countries is characterized by mutual recrimination. The relationship is, however, a complex one which defies blanket solutions.

The basic question that must be asked, and concerning which there is appalling little evidence from which to derive a satisfactory answer, is whether or not the less-developed countries have benefited from the presence of the multinational enterprise. Do the multinational corporations dominate the host countries? Who receives the lion's share of the profits? Has the multinational corporation adversely affected the less-developed countries' balance of payments?

As mentioned earlier, the bulk of U.S. direct investment in the less-developed countries is in petroleum. Therefore, it is of some interest to our study of the relationship of the multinational corporation to less-developed countries to pursue such consideration. It is only in recent years that host countries have managed to use the multinational enterprise for their own purposes, not in a zero-sum situation but rather as participants in the rewards of oligopoly. After almost half a century of outright exploitation by the oil cartel since 1928, the oil-producing countries are beginning to control their oil. Members of OPEC (Organization of Petroleum Exporting Countries) have raised their share of the profits on crude oil production from 10–15% to 80–85%. Bargaining positions of the less-developed countries vary with the international environment. Venezuela acquired a favorable 50–50 profit accord during the oil shortages of World War II. The oil-producing countries of the Middle East gradually improved their market position with respect to the multinational enterprises until 1971, when these governments negotiated an agreement assuring them of 80% or more of the production cost of crude oil and the F.O.B. price on oil from the Middle East.[15]

A major factor in the change in the bargaining position of these states has been the competition among the multinational corporations that have entered the market since 1950. The governments that form this world oil cartel will reap an estimated $70 billion in earnings by 1980. Recent events demonstrate that the oil-producing states are capable of driving hard bargains with multinational corporations and resorting to nationalization of industries where the national interest is believed to be served. In 1972, Iraq and Syria nationalized the assets of the Iraq Petroleum Company in their territories. In 1973, President Ahmed Hassan al-Bakr of Iraq implemented nationalization of the Iraq Petroleum Company in return for compensation. Iraq is the fourth largest oil-producing

[15] Raymond Vernon, *Restrictive Business Practices: The Operations of Multinational United States Enterprises in Developing Countries*, United Nations Report, (UN, NY: 1972), pp. 4–7.

country in the Middle East. Western oil companies have signed participation pacts with Saudi Arabia and Abu Dhabi which are likely to establish a pattern for petroleum operations around the world. The governments will acquire an initial 25% equity interest in the companies' Persian Gulf production. The governments' interests will rise by 5 percentage points a year (6 points in 1982) so that the Persian Gulf states will have acquired a 51% ownership of the properties by January 1982. The Arab-Israeli war of 1973 has also added a new political element to the supply and demand for oil in the immediate future.

Turkey and Ecuador have also moved to strengthen the position of local producers with foreign competitors. The Turkish National Assembly passed a petroleum bill that will give priority to the state-owned petroleum enterprises over local and private concerns, halve exploration, and quintuple rentals. In Ecuador, Texaco and Gulf Oil, which jointly accounted for the only significant oil production in that country, were ordered to return half of the acreage given them by negotiated agreements. The two companies retained some 1.2 million acres which had yielded eleven new field discoveries and ninety-nine productive wells producing more than 220,000 barrels a day. The companies have sought compensation. Viewed both in terms of maintaining a rising share in profits and capital assets as well as enjoying an oligopolist position with respect to the rest of the world, the relationship of the oil-producing states to the multinational enterprises has been more like client-agent than master-slave.

Harry Magdoff[16] has noted that between 1950 and 1965 the flow of direct investment from the United States to Latin America amounted to $3.8 billion, whereas income on capital transferred to the United States came to $11.3 billion, a surplus of $7.5 billion in favor of the United States. In Europe, U.S. direct investment was $8.1 billion, with $5.5 billion in profits transferred back. Profit rates are in fact higher in Latin America and the Middle East because investments in the extractive industries such as petroleum are consistently higher than those in the service and manufacturing industries. George Lichtheim, a European socialist, has argued that these statistics "merely underscore the familiar fact that 'uneven development' is a source of surplus profit for the advanced countries including the USSR. It does not prove that no development takes place, merely that an extra price is paid for it during the critical transition period."[17]

These figures tell us little of the impact of the multinational corpo-

---

[16] Harry Magdoff, *The Age of Imperialism* (New York: Monthly Review Press, 1969), p. 198.
[17] George Lichtheim, *Imperialism* (New York: Praeger, 1971), p. 152, note 14.

ration on the aggregate balance of payments of the developing states. Professor Vernon poses two models of the balance-of-payments impact on less-developed countries. If it is assumed that investments were made for "import replacement purposes," then foreign investment will have had a beneficial impact on these states if there was a choice regarding whether to invest within the United States or go abroad. If the rationale for investment was for the purpose of not losing a valuable market to national producers, then the foreign investment would be detrimental to the balance-of-payments problems of the particular states.

A crucial factor in determining the future relations between MNCs and the less-developed countries is the question of technology transfer. A persistent theme in economic theory has praised large firms for their technological efficiency and rational allocation of resources. Professor Vernon's sample of 187 multinational firms revealed that they devoted 2.4% of their sales for research-and-development purposes, while the remainder of the *Fortune* list spent 1.85%. Much is still unknown concerning the amount of technology transfer, and in which kinds of industries.

The Report to the Committee on Finance of the United States, of which previous mention was made, furnished the most comprehensive data to date on the significance of technology transfer. Using income earned in royalties and fees as an index of technology exports, the exports exceed imports by a factor of 10. Ninety percent of the $2.3 billion in income of royalties and fees were accounted for by U.S. multinational corporations. Multinational corporations engage in a strategy of not exporting their first-line technology. This situation may be of greater significance to developed rather than less-developed countries, however, because in the developed countries there is substantial competition between multinational enterprises for international consumer markets, which may influence them to withhold certain patents and processes. It is thus interesting to note that it is the multinational enterprises in the high-technology class that continue to generate a favorable ratio of new

[18] An analytical framework to evaluate the transfers of "know-how" and "show-how" technology can be found in Robert B. Stobaugh, *The International Transfer of Technology in the Establishment of the Petrochemical Industry in Developing Countries*, UNITAR Research Report no. 12 (New York: UNITAR, 1971). See also Terutomo Ozawa, *Transfer of Technology from Japan to Developing Countries*, UNITAR Research Report no. 7 (New York: UNITAR, 1971); Jack Baransom, *International Transfer of Automotive Technology to Developing Countries*, UNITAR Research Report no. 8 (New York: UNITAR, 1971); Lawrence H. Wortzel, *Technology Transfer in the Pharmaceutical Industry*, UNITAR Research Report no. 14 (New York: UNITAR, 1971); Walter A. Chudson, *The International Transfer of Commercial Technology for Developing Countries*, UNITAR Research Report no. 13 (New York: UNITAR, 1971); Ciro E. Zoppo, "Toward a U.S. Policy on Nuclear Technology Transfer to Developing Countries," paper presented at the Southern California Arms Control and Foreign Policy Seminar, University of California, Los Angeles, July 1971. At best, the literature on technology transfer is controversial.

exports to new imports rather than the multinational corporations in the medium- or low-technology classes, such as food products.[18]

But is it the nineteenth-century doctrine of economic subjection with which the MNCs threaten the sovereignty of the less-developed countries? Although this remains a factor that policymakers must take into account, it is a diminishing one, and not the primary challenge to the viability of those states. The future challenges to national sovereignty will be in the cultural, not in the political or economic spheres of activity. And the threat of such challenges is likely to be mounted by the American and Japanese MNCs. Nor is this a recent phenomenon.

A multinational corporation may clash with ethnic subcultures, as was the case in Canada where Premier Bourassa of Quebec intervened in a language dispute between General Motors and the United Auto Workers at an assembly unit outside Montreal. GM rejected demands that French be made the language of work for 2,400 assembly-line workers.

The rationalization of other cultural styles, for which the rubric "Americanization" has been used as a kind of shorthand, is more diffuse than the GM-Quebec controversy. It can be anticipated in the phenomenal growth of American fast-food enterprises, as well as service and culture industries. Heublein, Inc., maintains hundreds of Kentucky Fried Chicken outlets in more than thirty countries. McDonald Corporation maintains outlets in Japan, Australia, Holland, and Germany, to name a few countries. Dairy Queen International, Inc., and Pillsbury Co. are also active multinational corporations that receive scant attention. Dairy Queen has signed a 50-50 joint venture with Marbeni Corporation of Japan and has constructed hundreds of Dairy Queen Ice Cream stands. Dairy Queen currently maintains hundreds of outlets in Canada, West Germany, Mexico, Australia, Iceland, Switzerland, and the Philippines. Pillsbury has actively expanded its Burger King operations overseas. Nestle's Alimentara, a Swiss firm, is the twenty-ninth largest corporation in the world in terms of sales. The company had a total income of $4.2 billion in 1972, 53% from Europe, 33% from the Americas, 11% from Asia, and 3% from Africa. The firm maintains hundreds of subsidiaries which operate at least 300 factories and employ about 110,000 people in sixty countries. Nestle's products, such as Nescafé and Nesquick, are sold throughout the world. Has the candy bar become a transnational actor? Will the organizational imperatives surrounding the processing and distribution of Kentucky Fried Chicken create more social disequilibrium than the export of Marxist or capitalist models of development, or are these only idle thoughts?

The Crisis-of-Development Theory

The basic rationales that have been invoked to explain or encourage direct investment by states and multinational corporations in less-developed countries of the world have been overtaken by events. The national interest of the major states in the global system lies increasingly in the economic interdependence of consumer markets and the limitation of the proliferation of nuclear weapons. Ideological competition for the Third World appears to have been an idea whose time has come and gone. The geographic investment patterns of the multinational corporations reflect similar realities. Even where multinational enterprises have made investments, they are usually in extractive industries which do little to encourage growth in agricultural or industrial markets within the state. Throughout the world, the division between the rich and poor states appears to widen (see Figure 13-1).

Is there a utilitarian rationale for the development assistance? If not, which actor in the global environment is capable of acting upon other kinds of rationales? The Report of the Commission on International Development offers one alternative:

> So we return to the question: Why should the rich countries seek to help other nations when even the richest of them are saddled with heavy social and economic problems within their own borders? The simplest answer to the question is the moral one: that it is only right for those who have to share with those who have not.[19]

This is a difficult rationale for assistance in a world largely bent on discovering an "enlightened self-interest" for assisting the poor. Regrettably, in the past, arguments stressing an illusory "national interest" associated with development have been made with relatively little impact, even during the height of the Cold War when such pronouncements were taken with more seriousness.

The multinational corporation is neither inherently evil nor beneficent. Its movements are governed by a narrow frontier of economic impetuses. Some writers suggest that the multinational enterprise is the best hope for the less-developed countries, but for the reasons we have already explored this does not seem very likely.

In the final analysis, it will have to be the state acting through multilateral organizations, bilateral arrangements, perhaps through the multinational corporations themselves, if development assistance is to be made to the less-developed countries on the necessary scale. The multi-

---

[19] Commission on International Development, *Partners in Development* (New York: Frederick A. Praeger, 1969), p. 8.

GROSS NATIONAL PRODUCT PER CAPITA OF DEVELOPING AND SELECTED DEVELOPED COUNTRIES, 1970 AND 1975
(In 1974 U.S. Dollars)

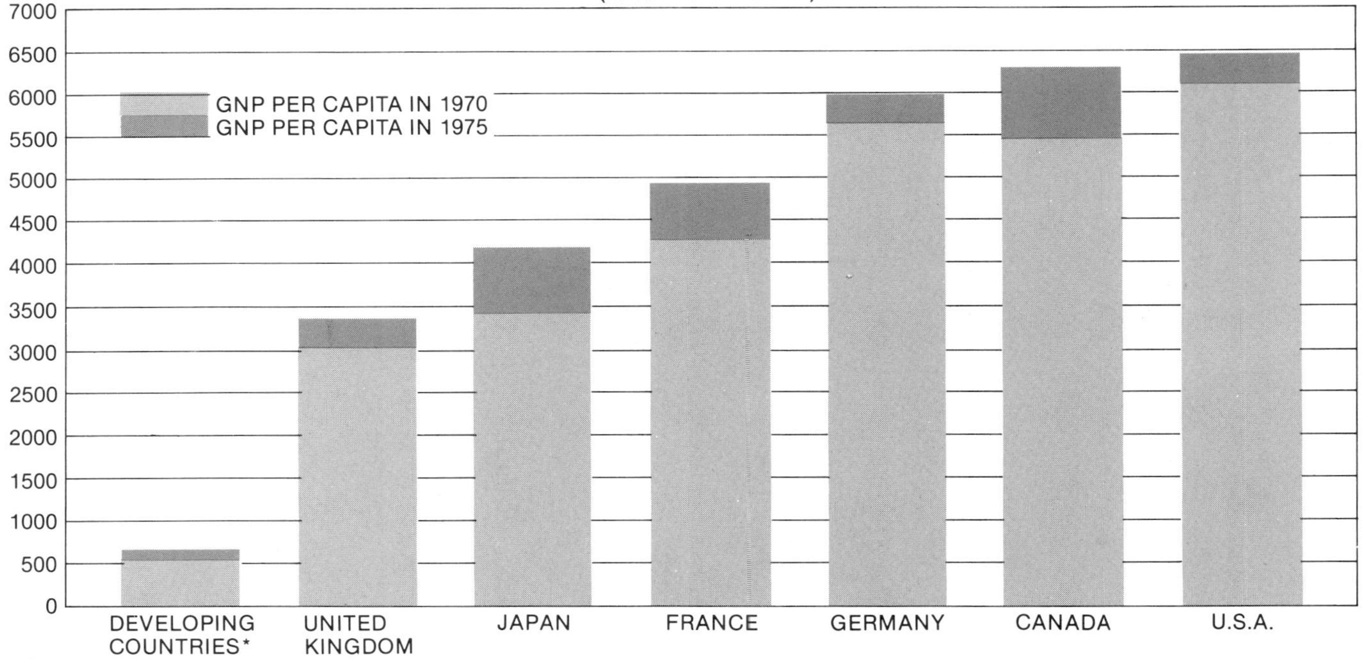

*Includes the developing countries listed in *Trends in Developing Countries*, (Washington, D.C.: World Bank, April 1978.) Excludes capital surplus oil exporting countries and centrally planned countries.

national corporation is not a substitute for development theory. It can be an agent for growth but little else. Only people, acting through their governments, and governments acting upon their ideals can furnish commitment and direction. Only the state can base its motivation on a spectrum of concerns which include humanitarianism. Thus while the territorial state is slowly losing its function as a guarantor of security, it can acquire and reemphasize a different function if it so chooses. But it is a decision that only states or organizations of states can make. Multinational corporations provide possibly one means toward that end.

Regulating the MNCs

The rapid growth of MNCs in recent years has attracted public attention in the United States, Western Europe, and Japan, where the vast majority of corporations are based, and throughout the world. In the United States, in 1972, the U.S. Senate Foreign Relations Committee voted to conduct an investigation into the activities of ITT in Chile and to examine the general role and impace of MNCs. A subcommittee on MNCs was established which commenced its hearings in March 1973. Similar inquiries have also been conducted in a number of other countries.

The work of the Commission on Transnational Corporations (CTC) of the United Nations on the formulation of a code of conduct represents that body's concern to create a universal instrument to regulate the activities of MNCs. This United Nations endeavor originated in the Economic and Social Council resolution 1721 of 1972, which requested the Secretary General to establish a Group of Eminent Persons to study the impact of MNCs on world development and international relations. The Group of Eminent Persons held meetings in New York and Geneva between 1973 and 1974 and recommended the creation of the Commission on Transnational Corporations and of a Research and Information Centre within the Secretariat. The commission was established in 1974 and held its first session in New York in 1975 during the same year the Research and Information Centre became operational.

The commission decided to assign top priority to the formation of a code of conduct, and the Centre was requested to submit to the second session of the commission a number of reports on the subject.

The analysis of material relevant to the formulation of a code of conduct began in 1976 during the second session of the commission when it received the reports submitted by the Centre. During that same session the commission established the Intergovernmental Working Group on a Code of Conduct which began its work in 1977.

In addition, several commissions and committees of the Economic and Social Council are concerned with the operations of MNCs, including the Statistical Commission; the Committee on Housing, Building, and Planning; the Committee for Development Planning; and the Advisory Committee on the Application of Science and Technology to Development. UNCTAD and UNIDO under the General Assembly of the United Nations are increasingly involved in issues related to MNCs. Finally, a number of the specialized agencies—ILO, IMF, FAO, World Bank, IFC, and GATT—are examining various aspects of operations of multinational corporations.

As the largest multinational corporations begin to dominate the world economy, it does not seem unlikely that they may gain more political power. The Japanese example has shown the contemporary world how the lack of military capability has not impeded the power of Japan to influence others; the source of this power being Japan's economic strength. Similarly the MNCs may exercise their economic power to achieve certain (their) political ends.

Many scholars welcome the growth of the MNCs and point to the corporations as being powerful agents of global economic integration. These scholars believe that the MNCs could be instruments of peace because their business dealings will become increasingly global in nature and purpose. Other scholars believe that the multinational corporate system will not be able to satisfy the needs of the world's population, nor will it necessarily promote the interests of world peace and equality. This new elitism and the presumed inability of the multinational corporate system to provide adequately for the needs of the world's population might perhaps be a source of conflict in the future.

The future development of the MNCs seems certain to impact the global system. It seems reasonable to assume that the MNCs will play an important role in the future global political system.

Recommended Readings

APTER, DAVID E., and LOUIS W. GOODMAN, eds. *The Multinational Corporation and Social Change.* New York: Frederick A. Praeger, 1976.

BALL, GEORGE, ed. *Global Companies.* Englewood Cliffs, N.J.: Prentice-Hall, 1975.

BARNET, RICHARD J., and RONALD MULLER. *Global Reach: The Power of the Multinational Corporations.* New York: Simon & Schuster, 1974.

BEHRMAN, JACK, and HARVEY WALLENDER. *Transfer of Manufacturing Technology Within Multinational Enterprises.* Cambridge, Mass.: Ballinger Publishing Co., 1976.

BLAKE, D., and R. WALTERS. *The Politics of Global Economic Relations.* Englewood Cliffs, N.J.: Prentice-Hall, 1976.

KAPOOR, A., and P. GRUB, eds. *Multinational Enterprise in Transition.* Princeton, N.J.: Darwin Press, 1972.

LILLICH, RICHARD B., ed. *The Valuation of Nationalized Property in International Law* (3 volumes). Charlottesville: University Press of Virginia, 1972–1975.

LITVAK, I., and C. MAULE, eds. *Foreign Investment: The Experience of the Host Countries.* New York: Frederick A. Praeger, 1970.

MAGDOFF, HARRY. *Age of Imperialism.* New York: Monthly Review Press, 1969.

MODELSKI, GEORGE. *Multinational Corporations and World Order.* New York: Sage, 1973.

SAID, ABDUL A., and L. SIMMONS, eds. *The New Sovereigns: Multinational Corporations as World Powers.* Englewood Cliffs, N.J.: Prentice-Hall, 1975.

SERVAN-SCHREIBER, JEAN-JACQUES. *The American Challenge* (trans. R. Steel). New York: Atheneum, 1968.

TURNER, LOUIS. *Multinational Corporations and the Third World.* New York: Hill and Wang, 1973.

VERNON, RAYMOND. *Storm Over the Multinational Corporations: The Real Issues.* Cambridge: Harvard University Press, 1977.

WALLACE, DON, JR. *International Regulation of Multinational Corporations.* New York: Frederick A. Praeger, 1976.

Ethnic Nations and Terrorist Groups

14

The nation-state is no longer regarded as the paradigm of human organization. Curiously enough, while philosophers and political scientists since Bodin have pointed to the need to move beyond the nation-state into supranational legal, economic, and political organizations, it is difficult to identify an experiment, other than the European Community, where a supranational political consciousness has been achieved. Not only has the movement toward supranationalism been averted in environments conducive to theories of supranationalism, but also with the emergence of a politics of disassociation a disenchantment with the political institutions of the nation-state and an emphasis on ethnic, cultural, and political sovereignty has persisted and occasionally exploded in many parts of the world.

Ethnic Nations *

The reasons for the conspicuous rise in ethnic politics are not always apparent. Ethnic movements have developed in environments that our theories and methodologies have told us are unlikely spawning grounds for secession and violence. Communications theory, with its contribution to our perception of the processes of nation-state building, has become increasingly suspect as a touchstone for interpreting the dynamics of state building. There seems to be a recognition that a nation-state is an intuitive expression of a people's perception of proper social and political organization. That such perceptions can and do change despite the social

---

* This section is adapted from A. A. Said and L. R. Simmons, *Ethnicity in an International Context* (New Brunswick, N.J.: Transaction Books, 1976).

cement believed to be supplied by good communication networks and economic integration is one profitable inference to be drawn from the resurgence of ethnic activity.

As we stated earlier, the state, as an organizational expression of the historical preoccupation with physical security, has been progressively undermined by the development and proliferation of conventional and nuclear weapons. The state is essentially a territorial form of organization in a century where security is no longer a function of geopolitics but of technology.

No longer the central organizing principle of physical security, the social psychology of authority, as it manifests itself in state patriotism, is undergoing a historical transformation. Antistatist politics as it appears in ethnic disassociation is one expression of this transaction.

Liberal theories of development have never embraced the idea of ethnic diversity with intellectual enthusiasm. Diversity was seen in terms of the coexistence of political systems, not ethnic nations. Quite often the modus operandi of the quintessential state builders encouraged if not insisted on the detribalization of world politics, which is no doubt a source of discomfort, for theories of development emphasize the necessity of rationalizing economic and political systems to achieve economic growth.

The future of ethnic conflict is, of course, closely tied to the future of the multiethnic state. A sample of 132 states shows that only 12 (9.1%) can be considered ethnic free. Twenty-five states (18.9%) are comprised of an ethnic nation-state that represents more than 90% of the state aggregate population, and in another 25 states the largest ethnic nation accounts for possibly 75–89% of the population. However, in 31 states (23.5% of the total) the significant ethnic group constitutes only 50–74% of the population, and in 39 states (29.5%) the largest group does not account for half the state's population. It has been estimated that in 53 states (or 40.2%), the population consists of five or more significant ethnic nations.

Never before have issues of human rights and cultural self-determination attracted so much popularity and scholarly attention. What are the human rights of these ethnic nations? What should be the position of the analyst and practitioner in response to secessionist movements such as those that occurred in Pakistan and Nigeria? Should the prerogatives of the sovereign state swallow the rights of the ethnic nation? Can the two be reconciled?

Despite one's position on this dispute, the ethnic and the emerging neoethnic group will not disappear from world politics. As emerging actors in the global system, they are indications that our perceptions of world relations and the causes of war and peace lag behind the consciousness of the individuals and nations we study. The ethnic nation cannot yet compete with the state in nuclear warheads and warships, but it continues to exercise formidable influence over the primary authority patterns of individuals. It is from this exercise of power that revolutions are born.

Nations vs. States

A revived sense of ethnic identity has grown in the last few decades, and ethnic politics has emerged as a significant factor in the global system. In recent years the antagonism of indigenous ethnic communities in Cyprus, Iraq, Malaysia, Ireland, Nigeria, Pakistan, and Canada (to name only a few) have wrought important changes in the relations among states. The ethnic conflicts of Ireland, the bloody struggle of Biafra, the secession of Bangladesh, and the transformation of ethnic discontent into ethnic nationalism worldwide have placed their mark on domestic and global politics.

There are perhaps as many as 862 ethnic nations living within the nation-states of the world: 239 in sub-Saharan Africa, 95 in the countries surrounding the Mediterranean, 93 in the Far East, 128 in the insular Pacific, 218 in North America, and 89 in Central and South America.[1] What future impact will they have as and if the nation-state continues to be a declining form of economic and political association?

The modern nation-state is struggling to overcome the internal contradictions between the nation and the state. These contradictions become fully visible when loyalty to the state and loyalty to one's nation conflict. In this conflict are forged the incandescent passions of secession and civil war and the unconscionable talent of some ethnic nations to completely destroy others. The state can be defined in terms of territory, population, and government, and its formation can be predicted in contemporary world politics, since it signifies the victory of positivism in the political affairs of individuals. An entity is generally recognized as a state when it exerts political control over a specific geographical area. Sovereignty is not a derivative of natural or divine law. Control is accompanied by international recognition in the transactions among states; loss of control is invariably a precursor of loss of recognition. The state is a positive contraption, both artifice and atrificer of the nineteenth-century fruition of the positivist approach to human affairs. But the nation is a conscious expression of people's shared sense of "peoplehood," reflecting what Kurt Lewin has described as the "interdependence of fate." The political self-consciousness of nations is a product of the nineteenth

---

[1] George Peter Murdock, *Ethnographic Atlas* (Pittsburg: University of Pittsburg Press, 1967).

century. Sir Ernest Barker stated the issue with enviable precision: "A nation must be an idea as well as a fact before it can be a dynamic force."[2]

We are entering a new era where state-nationalism as it has been known for the past few hundred years is undergoing serious, perhaps fatal, stress. It may seem presumptuous to talk of the end of the nation-state in an era characterized by references to rising nationalism, but history is made of such contradictions. After the successful defense of monarchy in Europe during the middle of nineteenth century, the defeated parliamentarians were, in fact, destined to be vindicated within two generations. In our era, the secession of Bangladesh, the Kurdish independence movement, and the struggle in Northern Ireland mark a fundamental shift in world politics.

The proliferation of new states after World War II has obscured the problem of scale and underscores the absurdity of describing both the People's Republic of China and the Bahamas as nation-states. The real global system consists of no more than twenty or thirty national and transnational actors who have any significant impact, and the top five actors have over half of the world's human and natural resources. The nation-state as a unit of analysis makes differences of degree so vast as to constitute differences in kind. Ethnic nations, in contrast, are more clearly defined and therefore constitute a real as opposed to a juridicial construct for analysis.

The dominant causal agent behind the emerging global political system is the technological revolution in communication that permits previously isolated ethnic nations to become more visible and, in certain cases, interact across national boundaries. Perhaps mass communication, instead of unifying humankind, is paradoxically differentiating it into progressively smaller communities.

The new global system is simultaneously more parochial and less geographic. Ethnic nations find more affinity along lines other than the national boundaries of traditional nation-states. The human need for a sense of community is gradually dissolving the bonds of geography that unite diverse groups within states. Community in this sense is of the ethnic nation or of communes, individuals who find their interests coinciding outside the political context of a nation-state. What this means in practical terms is that a community may rejoice at victories other than those of its state, since the defeat of its state will be a victory for its vision of community. The internal struggle within each state seeks its analogue in external politics. The domestic dispute requires the creation of a foreign policy dispute.

[2] Ernest Barker, *National Character and the Factors in Its Formation* (London: Methuen, 1927), p. 173.

We have entered the age of ethnicity in world politics. In such an environment, where distance as a barrier to national and transnational culture groups is a diminishing consideration and relationship becomes paramount, individuals rely less and less upon the nation-state as an agent for fulfillment. A politics of ethnicism is beginning to dominate the behavior of divergent cultures that will have a wide impact upon their respective nation-states. This development will also demand new theoretical models to explain their respective nation-states and their interaction. Ethnicism confutes the viability of a national ethos and suggests the importance of understanding ethnic nations in understanding world politics.

The conflict politics among states of the future will often be a response to the politics of ethnic disassociation. The present phenomenon of ethnic conflicts cannot be adequately analyzed within the context of traditional concepts of international relations. Concepts of balance of power, bipolarity, or even polycentrism as loci of conflict become less meaningful. As Andrew Greely has observed:

> The conflicts that have occupied most men over the past two or three decades and which have led to the most horrendous outpouring of blood have had precious little to do with this ideological division... In a world of the jet engine, nuclear energy, the computer, and the regionalized organization, the principal conflicts are not ideological but tribal. Those differences among men which were supposed to be swept away by science and technology and political revolution are destructive as ever.[3]

The nation-state is no longer viewed as the ultimate community, nor is it even the primary source of loyalty in many instances.

Roots of Ethnic Conflict

Core cultural values persistently reject absorption into a higher level of identification. Awareness of one's ethnicity may well be, largely, a function of coercive assimilation. Thus when social groups are mobilized, congeniality and cooperation do not necessarily occur. Increased contact, exposure, and communication may exaggerate one's self-image, magnify cultural differences, produce conflict, and induce political disassociation. Additionally, economic development—an increase in material goods and services—does not immunize a society from ethnic conflict. The concomitants of economic growth—urbanization-secularization-industrailization—may lead to competition over limited opportunities and

---
[3] Andrew Greely, "The Rediscovery of Diversity," *Antioch Review* (Fall 1971): 343.

resources. Previously stable interethnic differences have fit patterns of comparative advantage or coexistence, while the industrial-technical society tends to have a commonizing effect on economic behavior and produces competitive channels of achievement.

Analysis of ethnic conflict has been dominated by structural, social, psychological, and political anthropologists. Claude Levi-Strauss defines culture as "the complex whole which includes knowledge, belief, art, morals, custom, and other capabilities and habits by man as a member of society."[4] His contribution to anthropology enhances our knowledge of culture by identifying structure common to societies, diacritical features, language, conscious and unconscious levels of operation, kinship patterns, and myths. It is the task of the social scientist to understand the dynamics operating in the macro and micro levels of human behavior, and to relate the "Synchronic to the Diachronic, the individual to the culture, the physiological to the psychological, the objective analysis of institutions to the subjective experience of individuals."[5] Structural anthropology aims not so much at the compartmentalization and universalization of culture and its institutions, as at defining the relationships between the institutions and social behavior, and the variation of customs from structures. Implicit in this notion is that culture is not only a static-structural phenomenon, but a salient one as well.

Ethnicity reveals a structure analogous to that of culture. Fredrick Barth sees atomic groups as "biologically self-perpetuating, their members share fundamental cultural values, realized in overt unity in cultural form; they make up a field of communication and interaction and their membership identifies itself and is identified by others."[6] An ethnic group is a culture and yet may belong to a larger culture. A static concept of ethnic groups concieves their cultural differentiation as a function of social isolation, ecological factors, adaptive measures, invention, and selective borrowing.[7] Such an approach negates the high import of cultural interaction.

Ethnic consciousness is as much an objective process of diacritical realization as it is a subjective self-ascription vis-à-vis other social groups. A complex hierarchy of potential identification exists, but Barth stresses that "ethnic identity is superordinate to most other statuses, and defines a way an individual operationalizes and externalizes his reference group

---

[4] Claude Levi-Strauss, *Structural Anthropology*. (Garden City, N.Y.: Anchor Books, 1963), p.19.
[5] *Ibid* p.19.
[6] Fredrick Barth, ed., *Ethnic Groups and Boundaries*. (Boston: Little, Brown and Co., 1969), p.10.
[7] *Ibid.*, p.11.

norms."⁸ Adherence thus entails the analyzing of social life, and "implies a recognition of limitations or shared understanding, differences in criteria for judgement of value and performance, and a restriction of interaction to sectors of assumed common understanding and mutual interest."⁹

As structural anthropology accentuates the dynamic relationship between the individual and culture and its divergent consequences, social anthropology concentrates on the dynamic relationship of ethnic nations as they define social-psychological boundaries between and among themselves. Barth's insights are particularly useful here: "Boundaries persist despite a flow of personnel across them . . . categorical distinctions do not depend on an absence of mobility, contact, and information."¹⁰ On the other hand, adds Barth, "stable interethnic relations presuppose a structure of interaction: a set of prescriptions governing situations of contact, and allowing for articulation in some sectors or domains of activity, and a set of proscriptions or social situations preventing interethnic interaction in other sectors, and thus insulating parts of the cultures from confrontation and modification."¹¹

Thus begins to emerge the anthropoligical roots of ethnic conflict: the fluid relationships existing between ethnic nations catalyze sociopsychological identification and boundaries and do not necessarily induce conflict. Shared values are sometimes a component but not a sufficient condition of mutual understanding; the sectors of mutual activity entail competition as well as cooperation. Conflict and cooperation alike are indicators that the individual is living on the same plane; communication is thus predicated on a certain degree of community as illustrated in structural anthropology.

Psychological anthropology plays an important role in the configurations and matrix of ethnic interaction. It focuses on the teleological roots of ethnic conflict and the fundamental difference between ethnic nations,¹² and explores the relationship of human beings, their levels of interaction, and such crosscurrents as social change and economic development. Such currents infuse change and substance into cultural adaptation and contribute to the friction within and between cultures.

Francis Hsu's concept of psychosocial homeostasis clarifies the organic relationship between culture, ethnic contact, and the resulting phenomenon or, more specifically, ethnic contact and ensuing behavior. This

---

⁸ *Ibid.*, p.17.
⁹ *Ibid.*, p.15.
¹⁰ *Ibid.*, P.9
¹¹ *Ibid.*, p.16.
¹² Francis Hsu, "Psychosocial Homeostasis and Jen," *American Anthropologist* (Fall 1971), p.24

means "psychosocial homeostatis is the level of psychic and interpersonal equilibrium within a society."[13] This tool of analysis flows from a scientific desire for a "more precise formulation of how man lives as a social and cultural being"[14] and how cultural expressions take institutional and sociopolitical form in disequiliberated environment.

Predictability of ethnic conflict appears to be contingent upon those levels of articulation between cultures that are affective and those that are decreasingly utilitarian, along with varying intensities. One might not expect ethnic conflict between ethnic nation A and B even if nation A has a predominant advantage in political representation, if ethnic nation B is not politicized. Internecine behavior is as much a function of commonality of values as of a multiplicity. Thus, viewed from an ecological perspective, ethnic transactions are dependent on: (1) minimal competition for scarce resources (be they natural or occupational) where the area of articulation will be in trade; (2) territorial claims (in which articulation is politicized); (3) symbiosis and interdependence where articulation is multiple; and (4) partial competition for the same niche, where conflict is most likely.[15]

Structural and valuational motifs of interaction are integral to understanding the roots of ethnic conflict. As a corollary, the milieu of interaction is defined and redefined by sociopsychological boundaries that may involve cultural ascription, social prescription, and political proscription. Emerging from this contention is the concept of ethnopolitical culture, which reflects the structural and salient milieu as well as the values involved in interethnic communication and articulation.

Ethnicity and Development

Is it conflict that causes tribalism or tribalism that causes conflict? The biases of Western ideologies and methodologies have consistently led us to accept the former, while treating the latter as a causalty for the trash heap of history. Our religious faith in progress has prevented us from recognizing that while there is nothing inevitable about ethnic conflict, neither is it evident that nation-state builders will discover the precise formula to absorb so formidable an antagonist. Thus we are compelled to posit the ethnic nation as an irreducible dilemma for the state, one that under the proper (or dysfunctional) conditions can emerge as a truculent divisive force. Conflict, such as economic scarcity or political or cultural repression, can exacerbate these tendencies, but it is not

---

[13] *Ibid.*, p. 28.
[14] *Ibid.*, pp.24–27.
[15] Frederick Barth, ed., *Ethnic Groups and Boundaries* (Boston: Little, Brown and Co., 1969), pp.19–20.

demonstrable that an absence of these conflicts (were it possible) would mean the withering away of the ethnic nation.

Milton Gordon has reminded us that the term *ethnicity* has been used to embrace the unities of race, religion, and national origin. However, the common denominator of these categories is a "common social-psychological referent," which acts to create a consciousness of peoplehood. Thus the term *ethnicity* is invested with a broader significance than it has been given by some sociologists who use the term as a typology of national origin. Obviously, the raising of such a consciousness has direct implications in social, economic, and of course political behavior. How difficult it must be, for example, to persuade an ethnic nation to reweave the values, attitudes, and norms that characterize a group's authority patterns, since, as Gordon states:

> Common to all these objective bases . . . is the social-psychological element of a special sense of both ancestral and future-oriented identification with the group. These are the "people" of my ancestors, therefore they are my people, and they will be the people of my children and their children . . . in a very special way which history has decreed. I share a sense of indissolvable and intimate identity with *this group* and *not that one* within the larger society and the world.[16]

Clifford Geertz has elaborated upon the contrast inherent in such a definition, which he refers to as *communalism*.[17] In India, it is based on religious contrasts, in Malaysia we are primarily attracted to racial differences, and in Zaïre by tribal affiliations. Divisions based on economic, class or political disaffection may be the harbinger of civil strife, but alienation based on culture, language, race, and nationality are elements that comprise what Edward Shils has called the *primordial* ties and are the foci of authority and patriotism *within* the state that the ethnic group often seeks to replace or from which it seeks to disassociate.[18] Geertz identifies several ascriptive characteristics around which much ethnic conflict has revolved: *assumed blood ties*, like those that characterize the "hill tribes" of Southeast Asia and the Kurds; *race*, a volatile element in the transactions between the ex-colonial powers and the ex-colonial states; *language*, such as that served as the basis for the political crisis that toppled the Belgian government and threatens the Canadian unity; *religion*—Indian partition

---

[16] Milton Gordon, *Assimilation in American Life; The Role of Race, Religion, and National Origin* (New York: Oxford University Press, 1964), p.29.
[17] Clifford Geertz, "The Integration Revolution" in *Old Societies and New States*, edited by Clifford Geertz (New York: Free Press, 1963).
[18] Edward Shils, "Primordial, Personal, Sacred, and Civil Ties," *British Journal of Sociology*, Vol. 8 (June 1957).

is an outstanding example and the turmoil in Ireland a disturbing reminder; and *custom*, examples of which are the Bengalis in India and the Javanese in Indonesia.

Throughout this patchwork of social organization and behavior patterns, the ethnic nation is self-consciously defined by the kind of social-political differentiation and cultural autonomy that we usually associate with candidates for statehood. Thus we would expect theorists of modernization and state building to dedicate themselves to constructing a viable paradigm that recognized the tenacity of these social organizations and their logical implications for theories of modernization. But curiously this has not been the case. Standard works on development have addressed themselves to analysis of the military, the bureaucracy, social classes, and urbanization. In fact, as Andrew Greely has wryly observed regarding the United States, throughout the 1960s articles on ethnic nations and ethnic behavior were scrupulously ignored by journals of scholarship.

Perhaps the proclivities of Western scholars to treat the ethnic nation and ethnic politics as a transitional social organization in the stages of political growth are rooted in the scientific rationalism of the postfeudal European period. Floyd Matson has traced the intellectual history of the application of the Newtonian model to the social sciences from the applied science of "social mathematics" invented by de Witt through the zealous initiatives of the Saint-Simonians to apply the Newtonian world view to the study and manipulation of society.[19]

This ideal of progress—linear, rational, and positivist—was canonized by the development of the political economy of the nation-state, which as Jacques Ellul has pointed out "was constructed little by little, and all of its individual techniques were improved by mutual interaction... Who was to coordinate this multiplicity of techniques? Who was to build the mechanism necessary to the new economic technique? Who was to make binding the decision necessary to service the machines? The individual is not rational enough to accept what is necessary to the machines. Individuals rebel too easily. They require an agency to restrain them, and the state had to play this role. To this end, the state itself must be coherent."[20]

Ellul's framework of analysis—shared to an important degree by contemporary expositors of a "counterculture"—is a stark analysis and projection of the impact of scientific rationalism on the varieties of human behavior and social organization. But the early theorists of the nation-state were not attracted by its potential to control and predict human

---

[19] Floyd Matson, *The Broken Image* (Garden City, N.Y.: Doubleday, 1966), p. 17.
[20] Jacques Ellul, *The Technological Society* (New York: Vintage Books, 1964), p. 115.

behavior within a political and economic framework. Thomas Hobbes is one of these writers who exerted a great deal of influence on the development of the state. *The Leviathan* was forged in the crucible of disorder—religious wars—that plagued seventeenth-century Europe.

However, for Hobbes the concentration of power was not an end in itself. It was a means to seduce and eliminate the parochial social barriers of custom, religion, and ethnic fratricide that he perceived to be the foremost obstacle to human fulfillment in his century.[21]

Whether we are dealing with the extermination of Brazilian Indians or the contemporary ethnic conflict in South Africa, Ireland, or India, we are naturally attracted to the anomaly of the twentieth century—the impulse for Western modernization and the accelerating consciousness for self-determination among varieties of linguistic, religious, and geographical ethnic nations. The question that such a conflict poses for a normative political scientist may be phrased in this manner: Although I believe that states must assimilate ethnic nations Y and Z in order to provide the modern economic, health, and social services that they deserve as citizens of the twenty-first century, what about the possibility that nations Y and Z resist the devaluation of sovereignty? What rights, if any, do they have under my scheme for modernization? What limitation, if any, should be placed on the central authority in their attempts to force secessionist ethnic nations to adapt to the political economy of the state?

Each of us can pose a different question that places more or less emphasis on the fruits of modernization or the political or cultural exhilaration of ethnic sovereignty, but finally we must confront the root question of how we shall balance our commitment to human rights with the contemporary experience of "state building"—often a bitter by-product of civil war. Then again, as we are rediscovering in the social sciences, our view of the controversy may be considerably influenced by the state we are living in at a particular point in history. States wracked by ethnic conflicts are probably less inclined to view secession and civil war as expressions of some transcedent human struggle than states that experience an acceptable level of ethnic conflict that does not approach disassociation. Another problem is posed when a state or international agency, attempting to intervene in behalf of an ethnic minority, confronts the dilemma posed by Conor Cruise O'Brien:

> We tell, let us say, the *Tutsi* that the right he fancies he possesses to dominate the Hutu is not a real right. He replies in effect that as far as his culture is concerned it is right. We tell him it is not a right,

---

21 Robert A. Nisbet, *The Quest of Community* (New York: Oxford University Press, 1953), p. 130.

because it is contrary to democracy, an ideology to which our ancestors became converted in the nineteenth century. He says his ancestors did not become so converted; are we claiming that our ancestors were superior to his? Now, that is a forked question, and we have to be very careful how we answer it. If we say, "No, no, of course not my dear fellow," he can say in reply: By what right then are we telling him that he must act according to the acquired conviction of our ancestors who are admittedly no better than his own. If, on the other hand, we say, yes, our people represent a more advanced stage of civilization than his do, he may reply that this is exactly his own position in relation to the Hutu.[22]

The response of the state to disaffected ethnic minorities has not been generous by most Western standards. The Tibetans with the Chinese, and the Kurds with Iraq, are indispensable reference points for predicting the state response to ethnic conflict and the politics of disassociation. Self-determination movements are invariably viewed as threats to the survival of the state. States threatened by such acts of disassociation have treated the leaders of these movements as traitors and have interned them without regard for even their own concepts of due process.

States can usually expect to lend covert or overt assistance to other states confronting ethnic dissidents unless, of course, the dissident ethnic elements are perceived as instrumentalities in the foreign policy armamentarium of one state to disrupt the internal affairs of another state. Basque nationalism furnishes a good example of the former, Chinese foreign policy in Burma of the latter. The Basque region is on the border of Spain and France. Although the French deny providing assistance to the Spanish government, since 1970 France has increased the expulsion of Basque political refugees. Basques, on either side of the border, note that improved French-Spanish relations that culminated in the French sale of armaments to Spain have contributed to growing collaboration of the governments on the Basque problem.

Ethnic Nations and Foreign Policy

While it should by now be becoming increasingly evident that ethnic conflict in Ethiopia can make itself felt in the diplomatic struggle in the Middle East or that Basque terrorism that ignores the French-Spanish border can pave problems between two states, there is another dimension to the study of ethnic conflict that demands a brief inquiry. The state has been forced by historical circumstances to share the stage with other

[22] Conor Cruise O'Brien, "On the Rights of Minorities," *Commentary* 55, no. 6 (June 1973): 46.

actors, such as multinational corporations, transnational subcultures, and, of course, ethnic nations. Quite often these ethnic nations, dissatisfied with political and social conditions at home, have begun to pirate international passenger flights, assassinate diplomats in foreign lands, and even extort ransom from multinational giants such as Ford Motor Company. Kidnappings of business executives and diplomats have become a familiar feature in contemporary world politics.

The mobility of ethnic nations in the global environment and the highly integrated state of our technology makes disruption of world services an easy mark. This naturally calls forth a response by states—Communist, socialist, capitalist, and others—manifesting itself in new conventions and bilateral treaties with procedures for extradition and perhaps even international accords. This is only one local consequence of ethnic conflict for politics among states. Another is the manipulation of ethnic conflict in one state by another state. The Indian Parliament has acknowledged that hundreds of Nagas have been trained by the Chinese, armed, and returned to northeastern India. General Ne Luin of Burma has alleged that China has furnished sanctuary to Kachin dissidents and has contributed to the creditability of reports linking China to other secessionist movements within Burma.

It is also becoming increasingly evident that these rebellious secessionist-ethnic nations will traffic in contraband in order to finance guerrilla activities or to maintain their bases of political and cultural sovereignty within a state. This raises a fundamental question about the processes through which foreign policy takes shape. Governments still continue to pursue—with only slight deviation—practices formed in the nineteenth-century crucible of diplomacy. This procedure calls for direct transactions among governments who exercise political control over a geographical area. In an age of political consciousness characterized by retribalization and neoethnic behavior, this is a short-sighted posture. Difficult a task as it may be, foreign policy must be able to learn how to communicate with different ethnic nations within a single state if it wishes to achieve it objectives. This will require differentiating messages on a scale that would have been impractical a century ago. It will also require political contacts with dissident ethnic nations, occasionally at the expense of political relations with the constituted central government. Much, of course, will depend on the objectives to be achieved.

Neoethnic Groups

The ethnic nation is not an anachronism of feudal and preindustrial society. It demonstrates remarkable persistence even in postindustrial countries such as the United States. Odder still is that behavior resembling that associated with tribalism in the less-developed countries should plague states forged in the crucible of scientific rationalism and rationalist-liberal ideologies. Marxists and liberals have been quite insistent in their claim that the new order shall not make concessions to such protagonists of an anachronistic social consciousness.

And yet, an ethnic revival—or rediscovery of diversity, as Andrew Greely has described it—is underway in a post-industrial society least susceptible (in theory, of course) to such blandishments. Greely defines an *ethnic group* as a "collectivity based on presumed common origin, which shapes to some extent the attitudes and behaviors of those who share that origin, and with which certain people may freely choose to identify at certain times of their lives." [23] If we accept this definition, we are able to certify our understanding of behavior whose roots extend no further than the demography of eighteenth- and nineteenth-century Europe. But if ethnicity means relating to the physical and social environment, then what of those who experience community but who demonstrably lack the connection of blood or land? Are those societies that have apprehended the contours of an existential visage to be afforded no options for the redefinintion of community?

Modernization has often served as the precursor to mass movements and war, as individuals have sought to reestablish the social psychology of community in a radically altered environment. But as we approach the twenty-first century, individuals seem to have wearied of the millennial visions promised by the ideologies of the nineteenth century. We venture to suggest that no new intellectual radicalism has risen like the phoenix from the ashes of ideological fires, but that a popular radicalism, a *neoethnic* response to depersonalization and rationalization of the postindustrial society and certain changes in the traditional function of the nation-state has diffused into certain political and cultural sensibilities.

A politics of neoethnicism is investing itself in the styles, politics, and social organization in America that will have a wide impact on theories of national development and integration. Neoethnicism as a system is a transition from the national consciousness of the nation-state to more communal forms of identity and organization characterized by cultural patriotism, ethnic nationalism, and a revolt against anxiety. A primary agent of this transformation is the primacy of communication in the process of mobilizing unassmimilated minorities and subcultures, the growth of particularistic and minority nationalism, in a redefinintion of national consciousness. It has been described at its farthest points by a

[23] Andrew Greely, "The Rediscovery of Diversity," *Antioch Review,* Vol. 31 (Fall 1971): 343–65.

process of retribalization, the philosophical concession to communal imperatives characterized by the "interdependence of fate" and a proliferation of related life styles. In its paramount expression, it is the apostasy of the nation-state, an exhaustion with the cumulative preoccupations of national and world institutions and the preference for the pursuit and study of personal and parochial problems. It is expressed in a variety of ideologies, among a variety of classes. It has assumed both subtle and overt expressions and is stimulated by structural changes in the functions of the state.

The intensity of neoethnic politics among the young reflects the changing sensibilities in an age of maximum weaponry where the utility of the state as a territorial instrument for preservation has lost its cogency, and where security has become a function of technology, not of geopolitics.

This reorganization of security has acted as a catalyst in the reexamination of other state institutions and functions and has revealed an extraordinary degree of weariness with the institutions of the nation-state. In such a system, where the nation-state is no longer regarded as the "highest" form of organization, interest groups—cultural and racial minorities—not receiving satisfaction from the processes of the state are easily mobilized to pursue nonnational alternatives to political and cultural communities.

Thus, privatism, ethnicism, spirituality, community-oriented protest, consumer unionism, and communes testify to the decline of the nation-state ethic and absence of the subscription of diverse national, ethnic, neoethnic preferences to the creation of state initiatives and ideology. The deauthorization of the symbols and the ideology of the nation-state is not a temporary phenomenon, nor is it primarily a casualty of the Vietnam War. It is bound up in, although not necessarily intrinsic to, the neoethnic rage. But public temperament is in transition as well; decentralization, revenue sharing, and community control are manifestations of this postponement of national gratification and a commitment to the development of smaller, more manageable administrative units. Some of the young have been among the first to grasp the significance of this transition and shape themes that accommodate their perspective "youth cultures." As such, these themes prefigure issues as seemingly diverse as revenue sharing and freedom-of-choice school designs, "youth ghettos," the new sex consciousness of women, and the competition among ethnic nations and neoethnic groups for political and economic rewards, which had induced much of the current social conflict.

In conclusion, it appears that the intensification of ethnic consciousness and the subsequent fragmentation, rather than political consolidation and social integration, may well be a function of modernization. The concept of development, long considered to be an increase of GNP and PCI or a rise in production and consumption, may be redefined in terms of "liberation" from externally imposed values, socioeconomic-political inequities, or supression of cultural expressions. The energies and attentions of states may become absorbed by intense ethnic division resulting in less effective domestic and foreign policies.

As security becomes increasingly a function of technology and the imperatives of national security are viewed less in geopolitical terms, the lack of "external" threats may catalyze ethnic consciousness and negate those forces previously contributing to social cohesion and result in doubling the number of states in the early twenty-first century. Postindustrial societies may not be immune to neoethnicism because the causes appear to be anthropologically, sociologically, and psychologically rooted and seemingly not assuaged by positivism or "progress." The nation-state may become less an entity of reference and perceived less as the prime mover of development and sine qua non of political identification. Consequently, the concept of national interest may become more nebulous and less useful in predicting political behavior.

Terrorist Groups

Terrorism—the use of violence for political purposes—is a logical response to the present distribution of power and level of integration of social, economic, political, and communications systems, just as the balance of power was a logical response to the previous geopolitical system. The nineteenth century saw the rise of the nation-state and the twentieth century witnessed the emergence of internationalism. The growth of terrorism is related both to the changing nature of international relations and to the transnational politics of the twenty-first century.

Terrorism as a System

It is useful to distinguish terrorism as a system from terrorism as a technique. As a technique, terrorism is employed by pirates, common criminals, national liberation movements, and governments. Accordingly, it does not lend itself to meaningful analysis, since we face a problem of methodology—locating the dependent variable—and a problem of theory—terrorism in one instance is an act of liberation in another.

A productive analysis of terrorism must assume that terrorism is a system. The identification of acts of terrorism must be made on an empirical basis in every situation. As a system, it is useful to analyze terrorism in a four-part paradigm: (1) the level of integration of political, economic, social, and communications systems; (2) the distribution of power in the system; (3) the capacity of the system to oppress terrorism; and (4) the capacity of the system to respond to the perceived need of terrorism.

When a system becomes more integrated, the possibility for terrorism increases correspondingly. Out of 951 estimated terrorist acts between 1965 and 1975, 333 occured in the more integrated system of Western Europe. In the less-integrated systems of the Middle East, Asia, and sub-Saharan Africa, terrorist incidents recorded were 122, 43, and 38, respectively.[24]

The United States and Canada, two systems characterized by the highest level of integration, recorded only 126 terrorist incidents. This relatively low incidence may be explained by the capacity of these systems to respond to the perceived needs of terrorism. The low number of terrorist incidents (22) in the Soviet Union and Eastern Europe is largely due to the capacity of those systems to oppress terrorist acts.

Terrorists have emerged as volatile actors in world politics who enjoy several advantages over their inevitable adversary, the national-state. The disturbing message of terrorists gives them access to "air time," where their objectives and aspirations are easily comprehended, reduced, and transmitted by the world's media. In contrast, the objectives and aspirations of the state, like the state itself, are often confused, conflicting, uncertain, and difficult to reduce to unequivocal messages. The terrorist's capability to communicate specific demands and ideas almost always exceeds the capabilities of the state except in time of war, an uncommon moment of consensus within the state.

Goals and Objectives of Terrorists

The capabilities of the terrorists to achieve their objectives also have begun to approximate the effectiveness of the state. The terrorist's success has either been a function of bleeding the patience and morale of the home country, such as the IRA has done with the British public, or affecting the consciousness of the world community, as with the case of the Popular Front for the Liberation of Palestine. Terrorists' capability is a product of extrinsic factors, not the intrinsic strength of a popular movement as in the case with a national war of liberation. The combination of high media visibility and a capability basis upon extrinsic politics has made the terrorists a more believable and potent adversary. The introduction and proliferation of weapons of war have permitted the

---

[24] Central Intelligence Agency, *International and Transnational Terrorism* (Washington, D.C.: U.S. Government Printing Office), 1976, p. 12

terrorists to acquire sophisticated araments, surface-to-air missiles, and, in time, nuclear weapons.

While the terrorists' capabilities flow from extrinsic considerations, the objectives of terrorist groups in several parts of the world cannot be separated from the political environment where they have developed or the sociopsychological characteristics of those persons who are conscripted to serve their objectives. In the first case, terrorist groups in Rhodesia (Zimbabwe African National Union—ZANU), the Philippines (Moro National Liberation Front—MNLF), and Spain (Azkatasuna—ETA) have defined their operations in terms of the right of self-determination. Indeed, this putative right of self-determination that is still evolving in customary international law—not yet a product of convention—has provided the legitimizing ideology for many of these groups. Yet the position of the terrorist as an "unprivileged belligerent" under the Geneva Convention of 1949 has become a code word for secession and the politics of disassociation—anathema to the integration of many states. As long as states refuse to yield sovereignty to "nations" within their political jurisdiction, the grievances of many of their so-called terrorist groups will not be abated. The tension between the nation and the state—the source of a preponderance of the terrorist activity in world politics today—insures the longevity of many terrorist groups and the proliferation of others.

Recent terrorist activity has suggested a global link-up between terrorist groups to harass states to further their common purposes. If this is true, it is a harbinger of what we believe may evolve into increasing interaction and integration of objectives, strategies, and tactics. It is not inconceivable that some terrorist groups may temporarily forego their own movement objectives in order to open a united front against a target state. They could be induced by the promises of a "second front" to be opened at a future time.

The terrorist, like most other nonstate actors, has received scant attention in the theoretical literature of international relations. But the needs and objectives of the terrorists are limited, their mobility high, and the system they seek to disrupt technically advanced and vulnerable.

The emergence of terrorist groups as actors is less a function of their capability and more a response to the vulnerability of the global system. The highly integrated institutions in the global system are vulnerable only to minor disruptions which can produce widespread damage or fear. An integrated system provides the logistical and functional requirements which contribute to the vitality of terrorist groups. Terrorism is not a peculiar pathology. The demand for self-determination and the struggle against internal political oppression or external exploitation form the basis for terrorist groups.

As important as the role which the terrorist will perform in politics among states is what the response of the state will be to terrorism. How will states react to other states who permit their territories to be used as sanctuaries? Will states stage the equivalent of terrorist raids of their own, as in the case of Israel in Uganda? Is there a role for international law in the conflict between the terrorist and the state, or will each state deal with the terrorists by entering into bilateral treaties of extradition and trying captured persons as criminals under its domestic law? Should acts of terrorism be considered political crimes and immune from prosecution?

The plans of terrorists are not desultory acts of tactical violence. Terrorism reveals strategy and tactics. The strategy of terrorism is contingent upon the environment where terrorists operate—whether urban or rural, regional or international. The tactics used by terrorists in a preindustrial society differ from those employed in industrial or postindustrial societies. The target and audience of terrorism is determined by the capability and objectives of the terrorists at any given time. Terrorists that are relatively weak attack a symbolic target—persons or objects rather than the seat of power. A natural constituency of a terrorist group that is not sufficiently politicized becomes the target audience of terrorist activity. Hence, the target audience of the Black September terrorists in 1972 at the Munich Olympics was not the Europeans or the Americans, but the Arab and Palestinian people. As terrorism becomes a revolutionary movement, the targets become less symbolic and more pragmatic.

Terrorists recognize the inherently restricted nature of their options as well as the limited outcome of their activity. Accordingly, they transfer the stage of conflict to a larger arena and involve a new set of actors to maximize their options and alter a predetermined outcome.

Terrorism often comprises acts of self-defense by the weak and exploited and will persist as long as the global system lacks effective machinery to regulate the power of the more important actors—states and corporations. Terrorists commit political crimes through hijacking, murder, and kidnapping, while states and multinational corporations commit political crimes through their monopoly over power and wealth. The terrorism of a state is called war, while that of the multinational corporation is called profit.

The ineffectiveness of international law and such international conventions as the human rights covenants to assist those who assert their rights to human dignity, survival, and self-determination ensures the persistence of terrorism. Terrorism succeeds due to overreaction of governments and not because of the skill of the terrorists. Governments fall because of their inadequacy and not due to the capability of terrorists. In many instances it is the reaction of government to terrorism that poses serious problems for the future of global politics. Terrorism does not succeed by itself, but only when aided by those in positions of authority.

In this context, terrorism is not without its positive aspects: It dramatizes injustice, it causes reexamination of political and economic issues, and it is less cruel and costly than war.

Legal Control of Terrorism

A question which has preoccupied legal theorists is whether acts of terrorism should be regarded as political crimes or merely common criminal offenses. There is no agreed-upon legal definition of terrorism. Terrorism is viewed merely as "acts of international crime committed by means of terror, violence, and intimidation." [25] Even criminologists cannot agree on a universally acceptable definition.

We can distinguish three stages in the development of international legal concern with terrorism. During the first stage, which followed World War I, concern focused on the legal definition of terrorism. The second stage, extending over the 1930s, was characterized by attempts to regulate terrorism at the international level. The third and present stage centers upon the efforts carried on within the United Nations to deal with new forms of terrorism such as air piracy (Conventions of The Hague, 1971, and Montreal, 1972) and the kidnapping of diplomats (Convention of Washington, 1971).

The problem of differentiating between terrorism and political crimes has not been resolved. The first attempt to define terrorism in a court of law was undertaken by German courts in 1929, in a case of extradition. The signing of extradition treaties which differentiated between political crimes and terrorism underscored the need for a clearer definition of terrorism. The Unification of Penal Law in 1935 developed a definition of terrorism, which remains in use today, as an act in which the perpetrator has created "a common danger or a state of terror that might incite a change or raise an obstacle to the functioning of public bodies or a disturbance in international relations." [26]

In 1937, the Convention for the Prevention and Repression of Terrorism instituted the first attempt to control terrorism. The convention stipulated that each of the contracting states is obligated to consider acts of terrorism in its criminal legislation. Regulations within the convention dealt with extradition and preserved a state's right to "try its own citizen

---

[25] Theo Volger, "Perspectives on Extradition and Terrorism", in Cherif M. Bassiouni, *International Terrorism and Political Crimes* (Springfield, Ill.: Charles Thomas, 1975), p. 392.
[26] Tran-Tram, "Crimes of Terrorism and International Criminal Law, in Cherif M. Bassiouni and Ved P. Nanda, eds., *A Treatise on International Criminal Law* (Springfield, Ill.: Charles Thomas, 1973), p. 495.

even when he has committed a crime in another nation." [27]

The U.N. General Assembly voted in 1972 to establish a thirty-five-member committee to study the problems posed by terrorism. This action followed a long and intensive discussion caused by the presentation, on the part of the United States, of a general draft for a Convention on Terrorism. The draft attempted to prevent the spread of violence across borders to states not party to internal or external conflicts. The measure has been postponed repeatedly by the General Assembly.

Present legal concern with terrorism is confined to definition for the purpose of extradition and for the purpose of containment of terrorist acts. Many extradition treaties in force today have differentiated between terrorism and political crimes. Containment is of primary importance along with a means of enforcement.

Responses to Terrorism

In 1972, the president of the United States authorized the formation of the Cabinet Committee to Combat Terrorism. It coordinates most of the intelligence gathered about terrorist groups and their plans, the contingency plans for dealing with such threats, and the evaluation of such plans after they have been implemented.

The United States' response to terrorism consists of efforts designed to enhance the security of individuals and buildings and to encourage international initiatives to suppress terrorism. United States policy toward terrorism is governed by two guidelines—not give in to blackmail demands, and not to condone other states giving in to blackmail demands for any reason. Quite obviously, this policy ignores the causes of terrorism. Assuming that terrorist action is not taken against Americans or American interests by accident, there have to be reasons why the United States was chosen as a target. Furthermore, by ignoring the causes of terrorism the United States implicitly throws its support behind those parties that frustrate terrorist groups. As terrorist acts are illegal, any actions taken to prevent terrorism must be legal or at least understandable. This attitude increases attacks on American interests when terrorist groups believe the United States perpetuates their frustrations by ignoring the conditions that spawn those frustrations.

The general American response to terrorism has taken two directions: (1) to protect U.S. citizens abroad and foreign officials residing in the United States through security precautions and prior intelligence

---

[27] Bogdan Zlataric, "History of International Terrorism and Its Legal Control" in Bassiouni, *International Terrorism*, p. 484.

about terrorist acts; and (2) to stop terrorism through international agreements.

The international initiative of the United States has supported the ratification of the three "sister" conventions on air security by all states. The 1963 Tokyo Convention requires states to return a hijacked plane and its passengers; the 1970 Hague Convention stipulates that countries should either extradite or prosecute hijackers; and the 1971 Montreal Convention affirms that any sabotage of aviation (e.g., blowing up planes on the ground) be dealt with by prosecution or extradition of the offenders. Many states have signed these conventions.

Far less successful have been American attempts at the United Nations to adopt a convention to protect diplomats. The Convention on the Protection of Diplomats has come under attack from some Latin American states because the convention could prevent states from granting asylum in certain cases, a traditional right in Latin America.

The United States also attempted to prevail upon regional organizations (including NATO, the Organization of American States, and the International Civil Aviation Organization) to act on the international problems of terrorism. Expanded cooperation is planned for NATO allies, and members of the OAS and ICAO have passed resolutions without much significance.

Other legal means the United States has taken to counter terrorism consist primarily of bilateral agreements with other states. Most notable among these is an agreement with Cuba calling for reciprocal extradition of hijackers. There have been no attempts to fly hijacked planes from the United States to Cuba since the agreement was signed in 1973, in contrast to sixty-three attempts in the four years preceeding the agreement.

The United States exchanges information with Canada on the movements of terrorist groups and technological innovations to combat terrorism. The United States sends advisors to other countries to counter terrorist threats and trains foreign policemen under the auspices of the AID Office of Public Safety.

The primary concern of the American response to terrorism does not deal with the causes of terrorism. Efforts at the Untied Nations provide limited solutions to the problem of terrorism. Terrorism will continue in one form or another until specific changes are made within the internal structures of some states and the foreign policies of others. The United States may seek to influence states with terrorist problems to broaden the representative basis of their governments by informally recognizing some terrorist groups and trying to bring them into the political system. The legitimacy breeded by this recognition may tend to tie the terrorists to the political system and enhance the chances for cessation of hostilities.

Recommended Readings

ALEXANDER, YONAH. *International Terrorism: National, Regional, and Global Perspectives.* New York: Frederick A. Praeger, 1976.

ALEXANDER, YONAH, and SEYMOUR MAXWELL FINGER, eds. *Terrorism: Interdisciplinary Perspectives.* New York: John Jay Press, 1977.

BARTH, FREDERIK, ed. *Ethnic Groups and Boundaries.* Boston: Little, Brown, and Co., 1969.

BELL, J. BOWYER. *A Time for Terror: How Democratic Societies Respond to Revoluntionary Violence.* New York: Basic Books, 1978.

BELL, WENDELL, and WALTER E. FREEMAN, eds. *Ethnicity and Nation Building.* Beverly Hills, Calif.: Sage, 1973.

DEMARIS, OVID. *Brothers in Blood: The International Terrorist Network.* New York: Charles Scribner's Sons, 1977.

ENLOE, CYNTHIA H. *Ethnic Conflict and Political Development.* Boston: Little, Brown, and Co., 1973.

FISHMAN, JOSHUA A, CHARLES A. FERGUSON, and JYOTIRINDRA DAS GUPTA, eds. *Language Problems of Developing Nations.* New York: John Wiley & Sons, 1968.

GLAZER, NATHAN, and DANIEL MOYNIHAN, eds. *Ethnicity: Theory and Experience.* Cambridge: Harvard University Press, 1975.

KUROKAWA, M., ed. *Minority Responses.* New York: Random House, 1970.

LAQUEUR, WALTER. *Terrorism.* Boston: Little, Brown, and Co., 1977.

LISTON, ROBERT A. *Terrorism.* Nashville, Tenn.: Thomas Nelson, 1977.

RABUSHKA, ALVIN, and KENNETH A. SHEPSLE. *Politics in Plural Societies: A Theory of Democratic Instability.* Columbus, Ohio: Charles E. Merrill Books, 1972.

SAID, ABDUL AZIZ, ed., *Ethnicity and U.S. Foreign Policy,* New York: Praeger Pub., 1977.

SAID, ABDUL AZIZ, and L. R. SIMMONS, eds. *Ethnicity in an International Context.* New Brunswick, N.J.: Transaction Books, 1976.

SCHERMERHORN, R. A. *Comparative Ethnic Relations: A Framework for Theory and Research.* New York: Random House, 1970.

Human Rights

15

Human rights may be difficult to define but they are impossible to ignore. We may quibble about the form of government, but torture, hunger, and political imprisonment are the same by any other name. Violations of human rights are not a monopoly of a single government or a group of states. They are global.

Human rights are concerned with the dignity of the individual—that level of self-esteem that is secure and self-accepting. The Universal Declaration of Human Rights (1948), the (European) Convention for the Protection of Human Rights and Fundamental Freedoms (1950), the International Covenant on Economic, Social, and Cultural Rights (1966), and the International Covenant on Civil and Political Rights (1966) are part of the process of enlarging the dignity, freedom, opportunity for creativity, and welfare of individuals and the development of an environment and the appropriate institutions to promote these goals.

While the pursuit of human dignity is universal, it is defined by the culture of a people. Politics is a cultural activity and reflects tradition and environment. The debate on human rights assumes that, in spite of the differences which characterize the diversity of cultures, political conduct can be conceptualized by certain common norms and attitudes. In the modern global system, Westerners have concentrated on discovering common denominators rooted in the Judeo-Christian traditions from which a calculus of human rights would emerge. This emphasis on Western common denominators has posited a parochial view of human rights, neglecting the traditional cultures and present conditions of the Third World.

In the West, the increasing totality of the nation-state, the declining need on the part of the state to perform the functions of security, and the integration and standardization required by technification underscore the issue of human rights. The expanded state narrows individuality, the historical preoccupation with external security is replaced with personal insecurity, and technification obscures self-definition.

In the Third World, the institutions that performed the traditional functions of social and political organizations have declined and the new structures patterned after the Western or Marxist models have not been established firmly. While the need to satisfy and promote human rights persists, this function has not found a role in the present political system. This situation, however, cannot last, for the search for dignity is an intuitive human expression.

Today's political life in the West, in the socialist states, and in the less-developed countries, on the domestic level and in the global system, is not burdened by many constants. The increasing complexity of Western society, the emphasis upon production in socialist states, the urge for modernization in the Third World, and the disparity in growth between rich and poor states have ascribed higher priority to efficiency than to human dignity. In the process, violations of fundamental human rights have assumed global dimensions.

International Concern for Human Rights

The Congress of Vienna in 1815 demonstrated international concern for human rights for the first time in modern times. The Congress dealt with religious freedom as well as civil and political rights and heard petitions by individuals and groups for international protection of those rights. Additionally, participants in the Congress agreed in principle to abolish slavery. This was followed by a number of antislavery acts and treaties: the Berlin Conference on Africa in 1885; the Brussels Conference of 1890; the Saint Germain Treaty of 1919; and the Geneva Conference of 1926. Great Britain's Abolition Act of 1833 ended slavery in the British Empire. Russia, France, Prussia, Austria, and Great Britain signed the Treaty of London in 1841 to abolish slavery. In 1845, France and Great Britain agreed to cooperate to end slave trade.

The Hague peace conferences of 1899 and 1907 introduced the notion of the right of individuals to appeal to the Court of Appeal (although the proposition was not ratified). The Central American Peace Conference of 1907 provided for the right of aliens to appeal to the courts where they resided. The problem of minorities' rights, however, was emphasized at the expense of other human rights such as those of women and children.

During the first two decades of the twentieth century, World War I, the efforts of peace groups, the impact of the Fourteen Points of

President Wilson, and the Bolshevik Revolution underscored the principle of international agreement to regulate the sovereignty of states. The Peace Conference at Versailles in 1919 demonstrated its concern for the protection of minorities. Several treaties were concluded with the new states stressing minorities' rights, including the right to life, liberty, and freedom of religion, the right to the nationality of the state of residence, complete equality with other nationals of the same state, and the exercise of civil and political rights.

Minorities' rights were placed under a system of international guarantees, with the Council of the League of Nations acting as guarantor. These rights were obligations of international interest and could not be modified without the assent of a majority of the Council. Violations were to be referred to the Permanent Court of Justice. The court, however, had no binding force. Rights of individuals were not covered by the system of minorities' rights. Only states could seek redress for violations of rights.

The International Labor Organization has made important contributions to the development of human rights. It has established conventions on the right to organize and collective bargaining, abolition of forced labor, and ending discrimination (employment and occupation). The ILO has been a pacesetter for other specialized agencies.

The Dumbarton Oaks proposal of 1944 for the establishment of the United Nations asserted as one of the purposes of the organization to "promote respect for human rights and fundamental freedoms." Unlike the Covenant of the League of Nations, which did not refer to rights of individuals, the United Nations Charter underscores the principle of human rights.

The Charter, however, fails to define human rights in specific terms and does not provide for adequate legal machinery to assure the effective implementation of its provisions. The role of the United Nations is further curtailed by Article 2(7) of the Charter, which upholds the concept of state sovereignty, preventing control or intervention by the United Nations in domestic matters of states. In 1946 the Security Council of the United Nations established the Commission on Human Rights and charged it with the duty of drafting an international declaration on the rights of individuals. The Universal Declaration of Human Rights was adopted by the General Assembly in 1948.

The Universal Declaration of Human Rights is an informal instrument appended to the Charter of the United Nations. Its purpose is to explain the contents of the human rights provision of the Charter and thus to be a preliminary formulation of the fundamental freedoms which require recognition internationally through a series of binding covenants. It consists of thirty short articles, dealing with civil and political freedoms as well as economic, social, and cultural rights. Its scope is broad. It is in a certain sense an act of faith in a better future for humanity. In an effort to conciliate clashing ideologies of member states, the terms defining each right have been kept general and noncommittal.

The success or failure of international protection of human rights is contingent upon performance. The adoption of the Universal Declaration of Human Rights with its definition of standards of fundamental freedoms lacked an international obligation binding on U.N. members to assure that their own legislation afforded protection of rights enumerated in the declaration.

The declaration, however, is only a statement of general moral principles. It invokes moral values setting forth a common standard of achievement among the states of the world, but it is not a treaty and does not have binding international force.

The adoption of the Universal Declaration of Human Rights necessitated a differentiation between rights and freedoms that had to be defined with legal accuracy and others that were described in general terms. This was accomplished in the drafting of two separate covenants, isolating the political and civil liberties from economic, social and cultural rights. The covenant dealing with the latter rights imposed on member states the duty to submit reports on their progress in the protection of human rights. The covenant on political and civil rights stimulated extensive debates as it contemplated the creation of a nine-member Human Rights Committee that would receive complaints of violations submitted by any member state against any other signatory member.

A proposal to grant individuals the right to petition an international body for relief against a state violating their human rights was abandoned for fear that the covenants may become political instruments rather than effective procedures in the protection of the fundamental freedoms of individuals. Accordingly, the United Nations has consistently refused to reach any agreement which would institutionalize strong measures of international control for the protection of individual freedoms. Finally, in 1966 the U.N. General Assembly unanimously approved two Human Rights Covenants.

Beyond international organizations, two regional organizations, the Council of Europe and the Organization of American States, have addressed themselves to human rights. The Western European states have been most sensitive to the development of institutions to promote human rights. The statute of the Council of Europe of 1949 asserts that human rights and fundamental freedoms are the basis of the emerging European system. The signatory states affirmed "their devotion to the spiritual and moral values which are the common heritage of their peoples and the true source of individual freedom, political liberty and the rule of law." Acceptance of the provisions on human rights is a condition for membership in the Council of Europe.

The European Convention on Human Rights of 1950, entered into force in 1953, was the first attempt to give specific legal content to human rights in an international agreement. The European Commission of Human Rights created in 1953 and its associated bodies, the European Court of Human Rights and the Committee of Ministers, represent important progress in the area of human rights.

The commission, the court, and the Committee of Ministers review the decisions of national tribunals, but do not perform the functions of an appeal court. The deliberations of the court are secret, but the final findings are pronounced in open session. The decision of the court is not binding, and the convention does not confer upon the Council the power to enforce the judgment of the court.

The Inter-American System of Human Rights is another regional model of concern for human rights. In the Declaration of Mexico of 1945 the American republics asserted the need to harmonize the rights of individuals with the interests of the community. The declaration called on the Inter-American Judicial Council to develop a draft on the International Rights and Duties of Man. The Bogota conference of 1948 produced the American Declaration of the Rights and Duties of Man. More than a decade later the Santiago Conference of 1959 produced the Inter-American Convention on Human Rights which provided for the establishment of the Inter-American Commission on Human Rights and of a Court of Human Rights which came into existence in 1960.

The Inter-American Convention of Human Rights has not yet been ratified by the United States. President Carter has announced that he will seek approval of the United States Senate for ratification. The custom of Latin American governments to invoke the constitutional device known as the stage of seige combined with repression by military dictatorships undermines the intent of the Inter-American human rights system.

Finally, nongovernmental organizations (NGOs) such as Amnesty International, the International League of Human Rights, the Minority Group, and others perform important investigative and communicative functions in the area of human rights. NGOs maintain a consultative status with the United Nations and its specialized agencies and international conferences. The contributions of NGOs, including fact finding, monitoring, and reporting human rights violations on the national and international level, are impressive. These agencies create a flow of information as well as exert pressure through lobbying in national states as well as international forums.

The Western Context of Human Rights

The fundamental problem of political life—the tension between the rights and liabilities of the individual and the duties and powers of government—has characterized the development of the state. Since ancient Greece, the West has approached this polarity within the framework of Platonic organicism and sophistic nominalism. For the Platonists, the individual beyond a political community had no rights; it was through the *polis* that individuals gained the spiritual and political attributes which made them human rather than barbaric. Therefore, concern for the whole of the political community preceded the claims of any individual. This type of political community was organic, since the individual functioned merely as a part of an organic whole and gained significance only in reference to that whole.

The sophists, on the other hand, based the state upon a contract acknowledging that the individual had natural rights apart from the political community. The state arose only when individuals saw that it would benefit them to surrender their purely selfish intersts in order to better secure their existence. For the sophists the community was predicated upon a philosophy of nominalism: the members *did* have an identity beyond the political community. The rationale of the state was not to achieve an organic harmony and a common good, but rather to maximize the interests of the individual members of the state.

The Platonic-sophistic dichotomy was reproduced with greater sophistication by the nominalists of the seventeenth century and the organicists of the nineteenth century. Seventeenth-century nominalism represented a final break with medieval organicism, which, following the dissemination of Aristotelian doctrines, provided the philosophical basis of political life in Europe. By the seventeenth century the community had become dissolved into a discrete mass of individuals with distinct self-interests. Hobbes built his state upon the selfishness of individuals. Even Locke made the individual enter political life for the benefits that accrue therefrom. The individual left the "state of nature"—in which life, Hobbes and Locke concurred, was "short, nasty, and brutish"—through the mechanism of the social contract. The political community was then held together by an intricate balance of power which gave rise to a harmony of interests and became the basis of laissez-faire economics and liberal politics. The interests of the individual and the community coincided.

The return to the organic notion of political community from seventeenth-century nominalism took place in the works of Kant, Hegel, and Rousseau. Kant asserted that human values and perception are structured by objective categories which one brings into the world at birth.

Accordingly, the individual has a categorical identity—as a member of a class, nation, race—which ultimately determines one's actions. Rousseau substitutes the general will for the will of all. The difference between the will of all and the general will is that the latter has a nonhistorical origin which bears no necessary relationships to the interests of the members of the political community to which it applied. The will of all, on the other hand, is simply the will of the majority of the people. Finally, Hegel formalized the course of history. There is an absolute in history, he maintained, which dictates human action. Freedom is simply action in accord with historical necessity. Human values and human purpose are rendered operationally irrelevant by the inalterable course of history.

The transition from seventeenth-century nominalism to nineteenth-century organicism begins with the reversion against the French Revolution and develops during the Industrial Revolution. With the emergence of the reign of virtuous terror in France, Europeans who had supported the original ideals of the revolution recoiled in the direction of doctrines of organicism. The exponents of the new organicism—Burke, Demaistre, and Fichte—argued that political community is established by nature and cannot be altered by political action. The values of the group to which the individual belongs are transhistorical. The course of history determines the significance of the group. Thus, nineteenth-century conservatives advanced the concept of the absolute. Burke found it in tradition, Fichte in the nation, Gobineau in the race, and Madison Grant in the aristocracy. Individuals' denial of a transcendent absolute, conservatives have imagined, has rendered them incapable of sustaining political order.

Even Marx, for instance, adopted all the trappings of nineteenth-century organicism. The individual for him was born with an objective identity dictated by the division of labor, a corollary of the prevailing system of production which was a by-product of historical necessity. An eventual classless society was assured by the unalterable course of the historical absolute.

In the twentieth century the conservative longing has found articulate and learned exponents. William Y. Elliott has written of the attack by pragmatism and pluralism on the absolute sovereignty of the constitutional state. Henry Kariel has lamented the twentieth-century image of the political individual, whose actions are environmentally determined and who is consequently incapable of positing transcendent political values. Richard M. Weaver, a consistent enemy of relativism, argues that the individual is dehumanized without the tyrannizing norms of culture.

The evidence of political life in the twentieth century, however, seems to refute the diagnosis of the conservatives. The paramount reality of twentieth-century politics, the "true believer," is distinguished precisely by a penchant to grasp an absolute though selfless dedication to the movement which embodies it. The selfless individual has appeared as the Bolshevik, the Nazi, the American, the Maoist. It is not the lack of absolutes, but the institutionalization of these absolutes, which has underscored the tension between the individual and the state.

The twentieth century lacks a public realm, as the classical Greeks understood it. The realm of freedom where individuals render their notions of the good political order has narrowed. The trend is toward ideological, "consensus" politics; membership in the political community of rights and duties is denied to those who remain beyond the pale of the prevailing dogma. In the absence of this realm of freedom, twentieth-century man has been reduced to an instrument of necessity. Now, however, necessity appears in the guise of ideologies, surrogates of true political expression. Even the organic needs which gave the private realm in classical Greece its rationale are less compulsive than the ideological absolutes; to them selfless man has sacrificed his organic existence.

Thus the erosion of individual rights, the fruits of which were left for twentieth-century individuals to bear, took place in the nineteenth century; Kant, Rousseau, and Hegel supplied the tools of the erosion. Freedom in the classical sense, in other words, has been the victim of the expression of nineteenth-century attitudes and ideologies in the twentieth-century political realm. The present crisis of human rights in the West is a function of ideological politics. The need for a new relationship between a freedom which recognizes man's essential spiritual nature and an expanded necessity imposed by the nineteenth-century heritage exerts strong pressure upon present-day society.

The needs of the individual conflict with the demands of the state which transformed the moral and political centers of authority, emasculating the political authority of the church and the family. The state has inherited many of the primary functions which these social organizations fulfilled. Accordingly, in Western society human rights issues center around both the nature of the social structure and demands for new life styles. The social structure of the state reflects the distribution of economic and political rewards among various competing interest and ethnic nations. Life styles, on the other hand, refer to individuals who have grown dissatisfied with their roles and functions in society and the quality of the life they lead. They have developed new needs. The politics of life styles involve very different considerations from the politics of social structure.

In such an environment, clothing, preference in music or drugs, homosexuality or heterosexuality—these become human rights issues. More specifically, individuals become more concerned with their self-determination and with the right for the private life. They want to preserve their individuality and what they consider important from the tyranny of atomization, automation, and alienation.

Marxist and Neo-Marxist Views of Human Rights

Marxism is an elaboration of the concept of humanism that was developed during the Renaissance asserting the basic dignity and worth of the individual and emphasizing a person's capacity for self-realization through reason. Karl Marx emphasized economic rights, affirming that the collapse of the capitalist system was inevitable and that the proletariat (the working class) would seize the means of production and establish a new socialist system. This socialist system would then work toward the attainment of communism under which all would share equally the benefits of the new society. The exploited proletarian class would construct a new classless society where all individuals would be treated equally and justly.

The global character of Marxism has provoked a diversity of opinion on the subject of Marxist humanism. In the Marxist societies (led by the Soviet Union), a more "traditional" approach to the subject of Marxist humanist thought has been emphasized. Traditional Marxist humanism focuses its attention on class struggle and the liberation of the working class. The class struggle is the force that molds the consciousness of the working class and allows the working class to free itself from the oppression of the exploitative classes. As one traditional Marxist, Ladislav Shtoll, writes, "It will not be amiss to recall Engels' *The Condition of the Working Class in England* where it is stressed that the workers can maintain their human dignity, their human countenance, only if their whole life is filled with a burning hatred for the exploiter class."[1] The traditional Marxists contend that there is no genuine humanism under the capitalist system because of the oppressed condition of the working class. Under the capitalist system, the worker is viewed only in terms of market value, not as a human being with a myriad of needs and cares. Thus, under such a system, the basis for a humanist society could never be constructed. As another traditional Marxist writer phrased it, "The problems of humanism . . . are, in the final analysis, reduced to the need for a just organization of society."[2]

While traditional Marxists stress the class struggle and the monolithic unity of the communist movement, other Marxists are beginning to explore new routes to communism. These "Neo-Marxists" are devoted

[1] Ladislav Shtoll, "The Class Struggle and Humanism," *World Marxist Review* 1, no. 3 (1958): 28.
[2] Roger Garaudy, *Marxist Humanism* (Paris: Edition Sociales, 1957), p. 88.

to developing a more humane socialism independent of the present centers of Marxist thought in Moscow and Peking. The Neo-Marxists are opposed to the harsh and repressive Stalinist system and demand autonomy for each national Marxist movement. The slogan of the Neo-Marxists has been "Socialism with a human face." As Wolfgang Leonhard has observed, "Humanist Marxists reject the Soviet idea that a socialist society must be based on a planned state economy and be characterized by moral and political unity under the leadership of an all-powerful party and its apparatus. Instead, they visualize socialism [as] a living, free pluralist society, based economically on the self-management of producers (entailing workers' councils in the factories), and characterized politically by legally secured democratic liberties for its citizens and by free discussion among different groups."[3] Obviously, many of these ideas contradict the Marxist-Leninist philosophy of a strong, centralized Communist party and the dictatorship of the proletariat as the method of government in a socialist state.

It is also significant that the Neo-Marxists do not overemphasize the class struggle. The Neo-Marxists aren't exclusively concerned with changing the economic structures of society. Rather, the Neo-Marxists stress democracy, freedom of discussion, and the problem of alienation. Michael Harrington observes, "In communist society, alienation persists; indeed, it is writ large. The totalitarian state becomes the very incarnation of all those powers which weigh upon man, which rob him of his individuality and personality. There is anticapitalism, to be sure, but an anticapitalism which is corrosive of human dignity in much the same way as its antagonist."[4] Further on, he writes: "As soon as one realizes that socialism is not simply directed against economic irrationality but that its deepest springs flow from positive humanism whose task is the conquest of alienation, it becomes obvious that Russian society has nothing to do with socialism."[5]

Neo-Marxist thought has risen to prominence in Western Europe (among the Eurocommunist parties) and in Tito's Yugoslavia, where exception from the Soviet model was taken in 1948. The Neo-Marxist stress on democratic methods of governing and greater freedom could be interpreted as a reaction to the rigidity of Stalinism. It could also be viewed as the fear, on the part of other Communist parties, of being dominated by the Soviet Communist party. This fear is based on the

---

[3] Wolfgang Leonhard, *Three Faces of Marxism* (New York: Holt, Rinehart and Winston, 1974), p. 259.
[4] Michael Harrington, "Marx as Humanist," in *Marxism*, edited by Michael Curtis (New York: Atherton, 1970), p. 145.
[5] *Ibid.*, p. 150.

historical experience of communism in Russia and of Soviet policies vis-à-vis Eastern Europe.

The traditional Marxists reject the possibility of other paths to communism—that is, democratic elections vs. violent revolution. They believe that only by changing the economic structure of society and economic relations between individuals can a new humanity be founded and a more humane society emerge. While Neo-Marxists recognize that economic structures must be changed to promote the new humanism, they emphasize values of individuality and freedom.

Human Rights in the Third World: The Islamic States as an Illustration

Existential conditions in the Third World differ from the West. Increased institutionalization of the national state has accentuated the confrontation between the Western individual and the state. In the West, human rights tensions derive from the frustrating efforts to fit the contemporary environment into the state. Tensions in the Third World represent their equally frustrating effort to fit the state into their traditional institutions. Human rights concerns in the Third World center more around the nature of the social structure and less around life styles. Poverty, hunger, disease, illiteracy, low productivity, mass unemployment, glaring disparities in the distribution of benefits—these underline the existential plight of the Third World.

The "nation-state" and a progressive (as opposed to a static) vision of reality have inspired explorations, and sometimes produced friction, in the relationships between traditional cultural patterns and the structures of government. The Third World is in a marked intellectual and political institutional discontinuity with the old. The family and the community have outlived their usefulness as organizing principles and as safeguards for certain basic human rights. Nothing has replaced them, except perhaps angry and sometimes ugly cynicism. Human rights in the Third World are thus in a stage of ferment. There is confusion and, at times, anarchy.

The national-state model has required Third World governments to enter into competition with traditional authority. This in turn has prompted the attempt to introduce new values, interests, and goals in an effort to supplant traditional ones. While the old has been destroyed, the new has not yet appeared. The reasons are technical as well as ideological. The new states have no commonly accepted values—hence their new national structures are easily perishable. Political systems in the Third World merge, in the overriding context of Leninism and militarism, with an ever-widening public sector. Hardly any Third World government has been able to institutionalize itself firmly, to establish liberal or popular institutions, or to relax its vigil against subversion, imagined or real. The central structures of government are modern in form only, not in substance. Government is minimal in organization and effect.

The purpose and functions of the state in most of the Third World differ from the Western model. The role of the state in Islam, for example, serves as a useful case study. Unlike the modern Western national state, the Islamic state is obliged to enforce principles of the Shariah (Islamic law) in the territory under its jurisdiction. The implementation of the Shariah means, among other things, that the Islamic state must create environments conducive to the socioreligious needs of the people. Another salient difference between the Western state and the Islamic state is that in the latter sovereignty belongs to God alone. Both the rulers and the ruled are working for the glory of God, whose wishes and commands must be fulfilled for achieving happiness here and in the hereafter. Since sovereignty belongs to God alone, the process of legislation becomes less significant in an Islamic state than in the Western state.

In Islam, the state surrenders its soveriegnty to God and accepts the position of Caliphate (viceregency) under God's suzerainty. The power of the Caliphate does not reside in any person or a community, but in those who believe and do good. Since the purpose of the individual is the service of God, the existence of an organized community of believers requires the establishment of government. Accordingly, the legitimacy of government is its ability to ensure the service of God through counsel among the Muslims.

The Islamic state is a blend of theocracy and democracy. It is theocratic as it is predicated upon the doctrine of sovereignty of God. However, it does not delegate the viceregency of God to a priesthood. The Caliphate is vested in the believers who are virtuous. The state is democratic since the right to govern derives from counsel among the believers, a form of general will. However, the rights of the people to change the law of the state are limited.

Viewed against this background, the state in Islam does not exist merely to maintain law and order and provide external protection for its territory. It strives to realize social justice and promote public good. The viability of the state depends upon its ability to balance the relationship between individuals and government, ensure that the government does not become absolute, reducing the individual to slavery, and prevent individual freedom from threatening the interest of the community.

Since the Islamic state derives its justification from the Shariah it is the state's duty to enhance human dignity and alleviate conditions that hinder individuals in their effort to achieve happiness. However, in practice Islamic legal theory provides no adequate machinery to safeguard individual rights against the state. Modern Turkey has dealt with this problem by establishing a system of guaranteed individual liberties in the secularization of the state. Pakistan, on the other hand, has sought to establish a system of individual rights through a liberal interpretation of the original sources of Islamic law. The vast majority of the other Islamic states have adopted Western concepts of individual rights. Only Saudi Arabia applies the Shariah fully.

The record of human rights in modern Turkey is relatively better than in most of the other Islamic states. Pakistan, on the other hand, has been beset by domestic strife, depriving it of the opportunity to test its system of individual rights. In the Islamic states that have patterned their political systems after Western or Marxist models, there is constant confrontation between individual rights and liabilities and state duties and powers. In Saudi Arabia, where the Shariah has been applied without interruption since the seventh century, rights are enjoyed within the context of Islamic values and denied to those who remain outside the prevailing dogma. Put differently, the only rights enjoyed are those prescribed by the original sources of Islamic law.

The Western liberal emphasis upon freedom from restraint is alien to Islam. While in the Western liberal tradition freedom signifies the ability to act, in Islam, it is the ability to exist, or to become.

According to Islam, human beings are created in the image of God and are also God's representatives on earth and are empowered by the Divine Being to govern themselves. God has created human beings who seek perfection, following the perfected, and mastership of the will. Human beings have certain God granted rights, and right by definition is the exercise of power. The human being as the reflection of God who is complete freedom and complete necessity, participates in both this freedom and this necessity. Personal freedom lies in surrendering to the Divine Will and in purifying oneself inward to become liberated from all external conditions which limit one's freedom.

Since absolute freedom belongs to God alone, the individual realizes freedom by seeking God, the author of human freedom. There is no freedom possible through rebellion against this principle which is the source of human existence. To rebel against this principle in the name of freedom is to become separated from the potency and grace of the Divine. It is to lose inner freedom for that of the material world where the only freedom is to pursue happiness devoid of purpose.

These principles inform Islamic thought on freedom, but their formulation depends upon the perspectives advanced by the jurists, the theologians, and philosophers within the Islamic tradition. The jurists see human freedom as a result of personal surrender to the Divine Will, rather than as an innate personal right. For them, since human beings are created by God and have no personal power to create they are dependent on God and therefore can only receive what is given to them by the sources of their own being. Human rights are a consequence of human obligations and not their antecedent. Individuals possess certain obligations toward God, nature, and other humans, all of which are defined by the Shariah. As a result of fulfilling these obligations individuals gain certain rights and freedoms which are again outlined by the Shariah. Those who do not fulfill these obligations have no legitimate rights, and any claims of freedom that they make upon society lack justification.

The theologians can be divided into two groups: One group negates human freedom completely in favor of a determinism which is all-embracing, while the other accepts human freedom and rejects total determinism. The debate concerning free will and determinism is a central one to theology and most Muslim theologians have participated in it. While Muslim theologians concur on the absence of an outward material factor determining human freedom since any freedom sought from an external agency renders the individual an instrument of that agency, they disagree on the relationship of human will to the Divine Will and the extent to which the latter determines the former. The debates of the theologians reflect this general religious concern for submission to the Divine Will and conformity to Its injunctions.

The philosophers in general react strongly against the theologians on this question and assert fully the reality of human freedom. They approach the issue from the point of view of the Shariah. For the Shariah is a reality as is the Islamic community and the legitimacy of political rule derived from the source of revelation. The reality of human freedom is asserted by them, but in the context of the community of Islam and not from the point of view of Western liberalism.

The pursuit of freedom in Islamic civilization on the level of action and thought has been less successful than in the spiritual domain. On the level of political action the immediate question which arises is that of political freedom regarding forms of government which since the first Islamic dynasty in the Seventh Century onward were much more militaristic than they were religious. There remains within Islamic society a continuous tension between the political authority of the ruler and the religious scholars (ulama') who play a major role in protecting the Shariah and, therefore, those freedoms of the individual guaranteed by the Shariah.

The theological and religious debate about free will and determinism in the Islamic tradition produced periods of submission characterized by anarchy and assassination. While some Muslim rulers firmly adhered to dogma other Muslims blindly rebelled against it. This historical process resulted in the neglect of the political life of the Muslim individual.

Human Rights in the World Order

The entire global system today is gripped by frustrations and crises. At first glance, it appears as if the rapprochement of the superpowers has produced peace. In fact, the superpowers' reconciliation purchases minimal security in exchange for shares in the vital interests of the less-developed countries. Already exponents of a new world order are asserting that the new detente of the superpowers—the United States, the Soviet Union, and the Peoples' Republic of China—demonstrates superpower indifference toward the rapidly growing gap between the rich and powerful states and an indifference to the humanist ideals of peace and equality framed in the declarations and covenants on human rights.

As my colleague Brady Tyson has remarked, rather than a liberal, democratic, egalitarian order of law to replace the anarchy of the nation-state system, a global corporatist order appears to be developing, which is neither liberal nor democratic. A corporatist system is one where interest groups are represented by their elites in concert with other interest group elites, and the concert of elites develops its own interests while maintaining control over their respective groups. That is, the heads of several interest groups, the army, big business, and banks form an alliance to preserve stability in their common universe and thereby virtually eliminate or severely limit competition among the groups they head.

The security managers of the three superpowers in pursuit of their respective interests have formed an informal network of understanding and communication to assure that competition among them will not be allowed to become destructive and that potential rivals will be contained before they can threaten the dominance of the big three or any one of them. It is sort of a superpower cartel for the restraint of competition, for limiting the power to change the rules of the game to the three major actors. And, of course, there is no international antitrust legislation of any significance.

From the standpoint of world development, it is tragic that the period of superpower conflict was very often used to enhance the prosperity of the superpowers and militarize rather than develop the Third World. The era of the emerging rapprochement may tend to deescalate the international military conflicts in the Third World, but it is not likely on the other hand to increase development assistance from the rich states to the poor states. For one reason, the development process tends to be destabilizing, and that is apparently not a goal at this time of any of the superpowers.

Thus, the inevitable tendency in such a three-superpower arrangement will be to reduce the area of maneuverability of the less-developed countries and to maintain or force them into client relationships with one of the superpowers. Military modernizers who will avoid exciting "extravagant" popular expectations such as those in the Universal Declaration of Human Rights will probably continue to appear and to flourish in the Third World, sponsored by one or the other of the superpowers.

It is useful to compare the 1930s to the 1970s. Like the '30s, the '70s are a time of severe testing of liberalism and constitutionalism. In the two cases the reasons are nearly identical; social dislocations caused by lack of planning provoked by technological change, national and corporate competition and power—and profit hunger. Liberalism and constitutionalism have easily become the prisoners of their own traditional processes and have failed to keep up with the necessity to adapt to new conditions. In the '30s the challenge of international communism created a counterrevolution from the right, which was only contained by World War II. In the '70s the challenge of protest movements without a program has been taken advantage of by a counterrevolution ("the new right") that is yet to be contained.

While the global political order is dominated by corporatism, the global economic order assumes the form of industrial feudalism. The present global system consists of no more than about twenty-five states and fifty multinational corporations who have any significant impact, and the top five states have over half of the world's human and natural resources.

The situation of the United States, with a GNP around $2 trillion, nearly 40 percent of the world's industrial production, and 75 percent of its computer capacity, raises the issue of who has the rights to world resources. America's power is increasingly exercised by a pluralistic, diffuse, and differentiated elite, residing throughout the world but increasingly Americanized in style and outlook. Today, the United States occupies a position similar to Rome during the Middle Ages—a nominal center of power forced to exercise influence through indirect diffused means and multinational corporations. The industrial states with a population of 600 million have an income between $2000, and $8000 a year, constitute less than a fourth of world population and enjoy more than three-fourths of its annual GNP. By contrast, 2 billion persons living in the Third World earn less than $200 per capita per year. In the Third World, about 800 million people lack minimal requirements of food, medical care, housing, and literacy. They subsist on $75 annual income.

Several of the multinational corporations (such as Royal Dutch/Shell, Standard Oil, Texaco, Mobil, Gulf, and IBM) exert more collective influence than all but a handful of states, principally the industrial ones.

The pattern of investment and activity of these corporations affects issues of war and peace and determines the long-term prospects for world economic development and allocation of world resources. Decision making by these companies has as much or more impact on the human conditions, and international conflict and cooperation, than do the foreign policy decisions of states such as Brazil, Iran, or the Philippines.

This maldistribution of wealth is accompanied by a maldistribution of information. The same industrial states and multinational corporations also enjoy political and economic control over the international exchange of information. The advanced industrial states have come to rely less and less on such markets as extractive industries and are bound together in a fierce competition to secure new technologies to maintain their superiority. With the abatement of unregulated competition among the superpowers, the appeals and publicity about the plight of the Third World, about hunger, poverty, and underdevelopment, will probably die down. But given the continuing population growth and the capital-intensive—and technology-intensive—nature of the usual postindustrial modernization process, these problems are hardly likely to diminish. Hunger and poverty will be out of sight and out of mind. The United Nations and its specialized agencies can hardly be expected in the face of the new situation to maintain even their present low level of impact. These agencies exist, or act on key issues, only by sufferance of the major powers.

Toward Global Human Rights

There are many views of human rights, but hardly a clear focus. Human rights in the West are expressed in demands for the redress of grievances and for the satisfaction of new needs, while in the past they represented a desire to be left alone. The Greco-Roman and the Judeo-Christian traditions asserted both rights and duties, as expounded in the "natural law" arguments of the times.

Thus, in the West, we see a movement away from the person's duties to the state through the individual's pleas to be left alone, and toward demands by individuals that the state perform more duties. As each stage develops, the number of individual rights expands while the province of individual duties narrows. On the other hand, the demand for the expansion of the duties of the state is satisfied only through the enlargement of state powers. These contradictory aspects run deep in the present human rights debate in the West. This contradiction has placed the state in a cross-fire between individuals and groups demanding equal rights. The essential contradiction is that government intervention to meet demands of an individual or a group decreases the rights of other individuals or groups in exact proportion to its success. The trend will persist until such time as there occurs a change in the allocation of power.

We must also recognize the connection between the type and number of rights and the nature of the environment. In the West there has been a definite shift from an abstract concept of universal rights toward a concrete concept of essential rights. The shift is indicative of societal conditions that must be taken into consideration in the dialogue on human rights. The West is in a stage of development substantially different from much of the Third World. The problems associated with Third World development have not been experienced in the recent history of the West.

In the Third World, human rights focus upon such essentials as hunger, inadequate sanitation, and lack of shelter. In the meantime, protagonists of change in the less developed countries suffer indignities of torture and political imprisonment. Their demand for human rights continues to expand. Eventually, the Third World will experience the same cycle of evolution of human rights as in the West, but in reverse order—from concrete essential rights to abstract universal rights to concrete rights again. In the process certain human rights conflict in specific circumstances, the reasons for the differences in particular lists of rights being both historical and functional. The need for tradeoffs between the ideal and the possible forces the Third World to assign priorities. However, it is not too early for the Third World to assess the price of modernization. It is imperative to ask which value will cost the least.

The development of a global conception of human rights suffers from lack of agreement on sources of human rights including the very foundation of international law. The uncertainty about the content of the doctrines of human rights including the lack of a philosophical common core poses additional obstacles. In fact, the very conception of the organization of society differs from one culture to another. The West places more emphasis on rights while Islam values obligations. The Western tradition posits freedom in order to avoid the outcome of a despotic system, while Islam emphasizes virtue as a goal to perpetuate tradition of society that often supports a coercive system. The West emphasizes individual interests while Islam values collective good. In the areas where natural rights transcend cultural values, as in the right to survival, the vested interests of foreign policy elites serve as a basis for disagreement in the exercise of human rights. Such political use of human rights increases the possibility of the perversion of the concept.

The United States enjoys leadership responsibilities to meet the challenges of human rights, both domestically and internationally. The domestication of international politics and the internationalization of domestic politics gives the struggle for human rights global affinity. The human need for a sense of community dissolves the bonds of geography that separate American affluence from Third World poverty.

America is still a moral exemplar to the world. There is no inherent contradiction between power and morality. Power becomes destructive only when committed to the service of a narrow conception of morality. Power may be used for moral or immoral purposes. United States power provides the possibilities to overcome the despair of the Third World or the mindless optimism of advocates of technocratic images of the future. American power can serve such foreign policy goals as the development of harmonious interaction between the individual and nature and the promotion of human solidarity.

The issue confronting United States foreign policy is not intervention versus nonintervention. The commitment to human rights requires a foreign policy process to promote them. It is the style of American intervention that is at issue.

What is required is dignity that corresponds to American stature. This entails a posture where United States foreign policy reflects its observed rank among states. A powerful and rich country is not obsessed with the politics of scarcity in dealings with the world. Only small and poor states are motivated by survival, and rightly so. The political viability of humanity, not of a political regime, must be a criterion of American commitment. The ecology of the planet, not shrimp beds off a remote coast, must be the focus of American interest. America enjoys a broad spectrum of action appropriate to its commitment. Otherwise, Americans dedicate their foreign policy to the noble purpose of making ends meet.

The American hard talk about human rights is not a substitute for acting hard. The boundary of sacrifice does not stop at the American shores. When Americans share their growth with the less-developed countries, they join the partnership of human rights.

Recommended Readings

AMNESTY INTERNATIONAL. *Report on Torture.* New York: Farrar, Straus and Giroux, 1977.

BROWNLIE, IAN, ed. *Basic Documents on Human Rights.* Oxford: Oxford University Press, 1971.

CLAUDE, R. *Comparative Human Rights.* Baltimore: Johns Hopkins Press, 1976.

DUCHACEK, IVOD. *Rights and Liberties in the World Today: Constitutional Promise and Reality.* Santa Barbara, Calif.: ABC-CLIO, 1973.

FORSYTHE, DAVID P. *Humanitarian Politics: The International Committee of the Red Cross.* Baltimore: Johns Hopkins Press, 1977.

FRAENKEL, JACK. *The Struggle for Human Rights.* New York: Random House, 1975.
JENNINGS, J., and M. FISHER. *Inquiring About Freedom.* Grand Rapids, Mich.: Fideler, 1975.
KITTRIE, NICHOLAS. *The Right to Be Different.* New York: Penguin Books, 1973.
LILLICH, R., and R. BILDER. *Human Rights and United States Foreign Policy.* Charlottesville: University Press of Virginia, 1977.
MCGREGOR, IAN. *Human Rights.* London: Batsford Press, 1975.
MOSKOWITZ, MOSES. *International Concern with Human Rights.* Dobbs Ferry, N.Y.: Oceana Publications, 1975.
POSSONY, S., and K. GLASER. *Victims of Politics: Human Rights, Discrimination, and Oppression in the World Today.* New York: Columbia University Press, 1978.
DEL RUSSO, ALLESSANDRA L. *International Protection of Human Rights.* Washington, D.C.: Lerner Law Book Co., 1971.
SAID, ABDUL A., ed. *Human Rights and World Order.* New Brunswick, N.J.: Transaction Books, and New York: Frederick A. Praeger, 1978.
VAN DYKE, VERNON. *Human Rights, the U.S., and World Community.* Oxford: Oxford University Press, 1970.

Conclusion: Beyond the Geopolitical System

Concepts are thought forms made of observation and experience. The process of conceptualization consists of the ordering of events by the mind and does not inhere to the events themselves. It is a process with limitations. Our concepts settle so deeply into our consciousness that they become distorted and fail to explain new events which may be analyzed more usefully in a different manner. The concept of nineteenth-century territorial imperialism, for example, does not explain the present expansion of multinational corporations. Through continued usage, concepts acquire a spillover effect and result in misleading interpretations. The concept of Cold War does not interpret present-day American-Soviet rivalry. With the passage of time concepts outlast the events they sought to describe. The concepts of the Monolith of Communism and the Free World are poor descriptions of present Soviet and American foreign policy contexts.

While our need for analytic concepts is constant since we must develop and apply categories for understanding, the content of concepts changes. The concepts, as well as constants and variables which have dominated the discussion and analysis of world politics since the nineteenth century, continue to enjoy popular currency in an age where rational security is increasingly a function of technology, not of geopolitics. Although some writers have suggested that our present world resembles the world of 1815, not the world of 1914, it resembles neither: It is not a world of calculated growth and stability or a stage upon which the passions of nationalism assume significant roles. It is not a world beyond ideology, but a world seeking to restore to individuals a coherent picture of the environment and a meaning to life which exceeds the simplistic nationalism of an earlier era. It is a world which relies less and less upon the nation-state as an agent for fulfillment, and a world where distance as a barrier to transnational culture groups is a diminishing consideration and relationships between these groups are paramount. Ideational integration has truly become the primary concern of mass movements and other human activities. The symptoms of rootlessness and cultural instability have become as much a part of the politics of postindustrial societies as they are the preoccupations of less-developed countries.

A dichotomy of purpose and design is beginning to separate policy-makers in the global system from broad cultural currents which transfigure our world. The former continue to emphasize such concepts as "balance of power" and the limitation of strategic nuclear weapons, while increasingly popular goals are focused upon restricting the unlimited spread and application of social technology, with its impact upon the individual's integrated conception of self. Thus, our traditional concepts are too narrow to capture the breadth of global politics while our new analytic tools are cast in the molds of old issues.

A politics of cosmopolitanism is beginning to influence the behavior of states and inspires a view of the world as a whole rather than as a collection of isolated parts. Cosmopolitanism undermines the viability of traditional concepts and theoretical models of world politics and suggests the importance of such new actors as multinational corporations, ethnic nations, terrorist groups, and nongovernmental organizations in understanding transnational relations.

Human organizations have neither finality nor a perfected form: Their changes are a record of our experience and of our changing needs. In response to the chaos resulting from the collapse of the Roman administration in the fifth century A.D., Europeans developed the institution of feudalism. The new conditions in Europe during the breakdown of the medieval synthesis saw feudalism gradually replaced by another organizational concept, the national state. Today, the impact of new technological conditions on the state system has launched us on a new process of organization in response to the new requirements and conditions of global politics.

The development of the nation-state encouraged a transformation of moral and political centers of authority, undermining the political authority of the church and the family. It also inherited many of the primary functions which these social organizations provided—most importantly, the maintenance of security. Since the nineteenth century the foreign policy of states has been preoccupied with this quest for security from external sources of disequilibrium. Political and cultural millennialism has been a persistent, unsettling feature of international system. The apprehension of one state by another has been the gravamen of traditional international politics. State nationalism evolved into imperialism.

The celebration of the state was not the only impetus to political millennialism, the idea of empire, both temporal and spiritual, being traceable to the first stirrings of history. But it did furnish focus, rationale, and organization for the conflicting aspirations of individuals which earlier mass movements, such as the religious millennialism of Western Europe, had lacked.

The mercantile aspirations of the Portuguese and the Spanish, the development of British capitalism and the British empire in India, a French empire in Africa, a Russian imperium in Central Asia, American imperial expansion beginning in the 1890s, Japanese and German militarism in the 1930s—all share a universal theme in world politics: the expansionist impulse.

Foreign policy and world politics have been characterized by a compulsive preoccupation with the physical vulnerability of the state. If we were to seek out a common denominator that transcends the foreign policy formulations of both the strong and the weak, it would be the concern for geopolitics, and the foreign policy of states that has been influenced by the geopolitical context. It has been concerned with the exercise of a particular species of politics-geopolitics, a strong compelling emphasis on the control of strategic land masses and waterways, and, of course, alliances.

An environment that placed inordinate emphasis on the role of geopolitics also invested its analytical concepts and methodologies with this narrow historical experience. The study of international relations became the study of transactions between territorial states. The drama of world politics became, in Palmerston's celebrated observation, the pursuit of permanent national interests, so defined in geopolitical terms. The content of international relations was merely a reflection of the content of foreign policy—threats, compromises, the creation of alliances and buffers, the cultivation of an elite foreign service, voyages by navies to show the flag, economic and cultural imperialism, ideological competition, and awakening nationalism—all of which have revolved, if only tenuously at times, around the quest for external security by the nation-state.

The indices that have been used to measure the conduct of specific foreign policies have been derived often from geopolitical bases of analysis, such as measuring conflicts and interventions between territorial states. The rationale behind giving foreign aid to less-developed countries, a preoccupation of recent years which originally was cast in terms of buying security and preventing the export to other states of worrisome political and economic models, still lingers on in subtle yet definite forms. Most importantly, the concept of capability in world politics, however illusive, was cast in terms of the military and economic power of states.

Thus the constants and variables which have dominated the discussion and analysis of transnational relations since the nineteenth century continue to enjoy currency. The theoretical foundations of such concepts as national interest, nation state, power and balance of power, which are invoked to explain contemporary transnational phenomenon, are artifacts of a remote environment concerned with the rivalries between states.

The nomenclature of politics has changed remarkably little, but the global environment from which the terminology derives its significance has experienced a major transformation which can be explained by the declining role of external security issues in the affairs of many states.

Political millennialism is no longer an important factor in transnational relations. Although the world has not moved beyond ideology, the possibilities of international geopolitical movements designed to subjugate one state to another is a declining factor in the decision-making calculus of states.

The traditional foci of international relations, geopolitical subrogation, and economic colonialism, however indistinguishable they have occasionally become, are in decline as strategic variables that affect the decision-making process of states. External security issues have not become unimportant, but it would be self-deluding to concentrate on subsystems of objective conflict at the expense of an understanding of the new world environment.

It is also likely that as we approach the twenty-first century and nuclear weapons begin to diffuse in the global environment so that terrorist groups may yet acquire them, we face an unprecedented juncture in our historical understanding of the definition of power. Military power will not be pursued as much as simply taken for granted. As military power becomes increasingly nondisposable, our conception of the nature of power in the twenty-first century will be radically transformed.

By placing some historical distance between ourselves and the geographic theories of international relations, with their emphasis on the state as the preeminent actor in world politics, the task of analyzing the significance of the emerging cosmopolitanism becomes easier. The primary characteristic of this system is its emphasis on nonsecurity issues. The newspapers, speeches, and journals which emanate from both the less-developed and developed areas, echo preoccupation with new issues in world politics.

The nation-state obviously can no longer independently fulfill its former objects of providing security, protection, and welfare. Nonetheless, the nation-state remains the basic unit in the global system, and powerful forces work toward its maintenance. The fact that the state is intimately involved in so many facets of national life creates a self-perpetuating national administrative infrastructure which will prove difficult to dismantle. Perhaps the only accurate conclusion which can be drawn at this juncture in history is that the content has changed. The more virulent forms of sovereignty and nationalism which have prevailed since the nineteenth century are under severe stress. We have found that cooperation is not only compatible with sovereignty, but that it is indispensable for our continued survival. While the evolution of the nation-state goes on rapidly, new forms of organization will continue to test its validity.

In this age of acceleration and nuclear technology, the challenge of global survival or global destruction has brought humanity close together in the attempt to find solutions to the problems that divide the world. Human needs have thus become universalized, and nation-states have been forced to work collectively. The propensity of national actors to broaden their national interests cannot be underestimated, however.

The dynamic nature of change in the present milieu of global politics is intensifying the search of people and governments for new types of organization. The combined consequences of the technological revolutions make organizational modernization in the present global system imperative. As governments have broadened their areas of effective control, corresponding areas of international and transnational activity must be subjected to regulation and standardization. The rapid pace of these activities cannot be satisfied with traditional devices of international politics.

Our right and ability to defend our person, property, and family has been, throughout history, the ultimate exercise and proof of freedom. The distinction between self-defense and aggression for defensive purposes has always been unclear. Being social animals, we have extended this principle to the various forms of communal organization which have characterized human heritage. Following the emergence of the nation-state as the primary unit or organized society, exercise of self-defense was collectivized and took the form of modern war. In this form, however, the freedom which we intended to preserve was cruelly wrested from us. The state, artificially created to bring us security, clearly has outgrown its usefulness. Although we could find a relative degree of security from our immediate neighbors within the state, the dangerous dynamics of intergroup existence still had to be controlled. For this purpose, international and transnational organizations, in myriad forms and for multifarious interests, have been created.

From a theoretical viewpoint, the development of new organizational forms has been embodied in the efforts toward global organization, which have been conducted from two major positions—the federalist and the functionalist. The federalists seek a world government, basing their hope for world order on the premise that all states must ultimately convert voluntarily from long-held sovereignties to allegiance to some form of universal parliament or council. The functionalists, on the other hand, postulate that the future can be assured only by gradual expansion of cooperation on broader levels in response to specific needs. Functionalist theory holds that cooperation in technical, economic, and generally nontechnical areas will produce a spillover effect eventually undermining and transforming the political form of the state.

International organizations involving voluntary submission by sovereign states to an outside and common authority are relatively new on the world political scene, but the logic and force of transnational exchange ensure their long life. Furthermore, it appears likely that the trend toward wider forms of global organization will continue until, minimally, the war-making capacity of the state is eliminated and we can turn to the solution of other abiding problems.

Prior to the League of Nations, the general historical practice had been to formulate international agreements for the purpose of either defensive or offensive concerted action against a particular power or alliance. The League opened a new era of international organization, because no previous international agreement had sought to encompass the whole of the international system, nor had any international compact undertaken to embrace as broad a range of interests. When the United Nations replaced the League after World War II, it was not thought at all remarkable that this second try at general international organization should take on an even broader scope of responsibility.

The real novelty of modern international organizational forms can be best observed beyond the traditional levels of politics and security. Present-day organizations such as the Food and Agricultural Organization, the World Bank, and the International Monetary Fund on the government level, and the World Federation of Trade Unions, the International Cooperative Alliance, and the World Federation of Democratic Youth in the nongovernment sector, and International Business Machines in the private sector—these are representative of the character of the new form of international organization: None of these action areas were conceived of in the early days of the state system; all are reflective of current trends and requirements. Functionalism, breadth of scope, and specialization are the major characteristics that differentiate contemporary organizations from such earlier international arrangements as the Dutch East India Company, the Concert of Europe, the Holy Alliance, and other eighteenth- and nineteenth-century European associations.

The evolution of organizational forms has touched off a growing controversy over the relative advantages of regional as opposed to universal systems. Supporters of regionalism contend that the universalist ideal is far too ambitious and perilous because it assumes allegiance to a community which does not, in fact, exist. Universalists claim that the regional approach is no more than an extension of the old and dangerous balance of power, doomed by its nature to a repetition of failure. Recognizing the revolutionary changes and the needs of modern society, universalists maintain that only through equally revolutionary political breakthroughs can we hope to find peace. Regional organizations, however, have continued to coexist with such universal bodies as the United Nations.

The functionalists gained their greatest impetus from the astounding success of the European Common Market. Developments in Western Europe have also strengthened the idea of regionalism. Most contemporary international and transnational organizations have utilized a combination of the regional-functional approach.

An implicit assumption in this book, made explicit at many points, is that the political world today is undergoing extensive, rapid, and, in some cases, violent change. New forces of far-reaching import have been released on humanity, and policymakers are grappling with the consequences. The structures and patterns of world politics, like those of any social system, were originally developed on the basis of and in response to certain prevailing social conditions. Now that those conditions have changed so drastically, serious questions must be asked about the relevance of familiar institutions to unfamiliar circumstances.

The global political system is a relatively loose and underinstitutionalized order, calculated to limit without nullifying the inescapable dynamics of state interaction. The inhibitions on state freedom of choice were long ago set at the precise minimum necessary to preserve the integrity of the system while allowing for a wide range of adjustment and stability. Created in the era of the absolute monarch and the musketeer, the systems and processes of world politics proved capable of adapting to such explosive forces as the rise of nationalism, the development of world empire, and the creation of mass armies. Why, then, are we suggesting that their viability has been seriously compromised today?

This question has also been repeatedly answered in the preceding pages. Contemporary challenges overtax the competence of the state form, and international conflict constantly threatens to go beyond the limits of tolerability and safety. The new means of action open to states are too dangerous to use, while the old techniques are inappropriate to new problems. The great questions of today's global life find no answers within the traditional confines of the state system. Nor can it suffice merely to regard such insistent problems as the escape from destruction, the adjustment of growth in developed societies, the challenge of development of the Third World, and the implications of nuclear energy as insoluble and therefore not fit matters for concern. So powerful are the new dynamics of global life that either answers will be found for them or they will find their own answers. The issue facing us is whether we will ultimately be dominated by them.

In these terms the problem of organizing human effort for solution of these long-term problems becomes central. The familiar state form has both legal and mystical underpinnings, but in the last analysis its only rational justification is utilitarian. In other words, it must get the job done. If it fails, other structures and other principles must be found to replace it.

The process of experimentation has already begun. New organizational forms have been developed, new processes initiated, and new solutions attempted. Only a very few of these, however, incorporate a fundamental break with the past. Most remain tentative steps that seek to preserve the psychic component of sovereignty while restricting its actual force. It is a tribute to human ingenuity that so many ways have been found to have our cake of sovereignty and eat it, too.

No serious observer feels today that such half-measures have proved their effectiveness. Such proof may yet be forthcoming; it is premature to argue flatly for outright abandonment of the sovereign state in favor of an unproved vision of world government. But it is clear that no overall rationale for global politics yet suggested or attempted meets the requirements of the contemporary era. What has taken place up to now is a massive purchase of time for innovation and—hopefully—hard thought. The era of difficult decisions and of new techniques of action lies ahead.

Some way must be discovered to cope effectively with the new forces of world politics if we are to free ourselves from the tension of contemporary life and move out from under the mushroom cloud of nuclear destruction. New ways of organizing human effort across national lines must precede any direct attack on the problems. The glaring fact of global politics is that an era has ended. The traditional geopolitical system has become a historical curiosity. Environmental change has outstripped institutional structures. But we are adaptable creatures with a highly developed genius for survival. The global system will be eventually forced into a shape more appropriate to the demands of the twenty-first century. Politics will remain the core relationship among actors, since competition and conflict will not disappear. But it will be a game played with new rules and for different stakes, with a much larger number of players and with a broad consensus of peoples and governments. Success in the new system will go as it did in the old—to those who best learn and apply the rules. We can dedicate ourselves to this end. The penalty for failure may be disaster; the reward for success may be a better life on this planet for everyone.

It is more difficult to forecast how future global politics will feel than how the future global system will look. The global system may not look very different from its present state-based structure. The broad issues of global politics probably will not change markedly from those of today. What will change is the content of the structure, the shift in significance we assign to issues and how we resolve them.

These, then, have been our reflections on the changing nature of world politics. You are now well acquainted with our map-making adventure. Our effort must serve only as a point of departure for you. The new environment is a flexible, dynamic, and amorphous system, much less predictable and much more complex than the traditional one. The prizes to be won under the new conditions are novel and unprecedented, but they are worth winning all the same. We are the heirs of the old order, but our legacy would be that much greater if we could also be the architects of a new order founded upon human solidarity and the wholeness of human life.

Recommended Readings

BELL, DANIEL. *The Coming of the Post Industrial Society.* New York: Basic Books, 1976.
EDWARDS, DAVID. *Creating a New World Politics.* New York: David McKay Co., 1973.
FALK, RICHARD A. *A Study of Future Worlds.* New York: Free Press, 1975.
FROMM, ERICH. *The Revolution of Hope.* New York: Harper & Row, 1974.
GROOM, A., and PAUL TAYLOR, eds. *Functionalism: Theory and Practice in International Relations.* New York: Crane, Russak, and Co., 1975.
HARMAN, WILLIS. *An Incomplete Guide to the Future.* San Francisco: San Francisco Book Company, 1976.
HEILBRONER, ROBERT. *An Inquiry into the Human Prospect.* New York: W.W. Norton, 1974.
HENDERSON, HAZEL. *Creating Alternative Futures: The End of Economics.* New York: Berkley Pub., 1978.
HUXLEY, ALDOUS. *Brave New World.* New York: Harper & Row, 1969.
KAHN, HERMAN, et al. *The Next Two Hundred Years.* New York: William Morrow and Co., 1976.
LEONARD, GEORGE B. *The Transformation: A Guide to the Inevitable Changes in Humankind.* New York: Dell, 1973.
ROSZAK, THEODORE. *Where the Wasteland Ends: Politics and Transcendence in Post Industrial Society.* Garden City, N.Y.: Anchor Books, 1973.
SCHUMACHER, ERNST F. *A Guide for the Perplexed.* New York: Harper & Row, 1977.
TEILHARD DE CHARDIN, PIERRE. *The Future of Man* (trans. Norman Denny). New York: Harper & Row, 1964.
TOFFLER, ALVIN, ed. *The Futurists.* New York: Random House, 1972.

Index

Abolition Act of 1833, 303
Action: capability in, 58–74; definition of theory of, 9; limitations on, 151–69; organization for, 40–45
Action theory, 9
Actors (*see also* Nation-State, States). concept of, 9, 14; as bloc, 125, 126–27; as international organizations, 125, 127–30; as nongovernmental organizations, 125, 132–33; as non-state, 125–26; as regional, 125, 126, 130–31; as transnational, 125, 131–32
Adjudication, procedure of, 145–46
Adjustment: conflict and, 135–51; procedure of, 79
Agreement, technique for, 79; (*see also* Decisions)
Agricultural capacity as capability factor, 67, 69–70
Aid (*see* specific types)
Alliances, use of, 112, 114 (*see also* Bloc actors)
Almond, Gabriel, 11
Alternatives, choice among, 48–49
Ambassadors, functions of, 43–44
Amnesty International, 125, 133, 306
Amuzegar, Jahangir, 247
Anarchy of international system, 98, 102–3, 109, 114
Anticolonialist, ideology of, 87, 118 (*see also* Third World)
Antihierarchy, concept of, 207–8
Appropriate technology, analysis of, 220
Apter, David, 11
Arbitration, procedures of, 154
Armaments (*see* Military doctrine; Military force; Warfare; Weaponry)
Arms control (*see* Arms race)
Arms race, 176 (*see also* Warfare; Weaponry): disarmament and, 191–96; logic of, 192
Arms transfers (*see* Arms race)
Aron, Raymond, 11, 240, 242
Ascriptive politics, 25–27

Balance of payments, 83
Balance of power, 9, 15, 32, 109–14, 135, 323 (*see also* Equilibrium theory; Power): bipolar basis, 109–11, 178, 208–9; integrated, 109, 111; multiple, 109–10; simple, 109–11
Balance of terror, 177–80, 195

Balancing-objective conflict, 139–41, 148
"Balkanization" of international order, 211
Barker, Sir Ernest, 282
Barth, Fredrick, 284–85, 286
Beard, Charles, 11
Behavior, concepts of, 4
Bell, Daniel, 199
Bendix, Richard, 242
Berlin Conference on Africa (1885), 303
Bipolar system, 109–11, 178, 208–9
Bloc actors, 125, 126–27, 209
Blockade, 148
Boulding, Kenneth, 11
Boycott of trade, 84, 148
British Commonwealth of Nations, 130
Brown, Lester R., 268
Brussels Conference of 1890, 303
Buffer zones, use of, 112–13

Cabinet, 40
Cabinet-Executive office, 41
Calculus of ends, 15 (*see also* Ends-means analysis)
Capability, factors of, 9, 15, 58–74
Capitalism, 12, 199, 242–43
Carr, E. H., 11
Central American Peace Conference (1907), 303
Central Treaty Organization, 114
"Challenge and response" theory, 9
Classes of states, 106–7, 117, 180
Clausewitz, Karl Von, 121, 138
Classically-oriented theorists, 11–14
Climatological data, 68
Coercion (*see also* Force; Military doctrine; Military force; Warfare): in capability, 60; right of, 173; technique of, 78, 81, 83–84, 103, 147–48; as a term, 15
Cold War, 81, 82, 83, 108, 158, 190, 248, 276, 322
Collective security, concept of, 111 (*see also* Security)
Commission on Transnational Corporations (CTC), 277
Commitments, precedents and, 56–57
Common Market, (*see* European Common Market)
Commonwealth of Nations, 130
Communication, revolution in, 85 (*see also* Propaganda)

331

Communications Satellite Corporation (COMSAT), 225
Communism: propaganda by, 230; theories of, 12, 35, 41, 87, 150, 190, 203, 204–5, 211, 241–3, 248, 308, 310–12
Community, 11, 98
Compensation as technique, 112–13
Computers, new patterns in, 216, 235–36
Concert of Europe, 327
Conciliation as procedure, 145
Conference of Foreign Ministers, 107
Conflict (*see also* Force; Military doctrine; Military force; Warfare): adjustment of, 143–48; nature of, 135–43; resolution of, 149–51
Conference on Security and Cooperation in Europe (Helsinki Agreement), 165
Congress of Berlin (1878), 107
Congress of Verona (1822), 107
Congress of Vienna (1815), 106, 107, 303
Consensus, need for, 52–53, 58–60, 66, 71–73, 98, 100, 118, 153–59, 177, 232
Constitutionalism, 12
Consumers, expectations of, 232–33
Consumption, new patterns in, 216–17, 232–33
Content analysis, 8
Conventional war, terms of, 190–91 (*see also* Warfare)
Convention for the Prevention and Repression of Terrorism (1937), 298
Convention for the Protection of Human Rights and Fundamental Freedom (European), (1950), 302
Conventions of the Hague (1971), 298
Convention of Washington (1971), 298
Convention on the Protection of Diplomats, 300
Convergence theory, 240
Copernicus, 6, 119
Cost/risk factors: military techniques and, 89–91; in policy-making, 32, 51–54, 143, 167–68, 174
Council of Europe (1949), 305
"Counterforce," concept of, 186
Counterinsurgent techniques, 87–88, 191
"Countersociety" ("countervalue"), theory of, 186
Credibility of military force, 179–80
Credits, freezing of, 83–84
Cultural issues, conflict of, 139–41
Cultural tradition, international law and, 164–66
Culture: definition of, 284; as imperialism, 88–89; as psychological technique, 85, 88
Currency: control of, 83; devaluation of, 84
Current events, study of, 3
Cybernetics, 8

Decisions (*see also* Policy-making): analysis of, 8; by consensus, 177; disappearance of, 176–77; on disarmament, 195; foreign policy and, 31–36; implementation of, 76–92; process of, 46–47
Declaration of Legal Principles Governing the Activities of States in the Exploration and Use of Outer Space, 225
Declaration of Mexico (1945), 306
Democracy, 240: forms of, 203, 205–7; initiative and, 35–36; liberalism in, 211
Deterrence: birth of, 15; doctrine of, 185–86, 189
Deutsch, Karl, 8, 11, 239
Development, problems of 16, 247–56, 274 (*see also* Economic policies): approaches to, 247–52; beyond economics toward adaptation, 252–53; goals of, 255; infrastructure of, 255–56; problems and prospects of, 254–56

Development assistance, 83, 84 (*see also* Economic policies)
Devlin, David, 260
Diplomacy: history of, 2–3; law of 161; as political technique, 77–81; settlement and, 144–45
Diplomatic personnel, 41, 42
Diplomatic service, 43–44
Diplomats, 79–81
Direct negotiations, 144
Disarmament: arms race and, 191–96; failure of, 194–96
Disorder, pole of, 101
Distribution, new patterns in, 216, 232–34
Divide and rule as technique, 112–13
"Dollar diplomacy", 112
Dumping as trading practice, 84

Easton, David, 11
Economic policies, 81, 243–56: aid suspension and, 84; capability judgements and, 62; in implementing decisions, 76, 81–85; individual welfare through, 30; ministry in, 41, 44; population explosion and, 227–28; structure for, 67, 71
Ecosystem, 216–36
Educational level as capability factor, 67, 72
Ellul, Jacques, 288
Embargo, 148
Embassies, organization of, 43–44
Ends-means analysis, 9, 15, 28–29, 31, 32–33, 58, 59, 135, 138, 155 (*see also* Objectives)
Energy revolution, 217–20 (*see also* Nuclear energy, analysis of; Technological revolution, results of)
Environmental factors, 9, 10 (*see also* capability, factors of)
Equality in international politics, 101–4
Equilibrium theory, 9, 15, 109, 139, 148 (*see also* Balance of power)
Establishment, recommendations of, 41
Ethnicity, 16, 118, 125, 131–32 (*see also* Ethnic nations)
Ethnic nations: development and, 286–90; foreign policy and, 290–91; neoethnic groups, 291–94; politics of, 279–83; roots of conflict, 283–86
European Atomic Community, 130, 219
European Common Market, 130, 328
European Community, organization of, 125, 130, 260, 279
European Convention on Human Rights (1950), 306
Expansionist policies, 139–40
"Expectation" theory, 9
Export licenses, 83
Expropriation, 164

Fascism, 87, 150
Federalism, 326–27
Feudalism, collapse of, 122
Finance ministry, 44
"Firepower," concept of, 183
Food and Agricultural Organization, 327
Force (*see also* Coercion; Military doctrine; Military force; Warfare): conflict and, 149–51; control of, 161–62; right of, 173; threat of, 162–63, 166; use of, 165
Foreign aid (*see* Economic policies)
Foreign exchange blocking, 83
Foreign minister, 42–44, 107
Foreign policy (*see* Policy)
Fossil fuels, analysis of, 217
Freedom as objective, 32

French Community, 130
Functionalism, 239, 326–28

Galbraith, John Kenneth, 240, 242
Game theory, 8, 9
Garaudy, Roger, 310
Geertz, Clifford, 287
General Agreement on Tariffs and Trade, 130
Geneva Conference of 1926, 303
"Geopolitics," theories of, 67, 68
Global politics (*see also* International politics): contemporary conditions of, 116–33; equality and inequality in, 101–4; ideas and patterns of, 97–114; new institutions of, 125–33; regularities of, 109–14
Goals (*see also* Interests, national; Objectives; Purpose, two categories of; Warfare): as common, 79, 98, 150; definition of, 29, 47; selection of, 29–31, 33, 34, 99, 100
Good offices, 144
Gordon, Milton, 287
Greeley, Andrew, 283, 288, 292
Gross national product (GNP), 253, 260, 261, 262, 266–68, 317

Haas, Ernst, 239
Hague Convention (1970), 300
Harrington, Michael, 311
Hartz, Louis, 11
Hasempflug, Haja (*see* Karl Sauvant)
Haushofer, Karl, 68
Head of government, 41–42
"Heartland" theory, 68
Hegemonic-objective conflict, 139, 141–42, 148
Hidy, Ralph W., 259
Historical experience, 139, 141
Holy Alliance, 155, 327
Hsu, Francis, 285–86
Human law, 160 (*see also* International law)
Human Rights, 16, 118, 254–56, 302–20: international concern for, 303–6; Marxist and neo-Marxist views of, 310–12; in the Third World (The Islamic States), 312–16; toward global human rights, 318–20; Western context of, 307–10; in the World Order, 316–18
Hundred Years War, 210

"Idealist" approach, 4–5
Ideology (*see also* specific ideologies): foreign policy and, 200–202; myth and reality of, 202; nature of, 199–200; prestige and, 198–215; problems of, 16; promotion of, 31; in world politics, 198–99, 203–14
Image projection, 9, 230–31 (*see also* Culture, as psychological technique; Persuasion, techniques of; Propaganda; Psychological techniques)
Imperialism, 12, 32, 139–40, 262
Inaction, strategy of, 76–77
Independence, as concept, 15
Individual, good of, 23
Industrial capacity as capability factor, 67, 69–70 (*see also* Technological revolution, results of)
Inequality in international politics, 101–4 (*see also* Balance of power; Equilibrium theory)
Influence: in capability, 60; spheres of, 112, 113; as term, 15, 265
Information, incompleteness of, 53–54
Initiatives, responses and, 35–36
Inquiry, commission of, 144–45
Institutions of international politics, 125–33 (*see also* specific institutions)

Integration, 16, 238–39
Intelligence agencies: information from, 54, 63; in policy-making, 45
Inter-American System of Human Rights, 306
Interaction theory: categories of, 15–16; definition of, 9
Interdependence, 16, 239, 240–43
Interests, national (*see also* Objectives; Purpose, two categories of; Warfare): application of, 29, 32, 38; morality and, 156–57; values of, 27–28
International Atomic Energy Agency, 130, 219
International Cooperative Alliance, 132, 327
International Court of Justice, 146, 147, 165
International Covenant on Civil and Political Rights (1966), 254, 302, 305
International Covenant on Economic, Social, and Cultural Rights (1966), 254, 302, 305
International Labor Organization, 304
International law: basis of, 153, 159–66; cultural tradition and, 102–3; human law and, 160; political conception of, 161–64; question of, 147; recent trends in, 166; subject matter of, 160–61; third world attitudes toward, 164–66
International Monetary Fund, 327
International organizations, 125, 127–30, 326–28
International politics (*see also* Balance of power; Global politics; Policy-making; Politics): domestic politics and, 24; foreign policy and, 23–25
International relations: development of, 2–5, 11–14, 100–1; present state of, 5–10; rules and procedures of, 161
Interstate relationships, opposition in, 100–1
Intervention as technique, 112
Islam, human rights in, 312–16, 319
Isolationism, 32

Judicial methods of settlement, 145, 147
Jurisdiction, rules of, 160–61

Kelman, Herbert, 11
Kennan, George, 240
Kepler, 119
Kindelberger, Charles, 263

Lasswell, Harold, 11
Law (*see* International law; specific procedures)
League of Arab States, 130
League of Nations, 3, 109, 127–28, 146, 158, 304, 327
Leonhard, Wolfgang, 311
Levi-Strauss, Claude, 284
Lewin, Kurt, 281
"Liberation wars," 182 (*see also* Revolution; Warfare)
Lichtheim, George, 271
Limited actors, 153–69
"Limited" wars, 148, 176, 182, 189–91 (*see also* Warfare)
Lindsay, A. D., 11
Lippmann, Walter, 11
Litvak, Isaiah A., 268
Lukacs, Georg, 240

MacKenzie, F. A., 258
McClelland, David, 11
Machiavelli, Niccolo, theories of, 99–121
Machtpolitik, 4, 104 (*see also* Power)
Mackinder, Sir Halford, 68
Magdoff, Harry, 271
Marcuse, Herbert, 243
Maritain, Jacques, 11
Marxism (*see* Communism)

Index

Mass communication, 216, 229–32 (see also Propaganda): destructive and constructive applications, 231–32; image projection in foreign policy, 230–31; in world politics, 230
"Massive retaliation" (see Response)
Mathematical formulation of internal relationships, 7–8
Matson, Floyd, 288
Means, ends and, 28–29, 31, 33–34, 58, 59, 135 (see also Objectives)
Mediation, procedure of, 144
Methodlogical formalism, development of, 13
Military doctrine: crisis in, 184–85; dilemma in, 173–96; economic techniques and, 82; in implementing decisions, 76–77, 89–93; importance of, 183–84; leadership in, 44–45; of limited war, 148, 176, 182, 185, 189–91; population analysis for, 68–69; of total war, 185–89
Military force (see also Technological revolution, results of; Warfare, Weaponry): as aid, 82; balance of, 108; in capability judgments, 61–62, 65–66, 70–71; as coercive capacity, 61; cost/risk factors and, 89–91; developments in, 181–83
Mitrany, David, 239
Modelski, George, 261
Modernization, 254–55 (see also Economic policies)
Montreal Convention (1971), 300
Morale as capability factor, 67, 72–73
Moral goals (see also Consensus, need for): consensus on, 153–59; decisions as, 100
Morgenthau, Hans J., 4, 11, 15–16
Mukerjee, Tapan, 260
Multinational Corporations (MNC): 9, 16, 125, 131, 245, 258–78: crisis of development theory, 274–76; goals of, 262–65; historical evolution of, 258–62; nation-states and, 265–73; regulation of, 276–78
Multiple balance of power, 110 (see also Balance of power)
Mutual and Balanced Force Reduction, 194

National interest, 27, 46
Nationalism (see also Sovereignty): birth of, 102, 118; characteristics of, 12, 80, 210–13; conflict of, 139–41; in Europe, 210; problems of, 16, 155–56; production and, 233; propaganda and, 232; results of, 149; rise of, 23; in third world, 212–13; war and, 90; weakening of, 158–59
National state, 9, 312 (see also Nation-state; State)
National style in policy-making, 55–56
Nation-state (see also Economic policies; National state; State): definition of, 120; emergence of, 118–20; multinational corporations and, 265–73; obsolescence of, 281–83, 309, 323, 325–29; in system, 105, 118–21
Natural law, 160, 162
Neutrality, concepts of, 161, 178 (see also Nonalignment)
Nisbet, Robert A., 289
Nominalism, 307–10
Nonalignment, concept of, 127, 209
Nongovernmental organizations, 125, 132–33, 306
Non-state actors, 125–33
Non-western world (see Third world)
North Atlantic Treaty Organization, 114, 300
North-South Relations, 16, 243–47: New International Economic Order, 244–46; North-South Dialogue, 243–47
Nuclear energy, analysis of, 217–19 (see also Technological revolution, results of; Warfare)
Nuclear Non-Proliferation Treaty (1968), 194
Nuclear Test Ban Treaty (1963), 194

Objectives (see also Goals; Policy-making; Purpose, two categories of; Warfare; specific objectives): in capability, 73–74; choice of, 65–66; common, 40, 59; cultural techniques and, 88–89; incompatibility of, 163; nature of, 28–29, 47, 136; need for, 27–31, 50–51; of states, 29–33, 38–39
O'Brien, Conor Cruise, 289–90
"Operating missions," conflicts in, 44
Order, pole of, 101
Organicism, 307–10
Organization: concept of, 118–21; for international action, 40–45; problems of, 15
Organization of African Unity, 130
Organization of American States, 130, 300, 305
Organization of Petroleum Exporting Countries, 217, 245, 270
Osgood, Charles, 11

Pacem et Terris, 254
Pacific settlement, methods of, 144–47
Pan American Rule, 165
Paris North-South Conference, 246
Payment, balance of, 83
Peace as objective, 32
Peace of Paris (1919), 106
Peace of Westphalia (1648), 106, 122
Permanent Court of Arbitration at the Hague, 146
Permanent Court of International Justice, 146
Persuasion, techniques of, 78–79, 81–83, 203 (see also Coercion; Propaganda)
Planning, ministry of, 45
Policy: ends and means in, 28; international politics and, 24–25, 258; nature of, 21–39; objectives in, 27–39; priorities in, 32–34; propaganda and, 85–87; social values and, 23–24; value content of, 24
Policy-making (see also Capability, factors of; Decisions; Settlement): foreign and domestic, 150–51; government and, 40–57; ideology and, 200–202; morality and, 156; process of, 31–36, 45–50, 59–60; prudence in, 153, 167–69; war and, 89–90
Policy paper, contents of, 32
Political action (see Action)
"Political gaming," devices of, 54–55, 61, 167–68
Political structure as capability factor, 67, 71–72 (see also Organization)
Political system (see System of states)
Political technique (see Diplomacy)
Politics (see also Global politics; International politics): definition of, 21–27; nature of, 21–22; population explosion and, 227–28
Population: as capability factor, 66–69; causes of, 216, 226–27; political, social, and economic effects of, 227–28; pressure of, 229; problems of, 226–29; solutions to, 228–29
Power: assumption of, 105; balance of, 32, 110–14, 135, 139, 149
bipolar, 109, 110; integrated, 109, 111; multiple, 110; simple, 109, 110–11, 178
capability and, 60–61; as common objective, 31; concept of, 15, 107–9, 265; morality and, 156–57; responsibility of, 106; status of, 106–7.
Precedents, commitments and, 56–57
President, 41–42
Presidium, 41

Prestige: as common objective, 30–31; ideology and, 198–215; race for, 213–15
Priorities: knowledge of, 80; need for, 32–34
Probability, role of, 167–68
Problem, appreciation of, 50–51
Production: as capability factor, 67, 69–70; new patterns in, 216, 232–34
Propaganda (*see also* Mass communication): capability judgements and, 62; economic techniques and, 82; as foreign policy tool, 85–87; in mass media, 229–32; nature of, 85; as psychological technique, 77, 85–87; use of, 45
Protest, registration of, 78
"Proxy wars," 179
Prudence, calculus of, 161, 167–69
Psychological techniques (*see also* Culture, as psychological technique; Persuasion, techniques of; Propaganda; Subversion, role of): in implementing decisions, 77, 85–87; warfare through, 141–42
Ptolemy, 6
Public funds, allocation of, 44 (*see also* Economic policies)
Purpose, two categories of, 36–39 (*see also* Goals; Objectives)

Quality in capability analysis, 67, 70
Quantity in capability analysis, 67
Quota policy for commodities, 83

Racial issues, conflict of, 139, 141 (*see also* Third world)
Raw materials, preemptive purchase of, 84 (*see also* Production)
"Realist" approach, 4–5
Reconstruction, problems of, 189
Reductionism, trend of, 12, 13
Reformation, influence of, 198
Regan, Gerald, 268
Regional actors, 126, 130–31
Regulating mechanisms of international politics, 15
Religious issues, conflict of, 139, 141
Reparations, 147
Reprisal, 148
Research techniques, area of, 7 (*see also* specific techniques)
Resource endowment as capability factor, 67, 69
Response: initiatives and, 35; nature of, 185–86
Retorsion, 148
Revisionism: policy of, 38–39, 49–50, 111, 140; wars and, 38
Revolution (*see also* Technological revolution, results of; Third World): incidence of, 140; technique of, 87, 191
Revolutionary council, 41
Richardson, Lewis F., 8
Rio Pact, 114
Rising expectations, revolution of, 118
Risk (*see* Cost/risk factors)
Rose, Sanford, 260
Rostow, Walt W., 240, 241

Saint Germaine Treaty of 1919, 303
Sakharov, Andrei, 240, 242–43
Sauvant, Karl, 244–45
Sea Bed Treaty, 194
Sea, law of, 164, 165
Sea power theory, 68
Second strike, capability of, 187
Secretary of State as foreign minister, 41
Security: as collective, 111; as common objective, 29–30, 32; military force for, 45

Self-preservation as common objective, 29–30, 33, 109
Settlement (*see also* Decisions; Policy-making): law of, 161; methods of, 144–45
Shils, Edward, 287
Shtoll, Ladislav, 310
Simple balance of power, 110, 111
Single-factor theory of capability, 65
Situations, analysis of, 47, 156 (*see also* Capability, factors of)
Snyder, Richard, 11
Socialism, 207–9
Social issues, conflict of, 139, 141
Social structure as capability factor, 67, 71
Social value (*see also* specific values): foreign policy and, 23, 24; to national interest, 27, 32–33, 36; as political root, 22–23
Society: definition of, 98; good of, 24
Solar energy, analysis of, 219–20
Sorokin, Pitrim, 241
Sovereignty: behavior and, 168; immunity and, 165; inequality and, 103; law and myth of, 102, 118; principles of, 15, 98–99, 153, 166
Space, conquest of, 216, 220–26 (*see also* Technological revolution, results of): breakthrough, 221–22; cooperation, 224–26; political and military considerations, 223–24; space race, 222–23
Specialized agencies, 129–30
Spheres of influence, 112, 113
Statehood, law of, 160–61
States (*see also* National State; Nation-state; Organization; System of states; Third World): classes of, 107–107, 124, 180; equality and inequality of, 103–4, 116–25; good of, 24; in system, 99–100, 136; of world, 116–25
Status, end of, 180
Status quo, policy of, 37
Strategic Arms Limitation Talks (SALT), 193–95
Strategic position as capability factor, 67, 73–74
Strategy: as conservative enterprise, 167; definition of, 50–51
Structural Anthropology, 284–85
Structure, as capability factor, 67, 71 (*see also* Organization)
Style in policy-making, 55–56
Subversion, role of, 87, 141, 203
Survival: as common objective, 41; defense and, 188–89
System of states, 97–101, 116–25 (*see also* Organization; States): analysis of, 9–10; coercion and, 173; as contemporary global, 117–18; diversity and integration of, 118–21; war and, 174–83
Systems analysis, 9–10

Tariffs, 83
Taxation, increase in, 44–45
Technical level as capability factor, 72
Techniques (*see* specific techniques)
Technological revolution, results of, 16, 90, 91, 104, 116, 124, 137, 149, 158, 159, 166, 216–36, 326
Territorial jurisdiction, 160–61
Territory, occupation of, 183
Terror, balance of, 177–80, 195
Terrorism, 16, 118, 298 (*see* terrorist groups)
Terrorist groups, 125, 132, 294–300: goals and objectives, 295–98; legal control of, 298–99; responses to, 299–300; as a system, 294–95
Theory (*see also* specific theories): nature of, 7; relevance of, 16–17; utility of, 1–2
Threshold Test Ban Treaty, 194

Third world: developments of, 248–51; economic methods to, 82, 83; human rights in, 303, 312–16, 319; nationalism in, 117, 118, 127; nation-building in, 117; theories of, 207–10; toward international law, 164–66
Time, pressure of, 54–55
Tinbergen, Jan, 240, 241
Tocqueville, Alexis de, 240
Tokyo Convention (1963), 300
Tool skill, capability factors of, 72
Total war (*see also* Military doctrine; Military force; Warfare): doctrines of, 185–89
Trade, policy of, 82–83 (*see also* European Common Market; European Community, organization of)
Transnational actors, 9, 16, 131–32
Treasury Department in international affairs, 44
Treaties (*see also* specific treaties): interpretation of, 147; law of, 160–61, 163–64; as "unequal", 165
Treaty of London (1841), 303
Treaty of Utrecht (1713), 106
Tyson, Brady, 316

Ultimatum as coercion, 78
Unification of Penal Law (1935), 298
United Nations: agencies of, 107, 111, 129–30, 145–47, 219; charter of, 102, 128–29, 144–45, 304; collective security in, 111; establishment of, 128–30, 158; importance of, 108; interventions of, 182–83; membership of, 117; role of, 42, 159, 162, 163, 177, 327; sovereign equality in, 102, 104, 109, 128–29
Universal Declaration of Human Rights (1948), 254, 302, 304, 305, 317

Values (*see also* Objectives): choice of, 61–62, 105; coercion and, 60; maximization of, 21–27, 97; primacy of, 175–76; system of, 9, 77, 156–57
Veblen, Thorstein, 240
Vernon, Raymond, 260, 271–72
Victory, invalidation of, 175

Warfare (*see also* Coercion; Military doctrine; Military force): appropriateness of, 91; consensus and, 52–53; as cost/risk factor, 51–52; definition of, 60; discriminatory force in, 147; in foreign policy calculations, 89–90; in implementing decision, 76–77, 89–93; law of, 160–61; in modern world, 173–96; as "normal", 101; political effects of new, 177–83; problems of, 16, 166; revisionism and, 38; system and, 174–83; use of, 203–5; as violent conflict, 136–39
Warsaw Pact, 114, 125
Weaponry (*see also* Technological Revolution, results of; Warfare): developments in, 137–38; use of, 112, 113–14
Weber, Max, 240
Weiner, Norbert, 8
Well-being as common objective, 30
Workforce as capability factor, 67, 68–69, 70
World Bank, 327
World Federation of Democratic Youth, 132, 327
World Federation of Trade Unions, 132, 327
World War I, 2, 106, 110, 112, 127–28, 138, 211
World War II, 34, 80, 107, 110, 112, 117, 123, 124, 127, 138, 174–77, 184, 203, 205, 206, 211, 228, 259, 260